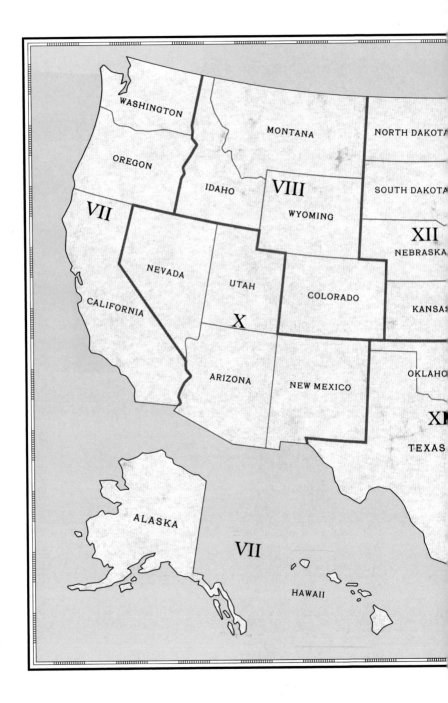

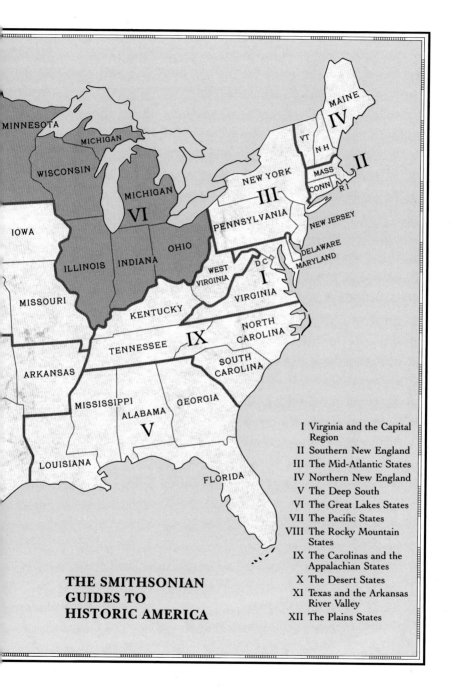

MINNESOTA

MICHIGAN

WISCONSIN

MICHIGAN

VI

IOWA

ILLINOIS INDIANA OHIO

MAINE

IV

VT

N H

NEW YORK

III

MASS

CONN

R I

II

PENNSYLVANIA

NEW JERSEY

MISSOURI

WEST VIRGINIA

D C

I

DELAWARE

MARYLAND

KENTUCKY

VIRGINIA

TENNESSEE

IX

NORTH CAROLINA

ARKANSAS

SOUTH CAROLINA

MISSISSIPPI

ALABAMA

GEORGIA

V

LOUISIANA

FLORIDA

I Virginia and the Capital Region

II Southern New England

III The Mid-Atlantic States

IV Northern New England

V The Deep South

VI The Great Lakes States

VII The Pacific States

VIII The Rocky Mountain States

IX The Carolinas and the Appalachian States

X The Desert States

XI Texas and the Arkansas River Valley

XII The Plains States

**THE SMITHSONIAN
GUIDES TO
HISTORIC AMERICA**

THE
SMITHSONIAN
GUIDES TO
HISTORIC AMERICA
THE GREAT LAKES STATES

TEXT BY
SUZANNE WINCKLER

SPECIAL PHOTOGRAPHY BY
BALTHAZAR KORAB

EDITORIAL DIRECTOR
ROGER G. KENNEDY
Director Emeritus, the National Museum of
American History of the Smithsonian Institution,
former Director of the National Park Service

Stewart, Tabori & Chang
NEW YORK

Published in 1998 by Stewart, Tabori & Chang, a division of U.S. Media Holdings, Inc., 115 West 18th Street, New York, NY 10011.

Due to limitations of space, additional photo credits appear on page 480 and constitute an extension of this page.

Front cover: main photo—Rolling farmland, southern MN.
inset 1—Farm building and fence in winter near Marine on St. Croix, MN.
inset 2—Barnraising near Massillon, OH.
inset 3—Map by Guenter Vollath.
inset 4—Henry Ford Museum, Dearborn, MI.
Half-title page: Saint Paul, 1855, by S. Holmes Andrews.
Frontispiece: Northwest Fur Post, near the Grand Portage Trail, MN.
Back cover: Tippecanoe County Courthouse, Lafayette, IN.

Series Editors: Henry Wiencek (first edition), Donald Young (revised edition)
Editor: Mary Luders
Photo Editor: Mary Z. Jenkins   **Assistant Photo Editors:** Ferris Cook, Barbara J. Seyda
Art Director: Diana M. Jones   **Cover Design** (revised edition)**:** Nai Chang
Designers: Paul P. Zakris (first edition), Lisa Vaughn (revised edition)
Associate Editor: Brigid A. Mast   **Editorial Assistant:** Monina Medy
Design Assistant: Kathi R. Porter   **Cartographic Design & Production:** Guenter Vollath
Cartographic Compilation: George Colbert   **Data Entry:** Susan Kirby
Text revisions throughout this edition by the series editor.

Library of Congress Cataloging-in-Publication Data

Winckler, Suzanne, 1946–
    The Great Lakes states / text by Suzanne Winckler ; special photography by
Balthazar Korab. — Rev. ed.
        p. cm. — (The Smithsonian guides to historic America ; 6)
    "Text revisions throughout this edition by Donald Young"—T.p. verso
    Includes index.
    ISBN 1-55670-637-5
    1. Lake States—Guidebooks. 2. Historic sites—Lake States—Guidebooks. I. Korab, Balthazar.
II. Young, Donald. III. Title. IV. Series.
F551.W56   1998
917.704'34—dc21   96-40543

Distributed in the U.S. by Stewart, Tabori & Chang, 115 West 18th Street, New York, NY 10011.
Distributed in Canada by General Publishing Co. Ltd., 30 Lesmill Road, Don Mills, Ontario, Canada, M3B 2T6. Distributed in all other territories by Grantham Book Services Ltd., Isaac Newton Way, Alma Park Industrial Estate, Grantham, Lincolnshire NG31 9SD, England. Sold in Australia by Peribo Pty Ltd., 58 Beaumont Road, Mount Kuring-gai, NSW 2080, Australia.

Printed in Japan

10 9 8 7 6 5 4 3 2 1

Revised edition

CONTENTS

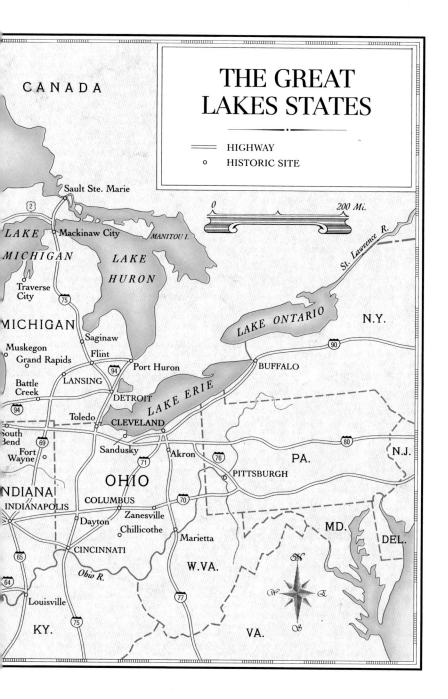

THE GREAT LAKES STATES

—— HIGHWAY

○ HISTORIC SITE

CANADA

0   *200 Mi.*

Sault Ste. Marie

(2)

LAKE   Mackinaw City   *MANITOU I.*

MICHIGAN   *LAKE*

       HURON

Traverse
City   (75)

St. Lawrence R.

MICHIGAN

Muskegon   Saginaw

Grand Rapids   Flint

LAKE ONTARIO   N.Y.

(90)

Battle   LANSING   (94)   Port Huron   BUFFALO
Creek

(94)   DETROIT   *LAKE ERIE*

Toledo   CLEVELAND

South
Bend   (69)   Sandusky   Akron   (76)   PA.
Fort   (71)   (80)   N.J.
Wayne   PITTSBURGH

INDIANA   OHIO

INDIANAPOLIS   COLUMBUS   (70)
           Dayton   Zanesville   MD.
              Chillicothe   DEL.
(65)   CINCINNATI   Marietta

Ohio R.   W.VA.

(64)
Louisville   (77)

KY.   (75)   VA.

INTRODUCTION

Roger G. Kennedy

Here is the Old Northwest, Frederick Jackson Turner country. Here is Middletown, U.S.A., and Sangamon County; the birthplace of Warren Harding and of Frank Lloyd Wright, of Ronald Reagan, Orson Squire Fowler, and Studs Terkel. It is a region in which diverse dreams have swirled and settled and formed crystals—villages like New Harmony and Zoar, Union Village, Nauvoo and Kirtland, Amana, Bishop Hill, and Saint Nazianz—and then, of course, Grosse Pointe, Shaker Heights, and Lake Forest. There are few Shakers in Shaker Heights, and little milling is done in Gates Mills, but the history is there, and in traveling the Great Lakes states, one comes upon startling reminders of Mormons and Icarians, Rappites and Amish, along with the Old Believers and the Eastern Orthodox. The Roman Catholics, Spanish and French, were the first to arrive. Then came Protestants of innumerable persuasions and Jews of several, all tinctured by their residence in older American areas before settling or pausing in the Midwest.

Because this is a region of considerable expanse—from Moorhead, Minnesota, to the eastern edge of Ohio is as far as from London to the frontier between Poland and Russia—one has to be very cautious making general statements about geography and climate. The terrain is not uniform. In the state of Michigan, Mount Arvon and the rest of the ridge that includes the Huron and Porcupine Mountains rise nearly 2,000 feet from the south shore of Lake Superior—enough to make a mountain man pant if taken too fast. And any simple notion that latitude or even altitude alone determines climate will be dispelled when one is chilled to the bone in Milwaukee one day in late fall when in the Michigan fruit belt, directly across Lake Michigan, an overcoat may not be needed. The prevailing winds from the west pass across the lake and sop up heat stored in that great basin during the summer, producing a miniclimate more like Virginia's than Saskatchewan's. So the land may be relatively smooth, but it is not flat; its people may seem on first acquaintance to share certain "midwestern" characteristics, but they are far from uniform; and its multitude of subclimates have altered the behavior and appearance of the area's many subcultures, rendering them even more varied.

All this may seem somewhat removed from "history," if what we generally mean by that word is written records of human activity. But we would miss much of the Midwest's magic if we restricted ourselves to literary records. Ever since Gutenberg, European-Americans have printed so much about their history that they have lost the capacity to learn about it from other than written sources. As a consequence, we have to work a little to recover that symbolic sense that was so powerful for our ancestors. Our preliterate predecessors could learn from stained-glass images, from statuary, from stories told by elders and minstrels, from liturgical drama, and from small objects in daily use, and they were reminded thereby of certain continuous truths.

The early history of the Middle West can be learned this way, too. The absence of written records is an inducement to relearn the language of objects, to reawaken a symbolic sense. When we visit the wonderful Ohio Historical Society in Columbus or the Field Museum in Chicago and examine the artifacts gathered from the thousands of years of human habitation in the Midwest that preceded the arrival of a written language, we are staggered by the power and skill of the artistry revealed in them.

Our desire to flex again our ability to learn symbolically, to begin to share the feelings of the people who made those objects, is increased when we encounter the profusion of architecture left by these peoples. The great mound at Cahokia, across the Mississippi from Saint Louis, is the largest of those remaining to us. Larger in extent than the Great Pyramid, it was a stepped platform for a ceremonial structure, now lost. The base alone was more than 1,000 feet by nearly 800, and 100 feet high. Many smaller earthworks remain in the area despite the work of plows, bulldozers, and parking-lot proprietors.

Ohio contains a rich diversity of ancient architecture, much of it—like the Serpent Mound in Adams County—in animal forms and in geometries that Aegean pottery makers were using at roughly the same time: octagons, ellipses, trapezoids, and circles. Wisconsin alone has more than 12,000 prehistoric buildings, Illinois more than 10,000. The eerie fact is that almost none of these were inhabited when European explorers first arrived and began to record their detailed impressions in the seventeenth century. Sometime during the preceding centuries there seems to have been a series of devastating disruptions of the life of the peoples of this region, leaving them vulnerable to outside conquest.

We know that the Iroquois engaged in a war to eliminate the competition of other tribes from the hunting grounds south of the Great Lakes and were so successful that large areas were depopulated. We know that the climate changed somewhat and also that European microbes preceded the Europeans themselves into this region, carried by Native Americans who had encountered those diseases on the coast. But we do not know all that happened to leave this area exposed like the abandoned places of the Old World—Petra, Persepolis, or Leptis Magna. Across a terrain of a thousand miles, Europeans found ruins only occasionally visited by the remnants of the people who had built them.

The land was not empty, but it was no longer occupied by the descendants of a thriving and vigorous agricultural society. In the thirteenth century the midwestern Native Americans lived in towns larger than any the European Americans would build until the eighteenth century. But by the seventeenth century the region had reverted to scattered bands of hunters and a very few agricultural settlements without ambitious or even permanent architecture. The Cahokia mound was built between A.D. 1025 and 1250; nothing like it was attempted again for four centuries. Never again did the Native Americans build anything so grand even as the smaller villages, like Angel Mounds in southern Indiana, with its mile of stockade with 53 bastions and rectilinear painted houses.

That the Native Americans were weakened does not mean that they were weak. Pontiac made this point to the British and Americans after he was deserted by his French allies in 1763. Rousing the tribes of the region, he waged war on a front a thousand miles long, taking every British fort except Detroit and Pittsburgh, inflicting casualties at least ten times his own losses, and forcing a radical change in British imperial policy. It is too easily forgotten that this successful Native American war actually convinced the government in London to constrain its citizens from further invasions of the territories Pontiac was defending. The working alliances he wrought, from Virginia to New York, were only to be dissolved when the British had him assassinated in 1769.

OPPOSITE: *The Lake Superior shoreline, Wisconsin. The Great Lakes provide the United States with a vast inland sea, which established the pattern of settlement in the area.*

Twenty years later, the Congress of the United States set out, in the Northwest Ordinance, to build a new society. In the Northwest Territory Americans might start fresh to form a better reality than that possible within the refractory original thirteen states, cluttered and clogged by inexpungible bad habits such as human slavery and an unsuitable appetite for the luxuries of Europe. Emboldened by such a prospect, they laid upon the land a grid—a geographic and psychological matrix into which their fellow citizens might place schools and colleges and churches, villages for those who liked villages and plantations for those who wished to avoid coming together too much—but all in modest sizes.

There was nobility in these plans, but in retrospect it appears as a flawed nobility. The founders shared in the human condition; they had angels' dreams, though with the rest of us their understanding was earthbound. Even as they were laying before the world their exalted aspirations, they betrayed how ugly were the racial realities of their time. They envisioned the Northwest Territory populated by free men and women, but some of them did not like to think of that population including free people who were black. (The Northwest Ordinance forbade slavery in the territory, but it contained a clause recognizing the right of owners to reclaim fugitive slaves—the new land would not be allowed to become a haven for slavery's refugees.) And they marked out, neatly, towns and houses, gardens, farms, and burial places, overlooking the presence of the numerous Native Americans who already had houses and villages, fields and burial places. From the 1820s onward, the region lying between the Ohio River and the Great Lakes received a rush of settlement from the East, some of it by water along the lakes and rivers, some along the National Road.

The northern tier of the region took upon itself a Yankee quality, building in the materials used traditionally by Yankees— pine horizontals painted white. When the usual things were not at hand, the settlers used exotic materials like cobblestones. The region of Yankee settlement is still marked by a distinctive glottal speech pattern and by a density of Greek Revival architecture; indeed, a region we could call "Greater New England" extends from New York's Finger Lakes into the Western Reserve of Ohio. This is, or was, actually the Western Reserve of *Connecticut,* a remnant of its colonial-era holdings west of Pennsylvania. West of the Western Reserve lie the Firelands of Ohio, compensatory acreage for property burnt during the Revolution by British raiders scorching out resistance on the Connecticut shore.

INTRODUCTION 15

The Yankee province continues into northern Indiana, around the corner of Lake Erie where Commodore Perry scored one of the few victories achieved by the Americans over the British in the War of 1812, and on across the band of counties in southern Michigan and northern Illinois. Greater New England includes the Saint Croix River Valley, dividing Minnesota from Wisconsin, the extreme reach of gentility in the contiguously settled United States before 1860. Minnesota's Taylors Falls, Afton, and Franconia and Wisconsin's Saint Croix Falls and Hudson were the last outposts of Yankeedom before it leapt a thousand miles of prairie and desert, eerie badlands, mountains, and western rivers. It came to earth again and founded its penultimate colonies in Oregon and Washington (the ultimate Yankee colony was on Oahu).

Brick had been the preferred building material of the Tidewater, the Upper South, and the central colonies, and it was generally found in the band of settlement descending the Ohio River and penetrating its small tributary streams. In the belt of counties along the Ohio River one feels as if one is in Virginia; many of the region's people came from there, or from Virginia's western dependencies, Kentucky and Tennessee. The brick band has extensions northward into Illinois and Indiana, swinging around the tip of Illinois and up the Mississippi into the mining region of southwestern Wisconsin and northwestern Illinois. There was a good deal of brick where the planters of the Deep South had heavily invested in Abe Lincoln's central Illinois. The brick-building tradition in the Midwest was occasioned by the declines of Virginia and South Carolina and the inhospitality to agriculture of Appalachia. Southern migration was less likely to be accompanied by the Yankees' shrewdness of mechanical invention or their sectarian utopianism, but it did sustain certain habits of courtesy that expressed themselves rather subtly in an architecture somewhat more deferential to its neighbors than was likely to be found in the North. It can be discerned in beautiful villages like Vevay and Madison, Indiana, and what is left of Lexington, Kentucky, and Shawneetown, Illinois. It is arresting to note how differently these two bands of settlement evolved. The Butternut areas, so-called because their people dyed their clothes with walnut or butternut oil, were dominated by the culture of the South and Pennsylvania. They tended to produce corn, sweet potatoes, and corn-based whiskey. James McPherson, the historian of the Civil War, has pointed out that they were also known for their antibank and antiblack sentiments and illiteracy. They voted overwhelmingly for

Democrats, and more of them were Baptist than anything else. The Yankee counties voted Whig and later Republican. They produced wheat, cheese, and wool. Statistics show that they had higher farm values, more improved land, farm machinery, and probank sentiment. They had more schools, and greater literacy, tended toward Congregational and Presbyterian churches, and opposed slavery.

The Butternut migration also gave its flavor to Galena, Illinois, a red-brick, templed little town curiously removed far to the northwest of its main current, and to Mineral Point, just across the border in Wisconsin, which was largely built of stone by Cornish tin-miners. Even those Butternuts who settled Wisconsin did not build like Yankees and they did not talk like Yankees; they had been trained for centuries to resist the English and their bland, deaspirated speech, inherited by the New Englanders.

There are not many places in the Great Lakes region where one can find evidence of the countryside before the coming of humankind. The land has been scarred, plowed, skinned, stripped, and paved. But there are gorges in the southern Ohio hill country where virgin timber can be found. South of Paoli, Indiana, there remain those "few black walnuts 130 feet high with trunks 5 feet in diameter, 70 feet high to the first limbs; oaks poplars etc. in proportion" that amazed the naturalist Andrew Hepburn in the mid-1900s. There are islands and patches of old-growth pines in the "north woods" of Minnesota, Wisconsin, and Michigan, though not nearly so many as were there when I guided canoe trips in the Boundary Waters in the 1940s.

Since the first person singular has entered this essay, it may not be amiss for me to suggest to you that from my point of view, the clearest justification for the conviction that human intervention in the landscape may ennoble as well as desecrate it is to be found in this region of America. To my eye, Louis Sullivan's bank in Owatonna, Minnesota, is America's Parthenon. William Gray Purcell's little house on Lake Place in Minneapolis, recently restored by the Minneapolis Institute of Arts, is far more important as a record of human achievement than most of the "period rooms" in the great museums of the nation. And a single visit to Frank Lloyd Wright's Taliesin in Spring Green, Wisconsin, should be enough to make Americans proud of their country—and induce them to wonder what were the qualities of the culture that could produce these masterpieces all within a decade of each other.

OPPOSITE: *Louis Sullivan's National Farmers Bank in Owatonna, Minnesota, the first of his distinctive Midwestern banks.*

C H A P T E R   O N E

OHIO

Ohio was the first of the Great Lakes states to be widely settled and the first to achieve statehood (1803). A study of its history can begin on its northern and southern boundaries, formed respectively by Lake Erie and the Ohio River. The river was the highway of settlement, the avenue of frontier commerce, and the dividing line between the North and South. The first and second cities in the Northwest Territory formed on its banks—Marietta in the summer of 1788 and Cincinnati six months later. The river's importance waned in the 1850s with the advent of trains and the construction of the Soo Locks at the formerly impassable falls between Lakes Superior and Huron. Now Lake Erie began to play a major role in Ohio's destiny, as the state emerged from a rural, agricultural economy to become a highly urbanized industrial giant.

Long before this transformation took place, 3,000 to 1,500 years ago, Ohio was the heartland of Indian cultures that left behind an array of artifacts and earthen mounds. Much remains unknown about these cultures, their waxing and waning being perhaps the foremost mystery. The Adena group flourished from around 1000 B.C. to A.D. 100, while the Hopewell culture, which may have evolved from the Adena, dates from about 200 B.C. to A.D. 500. Their preferred haunts were the lush valleys of the rivers that feed into the Ohio River, and a sampling of their magnificent earthworks can still be seen in southern Ohio. Many of these remains have been destroyed by the plow or backhoe, but thousands remain. Early settlers were keenly interested in the mysterious effigies and hummocks, which often contained caches of lovely objects, and some argued for their preservation. Beginning in the mid-nineteenth century, some of the first excavations in American archaeology were done at sites in Ohio's river valleys.

When French fur traders and missionaries began penetrating the Great Lakes in the late 1600s and early 1700s they encountered Indians who were themselves fairly new arrivals. In the late 1600s the Iroquois, supplied with British guns, waged a prolonged war on their competitors in the fur trade and drove the Huron and other tribes from the Lake Ontario area. These tribes took refuge in the western Great Lakes, where they forged alliances with the French, although they were attracted by the better prices and

OPPOSITE: *Evidence of the Hopewell Indians' far-flung trade can be found in this vivid bird's claw, made from mica mined in the southern Appalachians.* PAGES 26–27: *Religious observance and traditional farming methods characterize Ohio's Amish communities.*

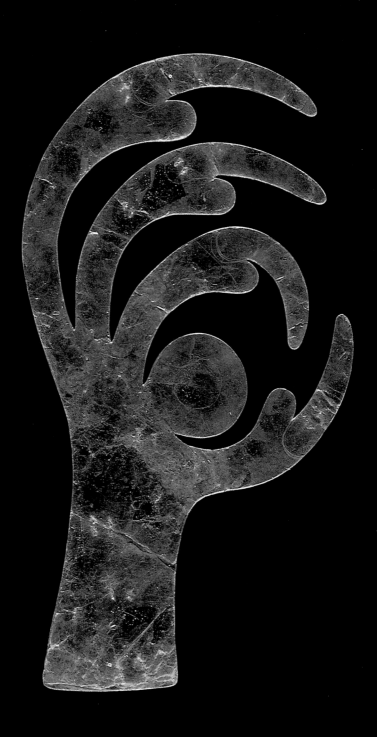

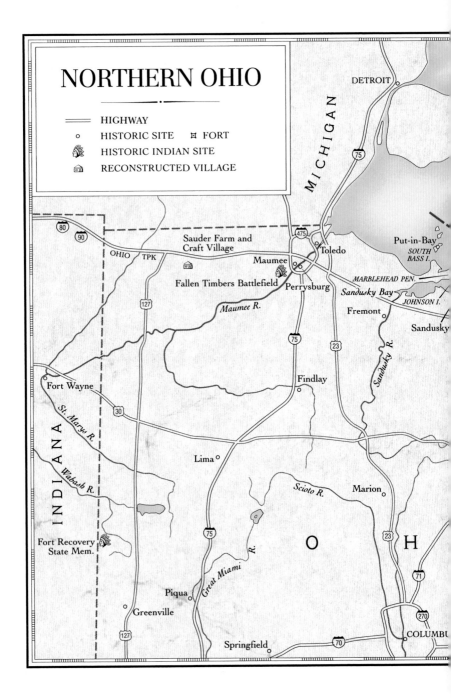

NORTHERN OHIO

- ═══ HIGHWAY
- ○ HISTORIC SITE ⛫ FORT
- HISTORIC INDIAN SITE
- RECONSTRUCTED VILLAGE

DETROIT

MICHIGAN

80 90

OHIO TPK

Sauder Farm and
Craft Village

475

Toledo

Put-in-Bay
SOUTH
BASS I.

Maumee

MARBLEHEAD PEN.

Fallen Timbers Battlefield

Perrysburg

Sandusky Bay

JOHNSON I.

127

Maumee R.

Fremont

Sandusky

75

23

Sandusky R.

Fort Wayne

Findlay

St. Marys R.

30

INDIANA

Wabash R.

Lima

Scioto R.

Marion

75

23

O   H

71

Fort Recovery
State Mem.

Great Miami R.

Piqua

270

Greenville

COLUMBU

127

Springfield

70

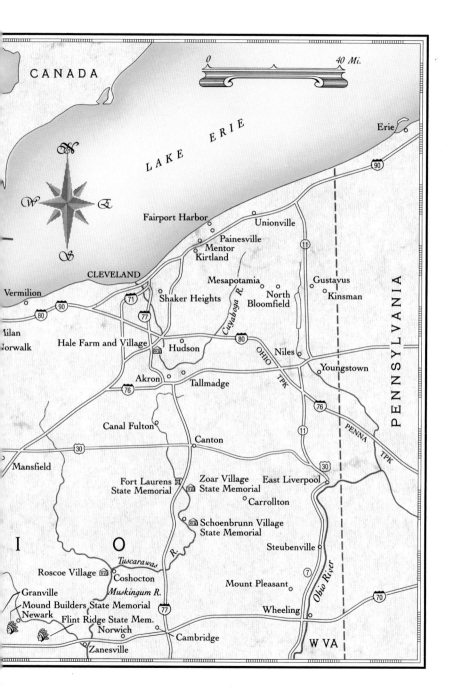

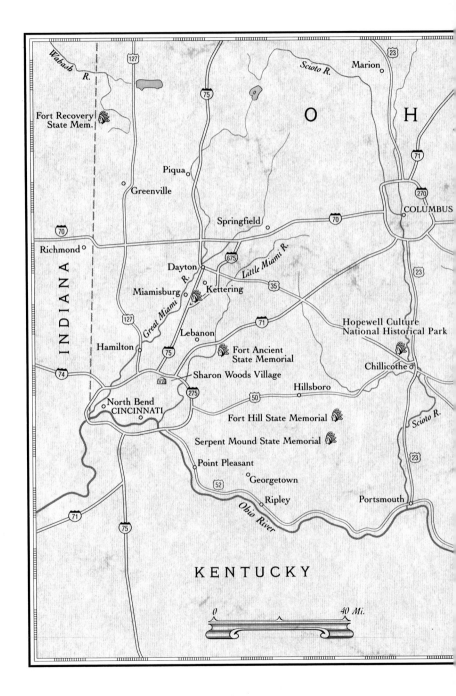

OHIO

Fort Laurens
State Memorial

Zoar Village State Mem.

East Liverpool

Carrollton

New Philadelphia

Schoenbrunn Village

Steubenville

7

Roscoe Village

Tuscarawas R.

Coshocton

Mount Pleasant

Granville

Mound Builders State Memorial

Newark

70

Wheeling

Norwich

Cambridge

Flint Ridge
State Memorial

Zanesville

ncaster

Ohio
Ceramic
Center

Muskingum R.

Hocking R.

33

Marietta

Ohio River

Athens

7

50

Parkersburg

Buckeye Furnace
State Memorial

77

WEST VIRGINIA

35

Gallipolis

7

PENNSYLVANIA

SOUTHERN OHIO

═══ HIGHWAY

○ HISTORIC SITE

⊟ FORT

  HISTORIC INDIAN SITE

  RECONSTRUCTED VILLAGE

greater supply of trade goods offered by the British. These skirmishes expanded in 1754 to the French and Indian War, which was fought primarily in western Pennsylvania and in a corridor from Montreal to Lake Champlain. Indians fought on both sides of the conflict, although more joined the ranks of the French. In 1763 the French lost the war and consequently their empire in North America.

The Indians, who had not been consulted as to the peace terms, lashed out at the victors in Pontiac's War, which lasted for five months in 1763. Indian resistance was organized, rallying under the Ottawa chief Pontiac, and many forts were seized. For two years Pontiac made his base on the Maumee River near present-day Toledo. The British were finally able to subdue the Indians, but they realized there would be no guarantee of peace without demarcating tribal lands. In 1768 the Iroquois, enticed by twenty boatloads of presents, signed the first Treaty of Fort Stanwix, which established the Ohio River as the permanent border between Indian country to the northwest and white settlement to the south and east. An estimated 60,000 Indians lived in the Great Lakes region at the time of the treaty.

With the outbreak of the Revolutionary War, both the British and Americans urged the Indians to remain neutral, but they were soon embroiled; once again mostly on the losing side. The new republic had no intention of holding the line of settlement at the Ohio River, and the Northwest Ordinance of 1787 defined the methods of colonizing the area. One of the first tasks was to remove squatters who had crept north of the Ohio River, both as a gesture to the Indians and as an attempt to ready the area for systematic settlement. To this end, Fort Harmar was built in 1786 at the mouth of the Muskingum, where two years later Marietta would be established. The Indians themselves proved a stronger deterrent to the squatters than did the federal troops. Between 1783 and 1790, Indian raiding parties along the Ohio River killed, wounded, or took prisoner some 1,500 settlers.

At the same time Indians were refusing all government demands for Ohio land cessions. Of this situation the governor of the Northwest Territory, Arthur St. Clair, wrote in 1788, "Our pretentions to the country [the Indians] inhabit has been made known to them in so unequivocal a manner, and the consequences are so certain and so dreadful to them, that there is little probability of there ever being any cordiality between us—The idea of being ultimately obliged to abandon their country rankles in their minds." In 1790 President George Washington directed federal troops to remove the Indians by force. The so-called Ohio Indian Wars, which occurred along the present-day boundary of Ohio and Indiana, lasted for four years. The wars began badly for the government. General Josiah Harmar's untrained, poorly equipped militia was soundly defeated in 1790 by a confederacy of Miami, Shawnee, Potawatomi, and Ojibwa fighting under the command of Miami chief Little Turtle. In 1791 Little Turtle and his coalition routed Arthur St. Clair at Fort Recovery in the worst military defeat in an engagement with Indians in American history. The tide turned with Washington's appointment of General Anthony Wayne, who began his march north from Cincinnati in 1793. In the 1795 Treaty of Greene Ville, which concluded the Ohio Indian Wars, the Indians relinquished claims on most of present-day Ohio. By 1817 they had turned over virtually all remaining lands in the state.

Meanwhile, Governor St. Clair was working with skill and energy to impose a moral, legal, and political framework on the formless Northwest. The Land Ordinance of 1785 provided broad instruction for the disbursement of lands and set aside land in each township for the maintenance of public schools, while the Northwest Ordinance of 1787 established more explicit guidelines: orderly government, a court system, an appointed governing body, the creation of a body of laws, and eventual statehood with increasing population. It also guaranteed freedom of religion and public education and explicitly prohibited slavery (though it implicitly accepted slavery in the territory south of the Ohio and contained the nation's first fugitive slave law).

Settlers poured into Ohio country. The population grew from 42,000 in 1800 to 230,750 by 1810; in 1803 Ohio attained statehood. Nevertheless, the region was hardly a settled or safe place, and the War of 1812 confirmed that neither the British nor the Indians were yet ready to give up their prior claims. Three important events of that war occurred in Ohio: General William Henry Harrison's troops repelled a British and Indian siege at Fort Meigs near present-day Toledo; Major George Croghan successfully defended Fort Stephenson at present-day Fremont; and Oliver Hazard Perry's decisive naval victory on Lake Erie near Put-in-Bay helped pave the way for Harrison's ultimate success at the Battle of Thames in Ontario.

In 1811 the *Orleans* became the first steamboat to ply the Ohio
River, while in 1818 *Walk-in-the-Water,* the first steamboat on Lake
Erie, journeyed from Buffalo to Detroit with stops at Cleveland
and Sandusky. These events presaged a new era of commerce, one
that promoted farming from a subsistence endeavor to a commercial one and that witnessed the rise of Ohio's port cities, especially
Cincinnati. With word of the construction of the Erie Canal, the
state embarked on its own ambitious canal-building program intended to link Lake Erie with the Ohio River. The Ohio and Erie
Canal went from Cleveland to Portsmouth, while the Miami and
Erie linked Cincinnati with Dayton and ultimately with Toledo.
These canals, opened between 1827 and 1847, brought great prosperity to Ohio, but they were supplanted within twenty-five years
by railroads, which were faster, more comfortable, and easier to
maintain (flooding and bank erosion were constant problems).

Many of Ohio's early settlers were from New England and the
Northeast. These Yankees were antislavery and, with the outbreak
of the Civil War, pro-Union—Ohio produced 30,000 volunteers,
more than twice its quota. Three Ohioans were prominent in
Union command: Ulysses S. Grant, who was born and raised in
Point Pleasant and Georgetown east of Cincinnati; William Tecum-
seh Sherman, a native of Lancaster in south-central Ohio; and
Philip Sheridan, who grew up in Somerset, just east of Lancaster.

Union setbacks in 1862 and the enactment of a conscription
law in 1863 gave rise to an antiwar movement that coalesced as the
Peace Democrats, a faction of the Democratic party whose members were often referred to as Copperheads. This movement was
strongest in portions of Illinois, Indiana, and Ohio that had been
settled by agrarians from the upper South. Known as Butternuts,
for the oil of butternuts or walnuts that they used to dye their
clothes, some were rural people who, while not particularly proslavery, had ties to the South and feared the competition of blacks.
Their leader, Dayton congressman Clement L. Vallandigham, was
arrested and convicted for disloyalty to the Union after meeting
with Confederate leaders. President Lincoln commuted his sentence to banishment to the South.

After the Civil War, Ohio began a dramatic shift from a largely
rural, agricultural society to an urban, industrial economy. The rise
of railroads and the parallel decline in river traffic account in part
for the change, but more important factors were the discovery of
iron ore around Lake Superior, the discovery of coal in western

Pennsylvania, and the opening of the Soo Locks in 1855 at Sault Sainte Marie. Iron ore and coal are the raw materials for steel production, and Ohio was positioned about midway between the sources of both. Cleveland in the Cuyahoga Valley and Youngstown in the Mahoning Valley emerged as the nation's major steel-manufacturing areas. The discovery of oil at Titusville, Pennsylvania, spurred research in petroleum-refining processes, and in 1870 Clevelander John D. Rockefeller and his partners formed Standard Oil. Steel and oil brought wealth to Cleveland and produced a powerful political bloc concerned with protecting its business interests in Congress. Its spokesman, the dapper and articulate millionaire Marcus Hanna, masterminded the presidential election of William McKinley in 1896. Reacting to the monopolistic growth of industries such as Standard Oil, Ohio senator John Sherman, brother of General William Tecumseh Sherman, authored the Sherman Antitrust Act in 1890.

This chapter begins in northwestern Ohio with Toledo, moves southward to Cincinnati, then turns eastward through the river towns and Indian sites of the Ohio River valley. The next section loops through the Western Reserve, part of Connecticut until 1800, where some areas still bear the stamp of the New Englanders who settled there. Finally the chapter moves to the interior of the state, a region that embraces both modest villages and the metropolis of Columbus, the state capital.

W E S T E R N   O H I O

TOLEDO

The Lake Erie port of Toledo, at the mouth of the Maumee River, was incorporated in 1837 following the yearlong Toledo War, a political skirmish between Ohio and the soon-to-be state of Michigan for rights to the port. It ended when Congress awarded the Maumee Bay region to Ohio and granted Michigan the Upper Peninsula. In the 1840s the Wabash and Erie Canal linked Toledo to the rich agricultural markets of Indiana, while the Miami and

OVERLEAF: *Toledo, an important Great Lakes port in the nineteenth century, became an international port for oceangoing ships with the opening of the Saint Lawrence Seaway in 1959.*

Erie Canal connected it with Cincinnati and the Ohio River. The canal traffic brought growth: Mills and factories sprang up along the Maumee River, and immigrants, especially Germans and Poles, poured into the city to work in them. A network of railroads followed the canals, and by the 1880s the city was the third-largest rail center in the country. Natural gas fields provided abundant and cheap fuel for industry, particularly for the manufacturing of glass, for which Toledo has been known since the 1880s. In 1895 the discovery of oil led to a local oil-refining industry.

The Greek Revival **Oliver House** (27 Broadway), designed by Boston hotel architect Isaiah Rogers, opened in 1859 and soon became Toledo's most fashionable hotel.

MAUMEE

The **Wolcott House Museum Complex** (1031 River Road, 419–893–9602) is a collection of six nineteenth-century buildings, including the Wolcott House, built between 1827 and 1836; an 1840s

ABOVE *and* OPPOSITE: *A log house moved from the banks of the Miami and Erie Canal is preserved on the grounds of the Wolcott House Museum Complex in Maumee.*

saltbox-style farmhouse; and a log house from the banks of the
Miami and Erie Canal. Each is furnished according to the appropriate period. The 1835 **House of Four Pillars** (322 East Broadway, private) is a stately Greek Revival structure that served as a
stop on the Underground Railroad. Its numerous residents included the author Theodore Dreiser and Union general James Steed-
man, a hero at the Battles of Chickamauga and Nashville. Portions
of the unexcavated earthwork remains of the British **Fort Miami**
can be seen between Michigan Avenue, River Road, Corey Street,
and the Maumee River.

Fallen Timbers State Memorial

This battlefield (two miles west of Maumee on Route 24) was the
site in 1794 of a brief but important clash between General Anthony Wayne's troops and a confederacy of Indians led by Chiefs
Turkey Foot and Little Turtle. President George Washington had
named Wayne commander-in-chief of the American army after a
series of military setbacks.

Wayne's disciplined troops, including 2,000 regulars and
1,000 Kentucky militia, marched toward the Maumee Valley from
Cincinnati in the fall of 1793, establishing outposts at twenty-five-
mile intervals along the way. One of the scouts who provided
Wayne with invaluable information during this campaign was fron-
tiersman William Wells, who spent his adolescence among the
Miami but returned in later years to act as scout, interpreter, and
Indian agent. Wayne's rapid and efficient sweep northward earned
him the name "Big Wind" among his Indian adversaries, and one
of his detachments scored a victory at Fort Recovery in June.

On August 20, 1794, scouts warned Wayne of Indians lying in
wait amid piles of tornado-strewn brush and timber just north of
Fort Deposit. Prepared for the ambush, his men routed the Indians, who fled toward the nearby British-held Fort Miami. The
British commander at the fort, fearing attack by the federal troops,
closed the stockade doors to his ostensible Indian allies, and they
dispersed. A **monument** marks the site of the battle. The 1795
Treaty of Greene Ville, which resulted from the Indians' defeat at
Fallen Timbers, arranged for the ceding of two-thirds of Ohio to
the federal government. The Indians' attempts to hold the line of
white settlement at the Ohio River were dashed.

FORT MEIGS

William Henry Harrison built Fort Meigs on a ridge along the Maumee River during the War of 1812. In May and July 1813 British troops, with substantial support from Tecumseh's Indian warriors, laid siege to the fort, and both times Harrison's forces, who numbered some 1,200, successfully defended it. The twin victories helped improve American morale after the loss of Detroit to the British and other defeats in the Northwest. The reconstructed ten-acre fortification includes seven blockhouses, cannon batteries, and earthen traverses. Exhibits give an overview of the War of 1812, depict life at the fort, and explain how it was constructed.

LOCATION: Route 65, Perrysburg. HOURS: June through August: 9:30–5 Wednesday–Saturday, 12–5 Sunday; September through October: 9:30–5 Saturday, 12–5 Sunday. FEE: Yes. TELEPHONE: 419–874–4121.

RUTHERFORD B. HAYES
PRESIDENTIAL CENTER

Rutherford B. Hayes, the nineteenth president of the United States, inherited this twenty-five-acre estate from his bachelor uncle Sardis Birchard, who helped raise him after his father died. The estate, known as Spiegel Grove, was Hayes's home from 1873 until his inauguration in 1877 and again after he left the presidency in 1881. He and his wife, Lucy, are buried here. The 1859 brick mansion is furnished with period pieces and holds research materials and a museum of Hayes family memorabilia in the Hayes Library. The fence enclosing Spiegel Grove includes six iron gates from the White House that date from 1873.

LOCATION: 1337 Hayes Avenue, Fremont. HOURS: 9–5 Monday–Saturday, 12–5 Sunday. FEE: Yes. TELEPHONE: 419–332–2081.

SAUDER FARM AND CRAFT VILLAGE

The land to the west of Toledo, now a region of fertile farms, was the last part of Ohio to be settled. Known as the Black Swamp, the area was an impenetrable forest bog until it was drained and cleared in the last half of the nineteenth century. In its heart is the

Sauder Farm and Craft Village, a compound of nineteenth-century structures, some authentic, some replicas, including an 1890s schoolhouse, a general store, a farmstead, and a printing office. A **museum** contains nineteenth-century tools, machinery, household items, and quilts, and costumed guides demonstrate nineteenth-century crafts.

LOCATION: Route 2, just north of Archbold. HOURS: Mid-April through late October: 10–5 Monday–Saturday, 1–5 Sunday. FEE: Yes. TELE-PHONE: 800–590–9755.

FORT RECOVERY STATE MEMORIAL

Although off the beaten track, the Fort Recovery State Memorial, which includes replicas of two blockhouses and a stockade, is one of the most historically significant sites in the Great Lakes area. In 1791, two years before the fort was built, an estimated 1,000 Indians led by Miami chief Little Turtle won a stunning victory over Major General Arthur St. Clair and his 1,400 troops at this location. When St. Clair was assigned the job of fighting the Indians, he was 55 and crippled by gout, and his army of regulars and militia were poorly equipped and trained. At sunrise on November 4, 1791, Little Turtle and his warriors closed in on the federal troops, who were encamped on high ground near the Wabash River, and killed some 600 men. The battle was the U.S. government's worst defeat in the long history of warring with the Indians.

In June 1792 General Anthony Wayne, a Revolutionary War hero who had failed as a politician in Georgia, replaced St. Clair as major general and embarked on a concerted campaign to defeat the Indians. Fort Recovery, built by his troops in the winter of 1793, played a crucial role in Wayne's ultimate success. On June 30, 1794, a group of Indians, again led by Little Turtle, attacked the fort—the battle was bloody and prolonged, but the federal troops finally turned back the Indians. The greatly improved skill of Wayne's troops was not lost on Little Turtle, who at this point urged conciliation with the United States. His fellow chiefs did not heed his advice, and Little Turtle lost stature among the confederation of Indians, although Wayne's victory at the Battle of Fallen Timbers would prove him right.

OPPOSITE: *Blockhouse No. 3 in the reconstructed Fort Meigs, originally built under the command of General William Henry Harrison and the site of two important American victories in the War of 1812.*

The museum at Fort Recovery contains exhibits of federal uniforms and Indian garb, displays explaining the Indian wars of the 1790s, and a large collection of artifacts. A 93-foot-tall monument commemorates the defeat of St. Clair in 1791.

LOCATION: Routes 49 and 119, Fort Recovery. HOURS: June through August: 12–5 Daily; May and first half of September: 12–5 Saturday–Sunday. FEE: Yes. TELEPHONE: 419–375–2311.

GREENVILLE

During the winter of 1793–1794, General Anthony Wayne carefully trained troops at Fort Greene Ville, as the place was then known, in preparation for the Battle of Fallen Timbers. In the summer of 1795 Wayne negotiated the Treaty of Greene Ville with Miami leader Little Turtle and the chiefs of other tribes, including the Delaware, Wyandot, Shawnee, Ottawa, and Potawatomi. The 1768 Treaty of Fort Stanwix, which had fixed the "permanent" boundary of white settlement south of the Ohio River, had already been abrogated, and with the Treaty of Greene Ville the Indians signed over two-thirds of present-day Ohio.

The **Garst Museum** (205 North Broadway, 937–548–5250), located in an 1852 inn, contains exhibits pertaining to the forts built in the area during the Indian campaigns and the signing of the treaty. There are also displays of Indian artifacts and memorabilia associated with sharpshooter Annie Oakley, who was born in the vicinity and is buried in Greenville.

PIQUA HISTORICAL AREA

The 174-acre Piqua Historical Area contains an array of sites and structures depicting the history of the Great Miami River valley. The oldest structure is a 2,000-year-old Adena mound. Artifacts and exhibits pertaining to the Woodland Indians who occupied the Ohio country from the seventeenth through the nineteenth century are housed in the Historic Indian Museum. The site of Fort Piqua, a supply post erected by General Anthony Wayne during his 1794 campaign against the Indians, is marked. Irish immigrant

OPPOSITE: *General Anthony Wayne and his officers negotiating the Treaty of Greene Ville with Miami Chief Little Turtle in 1795, shown in a detail of a rare contemporary painting.*

John Johnston was so impressed with the area when hauling supplies for General Wayne that he returned with his family to farm in 1811. He then served as Ohio Indian agent from 1812 to 1829. The Johnston Farm includes the restored brick house, built in 1810 in the traditional Hudson River style. It contains period furnishings. The Canal Boat Landing and a mile-long restored section of the Miami and Erie Canal recall the mid-nineteenth century, with rides on the canal in the *General Harrison,* a replica of an 1840s cargo boat.

LOCATION: 9845 North Hardin Road, Piqua. HOURS: June through August: 9:30–5 Wednesday–Saturday, 12–5 Sunday; September through October: 9:30–5 Saturday, 12–5 Sunday. FEE: Yes. TELEPHONE: 937–773–2522.

DAYTON

Dayton sits in the broad floodplain of the Great Miami River where its flow is augmented by three other streams—the Stillwater and Mad rivers and Wolf Creek. This lush and fertile area nurtured seminomadic Indians for centuries but proved precarious for a permanent nineteenth-century settlement. Dayton was repeatedly devastated by floods, the worst of which occurred in 1913. (A five-dam flood-control system was completed in the early 1920s.) Nonetheless the city thrived as a trade and industrial center. In 1879 Dayton citizen James Ritty invented the mechanical cashbox, and in 1884 John and Frank Patterson bought out Ritty and formed the National Cash Register Company.

Carriage Hill Reserve

Carriage Hill Reserve, on Dayton's northern edge, is a 900-acre park centered on a nineteenth-century Ohio farmstead. The **Daniel Arnold House** is the original brick structure built here by a German pioneer family in 1836. Other restored or reconstructed buildings include a summer kitchen, ice house, blacksmith shop, engine shed, wood shop, and log barn. The Arnold family cemetery is on the highest hill on the farmstead.

LOCATION: 7860 Shull Road, off Route 201. HOURS: 10–5 Monday–Friday, 1–5 Saturday–Sunday. FEE: None. TELEPHONE: 937–879–0461.

Old Courthouse Museum

The Old Courthouse is a Greek Revival limestone structure, one of the half-dozen finest public buildings in America. Designed by Howard Daniels, and his only known work, it was built between 1847 and 1850 and served as the county courthouse until 1884. Inside are exhibits on the National Cash Register Company, Miami Valley history, and memorabilia of the Wright brothers.

LOCATION: 7 North Main Street. HOURS: June through August: 10–4:30 Monday–Friday, 12–4 Saturday; Rest of year: Closed Monday. FEE: Yes. TELEPHONE: 937–228–6271.

Dayton's Old Courthouse, now a museum operated by the Montgomery County Historical Society, has a particularly fine portico of six Ionic columns.

In 1816, Colonel Robert Patterson, a Revolutionary War veteran and early settler of Dayton, built a large brick house, now the **Patterson Homestead Museum** (1815 Brown Street, 937–222–9724). The family farm housed three generations; grandsons John and Frank founded the National Cash Register Company. The Federal-style homestead contains antiques and period furnishings.

DAYTON AVIATION HERITAGE NATIONAL HISTORICAL PARK

Wilbur and Orville Wright lived in Dayton most of their lives. In 1992, Congress established the Historical Park to commemorate the legacy of the brothers and of their friend, the poet Paul Laurence Dunbar. The Wrights, self-educated in the science of aviation, built and flew the first flying machine. The Historical Park consists of scattered sites and associated sites.

A museum is at the **Wright Cycle Company** (22 South Williams Street, 937–225–7705), where the brothers operated a bicycle-manufacturing and printing business from 1895 to 1897. At another bicycle shop that they owned later, the Wrights built the plane that they flew at Kitty Hawk, North Carolina, for twelve seconds on December 17, 1903—the first heavier-than-air craft to fly under its own power.

Between 1903 and 1910, the brothers built three hangers at the **Huffman Prairie Flying Field.** Here, northeast of Dayton, they established the first permanent flying school, where more than one hundred of the world's first aviators learned to fly. The **Wright Memorial** at Wright-Patterson Air Force Base (Route 444) overlooks Huffman Prairie.

The **Paul Laurence Dunbar State Memorial** (219 North Paul Laurence Dunbar Street, 937–224–7061) is the home of one the first black writers to achieve recognition in America and abroad. He lived with his mother in this simple brick home in the West Side neighborhood from 1903 until 1906, when he died of tuberculosis at the age of 34. The house, which Dunbar purchased for his mother, contains many original furnishings, papers, and personal belongings, including a bicycle given to him by the Wright brothers.

Hawthorn Hill (901 Harmon Avenue, private) is the only home built by the brothers. Wilbur died in 1912, before its completion in 1914. Orville lived there until his death in 1948.

Carillon Historical Park

This museum park depicts the history of the Miami Valley from the arrival in 1796 of the first white settlers to the early twentieth century. Special emphasis is placed on industrial development and local inventions. The central attraction is the 1905 *Wright Flyer III*, the Wright brothers' third airplane and the first that was capable of turning. Exhibits in the Wright Cycle Company, a replica of the building in which Wilbur and Orville built their experimental aircraft, focus on their three careers as printers, bicycle makers, and pioneers of aviation, and the machine shop is equipped with period tools. Other exhibits in the park include the 1796 Newcom Tavern, the oldest building in the city, which served as an inn; a 1903 Barney and Smith railroad coach; an original lock from the Miami and Erie Canal; and a 1912 Cadillac, the first car equipped with a self-starter, a device invented by Dayton resident Charles Kettering.

LOCATION: 2001 South Patterson Boulevard. HOURS: May through August: 10–6 Tuesday–Saturday, 1–6 Sunday; September through April: Closes at 5. FEE: Yes. TELEPHONE: 937–293–2841.

The **U.S. Air Force Museum** (Springfield Street at Gate 28B, Wright-Patterson Air Force Base, 937–255–3286) details the history of aviation from the experiments of the Wright brothers to manned space flight with a comprehensive collection of military aviation items, including 200 aircraft and missiles, and exhibits profiling famous figures in aviation history.

The **Kettering-Moraine Museum** (35 Moraine Circle South, Kettering, 937–299–2722) contains exhibits of Wright memorabilia, Shaker crafts and furniture, and American decorative arts dating from 1720 to 1840. The adjacent Deeds Barn houses aviation and automotive artifacts, including Charles Kettering's self-starter.

Sunwatch Prehistoric Archaeological Park (2301 West River Road, 937–268–8199) preserves the culture of prehistoric Americans through reconstruction of one of their villages.

Miamisburg Mound (Mound Avenue, in the south end of Mound Park (614–297–2300) is an impressive Indian earthwork located in the city of **Miamisburg,** just southwest of Dayton. One of the largest conical burial mounds in eastern North America, it is 65 feet high and covers one and a half acres at its base. The mound sits on a 100-foot bluff overlooking the Great Miami River, offering a spectacular view of the river valley and wooded grassland below.

LEBANON

In 1805 a Shaker community that would survive for about a century was established a few miles from Lebanon. Handmade furniture and other Shaker artifacts can be seen at the **Warren County Historical Society Museum** (105 South Broadway, 513–932–1817), which also contains prehistoric Indian items, pioneer clothing, antique toys, farm tools, and period furnishings.

The nearby **Golden Lamb Inn** (27 South Broadway, 513–932–5065) is a hotel and tavern that has been operating continuously since 1803 and has played host to ten U.S. presidents as well as Mark Twain, Charles Dickens, Henry Clay, and Harriet Beecher Stowe. **Glendower State Memorial** (105 Cincinnati Avenue, 513–932–1817) is a handsome Greek Revival mansion, one of a magnificent row set on a hill overlooking the town. The house was built between 1836 and 1840 and contains period furnishings gathered from the Lebanon area.

Seven miles southeast of Lebanon is the **Fort Ancient State Memorial** (6123 Route 350, 513–932–4421), a Hopewell Indian site on a bluff overlooking the Little Miami River. The 764-acre park encompasses a series of earthen walls ranging in height from four to twenty-five feet; if the earthworks were placed in a straight line, they would extend nearly three and a half miles. The Hopewell culture was active between 100 B.C. and A.D. 500. Besides constructing the embankments, the Hopewell built mounds, gateways, and a 500-foot stone pavement within their enclosure. Several of the mounds are associated with astronomical alignments, giving the Hopewell a "calendar of events" system that allowed for religious or social observances during specific times of the year. About A.D. 1200, part of the site was occupied by the Fort Ancient Indians, who farmed in the rich floodplains and foraged for fish, clams, and wild edible plants. The museum describes the two cultures.

OPPOSITE: *Miamisburg Mound, near Dayton, is one of the highest burial mounds surviving from the Adena culture.*

One of eight photographic plates used for a panoramic view of Cincinnati's waterfront along

THE OHIO RIVER REGION

CINCINNATI

Cincinnati, the third-largest metropolitan area in the state, grew up as the chief river port on the Ohio, and as long as river and canal travel were the chief means of moving goods and people, the city reigned as the preeminent metropolis of the Midwest.

New Jersey trader Benjamin Stites made an exploratory swing through the Ohio country in 1786, and his favorable accounts prompted New Jersey politician and speculator John Cleves Symmes to make his own journey in 1787. Three communities quickly sprang up along the Ohio River.

In 1789 Fort Washington was built in Losantiville to protect settlers from the Indians. From this fort three successive campaigns were launched to quell the Indian tribes of the Ohio country. The first two—those of General Josiah Harmar in 1790 and

the Ohio River in 1848.

General Arthur St. Clair in 1791—were both disastrous failures. The third—General Anthony Wayne's well-organized assault in 1794—finally defeated the Indians, who a year later in the Treaty of Greene Ville relinquished most of their land in the area.

Cincinnati prospered in the aftermath. With the advent of steamboats (the first docked on the Cincinnati landing in 1811) the city became a major boat-building center. The opening of the Miami and Erie Canal to Dayton in 1829 (and subsequently to Toledo) enhanced Cincinnati's role as a trade and market hub, with pork as its best-known commodity.

With its heterogeneous population of New Englanders, Southerners, foreign immigrants, and a sizable community of freedmen, plus its reliance on the South for trade, Cincinnati became a hotbed of debate over the issue of slavery. Activists in the Underground Railroad included the influential abolitionist Quaker Levi Coffin and Presbyterian minister Lyman Beecher, the father of Harriet Beecher Stowe. Representing the opposite viewpoint, working-class residents feared that blacks would compete with them for jobs. The city was the scene of numerous bitter conflicts, including a race riot in 1829 and the destruction of an abolitionist's press in 1836. During the Civil War, Cincinnatians for the most part chose to defend the Union, while the city's loss of Southern markets was compensated for by a wealth of federal military contracts, including building gunboats for the Union navy. An active Copperhead faction remained in the area, however.

With increased reliance on trains after the Civil War, Chicago surpassed Cincinnati in importance. Nonetheless, Cincinnati continued to thrive. The crowded city began to spread from the confined flats along the Ohio—the so-called Basin—to the surrounding hilltops. The first bridge linking Cincinnati with Kentucky was completed in 1867, and the city financed and built its own railroad, the Cincinnati Southern. The Cincinnati Red Stockings, the first all-professional baseball club in the country, was organized in 1869. Manufacturing continued to expand, and Cincinnati counts among its entrepreneurs Procter and Gamble, who expanded a candle and soap business into diversified home products, and the Fleischmanns, producers of gin and yeast.

Following the move to the hills, a migration mainly of the affluent, the Basin declined to unhealthy and unsafe slums. In 1884, when a young man accused of murder received a reduced sentence, several thousand angry townspeople assembled to protest the verdict, which led to three days of fighting between the mobs and city police, militia, and the Ohio National Guard. Some fifty people were killed and much property damage was done, including the burning of the Hamilton County Courthouse. This dismal event, combined with labor strikes and continued crime in the city, foreshadowed the rise of George B. Cox, a tavern owner and master politician. The corruption accompanying his reign as political boss, from 1884 until his death in 1916, attracted the attention of such political muckrakers as Lincoln Steffens. After World War I, the Cincinnatus Association, a group of progressive civic leaders, was able to force a revamping of city government.

Fountain Square (Fifth Street between Vine and Walnut), in the heart of downtown Cincinnati, was designated a public square in 1871 over the protests of irate butchers whose Fifth Street Market was removed for the esplanade. Its centerpiece is the 1871 **Tyler Davidson Memorial Fountain.** A few blocks to the northwest is the **Cincinnati Music Hall** (1241 Elm Street, 513–621–1919), a splendid High Victorian Gothic structure designed by prominent Cincinnati architect Samuel Hannaford and completed in 1878.

The **Cincinnati Fire Museum** (315 West Court Street, 513–621–5553) preserves the memorabilia of the city's firefighters, including two motorized fire trucks made by the Cincinnati-based company Ahrens-Fox. The museum is housed in the Court Street Firehouse, an elaborate Second Renaissance Revival structure built in 1907. The immense red stone **Cincinnati City Hall** (801 Plum Street), designed by Hannaford and completed in 1893, is the city's only Richardsonian Romanesque building. The 1866 **Plum Street Temple** (Eighth and Plum streets), also known as the Isaac M. Wise Temple, combines Middle Eastern and Gothic motifs. Wise, rabbi from 1854 to 1900, was the father of American Reform Judaism and founder of Cincinnati's Hebrew Union College.

East of Downtown, Eden Park, the city's premier park, contains the **Cincinnati Art Museum** (513–721–5204), which exhibits ancient and medieval art from around the world and captures creative expression in paintings, prints, drawings, photographs, sculpture, costumes, textiles, and decorative arts.

Brooklyn Bridge–builder John A. Roebling's Cincinnati suspension bridge—the first bridge to span the Ohio River—was the world's longest suspension bridge when it was completed in 1867.

On the southern edge of downtown, near Riverfront Stadium, is the **John A. Roebling Suspension Bridge.** The panic of 1857 and the Civil War interrupted its construction, but when it was completed in 1867 its span of some 1,000 feet was the longest in the world. This engineering feat is considered a progenitor of Roebling's more famous project, the Brooklyn Bridge in New York City.

Taft Museum

Located in a ca. 1820 Federal-style house tucked away in a quiet pocket of downtown, the Taft Museum displays the private art collection of Anna Sinton and Charles Phelps Taft, who was the half brother of President William Howard Taft. The wide-ranging collection includes Chinese porcelains, maiolica, Flemish tapestry, and works by Luca della Robbia, Rembrandt, J. M. W. Turner, and Whistler, and the period furnishings include an extensive collection of Duncan Phyfe workshop pieces. Landscape murals by prominent nineteenth-century black artist Robert S. Duncanson decorate the entrance hall and foyer.

LOCATION: 316 Pike Street at East Fourth Street. HOURS: 10–5 Monday–Saturday, 1–5 Sunday. FEE: Yes. TELEPHONE: 513–241–0343.

The **John Hauck House** (812 Dayton Street, 513–721–3570), an Italianate townhouse-style mansion on a street once known as Millionaires' Row, was built in 1870 for coal merchant George Skaats, and purchased and remodelled ten years later by Hauck, one of Cincinnati's wealthy German brewers. The interior contains painted ceilings, parquet floors, and marble mantels and has been restored with period furnishings. A few blocks to the east, **Findlay Market** (Elder Street between Elm and Race streets) is the last of the city's nineteenth-century markets. The structure, although modified over the years, dates to 1852, and the market remains.

William Howard Taft National Historic Site

This commodious Italianate house was the birthplace of William Howard Taft in 1857. The son of lawyer, statesman, and foreign diplomat Alphonso Taft, William Howard likewise developed a keen interest in law and public service. With a college degree from

OPPOSITE: *The elegant carved stone facade of the restored John Hauck House, one of many surviving nineteenth-century houses on Cincinnati's Dayton Street.*

Yale and a law degree from Cincinnati Law School, he held a variety of legal and public positions, including civil governor of the Philippines in 1901. An ardent supporter of the Republican party, he became an intimate adviser to President Theodore Roosevelt and was himself elected president in 1908. When he sought a second term in 1912, his former ally Roosevelt formed the Bull Moose party and ran against him, creating a split in the Republican party that resulted in the election of Democrat Woodrow Wilson. In 1921, after serving as a law professor at Yale, Taft was appointed chief justice of the U.S. Supreme Court—a post he held until his death in 1930.

Outsized from birth—his mother remarked in a letter when he was two months old, "He is very large for his age, and grows fat every day"—Taft reached 350 pounds as an adult. An avid baseball player in his youth, he inaugurated the custom of the president throwing out the first ball at the beginning of each major league season. The house contains period furnishings and exhibits relating to Taft and his family.

LOCATION: 2038 Auburn Avenue. HOURS: 10–4 Daily. FEE: None. TELEPHONE: 513–684–3262.

The imposing **Cincinnati Union Terminal** (1301 Western Avenue, 800–733–2077), west of the downtown area, is a wonderful Art Deco structure with a ten-story rotunda in a rainbow of pastel colors that was completed in 1933. The terminal, whose walls have several large mosaic tile murals, was restored and then reopened in 1990 as the home of the **Cincinnati Museum Center.** This complex includes the **Cincinnati Historical Society Museum,** which features a riverboat landing from the mid-nineteenth century with sidewheel steamboat. It also has a World War II exhibit. Under the same roof, the **Cincinnati Museum of Natural History** is renowned for its limestone cavern, with underground waterfalls and live bats; ice-age exhibit; and the hands-on children's discovery center. The separate **Robert D. Lindner Family Theater** features a five-story, seventy-two-foot wide, 260-degree domed screen.

LOCATION: 1301 Western Avenue. HOURS: *Museums:* 9–5 Monday–Saturday, 11–6 Sunday. FEE: Yes. TELEPHONE: 800–733–2077.

Northeast of downtown is the **Harriet Beecher Stowe House** (2950 Gilbert Avenue, 513–632–5120), a nineteenth-century

Greek Revival structure where the author of the influential anti-slavery novel *Uncle Tom's Cabin* lived as a young woman. Stowe's father, Lyman Beecher, was a minister at the Presbyterian Lane Theological Seminary, which was founded in Cincinnati in 1829. The seminary was torn by debate over the slavery issue, and in 1834 half the student body decamped to join the ranks of strongly abolitionist Oberlin College near Cleveland.

The **Harrison Tomb State Memorial** (Cliff Road, one mile east of the intersection of Routes 50 and 128) stands in the small town of **North Bend.** William Henry Harrison arrived in the Cincinnati area in 1791 as an officer at Fort Washington and served as aide-de-camp to General Anthony Wayne. Harrison was the prime negotiator with the various Indian tribes of the Ohio country, securing for the federal government millions of acres of land for white settlement. Running as a Whig, he was elected ninth president in 1840 but died only a month after taking office. His grave is marked by a 64-foot sandstone obelisk.

Located in the northeast suburb of **Sharonville, Sharon Woods Village** (11450 Lebanon Pike–Route 42, in Sharon Woods Park, 513–563–9484) preserves numerous historic structures moved here from various sites in the Cincinnati area including the 1804 Kemper Log House, a two-story double-pen log house built by the first Presbyterian minister to practice north of the Ohio River; the Hayner House, a Greek Revival farmstead built in the 1840s; an 1870s suburban railroad station; a Carpenter Gothic house; and a Federal-style country home.

Twenty miles southeast of Cincinnati in **Point Pleasant** is **Ulysses S. Grant's Birthplace** (Routes 52 and 232, 513–553–4911). The three-room white frame cottage was built overlooking the Ohio River in 1817; Grant was born here in 1822. The house contains family memorabilia and period furnishings.

When Grant was a year old the family moved to nearby **Georgetown,** where his father operated a tannery. The **Ulysses S. Grant Boyhood Home** (East Grant Avenue and North Water Street, 513–378–4222), built in 1823, is a Federal-style, white brick structure containing period furnishings and Grant memorabilia. His father's tannery still stands across the street, and the two-room brick schoolhouse he attended is on South Water Street. Grant left Georgetown when he was 14 to attend boarding school.

During the nineteenth century neighboring **Ripley** was a center of steamboat production, and because prominent abolitionist

Reverend John Rankin lived nearby, its history is linked with the Underground Railroad. The **Rankin House State Memorial** (Rankin Road, off Route 52, 937–392–1627) preserves the vernacular brick home of the minister, his wife, Jean, and their thirteen children. Built in 1828, the house sits on Liberty Hill, a prominent rise overlooking the Ohio River. It is said that a light in the attic window of the Rankin house served to guide fleeing slaves across the river to safety. Harriet Beecher Stowe visited here in 1834 and later adapted Rankin's accounts of escaping slaves in her influential book *Uncle Tom's Cabin*. The house contains period furnishings and Rankin's personal effects.

SERPENT MOUND

This large and enigmatic effigy mound on a plateau overlooking Ohio Brush Creek is the best known of the prehistoric earthworks in the Ohio Valley. It measures 1,348 feet in length, about 5 feet high, and roughly 20 feet wide, although erosion has diminished its height and girth. The name refers to its slithering snakelike form: The "tail" end is coiled, while the "mouth" resembles distended jaws that seem to be grasping a large oval described variously as an egg or a frog. The exact age of construction is not known, but investigations of a nearby burial mound suggest it was built by Adena people who occupied the area between 800 B.C. and A.D. 400. The site was first excavated by Harvard professor Frederic Ward Putnam. In 1887, when destruction of the site was imminent, Putnam raised the money to save it. In 1888 the Ohio legislature passed the nation's first law protecting archaeological sites. The museum contains archaeological and geological exhibits, a diorama describing how the mound was constructed, a replica of an Adena burial mound, and some of the artifacts excavated by Putnam.

LOCATION: Route 73, four miles northwest of Locust Grove. HOURS: *Park:* Memorial Day through Labor Day: 9:30–8 Daily; April through Memorial Day and Labor Day through October: 10–5 Monday–Friday and 10–7 Saturday–Sunday. *Museum:* Memorial Day through Labor Day: 9:30–5 Daily; April through Memorial Day and Labor Day through October: 10–5 Saturday–Sunday. FEE: Yes. TELEPHONE: 937–587–2796.

OPPOSITE: *The Rankin House, in Ripley, was an important stop in the Underground Railroad.* OVERLEAF: *The significance of the Serpent Mound, constructed of stone and yellow clay by the Adena people, is still unknown.*

Some fifteen miles north of Serpent Mound, **Fort Hill State Memorial** (off Route 41, 614–297–2630) preserves a rare example of a prehistoric hilltop enclosure. An earthen and stone wall ranging from six to fifteen feet in height encloses 40 acres at the summit of a steep hill. Artifacts suggest that the wall may have been built by Hopewell Indians, who may also have had a village in the area. The earthworks lie at the center of a 1,200-acre nature preserve that is an isolated pocket of Appalachian flora and fauna. The museum has exhibits about Fort Hill's prehistoric earthworks as well as its natural history.

CHILLICOTHE

Long before the arrival of white settlers, this part of the Scioto River valley was a major center of the Hopewell culture, which flourished from 200 B.C. to A.D. 500. The wealth of ancient sites in the area inspired two Chillicothe residents, Ephraim G. Squier, a newspaper editor, and Edwin H. Davis, a physician, to investigate and map many of the prehistoric sites. Their 1848 book, *Ancient Monuments of the Mississippi Valley,* is a seminal work in the field of American archaeology and was the first publication of the Smithsonian Institution.

Founded by Virginians in 1796, Chillicothe takes its name from Chahlagawtha, the Shawnee village that previously occupied this site on the west bank of the Scioto River. The town served as capital of the Northwest Territory and was the state capital from 1803 until 1810, and again from 1812 to 1816. In the 1830s and 1840s Chillicothe thrived as a port on the Ohio and Erie Canal, then rail transportation began to supplant canal traffic.

The **Ross County Historical Society** (45 West Fifth Street, 614–772–1936) houses its collections in three nineteenth-century residences. Antiques, period furnishings, pioneer crafts, Indian artifacts, and exhibits pertaining to Ohio statehood are located in the **McClintock Residence** (45 West Fifth Street), built in 1838 with Federal and Greek Revival elements. The **McKell Library** (39 West Fifth Street) is one of a remarkable number of Federal and Greek Revival buildings in the town; it was built in 1838 and contains books and manuscripts. Various exhibits dealing with nineteenth-century activities of women are on display in the 1901 Craftsman-style **Franklin House** (80 South Paint Street).

OPPOSITE: *Adena, the Georgian house where the entrepreneur and politician Thomas Worthington entertained such luminaries as James Monroe, Henry Clay, and Chief Tecumseh.*

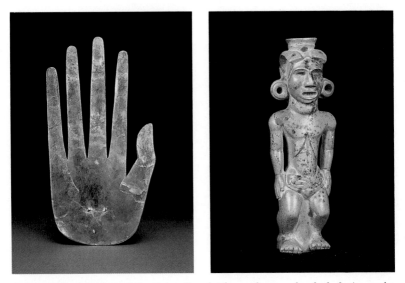

Ceremonial burial objects of the Hopewell and Adena cultures: a hand of of mica and a carved stone effigy pipe.

Adena

Situated on a hill with a view of the surrounding Scioto River valley, Adena was the estate of Thomas Worthington, an imposing force in early Ohio politics. Worthington, a wealthy land speculator, entrepreneur, and farmer, came to the valley from Virginia with his wife, Eleanor, in 1798, and they raised ten children here. As a member of the territorial legislature, he worked toward Ohio's statehood, and when that goal was achieved in 1803 he served as the state's first U.S. senator. He was elected governor in 1814 and served two terms. In the 1820s he entered the state legislature, where he helped initiate Ohio's canal system.

In the early nineteenth century, the estate at Adena encompassed 5,000 acres. The two-story, modified Georgian-style stone mansion was completed in 1807 and is furnished with period antiques. Outbuildings include a smokehouse, wash house, springhouse, tenant residence, and barn.

LOCATION: Adena Road, off Pleasant Valley Road, just northwest of Chillicothe. HOURS: June through August: 9:30–5 Wednesday–Saturday, 12–5 Sunday; September through October: 9:30–5 Saturday, 12–5 Sunday. FEE: Yes. TELEPHONE: 614–772–1500.

Hopewell Culture National Historical Park

Mound City is an ancient necropolis on the banks of the Scioto River. The thirteen-acre expanse, encircled by a low earthen berm, contains twenty-three Hopewell burial mounds, one of the largest extant concentrations of this type. The ceremonial methods used during interment are unusual—rather than simply bury the deceased, the Hopewell in this area cremated the body and interred the ashes and bones with a variety of ceremonial objects, such as decorated vessels, effigy pipes, elk and bear teeth, shell beads, and fossils, that may have designated the dead person's rank and status. Archaeologists believe the cremation method of burial was reserved for the elite members of the Hopewell society. When a crematory basin was filled—the largest site contained thirteen individuals—it was mounded over with dirt and capped with stone and gravel. **Mica Grave Mound,** named for the distinctive sheets of

Mound City, which has yielded an astonishing number and variety of artifacts.

glittering mica that were found in it, has a cutaway section that shows four burials and reveals the method of mound construction. The **Mound of Pipes** takes its name from the some 200 exquisitely carved effigy pipes that the early archaeologists Squier and Davis found there when they were excavating the site (the pipes are now in the British Museum).

Many of the mounds were disturbed or destroyed when the area was used for military training during World War I. Exhibits in the visitor center explain Hopewell burial rituals and display various ceremonial artifacts taken from the site.

LOCATION: 16062 Route 104, three miles north of Chillicothe. HOURS: June through August: 8–6 Daily; September through May: 8:30–5 Daily. FEE: Yes. TELEPHONE: 614–774–1125.

Tucked away in Wayne National Forest, about halfway between Chillicothe and Gallipolis, the **Buckeye Furnace State Memorial** (off Route 124, southeast of Roads, 614–384–3537) preserves one of the many nineteenth-century iron-ore smelters that once operated in the ore-rich area of southern Ohio and adjacent Kentucky known as the Hanging Rock iron region. The iron was precipitated from a molten mixture of ore, charcoal, and limestone heated in the furnace, a process that required vast amounts of raw materials. Built in 1851 of native sandstone and timber, the Buckeye Furnace alone used 12,000 cords of wood in one year to supply charcoal for the smelter. It was in operation until 1894. The site includes the original furnace, the restored engine house, and a replica of a company store and office.

GALLIPOLIS

Gallipolis was settled in 1790 by several hundred French Royalists who had been duped into accepting worthless deeds for their property from fraudulent representatives of the Scioto Land Company. Many of the court servants, hairdressers, footmen, grooms, musicians, and the like who were fleeing their country's revolution were unprepared for the harsh life in the wilderness, and within a few years half of the original French settlers had moved elsewhere. Those who chose to stay were forced to repurchase their land from the Ohio Company. **Our House Museum** (434 First Avenue, 614–

446–0586) is a tavern and inn that served as the social center of the community for many years. The three-story brick Federal structure was built in 1819 by Henry Cushing, a prominent early resident of Gallipolis, and contains period fixtures and furnishings.

MARIETTA

Marietta is the oldest organized American settlement in the Northwest Territory. In 1788, under the terms of the newly passed Northwest Ordinance, an adventuresome group of New England investors called the Ohio Company of Associates purchased 1.5 million acres in the southeast corner of what is now Ohio. The chief promoters of the purchase were Manasseh Cutler, an erudite New England preacher, and General Rufus Putnam, a Revolutionary War veteran and member of George Washington's staff.

In the spring of 1788 a flotilla of Ohio Company surveyors, carpenters, and artisans led by Putnam arrived at the confluence of

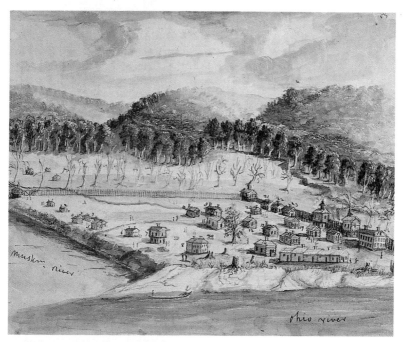

A 1792 view of Marietta shows a palisade protecting the four-year-old village, which was named after Marie Antoinette to honor French assistance to the American Revolution.

the Ohio and Muskingum rivers, where they founded Marietta and set into motion the westward settlement of the United States. Many of the settlers who followed were veterans who received land in lieu of cash for their service in the Revolutionary War.

Campus Martius:
The Museum of the Northwest Territory

Although Fort Harmar had been erected three years earlier at the mouth of the Muskingum, Putnam and his settlers constructed their own civilian fortification on a bluff overlooking the river and named it after Campus Martius, an ancient Roman military training camp. Campus Martius served as the seat of government for the Northwest Territory from 1788 to 1790 and as a refuge for Marietta settlers during the Ohio Indian wars of 1790 to 1794.

The museum, on the original site of Campus Martius, has exhibits of Indian crafts and costumes, early government and settlement, and an array of original furnishings, tools, agricultural implements, and decorative arts relating to the history of Marietta. One wing contains the **Rufus Putnam House,** the only structure from the original stockade still standing on its original foundation. Putnam was superintendent of the Ohio Company of Associates and the first surveyor general of the United States, in which capacities he drafted some of the earliest maps of the Northwest Territory. His 1788 two-story house, constructed of hand-hewn or sawed planks and posts, is a very handsome and well-crafted structure for its time and place. Many of its period furnishings date from its eighteenth-century fort days. Also on the site is the 1788 plank-and-clapboard **Ohio Company Land Office,** from which land grants were made and the territory surveyed and platted.

LOCATION: 601 Second Street. HOURS: March through April: 9:30–5 Wednesday–Saturday, 12–5 Sunday; May through September: 9:30–5 Monday–Saturday, 12–5 Sunday; October through November: 9:30–5 Wednesday–Saturday, 12–5 Sunday. FEE: Yes. TELEPHONE: 614–373–3750.

Ohio River Museum

This museum covers a broad spectrum of Ohio River history with exhibits that explain the natural history and early exploration of the river and the golden age of steamboat travel. Visitors can board the 1918 *W. P. Snyder Jr.*, the sole surviving example of a steam, stern-wheel towboat, which is moored on the adjacent Muskingum River. Also on the museum grounds are a replica of a flatboat, the type of river conveyance that carried eighteenth- and early-nineteenth-century settlers into Ohio before the advent of steamboats, and the pilothouse of the river steamboat *Tell City*.

LOCATION: 601 Front Street. HOURS: March through April: 9:30–5 Wednesday–Saturday, 12–5 Sunday; May through September: 9:30–5 Monday–Saturday, 12–5 Sunday; October through November: 9:30–5 Wednesday–Saturday, 12–5 Sunday. FEE: Yes. TELEPHONE: 614–373–3750.

The Castle (418 Front Street, 614–373–4180) is an exceptional ca. 1855 Gothic Revival-style home with Victorian furnishings.

Fascinated by prehistoric earthworks along the river bluff, settlers surveyed and mapped them—the first such sites in Ohio to be systematically described—and designated some as public squares. The thirty-foot-high Conus Mound, built by the Adena between 800 B.C. and A.D. 100, is in **Mound Cemetery** (Fifth and Scammel streets), where early settlers, including Rufus Putnam, are buried.

MOUNT PLEASANT

This small trade center was settled around 1800, and many of its early and prominent citizens were Quakers. The Society of Friends was one of the first organized groups to denounce slavery, and the town became a center of antislavery activity in Ohio and an important stop on the Underground Railroad. *The Philanthropist*, the first abolitionist newspaper in the country, was published here in 1817, and Benjamin Lundy's *Genius of Universal Emancipation* followed in 1821. The 1814 **Friends Meetinghouse** (near Route 150, 614–769–2893) is a spacious brick building that served as the first yearly meetinghouse for Quaker communities west of the Alleghenies. Annual gatherings were held in August, and some 8,900 Quakers convened here in 1826. With a seating capacity of 2,000, the massive structure was an engineering feat for its era. According to Quaker custom, it has separate entrances for men and women.

THE WESTERN RESERVE

MILAN

Milan was laid out in 1816 in the New England style by its Connecticut founders and became a booming wheat-shipping port in the 1840s after it was linked to Lake Erie by canal. The **Mitchell-Turner House** (128 Center Street) is, with the Avery-Downer House in Granville, one of the two most elegant and richly ornamented Greek Revival houses in America.

The **Thomas Edison Birthplace Museum** (9 North Edison Drive, 419–499–2135) preserves the little brick house where the inventor was born in 1847. The house is furnished with family belongings, and an adjacent building contains memorabilia and early models of some of Edison's inventions. The **Milan Historical Museum** (10 North Edison Drive, 419–499–2968) operates a five-building complex that includes a country store; a blacksmith shop; the 1840 Colonial-style Sayles House; the Newton Memorial Building, with exhibits of the decorative arts; and the main museum, displaying collections of glass, antique dolls, and costumes. A walking tour of the town's historic houses is available from the museum.

Seven miles south of Milan is the town of **Norwalk,** also founded in 1816 by settlers from Connecticut. The **Firelands Museum** (4 Case Avenue, 419–668–6038) commemorates the settlement of the Firelands, the 500,000 acres of land on the edge of the Western Reserve given to New Englanders in 1792 in compensation for properties destroyed by the British during the Revolutionary War. (The region comprises present-day Erie, Huron, and a portion of Sandusky counties as well as Marblehead Peninsula.) The museum contains period furnishings, pioneer farm and household implements, antique firearms, and various maps, artifacts, and documents relevant to the settlement. It is housed in the 1835 Preston-Wickham House, one of many buildings in the **West Main Street District** dating from the 1830s and 1840s.

SANDUSKY

Sandusky, on the south shore of a well-sheltered bay of Lake Erie, was laid out by Connecticut settlers in 1818 and contains an impressive number of nineteenth-century structures built of brick and

locally quarried limestone—most notably the commercial buildings, constructed between 1855 and 1890, that line **Water Street.**
German immigrants arrived in the 1850s and 1860s and established numerous successful wineries and breweries, such as the
Engels and Krudwig Wine Company (220 East Water Street),
which remained open until 1996. Built in 1863, the large stone,
brick, and frame structure was owned by the largest of the German
vineyards in the area.

The 1837 **Follett House Museum** (404 Wayne Street, 419–
627–9608) is a handsome Greek Revival mansion built of local
limestone for prominent Sandusky businessman Oran Follett. It
contains nineteenth-century household items, quilts, apparel, and
toys; items from the War of 1812 and the Civil War; and artifacts
from the Johnson Island Confederate Officers' Prison. This Civil
War prison, established in 1862 on an island across the bay, held an
estimated 12,000 prisoners during the course of the war. Although
nothing remains of the prison, the nearby **Confederate Cemetery**
contains the graves of some 200 prisoners who died on the island.
The island is accessible by a causeway from **Marblehead Peninsula,**
the arm of land that shelters Sandusky Bay.

Lakeside, on Marblehead Peninsula, is a Chautauqua resort
founded by the United Methodist Church in 1873. Among the
many Victorian-era structures are the Italianate **Hotel Lakeside**
(150 Maple Avenue, private), completed in 1875, and an array of
cottages and bungalows. On the peninsula's tip stands the **Marblehead Lighthouse** (off Route 163), constructed in 1821.

PERRY'S VICTORY AND INTERNATIONAL PEACE MEMORIAL

This park and museum commemorate Oliver Hazard Perry and
the Battle of Lake Erie, which occurred on September 10, 1813.
During the War of 1812, 27-year-old Perry was given a command
on Lake Erie. He stationed his flotilla at Put-in-Bay and awaited an
overture from the British navy. The enemy was sighted on the
morning of September 10, and Perry advanced in his flagship, the
Lawrence. When it was destroyed by the British, Perry, with four
men, transferred to the *Niagara,* which broke through the British
line and subdued the enemy in an intense fifteen-minute barrage.
The British surrendered at 3 PM, whereupon Perry sent to General
William Henry Harrison his terse and subsequently famous

message, "We have met the enemy, and they are ours." Perry's victory gave America control of Lake Erie and opened the way for Harrison's invasion of Canada and the Battle of Thames, which concluded the War of 1812 in the Northwest.

Erected between 1912 and 1915, the towering Peace Memorial is a 352-foot Doric column of granite topped with a bronze urn. From its observation deck visitors can view the battle site, ten miles to the northwest. The museum contains weapons and equipment from the War of 1812 and items pertaining to the construction of the Peace Memorial.

LOCATION: Put-in-Bay, South Bass Island. Accessible May through October by ferry from Catawba Point and Port Clinton. Air service is available year-round from Port Clinton Airport. HOURS: June through August: 10–7 Daily; May, September, October: 10–5 Daily. FEE: For observation platform. TELEPHONE: 419–285–2184.

Nineteenth-century resort-era structures in the tourist village of **Put-in-Bay** on **South Bass Island** include the picturesque 1873 **Round House** (Delaware Avenue), named for its distinctive domed roof; the ca. 1870 **Hunker Villa** (Route 357), a white frame Italian Villa–style structure with a captain's walk; and **Inselruhe** (Route 357), constructed in 1857 in the fanciful Steamboat Gothic style.

VERMILION

Located in one of the best natural harbors on Lake Erie, Vermilion had pretensions in the nineteenth century of competing with Cleveland, a hope dashed when its largest shipbuilder moved operations to the rival city. The **Inland Seas Maritime Museum** (480 Main Street, 216–967–3467) maintains a large museum of maritime history displaying marine engines, tools for constructing wooden ships, a Fresnel lighthouse lens, photographs, and models of various Great Lakes vessels (including the *Niagara*). A fully equipped pilothouse of a Great Lakes freighter overlooks Vermilion harbor.

CLEVELAND

Cleveland is the principal city in Ohio's Western Reserve, the northeast triangle of the state that was the remnant of vast lands promised to Connecticut by King Charles II in 1662. On July 22, 1796, Moses Cleaveland, one of the directors of the Connecticut

Land Company, and a team of surveyors arrived on the high, forested plain overlooking the east bank of the Cuyahoga River, just beyond the Appalachian foothills. Their mandate was to establish township boundaries in that portion of the Western Reserve east of the Cuyahoga (the lands to the west were still firmly in the hands of the Indians) and lay out a town site that would serve as the commercial and political center of the future villages. Cleaveland selected the east bank of the Cuyahoga where the river entered Lake Erie, a site that had obvious harbor potential, and the surveyors laid out a grid of streets converging on a village green. "These men," as historian Edmund Chapman writes, "knew no other way to lay out a town. It was their every intention to reproduce in the wilderness of the Western Reserve another such village as they had left in the east." They named the town for Moses Cleaveland (the a was inexplicably dropped), who returned to Connecticut in the fall of 1796.

For its first two decades Cleveland was a sleepy, sparsely populated town, but the opening of the Ohio and Erie Canal in 1827 made the city the major terminus on the waterway that eventually linked Lake Erie with the Ohio River. In the 1850s the railroads arrived and transformed Cleveland from a mercantile city to an industrial center, with all the attendant problems of rapid, uncontrolled growth. The railroads, for instance, were routed along the scenic river flats and lakeshore and across fashionable neighborhoods. Once Cleveland's most famous residential street, Euclid Avenue is now largely a commercial strip, the only historic site left being **Dunham Tavern** (6709 Euclid Avenue, 216–431–1060), a stagecoach stop on the Buffalo–Cleveland–Detroit Road that for many years was a social and political center of the area. Built in 1842, it is a frame structure containing period furnishings, Shaker items, glass, and textiles.

Linked by the railroads to the iron ranges of Minnesota and the coalfields of western Pennsylvania, Cleveland began producing steel. Waves of immigrants were attracted by the steel industry, and by 1890 Cleveland's population of some 260,000 was 37 percent foreign born. Czechs were the largest ethnic group, followed by Poles, Italians, Germans, Yugoslavians, Irish, and Hungarians. Built in 1897, the Romanesque–Second Renaissance Revival **Bohemian National Hall** (4939 Broadway) served as a cultural center and auditorium for the city's large Czech community. Churches were often the focal points of ethnic neighborhoods, and many remain throughout the city, including the primarily Czech Catholic church **Our Lady of Lourdes** (3395 East Fifty-third Street) and **St. Theodosius Russian Orthodox Cathedral** (733 Starkweather Avenue). The **Ukrainian Museum** (1202 Kenilworth Avenue, 216–781–4329) contains a large collection of artifacts and documents relating to Ukrainian culture in the United States.

In 1859 oil was discovered in Titusville, Pennsylvania, and Cleveland became the country's first refining center. Four years later, two partners in the produce business, Maurice B. Clark and John D. Rockefeller, teamed up with Samuel Andrews, an Englishman who had developed a new oil-refining process, to form the venture that would soon become the Standard Oil Company. With its large industries seeking to protect their corporate interests, Cleveland became a bastion of the Republican party in the late nineteenth century, and Cleveland money helped bankroll the campaigns of two presidents, James A. Garfield and William McKinley. Cleveland millionaire, Republican party boss, and politician Marcus Hanna attained national prominence for his electioneering and fund-raising skills during McKinley's presidential campaign.

Although it bears no resemblance to the pastoral village green it once was, Cleveland's ten-acre **Public Square** is the one visible legacy of the city's New England founders. Dominating the scene is the **Cuyahoga County Soldiers and Sailors Monument,** a commemorative to men from the area who had served in the Civil War. Completed in 1894, it is a stone building surmounted by a 125-foot granite shaft that holds aloft a 15-foot Statue of Liberty. The late Victorian structure is ornamented with bronze sculptures representing the four branches of the armed services. The oldest building on the square is the **Old Stone Church** (91 Public Square), a handsome Romanesque Revival structure built in 1855. The church interior, which was rebuilt in 1885 after a fire, includes frescoes, wainscoting, and a barrel-vaulted ceiling.

Casting an impressive shadow on the Public Square is the **Terminal Tower,** a Beaux-Arts skyscraper built in 1927 by brothers Oris P. and Mantis J. Van Sweringen, whose other major landmark in Cleveland is the residential community of Shaker Heights. The tower is an early example of the now commonplace

OPPOSITE: *Cleveland's fifty-two-story Terminal Tower, designed by the Chicago firm of Graham, Anderson, Probst & White, was the focal point of an innovative urban complex that included office building, railroad station, hotel, and department store. The Cuyahoga County Soldiers and Sailors Monument is in the foreground.*

"city-within-a-city" urban complex. Although its development coincided with the Great Depression, Terminal Tower carried into the twentieth century a good bit of the ingenuity and optimism of the nineteenth, which was fueled by Cleveland's great wealth in oil, steel, and railroads. The finest architectural expression of that exuberant era, and one of the most remarkable buildings in the country, is the **Cleveland Arcade** (401 Euclid Avenue). Completed in 1890, it is composed of two nine-story office buildings—one opening onto Euclid Avenue, the other onto Superior Avenue—joined by a five-story skylighted court appointed with ornate iron galleries, stairs, and balustrades. The arcade is light, airy, and immense (290 feet long, 60 feet wide, 104 feet tall), and the trusses of the arched ceiling—designed to distribute roof load to the outer walls as well as admit maximum light—demanded the expertise of the Detroit Bridge Company. The arcade was designed by John Eisenmann and George Smith and financed by a consortium of Cleveland financiers, including John D. Rockefeller, Louis H. Severance (a Standard Oil executive), and Charles F. Brush (developer of the arc light and electrical power station).

Another turn-of-the-century landmark in downtown Cleveland is the 1890 **Society for Savings Bank** on the Public Square, a ten-story stone building that combines Gothic, Romanesque, and Renaissance elements. It is one of the extant masterpieces of John Wellborn Root of the Chicago firm of Burnham and Root.

Under Mayor Tom Johnson's progressive and at times controversial leadership, Cleveland embarked in the early 1900s on an ambitious project to erect a monumental grouping of public buildings, a concept inspired by the 1893 Chicago Columbian Exposition. The designers of the group plan were architects Daniel Burnham, John M. Carrère, and Arnold W. Brunner. **Cleveland Mall,** as it is known, is a gathering of stately Beaux-Arts and Second Renaissance Revival structures set on a T-shaped expanse of land between East Ninth and West Third streets and Superior Avenue with a view of Lake Erie. Developed between 1903 and 1935, its major structures include the **Federal Building, Cleveland City Hall,** and **Cuyahoga County Courthouse.**

OPPOSITE: *The Cleveland Arcade has set-back balconies to allow the maximum amount of natural light to reach the ground level.*

John D. Rockefeller and Marcus Hanna are among those buried in **Lake View Cemetery** (12316 Euclid Avenue, 216–421–2665), which also contains two superlative edifices. The 1900 **Jeptha Wade Memorial Chapel** is a Greek Revival shrine, the interior of which was completely designed by Tiffany and Company, including large glass mosaic murals and windows. The 1890 **James A. Garfield Memorial** is a monumental tower capped with a conical roof that reaches a height of 180 feet. Built of local sandstone, it is a Richardsonian Romanesque structure with Gothic and Byzantine elements. A marble statue of Garfield stands in the center of the monument.

Western Reserve Historical Society Museum

The Western Reserve Historical Society Museum has extensive displays recounting the early history of the Western Reserve and the rise and ascendancy of Cleveland. The centerpiece of the museum is a series of period rooms dating from 1770 to 1920 and ranging in style from an Early American bedroom to a Renaissance Revival parlor to an Art Deco alcove. This portion of the museum is housed in two adjoining Italian Renaissance mansions, the 1918 **Leonard C. Hanna, Jr., House** and the 1910 **John Hay House.** The latter was designed by Abram Garfield, son of the president, for the widow of author and statesman John Hay.

Another wing contains the Frederick C. Crawford Auto-Aviation Museum, which displays early aircraft and an array of automobiles dating from 1895 to 1976. The society's library preserves on its north face the terra-cotta arch from the doorway of the 1893 Cuyahoga Building, a major landmark on Cleveland's Public Square. Designed by Daniel Burnham, the eight-story steel-frame building (the first in Cleveland) was demolished in 1982.

LOCATION: 10825 East Boulevard. HOURS: 10–5 Monday–Saturday, 12–5 Sunday. FEE: Yes. TELEPHONE: 216–721–5722.

The Western Reserve Historical Society Museum is located in **University Circle,** a beautiful parklike expanse of land that embraces Cleveland's major cultural institutions (Cleveland Museum of Art, Cleveland Museum of Natural History, Severance Hall of the Cleveland Orchestra) and the campus of Case Western Reserve

OPPOSITE: *The James A. Garfield Memorial in Cleveland's Lake View Cemetery includes a statue of the twentieth president by Alexander Doyle in an ornate setting.*

University. The area was developed from land donated to the city
in 1881 by Jeptha Wade, a founder of Western Union and builder
of the first transcontinental telegraph line.

Cleveland Museum of Art

Founded in 1913 and opened to the public in 1916, the Cleveland
Museum is among the finest in the nation, noted for the high
quality of its collections. Its American and European holdings are
balanced by a superb collection of Asian art, largely gathered
during the tenure of renowned Orientalist Sherman E. Lee, who
served as director from 1958 to 1983. The museum's broad American collections of furniture, silver, paintings, and photographs
include an eighteenth-century silver teapot by Nathaniel Hurd, a
chair by Samuel McIntire of Salem, an enormous (over nine feet
tall) and elaborately carved 1850s walnut sideboard, and portraits
by John Singleton Copley, Gilbert Stuart, and Charles Willson
Peale. The American painting collection is particularly strong for
its nineteenth-century works by Church, Cole, Inness, and Homer.

LOCATION: 11150 East Boulevard. HOURS: 10–6 Tuesday, Thursday–
Friday, 10–10 Wednesday, 9–5 Saturday, 1–6 Sunday. FEE: None. TELE-
PHONE: 216–421–7340.

The **Rock and Roll Hall of Fame and Museum** (East Ninth Street
at Erieside Avenue, 216–515–1920) is the only museum dedicated
to the legendary music and artists of rock and roll.

Shaker Heights is the planned residential community developed by
the Van Sweringen brothers during the 1910s and 1920s. A scenic
zone of woods, lakes (the original Shaker dams were rebuilt), and
winding boulevards, it is a classic example of the early-twentieth-
century "garden city" ideal and a far cry from the grid mentality of
Cleveland's New England founders. Through the use of deed
restrictions, the Van Sweringen Company maintained tight control
over building patterns and land use. The commercial heart of the
community is **Shaker Square** (Shaker and Moreland boulevards), a
grouping of Georgian Revival buildings around a traffic circle that
was developed between 1927 and 1929. The pastoral swath of land
between North Park and South Park boulevards contains vestiges—
earthworks, a millrace, foundations—of the North Union Shaker
Community, which existed here from 1822 to 1889. The **Shaker**

Historical Museum (16740 South Park Boulevard, 216–921–1201) displays Shaker furniture and artifacts as well as memorabilia of Shaker Heights.

JAMES A. GARFIELD HOME

Garfield's home, known as Lawnfield, is a one-story farmhouse built in 1832 and modified and expanded in the 1870s and 1880s to produce a rambling white frame structure with Stick-style elements. Garfield bought the house in 1876 and while running for president in 1880 conducted his "front porch" campaign from here. Elected as the twentieth president, Garfield was assassinated shortly after taking office in 1881. The house contains original furnishings and Garfield memorabilia, and a carriage house with five period carriages stands on the grounds.

LOCATION: 8095 Mentor Avenue (Route 20), Mentor. HOURS: 10–5 Tuesday–Saturday, 12–5 Sunday. FEE: Yes. TELEPHONE: 216–255–8722.

KIRTLAND TEMPLE

The Kirtland Temple, which sits on the brow of a hill in the town of Kirtland, was the first permanent church built by the followers of the charismatic Mormon leader Joseph Smith. The Church of Jesus Christ of Latter-Day Saints was organized in New York in 1830, and shortly thereafter Smith and his recent converts came to northeastern Ohio from New York and Pennsylvania. Tithing their skills as well as their money, the parishioners built the church between 1833 and 1836. One of the most beautiful buildings in the Western Reserve, it is a lofty stone and stucco structure with Federal and Gothic elements. Many of the decorative touches, such as the array of interior hand-carved motifs, are Mormon symbols.

LOCATION: 9020 Chillicothe Road. HOURS: February through December: 9–5 Monday–Saturday, 1–5 Sunday. FEE: None. TELEPHONE: 216–256–3318.

Fairport Harbor, a small lakefront community that was a thriving nineteenth-century port, is home to the **Fairport Marine Museum** (129 Second Street, 216–354–4825), housed in the 1871 Fairport Lighthouse. It contains navigational instruments, marine charts, items pertaining to the history of Fairport Harbor, and a fully equipped pilothouse from a Great Lakes ship.

The 1836 Mormon Temple in Kirtland marks the first stage in this religious group's cross-country odyssey from upstate New York to their ultimate settlement in Utah.

SHANDY HALL

One of the oldest homes in the Western Reserve, Shandy Hall was built in 1815 by Colonel Robert Harper, whose father, Alexander Harper, was an early settler in the reserve (he founded nearby Harpersfield in 1798). The house was occupied by members of the Harper family from 1815 until 1935 and was passed to the Western Reserve Historical Society with its contents virtually intact. The modest exterior of the vernacular frame structure belies a commodious interior—seventeen rooms appointed with family items, including American Empire furniture and French wallpaper.

LOCATION: 6333 South Ridge Road, Unionville. HOURS: May through October: 10–5 Tuesday–Saturday, 1–5 Sunday. FEE: Yes. TELEPHONE: 216–466–3680.

Visitors to Northeastern Ohio can capture the nineteenth-century New England atmosphere of the Western Reserve by driving back roads in the rural area between Youngstown and Cleveland. A string of well-preserved villages can be found along Route 87: **Mesopotamia, North Bloomfield, Gustavus,** and **Kinsman,** the last of these being the birthplace of the eminent trial lawyer Clarence

Darrow, the attorney who represented the school teacher John T. Scopes in the 1925 "Monkey Trial" in Tennessee.

YOUNGSTOWN

Youngstown was founded in 1796 by New Yorker John Young, who had purchased a township along Mill Creek and the Mahoning River from the Connecticut Land Company. A manufacturing center, Youngstown until recent years teemed with activity from the steel mills that lined the Mahoning Valley. The steel industry collapsed in the late 1970s, but a few steel mills remain. The mills attracted many immigrant workers.

Before the advent of the steel industry, Mill Creek provided waterpower for a series of grist- and sawmills that stood at the falls of the creek. The large stone-and-frame **Lanterman's Mill** (Mill Creek Park, off Canfield Road, 330–740–7115), the third structure to occupy the site, was constructed in 1845 by German flour millers who operated it until 1888. It has been restored.

The **Butler Institute of American Art** (524 Wick Avenue, 330–743–1107) is housed in a Second Renaissance Revival structure designed by McKim, Mead & White and built in 1919 by Joseph Green Butler, Jr., a Youngstown steel executive, to display his collection of American art. Nearby is the **Arms Family Museum of Local History** (648 Wick Avenue, 330–743–2589) depicting the lifestyle of former owners Olive and Wilford Arms. The **Youngstown Historical Center of Industry and Labor** (151 West Wood Street, 330–743–5934) will illustrate the life and work of steelworkers and how the iron and steel industry shaped the communities of the Mahoning Valley.

Located in the city of **Niles,** the **National McKinley Birthplace Memorial** (40 North Main Street, 330–652–1704) is a Neoclassical Revival structure designed by McKim, Mead & White and built in 1915. The memorial houses a museum that contains McKinley memorabilia, furniture, costumes, glass, and military items.

Hudson, the oldest community in Summit County, contains many nineteenth-century Greek Revival, Federal, and Gothic Revival buildings. Using Yale as their model, early Hudson residents founded Western Reserve College. After the college moved to Cleveland in 1882, the facility was taken over by **Western Reserve Academy** (115 College Street), a private preparatory school. The

Winslow Homer's 1872 painting Snap the Whip, *in Youngstown's Butler Institute of American Art (detail).*

campus is a textbook of nineteenth-century architectural styles. The handsome 1828 Federal-style **President's House** was built by Lemuel Porter, and many other campus buildings were executed by his son Simeon.

HALE FARM AND VILLAGE

Located within the scenic Cuyahoga Valley National Recreation Area, this open-air museum re-creates a Western Reserve farm and village from the first half of the nineteenth century. The complex has been developed on the original Jonathan Hale farm, which was settled by a Connecticut family in 1810. The handsome Federal-style Hale House, built in 1826 of brick made from clay on the property, contains period furnishings. Many other nineteenth-century structures have been gathered from various locations in the Western Reserve and restored around a village green. They include the 1830 Federal-style law office of U.S. Senator Benjamin Wade; the 1830 Robinson House, by master builder Jonathan Goldsmith; an 1851 Greek Revival meetinghouse; an 1816 log schoolhouse; the 1845 Greek Revival Jagger House; and an 1830 Federal-style saltbox house. Demonstrations of nineteenth-century crafts are conducted throughout the village.

LOCATION: 2686 Oak Hill Road, Bath. HOURS: Mid-May through October: 10–5 Tuesday–Saturday, 12–5 Sunday. FEE: Yes. TELEPHONE: 330–666–3711.

In **Tallmadge**, the **Town Square Historic District** preserves the oval-shaped village green, which was planned in 1809. On the green stands the **First Congregational Church**, a charming white frame structure with Federal and Georgian elements. It was built between 1821 and 1825 by Lemuel Porter, one of the important early builders in the Western Reserve.

AKRON

Akron, which derives from the Greek word for "high," sits on a rise that forms the divide between two watersheds. The site was on a well-worn portage path for Indians crossing to and from the Cuyahoga River, which flows north into Lake Erie, and the Tuscarawas, which flows south to the Muskingum and ultimately to the Gulf of Mexico. Simon Perkins, who was a promoter of the Ohio and Erie Canal and privy to its proposed route, acquired land on the divide and laid out the town in 1825. The canal opened in 1827 and Akron flourished accordingly.

Akron's most conspicuous product for many years was rubber tires. Benjamin Franklin Goodrich opened the first rubber factory west of the Alleghenies in 1870, and the industry boomed between 1910 and 1920 with the advent of automobiles. Other thriving nineteenth-century businesses included iron manufacturing, farm implements production, pottery (made from nearby deposits of superior clay), flour milling, and cereal making. Ferdinand Schumacher started making oatmeal in 1856, supplied the cereal to the Union Army during the Civil War, and began marketing Quaker Oats through grocery stores thereafter.

The **Simon Perkins Mansion** (550 Copley Road, 330–535–1120) was the estate of Simon Perkins, Jr., the son of Akron's founder. Built in 1835, the handsome stone Greek Revival structure is furnished with early and late Victorian pieces and contains costumes, glass, and pottery. Across the street is the **John Brown House** (514 Diagonal Road, 330–535–1120) where Brown, who

The three-story Great Hall, furnished in the Tudor style, part of the Stan Hywet estate. A "chaperone's window" above the fireplace leads into the master bedroom. OPPOSITE: *A birch allée in the Hywet garden.*

would later attain national fame as an abolitionist, raised sheep in the 1840s. The vernacular farmstead contains period clothing and firearms. The **Hower House** (60 Fir Hill, 330–972–6909) is a handsome and well-preserved Second Empire–Italianate mansion built in 1871 for Akron industrialist John Henry Hower. The lavish interior contains original family furnishings.

Stan Hywet Hall and Garden

The 70-acre Stan Hywet Hall and Garden is the opulent and well-groomed remnant of the former 3,000-acre estate of Frank A. Seiberling, cofounder of the Goodyear Tire and Rubber Company. The sixty-room mansion was built in 1912 in the Jacobean style; the furnishings include Tudor and Stuart furniture, antique silver, pewter, and sixteenth- and seventeenth-century Flemish tapestries. On the grounds are Japanese and English gardens, lagoons, and rhododendron-lined paths.

LOCATION: 714 North Portage Path. HOURS: 10–5 Tuesday–Saturday, 1–5 Sunday. FEE: Yes. TELEPHONE: 330–836–5533.

THE OHIO INTERIOR

CANTON

First settled in 1805, Canton was bypassed by the Ohio and Erie Canal but emerged as an important steel-manufacturing center by the turn of the century. William McKinley, born in nearby Niles in 1843, came to Canton in 1867 to set up a law practice and became active in politics, serving in Congress for fourteen years and as governor for four years. He was elected president in 1896 and reelected in 1900, but on September 6, 1901, while visiting Buffalo, New York, he was assassinated. The **McKinley National Memorial** (McKinley Monument Drive NW), located in a twenty-three-acre park, is a large circular stone mausoleum where the president is interred with his wife, Ida, and their two daughters, both of whom died at an early age.

The **McKinley Museum of History, Science, and Industry** (800 McKinley Monument Drive NW, 330–455–7043) contains a large collection of McKinley memorabilia; the Street of Shops, an exhibit of nineteenth-century interiors, including a lawyer's office and a print shop; a 1908 Martin glider; and displays of important area industries, such as the production of steel and roller bearings.

A Revolutionary War outpost, **Fort Laurens** (near Routes 212 and 77, just south of Bolivar, 330–874–2059) was garrisoned during the winter of 1778–1779 as part of an American strategy to counter the Indians and establish a supply line for an eventual attack on British-held Detroit. The garrison was encircled by British and Indian troops, and as supplies dwindled many men were killed during attempts to obtain food and firewood. In March a relief force arrived from nearby Fort McIntosh, and the enemy withdrew. While only an outline remains of the stockade, the museum exhibits many artifacts from the site as well as displays of uniforms and Revolutionary War weapons.

ZOAR

Founded in 1817 by German Separatists seeking religious freedom in the United States, Zoar is named for the biblical city where Lot

OPPOSITE: *The reconstructed ca. 1825 tinsmith's shop at Zoar, built in the 1960s on the original foundations, illustrates the Zoarite construction technique called "nogging," in which brick or sandstone was placed between reinforcing framing timbers.*

An 1889 barn-raising near Massillon was a major undertaking for the entire community.

took refuge after fleeing Sodom. Under the leadership of Joseph M. Bimeler, the Separatists purchased 5,500 acres along the Tuscarawas River and farmed the land communally. They put up saw, flour, and woolen mills, exported their surplus farm products, and contracted to build a portion of the Ohio and Erie Canal across their property. After the charismatic Bimeler died in 1853, however, the Zoarites lost initiative, and young members left the village. In 1898 common property was divided among the members and the society was dissolved.

The village is built around a geometric garden, the configuration of which has religious significance: The central Norway spruce symbolizes the tree of life and the twelve junipers encircling it represent the apostles. The houses and shops are half-timbered, brick, and log structures, many with Federal and Greek Revival elements. Built in 1835 as a home for the aged, the two-story brick Number One House was later used as a residence for the trustees of the village, including Bimeler himself; it contains period furnishings, textiles, and decorative arts.

LOCATION: Route 212, 3 miles southeast of exit 93 off Route 77. HOURS: April through May: 9:30–5 Saturday, 12–5 Sunday; June through August: 9:30–5 Wednesday–Saturday, 12–5 Sunday; September through October: 9:30–5 Saturday, 12–5 Sunday. FEE: Yes. TELEPHONE: 330–874–3011.

Located in **Carrollton**, the **Daniel McCook House** (Public Square, 330–627–3345) is a large brick Federal-style residence built in 1837. Major Daniel McCook's nine sons, along with the five sons of his brother, Dr. John McCook, became known as the Fighting McCooks for their military participation in various parts of the world but particularly in the Civil War, in which fifteen McCooks served, fourteen as officers. The house contains period furnishings, antique medical instruments, and military artifacts.

SCHOENBRUNN VILLAGE

Schoenbrunn Village, Ohio's first Moravian settlement, was established on the Tuscarawas River in 1772 by David Zeisberger and his followers. The Moravians, a pacifist German Protestant sect, had been invited by the Delaware Indians to establish a mission in the Ohio country. The missionaries built some sixty log houses arranged around a large log meetinghouse. Here they instructed the Indians in various skills and taught the children, using texts they had translated into the Delaware language. The Moravians and their Indian converts hoped to remain neutral in the increasing tension between the British-allied Indians and land-seeking white settlers, but with the outbreak of the Revolutionary War, they were vexed by hostile Indians and American frontiersmen alike. In 1777 they dismantled and abandoned Schoenbrunn and moved to two nearby Moravian villages, Gnadenhutten, twelve miles downriver, and Lichtenau, near present-day Coshocton. Over the next several years the Moravians continued to work with the Indians, but in 1781 the British sent Zeisberger and the other missionaries to Detroit to be tried as American spies and forced the Indians to relocate to a site on the Sandusky River. In February 1792 a group of about a hundred of these Indians were permitted to return to the Tuscarawas to get their belongings and harvest corn. En route they encountered American Colonel David Williamson and a force of ninety militia, who captured the Indians, accused them of aiding the British, and massacred sixty-two adults and thirty-four children. The Moravians attempted to reestablish their villages on the Tuscarawas, but the ensuing Ohio Indian wars and harassment from white traders frustrated their efforts. Their last mission town, Goshen, a few miles from Schoenbrunn, was abandoned in 1824.

Schoenbrunn Village, a replica of the original settlement, consists of seventeen log structures and includes a meetinghouse and schoolhouse, planted fields, and the original cemetery. The museum explains life at the village, chronicles the Moravians' involvement with the Delaware Indians in Ohio, and displays artifacts found on the site.

LOCATION: Route 250, exit 81 off Route 77, 1 mile southeast of New Philadelphia. HOURS: June through August: 9:30–5 Monday–Saturday, 12–5 Sunday; September through October: 9:30–5 Saturday, 12–5 Sunday. FEE: Yes. TELEPHONE: 330–339–3636.

ROSCOE VILLAGE

Roscoe Village, along with Coshocton, its rival across the Walhonding River, began to thrive as an export point for wheat and wool when the Ohio and Erie Canal arrived in 1830. Canal traffic peaked in 1851 and in the 1860s the railroad bypassed Roscoe Village for Coshocton. Roscoe Village fell into quiet decline and never recovered from a flood in 1913, which also destroyed most of the canal system. It has now been restored to its mid-nineteenth-century luster as a museum village. Five buildings on Whitewoman Street, the main thoroughfare, contain exhibits pertaining to the history of the village and the Ohio and Erie Canal. A one-room schoolhouse is located in the 1880 Jackson Township Hall. The Dr. Maro Johnson House is an 1840s Federal-style house with period furnishings. The Toll House, home of Roscoe Village's first toll collector, contains exhibits depicting family life during the canal era. Nineteenth-century crafts are demonstrated at the Craft and Learning Center, and the Village Smithy still functions as a blacksmith shop.

LOCATION: Hill and Whitewoman streets. HOURS: Shops and exhibit buildings: 10–5 Daily; Tours 10–3 Daily, closed January 1, Thanksgiving, and Christmas Day. FEE: For exhibit buildings. TELEPHONE: 614–622–9310.

The **Johnson-Humrickhouse Museum** (300 North Whitewoman Street, 614–622–8710) contains collections of American Indian art and artifacts, Oriental decorative arts, and nineteenth-century pioneer furnishings and implements. Visitors to Roscoe Village can take rides on the *Monticello III* (614–622–7528), a replica of a horse-drawn canalboat that regularly plies a restored section of the Ohio and Erie Canal.

NATIONAL ROAD/ZANE GREY MUSEUM

This museum includes various nineteenth-century vehicles, including a Conestoga wagon; other items related to overland transportation; and a diorama showing the building of the National Road, the nation's first federally funded thoroughfare. Memorabilia of the prolific adventure and western writer Zane Grey include manuscripts and first editions of his work, while exhibits include personal memorabilia from his travels in the American West and his brief career in dentistry. Over 250 pieces of Zanesville pottery are also on display.

LOCATION: 8850 East Pike Street, near Norwich. HOURS: May through September: 9:30–5 Monday–Saturday, 12–5 Sunday; March through April, October through November: 9:30–5 Wednesday–Saturday, 12–5 Sunday. FEE: Yes. TELEPHONE: 614–872–3143.

ZANESVILLE

Located at the confluence of the Licking and Muskingum rivers, Zanesville sits on one of the parcels of land given by Congress to Ebenezer Zane and his brothers in 1797 in payment for their construction of Zane's Trace, a road that ran across southeastern Ohio from Wheeling, West Virginia to Limestone, Kentucky. It was an important thoroughfare for the settlement of the Northwest Territory. From 1810 to 1812 Zanesville served as the state capital, until lawmakers decided to establish a permanent capital in the geographic center of the state. Via the Muskingum River, steamboats linked Zanesville with Marietta and the Ohio River, and the manufacture of locomotives and portable steam engines were important nineteenth-century industries. The town was also a stop on the National Road. The discovery of high-quality clay deposits in the area prompted the rise of the pottery industry here.

The **Increase Mathews House** (304 Woodlawn Avenue, 614–454–9500) is the oldest extant house in Zanesville. Dr. Mathews, the first physician in the area, came from Massachusetts and was a nephew of Marietta founder General Rufus Putnam. The one-story sandstone cottage was built in 1805, and additional stories were added in 1884. It now serves as the museum of the Pioneer and Historical Society of Muskingum County, with period furnishings, military items, kitchen implements, and memorabilia.

Zanesville was the birthplace of the nationally prominent architect Cass Gilbert (1859) and of adventure writer Zane Grey (1875), who was the great-grandson of Ebenezer Zane. The **Zane Grey Birthplace** (705 Convers Avenue), an Italianate structure built in 1871, is located in the **McIntire Terrace Historic District** (Blue, Adair, Maple, and McIntire avenues), an early residential neighborhood that retains many houses in a variety of nineteenth-century styles.

OHIO CERAMIC CENTER

The Ohio Ceramic Center explains the proliferation of potteries in this part of the state—some forty of them in the 1850s. They were known as Bluebird potteries because production started in the spring, when the clay could be mined, and coincided with the return of the bluebirds. The early potteries were part-time operations of farmers, who made containers and tableware for their own use and then began selling their surplus wares.

LOCATION: Route 93, 15 miles south of Zanesville between Roseville and Crooksville. HOURS: Mid-May through mid-October: 10–5 Wednesday–Saturday, 12–5 Sunday. FEE: Yes. TELEPHONE: 614–697–7021.

FLINT RIDGE STATE MEMORIAL

This 525-acre preserve encompasses extensive outcroppings of high-quality silica that was quarried by prehistoric Indians, who then worked the stone into projectile points, scrapers, awls, and other tools. The ridge is dotted with shallow pits, now filled with soil and vegetation, where the Indians dug below the surface to obtain unweathered deposits of the stone. Flint from this quarry has been found in many Adena and Hopewell sites; it was a popular trade item and has been found in prehistoric sites as far away as New York and Louisiana. The museum is constructed over one of the original pits, which serves as a life-size diorama with Indian figures engaged in quarrying flint. Other exhibits explain the geology of Flint Ridge, flint-working techniques, and prehistoric flint trade routes.

LOCATION: Route 668, three miles north of Brownsville on Route 40. HOURS: June through August: 9:30–5 Wednesday–Saturday, 12–5 Sunday; September through October:.9–5:30 Saturday, 12–5 Sunday. FEE: Yes. TELEPHONE: 614–787–2476.

NEWARK

Newark was platted in 1802 and named by its founder after his hometown in New Jersey. The **Sherwood-Davidson House** (Veteran's Park, North Sixth Street, 614–345–4898), a frame structure built around 1815, contains eighteenth- and nineteenth-century furnishings and the collections of the Licking County Historical Society. The most important building in town is Louis Sullivan's **Old Home Bank** (West Main and Third streets), a square stone building completed in 1914.

The **Newark Earthworks** was a rich assortment of earthen structures—circles, parallel embankments, a square, and an octagon—scattered over several square miles on a terrace overlooking the tributaries of the Licking River. They were executed by the Hopewell culture, which flourished in the Ohio Valley between 200 B.C. and A.D. 500. Many of the earthworks have been destroyed by agricultural development and the encroaching city, but a few have been preserved or restored in several tracts of land on the western edge of Newark. The major site is the 138-acre **Octagon State Memorial** (Thirty-third Street and Parkview), where the earthworks enclose 50 acres. The 66-acre **Mound Builders Memorial** (Route 79, south of Grant Street) encompasses a large circular wall of earth known as the Great Circle Earthworks. This structure is 1,200 feet in diameter, encloses 26 acres of land, and varies in height from 8 to 14 feet. Within the circle is an effigy mound, possibly representing a bird in flight.

The **Mound Builders Museum** (off Route 79, 614–344–1920) contains exhibits and artifacts relating to the art and culture of the Ohio Valley's prehistoric Indians, with special emphasis given to the Hopewell culture.

Granville was founded in 1806 by settlers from Granville, Massachusetts, and the town, set amid wooded hills, still retains a New England character. The **Robbins Hunter Museum/Avery-Downer House** (221 East Broadway, 614–587–0430) is a superb Greek Revival house built in 1842 and appointed with eighteenth- and nineteenth-century furnishings and decorative arts.

LANCASTER

Lancaster was established in the scenic valley of the Hocking River in 1800 by Ebenezer Zane and his brothers, who had been given this land and other tracts on the Muskingum and Scioto rivers in exchange for building Zane's Trace. Access to the Ohio and Erie Canal, the advent of railroads, and the discovery of natural gas in the area brought Lancaster prosperity throughout the nineteenth century. The **Square 13 Historic District** (Wheeling, High, Main, and Broad streets) preserves one of the original blocks laid out by the Zane brothers and contains many exceptional examples of nineteenth-century residential styles.

A self-guided walking tour of the district is available from the Fairfield Heritage Association, which is headquartered in the **Georgian** (105 East Wheeling Street, 614–654–9923), one of the finest houses in the Square 13 neighborhood. Completed in 1832, the brick structure is in the vernacular townhouse style of the Middle Colonies and Mid-Atlantic states. It contains furnishings of the 1830s and 1840s, some of which are original to the house.

Another distinguished Square 13 residence is the **Ewing House** (163 Main Street, private), a handsome structure built for prominent lawyer and politician Thomas Ewing in 1824. The young William Tecumseh Sherman came here to live at the age of 9, after the death of his father, and later married the Ewings' oldest daughter, Ellen. During the Civil War Sherman stayed at this house while recovering from exhaustion.

William Tecumseh Sherman was born in 1820 in the **Sherman House** (137 East Main Street, 614–687–5891), a modest frame house built in 1811 with an addition in 1816. His brother John, who was born here in 1823, became a prominent politician and statesman and was author of the 1890 Sherman Antitrust Act. The

OPPOSITE: *Samuel Maccracken's 1832 Lancaster house, now called The Georgian, was built by a talented local builder who adapted elements from Asher Benjamin's* Handbook for Carpenters, *a widely used manual of Georgian architectural designs.*

Victorian brick front was added after the family had left. The house has been restored to reflect the Sherman family occupancy of 1811–1842 with furnishings of this period and family memorabilia; it also contains Civil War exhibits.

Dawes Arboretum

The Dawes Arboretum is an extensive preserve of woods and gardens that offers a variety of educational programs and self-guided tours relating to nature, horticulture, and history. The **Daweswood House Museum,** an Italianate farmhouse built in 1867, became the country home of arboretum founders Beman and Bertie Dawes about 1917. An eclectic mix of nineteenth- and early-twentieth-century antiques and memorabilia reflects the lifestyle, interests, and history of the Dawes family.

LOCATION: Five miles south of Newark on Route 13. HOURS: *Grounds:* Dawn–Dusk Daily. *House:* Tours at 3:15 Saturday–Sunday. FEE: Yes, for house. TELEPHONE: 614–323–2990.

COLUMBUS

Columbus, the state capital, is situated on the banks of the Scioto and Olentangy rivers in the approximate center of Ohio. The site was selected by state lawmakers in 1812, in part because the thriving village of Franklinton, established on the west bank of the Scioto in 1797, had proven the economic viability of the location. The new capital was laid out amid swamps and bogs on the east bank of the Scioto and soon encompassed Franklinton. One of the few remaining original structures is the Federal-style brick **Jacob Overdier House** (570 West Broad Street, 614–469–1300), also known as the Harrison House. Built around 1810 it now holds the archives of the Franklin County Genealogical Society.

Columbus was hindered initially by inadequate transportation, a problem that was alleviated when a feeder canal connected it with the Ohio and Erie Canal in 1831 and the National Road was routed through the city in 1833. By the 1870s five railroads served the city. The focal point of downtown Columbus is the **Ohio Statehouse,** which stands just off the intersection of the city's two main thor-

OPPOSITE: *A statue of William McKinley—one of eight U.S. presidents from Ohio, a state known as the "Mother of Presidents"—on the grounds of the State Capitol in Columbus.*

WILLIAM
McKINLEY

TWENTY-FIFTH
PRESIDENT OF
THE VNITED STATES

"OVR EARNEST PRAYER IS THAT GOD
WILL GRACIOVSLY VOVCHSAFE PROS-
PERITY, HAPPINESS AND PEACE TO ALL
OVR NEIGHBORS, AND LIKE BLES
INGS TO ALL THE PEOPLES AN
POWERS OF EARTH."

oughfares, High and Broad streets. Built between 1839 and 1861—the project was impeded by a cholera epidemic and the panic of 1857—the capitol is a beautiful Greek Revival structure. It is America's finest example of architecture by committee; the member who most clearly influenced the ultimate form was Hudson River School painter Thomas Cole. Each facade is composed of a Doric colonnade with recessed loggia, and the building is topped with a distinctive drum-shaped cupola without a dome. The 1928 **Ohio Theatre** (39 East State Street) is a baroque movie palace designed by theater architect Thomas Lamb. It now serves as a theatrical and music performance hall.

Ohio Historical Center and Ohio Village

The Ohio Historical Center houses the exhibits, library, and headquarters of the Ohio Historical Society, the state archives, and Ohio Historic Preservation Office. Many objects from the center's extensive archaeological collection are on display, along with life-size dioramas depicting the daily life of prehistoric cultures. This is probably the finest museum in America devoted to pre-European history. There are also exhibits of Midwestern glass and Ohio ceramics, interior furnishings, and decorative arts. Natural history exhibits explain the environments that prevailed in Ohio in 1805.

Ohio Village re-creates life in the mid-nineteenth-century with replicas of a schoolhouse, town hall, print shop, hotel, farmhouse, blacksmith shop, livery stable, and barn, all laid out around a town square. Guides in period apparel give craft demonstrations, tend the livestock, work the fields, and perform other daily chores.

LOCATION: Route 71 and Seventeenth Avenue. HOURS: *Historical Center:* 9–5 Monday–Saturday, 10–5 Sunday. *Ohio Village:* April through November: 9–5 Wednesday–Saturday, 10–5 Sunday; December: 12:30–9 Wednesday–Sunday. FEE: Yes. TELEPHONE: 614–297–2300.

Columbus was an important military center during the Civil War. The largest post was Camp Chase, which served as a training ground for federal troops and later as the largest Confederate prison in the North. Some 26,000 prisoners had been held here by the end of the war. Nothing remains of the large stockade, but the

Camp Chase Cemetery (2900 Sullivant Avenue) contains the graves of 2,200 Confederate soldiers who died in the prison.

Exhibits in **Ohio's Center of Science and Industry** (280 East Broad Street, 614–228–2674) cover a variety of scientific, technological, and historical topics and include a coal mine, farm museum, diorama of U.S. presidents, and replica of a nineteenth-century street. One-half mile south of downtown, **German Village** (Livingston Avenue, Pearl Alley, Nursery Lane, Blackberry Alley, and Lathrop Street) preserves many of the commercial and residential structures of Columbus's largest nineteenth-century ethnic group.

MARION

Marion is a small industrial and agricultural center that was settled in the 1820s. The Marion Steam Shovel Company, established in 1884, manufactured earth-moving equipment, dredges, and draglines which were used to construct, among other projects, the Panama Canal and the gantry used to hold the space shuttle rockets.

Warren G. Harding Home and Museum

Warren G. Harding was born in nearby Blooming Grove in 1865 and came to Marion to pursue a career in publishing. He bought the Marion *Star* when he was 19 and served as editor and publisher for thirty-nine years. He was also active in state and national politics and was elected president on the Republican ticket in 1920.

Harding and his wife, Florence, built their Queen Anne–style home in 1890 and lived there until he was elected president. It has been restored and contains original furnishings and personal effects. The **museum,** in a bungalow behind the home that served as the press corps office during Harding's 1920 presidential campaign, contains memorabilia relating to Harding's life. He died in office in August 1923 while on a transcontinental trip to Alaska and is buried with his wife at the **Harding Tomb,** along Route 423 on the southern edge of the city.

LOCATION: 380 Mount Vernon Avenue. HOURS: June through August: 9:30–5 Wednesday–Saturday, 12–5 Sunday; September through October: 9:30–5 Saturday, 12–5 Sunday. FEE: Yes. TELEPHONE: 614–387–9630.

INDIANA

OPPOSITE: *In the Hall of Fame Museum at the Indianapolis Motor Speedway, an eight-cylinder supercharged Novi from the 1948 Indianapolis 500 race and the 1977 winner, A. J. Foyt's red Coyote.*

Indiana barely clings to the southern tip of Lake Michigan, and while that area is noted for its distinct and diametrical landscapes—towering factories and steel mills abutting wild lakeshore dunes—the state's development has not been greatly affected by its proximity to the Great Lake. Lake Michigan did, however, provide access for French explorers, a cast of early adventurers that included the state's first recorded European visitor, the illustrious Robert Cavelier, sieur de La Salle. In 1679 the Miami Indians showed La Salle and his party the portage from the Saint Joseph River to the Kankakee River, connecting Lake Michigan with the Gulf of Mexico, via the Illinois and Mississippi rivers.

Another river system—the Maumee-Wabash—linked Indiana with Lake Erie. To protect their fur-trading interests, in the early 1700s the French strategically established three fortified villages along the Wabash: Fort Miami, which evolved into the city of Fort Wayne; Fort Ouiatenon, near present-day Lafayette; and Fort Vincennes on the lower Wabash. For over a hundred years these sites were crucial in the struggle among the French, British, and Americans for control of the territory.

Vincennes in particular witnessed a parade of intrepid eighteenth- and nineteenth-century characters, including William Henry Harrison. In 1800 Vincennes was made capital of the Indiana Territory—an area that then comprised present-day Indiana, Illinois, Wisconsin, a large portion of Michigan, and part of Minnesota—and 27-year-old Harrison was appointed territorial governor, a position he held for twelve years. The indefatigable Virginian wielded enormous power, negotiating many of the treaties that transferred millions of acres of Indian lands to the federal government.

The Maumee-Wabash route also served as the backdrop for two major battles that irrevocably weakened the Indians' resistance to settlement in the Old Northwest. The first was the Battle of Fallen Timbers, which occurred in 1794 on the Maumee River in present-day Ohio. This battle led to the defeat of Indiana's most influential Indian leader, the Miami chief Little Turtle. The Miami Indians, who were the largest of the tribes inhabiting the area that became Indiana, lived in villages along the Maumee and Wabash rivers. Their stronghold was Kekionga, at the portage of the two rivers where Fort Wayne stands today. (The other large Indian tribe in the state was the Potawatomi, whose members lived primarily north of the Wabash and along Lake Michigan.) After their

Fur traders and pioneers, from Industrial Progress, *a series of murals painted by Thomas Hart Benton for the Indiana Pavilion at the 1933 Chicago Century of Progress Exposition. They are now in the auditorium at Indiana University.*

defeat, the Miami attempted to live in peace with the ever-increasing numbers of white settlers and they refused to join the Indian federation formed by the Shawnee chief Tecumseh to resist encroachment; their overtures failed. American troops destroyed many of their villages during the War of 1812, and in an 1818 treaty the Miami gave up most of their tribal lands in the central third of Indiana. The second clash was the Battle of Tippecanoe, fought on the Wabash River in 1811 near present-day Lafayette. Here William Henry Harrison defeated an alliance of fourteen tribes, including the Crow and the Sioux, that had been brought together by Tecumseh and his brother, the Shawnee Prophet. In a few hours of fighting, the Battle of Tippecanoe destroyed Tecumseh's dreams of a pan-Indian federation.

The Maumee-Wabash river system was also important economically. The Wabash and Erie Canal and other canal systems in Indiana were plagued with mismanagement and fiscal problems— the state went bankrupt in 1841 because of overindebtedness—and they were ultimately outdone by the railroads. They nonetheless provided an important outlet for Indiana's agricultural products and spurred the growth of numerous cities.

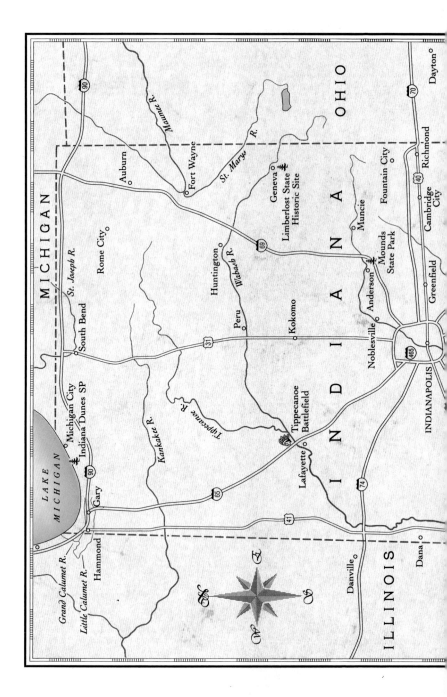

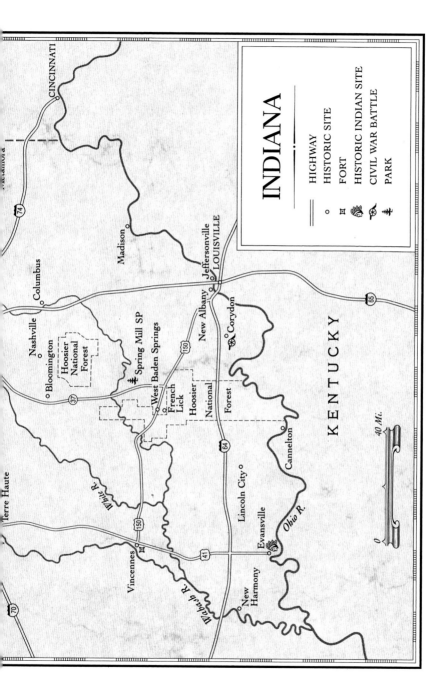

INDIANA

HIGHWAY
HISTORIC SITE
FORT
HISTORIC INDIAN SITE
CIVIL WAR BATTLE
PARK

CINCINNATI

74

Madison

Columbus

Jeffersonville
LOUISVILLE

Nashville

Bloomington

Hoosier
National
Forest

37

Spring Mill SP

West Baden Springs

French
Lick

150

New Albany

Corydon

Hoosier

National

Forest

65

K E N T U C K Y

64

Cannelton

40 Mi.

0

White R.

Terre Haute

Lincoln City

Evansville

150

Vincennes

41

Ohio R.

Wabash R.

New
Harmony

70

While the early French forts provided pockets of development on the Wabash, it was along the broad avenue of the Ohio River, which forms Indiana's southern boundary, that intense white settlement occurred during the first half of the nineteenth century. Many were from the upland South: Kentucky, Tennessee, Virginia, and North Carolina. They were in large measure yeoman farmers, not slave-holding planters. Thomas and Nancy Lincoln and their two children, Sarah and Abraham, were among this migration. The future president lived here from the age of 7 until he was 21, when the family moved to Illinois.

Southern Indiana is rugged country, a region of forest and thickets, dramatic limestone outcrops, and tucked away valleys, and it retains a backwoods quality distinctly different from the rest of Indiana. Rushing spring-fed streams provided sites for gristmills, and the quarrying of limestone became a major industry. The heart of the quarrying industry lies in and around Bloomington.

Beginning in the nineteenth century artists were attracted to the scenic beauty of southern Indiana, especially to the picturesque wilds of Brown County, between Bloomington and Columbus. People of means were also lured by the hot springs around French Lick and West Baden Springs, fashionable spas and gambling resorts until the Great Depression.

Indiana's economic and cultural center of gravity began to shift northward away from the Ohio River with the coming of the railroads. Rail transportation, initially viewed as a way to supplement river traffic, soon supplanted it, and the thriving ports along the Ohio began to wane. In 1824 Indianapolis, located in the middle of the state on an unnavigable river, was named the new and final capital, a move that seemed brash for its time. Railroads, however, guaranteed that Indianapolis would be more than a mere political hub, and soon the city emerged as the state's major trade, transportation, and manufacturing center.

Before the railroads, Indianapolis relied on the National Road, routed through the city in the 1830s. Today Route 40 follows that path, while Interstate 70 parallels it. The National Road has always served as a cultural demarcation in Indiana. The hills to the south were settled by Southerners and the plains to the north by Pennsylvanians, New Yorkers, and New Englanders. Indiana

OPPOSITE: *Abraham Lincoln's youth was spent in a pioneer cabin like this replica at the Lincoln Boyhood National Memorial near Little Pigeon Creek in southern Indiana.*

A nineteenth-century barn on one of the many farms near Rising Sun, in the fertile Ohio River Valley.

was settled largely by American-born people. Although Indianapolis, Fort Wayne, and Evansville had fairly sizable German populations in the nineteenth century, and canal and railroad building both drew a number of Irish, the state never attracted waves of foreign immigrants—no doubt because during the peak of European immigration in the 1840s and 1850s Indiana lacked a Great Lakes port of entry.

Although virtually no material evidence remains of the early French presence in Indiana, the state holds a wealth of structures that demonstrate its cultural and economic evolution beginning in the early nineteenth century on the banks of the Ohio River and moving northward to the early-twentieth-century steel mills along the Lake Michigan shore. Two different individuals attempted to establish utopian centers at New Harmony, and though both largely failed, they left behind the remnants of a beautifully planned nineteenth-century community. The city of Columbus has emerged in the twentieth century as one of the most fascinating planned communities in the country. Under the patronage of J. Irwin Miller, the chief owner of the Cummins Engine Company,

Columbus attracted many of the world's best architects to design buildings (beginning in 1942 with Eliel Saarinen). The city has become a textbook example of twentieth-century trends in modern architecture.

Following more or less the historical development of Indiana, this chapter begins in the southern part of the state in the Lower Wabash Valley and along the Ohio River. It then moves northward to the central portion of the state, an area dominated by Indianapolis but including Terre Haute, the limestone quarrying region around Bloomington, the scenic hills of Brown County, a stretch of the old Whitewater Canal at Metamora, and several nineteenth-century towns along the National Road. The last section covers the northern third of the state, an area that includes the highly industrial Calumet area around Lake Michigan, the city of South Bend, and the richly historic Upper Wabash Valley.

S O U T H E R N   I N D I A N A

VINCENNES

Now a small manufacturing and agricultural center, the first permanent settlement here dates from 1732, when François Morgan, sieur de Vincennes, established a fort to protect French fur traders and their Indian allies. The fortified village grew up along a buffalo trace, where the animals had beaten a path to cross the Wabash River. The original settlers, French-speaking immigrants from Quebec, were soon joined by French missionaries. The stately **Basilica of St. Francis Xavier** (205 Church Street, 812–882–7016) is the latest manifestation of the church they established over 200 years ago. Begun in 1826, the red brick structure is in the Jeffersonian Classical style. Vincennes passed to the British after the French and Indian War, and in the 1770s they established a new outpost, Fort Sackville.

George Rogers Clark National Historical Park

Slogging through the muddy lowlands during a midwinter thaw in February 1779, George Rogers Clark and his Virginia Longknives seized Fort Sackville from the British, then under the command of Lieutenant Governor Henry Hamilton, renaming it Fort Patrick

The George Rogers Clark Memorial in Vincennes commemorates Clark's capture of the British Fort Sackville and the United States' subsequent acquisition of the Northwest Territory. OPPOSITE: *Inside the memorial, a larger-than-life-size statue of Clark by Hermon A. MacNeil, surrounded by murals depicting scenes from Clark's life by Ezra Winter.*

Henry. The park overlooks the Wabash River and encompasses the original grounds of Fort Sackville. Its focal point is the massive granite and marble George Rogers Clark Memorial, built between 1931 and 1933, and inscribed with the phrase "The Conquest of the West." Inside, seven large murals depict Clark's campaign. The adjacent visitor center contains exhibits on the American frontier with emphasis on the history of Vincennes.

LOCATION: 401 South Second Street. HOURS: 9–5 Daily. FEE: Yes. TELEPHONE: 812–882–1776.

Grouseland

When the Indiana Territory was formed in 1800, Vincennes became its first capital and William Henry Harrison its first governor. In 1804 work was completed on a large, brick, Georgian-style house known as Grouseland, where Harrison lived until 1812. It was on this 300-acre estate near the Wabash River that Harrison

Virginia native and future president William Henry Harrison built the elegant Grouseland, his Georgian residence, soon after he moved to Vincennes.

met with the Indian leader Tecumseh and also planned the campaign that culminated in the Battle of Tippecanoe.

LOCATION: 3 West Scott Street, Harrison Historical Park. HOURS: March through December: 9–5 Daily; January through February: 11–5 Daily. FEE: Yes. TELEPHONE: 812–882–2096.

Nearby are the **Vincennes State Historic Sites,** including three near First and Harrison streets. The **Indiana Territory Capitol,** a clapboard structure, was headquarters for the governor and assembly for thirteen years. The **Elihu Stout Print Shop** is a replica; in 1804 he launched the *Indiana Gazette,* the state's first paper. The **Maurice Thompson Birthplace** honors the author of *Alice of Old Vincennes,* a 1900 novel set in the Revolutionary War. The **Log Cabin Visitor Center** (812–882–7422) has information.

The **Old State Bank Historic Site** (114 North Second Street, 812–882–7422), an 1838 Greek Revival structure, contains an art gallery and artifacts of local history. The ca. 1806 **Michel Brouillet House** (509 North 1st Street, 812–887–0199) is a rare extant example of the French vertical-log (*poteaux-en-terre*) construction, although its exterior has been covered with a protective siding. It contains period furnishings, a fur-trade exhibit, and prehistoric Indian artifacts from the area.

Three miles north of Vincennes is **Fort Knox II** (Fort Knox Road, off Route 41, 812–882–7422), the second of three military outposts on the Wabash River intended to protect American settlers here from Indian incursions. This site was garrisoned from 1803 to 1813 and it was from here that, on September 26, 1811, William Henry Harrison and a combined force of 1,000 soldiers, militia, and volunteers marched north to confront the Shawnee Prophet and his warriors in the Battle of Tippecanoe. Excavations outline the fort and interpretive markers explain its history.

NEW HARMONY

New Harmony is one of America's most illustrious and best preserved utopian communities. While today the town serves as a small trade center to nearby farms, it flourishes primarily as a cultural and intellectual hub, and its many historic structures attract scores of tourists.

In 1803 George Rapp, a Lutheran separatist from Germany, came to America in search of religious freedom. In 1814 he selected the bottomland forests along the Wabash River as the future site of his community. Along with his adopted son Frederick and some 800 people from Pennsylvania, Rapp carved out a utopian niche in the wilderness. The Harmonists or Rappites, as they were called, pursued a course of perfectionism and celibacy in anticipation of the second coming of Christ. Their exacting nature produced an efficient and tidy settlement—New Harmony was one of the earliest planned communities in America—and for a decade its balanced activities in agriculture, manufacturing, and commerce met with much economic success. New Harmony products, especially flannel cloth, were marked with a golden rose trademark and were well respected throughout the United States, Canada, and Europe. However, the malarial swamps of the Wabash River, a nationwide depression in 1819, and the nonappearance of Christ (which was making his disciples restive) prompted Rapp to move his followers back to Pennsylvania, where they formed the town of Economy.

In 1825 Rapp sold New Harmony to another utopian reformist, the Scottish textile magnate Robert Owen, for some $125,000.

A nineteenth-century streetscape in New Harmony, home of two utopian communities. OPPO-
SITE: *Fonts of type in a re-created print shop in New Harmony's 1822 Dormitory Number
Two.*

Owen had implemented labor reform in Scotland but felt the Old
World was not ready for his more radical views on religion, mar-
riage, family, and private property. With the help of his sons, the
eminent Scottish geologist William Maclure, and a bevy of scientists
and intellectuals, Owen attempted to establish a utopian community here. It failed in two years. Owen returned to England, but his
four sons and daughter remained and pursued many of their
father's reformist and educational ideals. His sons Robert and
David, for instance, were instrumental in establishing the Smithsonian Institution.

Numerous historic structures and sites remain, including the
ca. 1820 frame **David Lenz House** (North Street), the **Harmonist
Cemetery** (West Street), the **Labyrinth Garden** (Main Street and
Route 69), and the 1822 **Dormitory Number Two** (Church and
Main streets), a fine example of nineteenth-century utopian institu-
tional architecture. Also of interest are the 1830 **Owen House**
(Tavern and Brewery streets); the 1840 **Robert Henry Fauntleroy
House** (West Street), home of the elder Owen's daughter Jane and

her husband, which contains period furnishings; and the 1894 **Workingmen's Institute** (Tavern Street), established by William Maclure as one of the country's first free public libraries.

Visitors can inspect New Harmony on their own or take any of several tours conducted by Historic New Harmony/University of Southern Indiana. Tours leave from the **Atheneum** (North and Arthur streets, 812–682–4488), a 1979 Postmodern structure designed by Richard Meier.

EVANSVILLE

Evansville, the largest industrial and trade center in southern Indiana, began in the early 1800s as a ferry crossing on the Ohio River and grew with increased river trade and the coming of the railroads. It became particularly well known for its furniture manufacturing. Its nineteenth-century prosperity is manifested by many fine public structures including the 1885 High Victorian Gothic **Willard Library** (21 First Avenue, 812–425–4309), designed by James and Merritt Reid; Henry Wolters's 1890 **Old Vanderburgh County Courthouse** (201 Northwest Fourth Street), a blend of Beaux-Arts Classicism and Neoclassical Revival; and the 1890 **Old Vanderburgh County Jail and Sheriff's Residence** (208 Northwest Fourth Street), also designed by Wolters, a castlelike structure in the Eclectic style. The 1879 **Old U.S. Post Office and Customhouse** (100 Northwest Second Street, 812–424–4851), another fine example of the High Victorian Gothic style, was designed by U.S. Treasury architect William Appleton Potter.

The **Evansville Museum of Arts and Science** (411 Southeast Riverside Drive, 812–425–2406) exhibits Rivertown, a re-creation of late-nineteenth- and early-twentieth-century Evansville, including a chest made by Abraham Lincoln and the engine, lounge car, and caboose of a train that evoke Evansville's railroad era.

Angel Mounds State Historic Site

Angel Mounds, a large palisaded Indian settlement on a broad expanse along the Ohio River, was occupied between A.D. 1200 and 1450 and supported an estimated 3,000 inhabitants. These people, part of the Mississippian culture, built eleven large earthen struc-

OPPOSITE: *Evansville's 1890 Old Vanderburgh County Courthouse—now home to a theater group, a dance company, and art galleries—also contains the restored courtroom and governor's parlor.*

Reconstructed family dwellings at Angel Mounds State Historic Site, a prehistoric Mississippian settlement near Evansville.

tures, including one forty-four feet high and some four acres in area. The mounds, built in the form of truncated pyramids, were used not for burial purposes but as elevated sites for important buildings. The stockade, built in wattle and daub and composed of some 4,500 vertically placed logs, was over a mile in length. A portion of it has been reconstructed to show the materials used and method of construction. There are also replicas of the Indians' dwellings, meetinghouse, and temple. The interpretive center's exhibits and artifacts, including a replica of an archaeological dig, explain the life of the Mississippian culture. The village site covers 103 acres and is surrounded by 300 acres of woodland. A nature preserve includes trails.

LOCATION: 8215 Pollack Avenue. HOURS: Mid-March through mid-December: 9–5 Tuesday–Saturday, 1–5 Sunday. FEE: None. TELEPHONE: 812–853–3956.

The reconstructed stockade wall that surrounds the 103-acre Angel Mounds State Historic Site.

LINCOLN BOYHOOD NATIONAL MEMORIAL

In the winter of 1816, having lost their farm in a land dispute in Kentucky, Thomas Lincoln, his wife Nancy Hanks, and their children Sarah and Abraham, ages 9 and 7, settled in the forested hills of southern Indiana near Little Pigeon Creek. The following year Nancy Hanks died of milk sickness, a common frontier illness that came from drinking milk of cows that had eaten a toxic plant called white snakeroot. In 1819 Thomas married Sarah Bush Johnston, a Kentucky widow with three children of her own, and the combined families lived on the farmstead until 1830, when they moved to Illinois.

The 200-acre forested park includes a visitor center containing sculptured panels depicting important periods in Abraham Lincoln's life; the **Cemetery,** which holds the grave of Nancy Hanks Lincoln; and the **Lincoln Living Historical Farm,** a replica of a typical early-nineteenth-century Indiana farmstead. Crops are cultivated using frontier methods, and guides in period clothing demonstrate a variety of daily activities.

LOCATION: Route 162, Lincoln City. HOURS: 8–5 Daily. FEE: Yes. TELEPHONE: 812–937–4541.

CANNELTON

Now a small manufacturing center, Cannelton was a thriving Ohio River port in the nineteenth century and the site of an ambitious industrial project, the vestiges of which can be seen in the impressive **Cannelton Cotton Mills** (Front, Fourth, Washington, and Adams streets). Built in 1849 by a wealthy and idealistic Louisville entrepreneur, the factory was to have been the center of a model mill town that provided housing, schools, and churches for its workers. The massive four-story structure, its central entrance accentuated with twin spires six stories high, was designed by Thomas A. Tefft, a founder of the American Institute of Architects, and is one of the few extant examples of his work. Although the founder's vision was never realized, the mill operated for over a hundred years, running on steam produced by local coal mines rather than relying on waterpower.

To the north, through the Hoosier National Forest in the heart of southern Indiana's scenic hill country, are the small towns of **West Baden Springs** and **French Lick**. They are in an area of natural mineral springs, and from the mid-nineteenth century up until the Great Depression, the towns were fashionable spas. The 1902 **West Baden Springs Hotel** (west of Route 56, 800–450–4534), an engineering marvel, is an exceptional example of nineteenth-century metal-and-glass construction, with a circular six-story brick shell built around a domed atrium 195 feet in diameter. The **Indiana Railway Museum** in French Lick (Route 56 and Monon Street, 812–936–2405) displays a variety of steam and diesel locomotives and conducts train trips through Hoosier National Forest.

SPRING MILL STATE PARK

In 1817 a massive stone gristmill was constructed on this site, giving rise to a pioneer village. It prospered through the mid-nineteenth century from the milling of grain and lumber but fell into decline when the railroad was constructed just to the north. The village, now restored, continues to be centered around the fine, three-story mill. Constructed of local limestone, with native hardwood flume, wheel, floors, and trim, the mill is still functional, using water from a nearby cave for power. Inside are nineteenth-century china, glass, agricultural implements, firearms, and Indian artifacts. Other structures on the site include residences, apothecary and blacksmith shops, and a distillery, where demonstrations are given of milling, weaving, candle making, and other crafts.

Also in the park is the **Virgil I. Grissom Memorial,** a small museum commemorating Mitchell native Gus Grissom, one of the original astronauts in the U.S. space program, who was killed in a flight-simulation accident at Cape Kennedy in 1967. It contains a Gemini III space capsule and Grissom memorabilia.

LOCATION: Route 60, three miles east of Mitchell. HOURS: 8:30–4 Daily. FEE: Yes. TELEPHONE: 812–849–4129.

A water-powered gristmill built in 1817 still grinds cornmeal at Spring Mill State Park. Its stone walls are three feet thick.

The 1816 House Chamber in the Corydon Capitol, the original capitol of the newly formed state of Indiana.

CORYDON

Founded in 1800 by William Henry Harrison, the town took over the title of capital of Indiana Territory from Vincennes in 1813, and of the state in 1816 (it was moved to Indianapolis in 1824). The **Corydon Historic District** preserves the original grid plan of the town around a public square and many nineteenth-century structures, including the Federal-style 1817 **Posey House** (225 Oak Street, 812–738–6921) and the 1800 log **Branham Tavern** (419 North Capitol Avenue), erected by Harrison.

Constructed in 1816 of local blue limestone, the **Corydon Capitol** (202 East Walnut Street, 812–738–4890) provided chambers for the state House of Representatives, Senate, and Supreme Court. Inside are period fixtures and furniture. Near the capitol grounds is the **Governor William Hendricks Headquarters,** an 1817 Federal-style brick structure that served as the home and office of Indiana's second governor.

One mile south of town is **Battle of Corydon Memorial Park** (Old Business Route 135, 812–738–8236), site of the only Civil War battle fought in Indiana. Here, on July 9, 1863, Confederate general John Hunt Morgan and some 2,000 cavalrymen repulsed 450 members of the Harrison County Home Guard. Despite this defeat, southern Indiana civilians offered enough resistance to repel Morgan, who had underestimated the pro-Union sentiments in a part of Indiana reputed to be a hotbed of Copperheads (Northerners who sympathized with the South during the Civil War). Interpretive markers describe the various military actions and list the names of the known dead.

NEW ALBANY

The manufacturing center of New Albany grew up at the foot of a dramatic escarpment overlooking the Ohio River. Now a satellite to Louisville, Kentucky, New Albany flourished in the nineteenth century as a river port between Pittsburgh and New Orleans.

New Albany's 1867 Culbertson Mansion was built by a Pennsylvania native who made a fortune in dry goods and died one of Indiana's wealthiest citizens.

Culbertson Mansion

New Albany's steamboat era is beautifully represented by the Culbertson Mansion, a pale yellow brick structure in the Second Empire style built in 1867. The ornate interior includes parquet floors and a restored painted ceiling in the formal parlor and is decorated with period furnishings. It is part of the **Mansion Row Historic District** (Main Street between State and 15th streets and Market Street between 7th and 11th streets), an area of Victorian residences.

LOCATION: 914 East Main Street. HOURS: Mid-March through mid-December: 9–5 Tuesday–Saturday, 1–5 Sunday. FEE: None. TELEPHONE: 812–944–9600.

JEFFERSONVILLE

In 1802 William Henry Harrison plotted Jeffersonville along the banks of the Ohio, and it became known in the nineteenth century for the Howard Shipyards, which manufactured steamboats of legendary beauty and craftsmanship.

Howard Steamboat Museum

The Howard Steamboat Museum is housed in the Richardsonian Romanesque mansion of Edmunds J. Howard, son of James Howard, the shipyard founder. The elder Howard and his descendants operated the Howard Shipyards from 1834 until 1941, when it was purchased by the federal government to manufacture landing ship tanks for World War II. During the riverboat era, it turned out some 3,000 steamboats, including the *City of Louisville,* reputed to be the fastest steamboat ever built. The house, built in 1893, contains Victorian furnishings, shipbuilding tools, and steamboat artifacts and models.

LOCATION: 1101 East Market Street. HOURS: 10–3 Tuesday–Saturday, 1–3 Sunday. FEE: Yes. TELEPHONE: 812–283–3728.

The **Grisamore House** (113 West Chestnut Street, 812–284–4534) was built in 1837 as a double residence by David and Wilson Grisamore. Reflecting the transitional styles of the time, the handsome brick structure combines Federal elements, such as fan lights and end chimneys, with massive Greek Revival-inspired Doric columns at the entryways.

MADISON

In the nineteenth century the river port of Madison was an important gateway for settlers streaming into the Northwest Territory and a major pork-packing center, vying in importance with nearby Cincinnati. These activities combined to make it the state's largest town at mid-century. In 1847, the first railroad in Indiana, the Madison and Indianapolis, was completed between those two points, marking a turning point in Madison's fortunes. Railroads were soon siphoning off business from Madison and other towns along the Ohio. Now a small manufacturing center, Madison retains a great deal of its steamboat-era charm.

The architect Francis Costigan, Indiana's leading nineteenth-century architect, came to Madison from Baltimore in 1837 and designed many buildings, including two of the most striking mansions in the Ohio Valley.

Lanier State Historic Site

J. F. D. Lanier, a wealthy financier and railroad promoter, commissioned Costigan to design a home overlooking the Ohio River. Built from 1840 to 1844, the Greek Revival mansion has an octagonal cupola on the roof, a grand portico facing the river, and the delicate wrought-iron work characteristic of Madison homes. Inside are period furnishings and opulent ornamentation, and a spiral staircase (Costigan designed an even more impressive one for the Shrewsbury house a few years later).

LOCATION: 511 West First Street. HOURS: 9–5 Tuesday-Saturday, 1–5 Sunday. FEE: None. TELEPHONE: 812–265–3526.

Shrewsbury House Museum

The home of Charles Lewis Shrewsbury, a shipping magnate who was involved in lucrative Virginia salt mines, was designed by Costigan and built between 1846 and 1849. The Shrewsbury House is another elegant variation on Greek Revival elements, with intricate plasterwork in high-ceilinged templelike rooms. But the interior's most impressive component is its three-story freestanding spiral staircase. The house is furnished with period pieces.

LOCATION: 301 West First Street. HOURS: April through December: 10–4:30 Daily. FEE: Yes. TELEPHONE: 812–265–4481.

A three-story freestanding spiral staircase is the focal point of Madison's Shrewsbury House, designed in 1846 by Indiana's leading architect, Francis Costigan.

Historic Madison (500 West Street, 812–265–2967) publishes self-guided walking tours of Madison, conducts periodic tours of many of the historic residences in the city, and maintains several important structures and sites that are open to the public, including the 1818 red brick **Jeremiah Sullivan House** (304 West Second Street), a fine example of Federal-style architecture. Furnished according to the period, it is notable for its large stone-lined basement, which served as a kitchen and storeroom, exceptional for its time. The ca. 1820 **Talbott-Hyatt Pioneer Garden** (301 West Second Street), includes a reconstructed carriage house, stable, and potting shed. Adjacent is the **Talbott-Hyatt House,** another Federal-style house, built ca. 1819. The **Dr. William D. Hutchings Office and Hospital** (120 West Third Street), a Greek Revival structure built sometime between 1838 and 1848, was one of the earliest medical facilities in the region. Many of Hutchings's belongings are on display.

CENTRAL INDIANA

ERNIE PYLE STATE HISTORIC SITE

The well-known World War II correspondent Ernie Pyle was born on a farm near the small town of Dana in west-central Indiana in 1900. Pyle covered the war from the perspective of the foot soldier, and his on-the-scene reports from various battlefronts in England, Europe, North Africa, and the Pacific were widely syndicated in American newspapers. He was killed in 1945 by a Japanese sniper on a small island off Okinawa.

Pyle's restored birthplace, a vernacular frame structure, holds many Pyle family furnishings typical of a 1900 Midwestern house, photographs, and memorabilia.

LOCATION: North of Route 36, Dana. HOURS: Mid-March through December: 9–5 Tuesday–Saturday, 1–5 Sunday. FEE: None. TELEPHONE: 317–665–3633.

World War II correspondent Ernie Pyle was born in this simple farmhouse, which was moved from its rural location into Dana and opened as a state historic site in 1976.

TERRE HAUTE

Terre Haute, founded in 1816 on a bluff overlooking the Wabash River, takes its name from the French for "high land." The town was on the National Road and the Wabash and Erie Canal, and the subsequent railroads attracted substantial industry, including steel manufacturing and pork packing. Rich deposits of coal were mined here well into the twentieth century.

The **Historical Museum of the Wabash Valley** (1411 South Sixth Street, 812–235–9717), housed in an 1868 Italianate building, contains restored Victorian interiors, nineteenth-century textiles and costumes, Indian artifacts, and military implements. The museum also maintains the **Paul Dresser Memorial Birthplace** (First and Farrington streets), where the popular composer, who wrote the state song of Indiana, was born in 1858. He was the oldest of thirteen children and the brother of author Theodore Dreiser (as an adult Paul adopted a simpler spelling for his surname). The **Sheldon Swope Art Museum** (25 South Seventh Street, 812–238–1676) has a fine collection of American regionalist paintings of the nineteenth and twentieth centuries, including works by Thomas Hart Benton, Charles Burchfield, and Edward Hopper.

Eugene V. Debs Home

Eugene Debs was a leader of the American labor movement, a founder of the Socialist Party of America, and a five-time presidential candidate on the Socialist Party ticket. Born in 1855, he was a native and lifetime resident of Terre Haute. As the organizer and president of the American Railway Union, he led the successful strike against the Great Northern Railroad in 1894, following it up a month later with the Pullman strike in Chicago, for which he spent six months in jail. In 1918 he delivered an outspoken speech protesting World War I and garnered a ten-year prison sentence— and a hero's welcome after his sentence was commuted some two years later. He and his wife, Katherine, built their large Victorian home in 1890. The house contains period furnishings (some original), personal and campaign memorabilia, and exhibits on the history of the socialist and labor movements in America.

LOCATION: 451 North Eighth Street. HOURS: 1–4:30 Wednesday–Sunday. FEE: None. TELEPHONE: 812–232–2163.

BLOOMINGTON

Founded in 1818, Bloomington lies amid rugged and scenic outcrops of limestone, the quarrying of which fueled the early growth of the city. Now a manufacturing center, it is home to Indiana University, established in 1820.

The **Monroe County Historical Society Museum** (202 East Sixth Street, 812–332–2517) displays Indian artifacts, implements relating to quarrying, and nineteenth-century household items, clothing, and toys. Information on walking tours of Bloomington's several historic districts is also available. The elegant 1906 Beaux-Arts **Monroe County Courthouse** is the focal point of the **Courthouse Square Historic District** (Morton, Seventh, Washington, and Fourth streets), an area of numerous turn-of-the-century commercial structures. The early-twentieth-century residences in the **Vinegar Hill Limestone District** (First Street between Woodlawn and South Jordan avenues) denote the continued prosperity that quarrying and the growing university brought. Many of the houses are constructed of, or decorated with, local limestone.

Many of the murals depicting the cultural and industrial development of Indiana that Thomas Hart Benton painted for the 1933 Century of Progress Exhibition in Chicago are on display at the **Hall of Murals** in the entry hall of the **Indiana University** Auditorium (1200 East Seventh Street on the Indiana University campus, 812–855–1103). Also affiliated with the university is the **Elizabeth Sage Historic Costume Collection and Gallery** (203 Memorial Hall, 812–855–5223), which preserves more than 6,000 items of clothing.

NASHVILLE

Nashville is a little village hidden away in the rugged hills that make this part of Indiana justly acclaimed for its scenery—the region is known for its dogwood and redbud scenic drives. Among the many log houses in the area are Nashville's **courthouse** and the **Brown County Museum** (Museum Lane, 812–988–4153), a complex of log buildings, including a blacksmith shop, doctor's office, and jail.

Early in the twentieth century, artists, particularly out of Chicago, began to come to Nashville, and many of the Hoosier group of American regionalist painters created romantic renderings of the area. Nashville remains an artists' colony and retreat. The **Brown County Art Gallery** (1 Artist Drive, 812–988–4609) and the

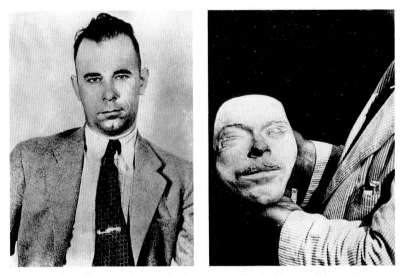

Gangster John Dillinger underwent plastic surgery to disguise his too-well-known face, as a comparison of his mug shot and a plaster death mask shows. The John Dillinger Historical Museum displays artifacts associated with America's "Public Enemy Number 1."

Brown County Art Guild (Van Buren Street, 812–988–6185) periodically display works of early Indiana artists.

The life and times of one of America's most famous criminals is documented in the **John Dillinger Historical Museum** (Franklin and Van Buren streets, 812–988–1933). Dillinger's letters, lucky rabbit's foot, and baseball shoes are displayed along with the wooden gun he used to escape from Crown Point and life-sized wax figures from both sides of the law.

T. C. STEELE STATE HISTORIC SITE

Landscape and portrait painter T. C. Steele, perhaps the best-known artist of the Hoosier group, came to Brown County in 1907, having had a peripatetic career in Chicago, Indianapolis, and Munich, Germany. The 200-acre woodland site encompasses the artist's home and studio and the gardens of his wife, Selma. The home contains furniture and decorative objects of the Steeles's; the studio houses over eighty paintings.

LOCATION: Eight miles southwest of Nashville, near Belmont. HOURS: Mid–March through mid-December: 9–5 Tuesday–Saturday, 1–5 Sunday. FEE: None. TELEPHONE: 812–988–2785.

COLUMBUS

Columbus was first settled in 1820 on the banks of the White River, an area that was then swampy and infested with malarial mosquitoes. The city's economy is now based on farming and industry, with the largest employer being the Cummins Engine Company, a major manufacturer of diesel engines. Among Columbus's numerous nineteenth-century structures are the Victorian commercial buildings on Washington Street, the handsome Second Empire 1874 **Bartholomew County Courthouse** (Third and Washington streets), and the 1870 Italianate brick residence that houses the **Bartholomew County Historical Society** (524 Third Street, 812–372–3541). But the city is best known for the impressive number of modern structures designed by many of the country's leading architects. It is the most comprehensive and successful effort to enhance the built environment of any community in America.

An imaginative proposal and the need for new schools in the 1950s made architectural sponsorship a public interest. The Cummins Engine Foundation offered to pay the architectural fees for new schools if the school board would select distinguished architects for the projects. More than fifty structures have been built in Columbus, designed by such architects as Edward Larrabee Barnes, Richard Meier, I. M. Pei, and Henry Weese. The building that initiated the effort was the **First Christian Church** (531 Fifth Street, 812–379–4491), designed by Eliel Saarinen and completed in 1942. Saarinen and his architect son, Eero, wrote, "As we compare this development of your church with that of the new architectural thought—according to which order your church is conceived—we find that they are very much alike, both as to meaning and course of development, for as your church emancipated itself from theology, so the new architectural thought has freed itself from traditional styles."

The visitor center of the **Columbus Area Chamber of Commerce** (506 Fifth Street, 812–372–1954) provides tour information and printed material on Columbus's architecture.

METAMORA

Founded in 1812, this small trade and tourist center on the Whitewater River had its heyday during the 1840s and 1850s, when the Whitewater Canal was in use. After nearly a decade of

The horse-drawn canalboat Ben Franklin *plies a preserved stretch of the Whitewater Canal in Metamora.* OPPOSITE: *Eliel Saarinen's 1942 First Christian Church in Columbus, with a Henry Moore sculpture in front, one of many buildings in the town designed by important contemporary architects.*

work plagued from the first by mismanagement, floods, washouts, and increasing competition from railroads, the project was completed in 1845. The Whitewater Canal, some eighty miles in length, connecting the National Road at Hagerstown with the Ohio River and Cincinnati, brought short-lived prosperity to Metamora and other towns along its route. The state, which did not increase taxes to support its bond indebtedness, went bankrupt, and as historian James H. Madison has written, "Indiana's reputation suffered a blow that stung long after the wooden canal boats and locks had rotted." The **Whitewater Canal State Historic Site** (Route 52, 317–647–6512) preserves fifteen miles of the waterway, including a feeder dam, locks, an aqueduct, a 1900 restored brick gristmill, and the ca. 1840 *Ben Franklin*, a horse-drawn canalboat.

THE NATIONAL ROAD

The National Road, which extended from Cumberland, Maryland, to Vandalia, Illinois, was the main overland thoroughfare in the Old Northwest in the early nineteenth century. Construction on the highway began in Maryland in 1811, and the survey for the road through Indiana was finished by 1828. Almost overnight a series of villages developed along the route. In the twentieth century, the National Road was replaced by U.S. Route 40 and then by Interstate 70. In Indiana, Greenfield, Knightstown, Lewisville, Dublin, Mount Auburn, Cambridge City, East Germantown, Centerville, and Richmond, all located on a fifty-mile stretch of Route 40 east of Indianapolis, retain numerous nineteenth-century structures from the National Road era.

In **Greenfield,** the ca. 1854 **James Whitcomb Riley Birthplace** still stands at 250 West Main Street. The 1898 **Hancock County Courthouse** (Courthouse Square), a blend of Richardsonian Romanesque and French Renaissance styles, and numerous nineteenth-century commercial structures are preserved in the **Greenfield Courthouse Square Historic District.** The 1853 **Old Log Jail** and **Chapel in the Park Museum** (Main and North Apple streets, 317–462–7780) can also be visited.

Huddleston Farmhouse Inn Museum

About 1840 the farmer John Huddleston purchased seventy-four acres of land and built a large brick farmhouse into a hillside on the western edge of Cambridge City. He and his family lived in the upper two stories, retaining the first floor as a public kitchen for travelers on the National Road. The house, which displays Federal and Greek Revival elements, contains typical mid-nineteenth-century farm furnishings and exhibits on the history of the farmstead and the National Road. It also houses a regional office of the **Historic Landmarks Foundation of Indiana.** The numerous outbuildings include a large barn used for programs and exhibits related to historic architecture.

LOCATION: Route 40, just west of Cambridge City. HOURS: May through August: 10–4 Tuesday–Saturday, 1–4 Sunday; September through December and February through April: 10–4 Tuesday–Saturday. FEE: Donation. TELEPHONE: 317–478–3172.

Founded in 1816, **Richmond** is an industrial center that grew to be the largest of the National Road towns in east-central Indiana. Several historic districts within the city preserve the nineteenth-century flavor of Richmond. The 1892 Richardsonian Romanesque **Wayne County Courthouse** (Third, Fourth, Main, and South A streets) is yet another example of Indiana's grandiose courthouses. Numerous Quakers settled in this part of Indiana, and one of their places of worship, the 1864 Hicksite Friends Meetinghouse, serves as the **Wayne County Historical Museum**

(1150 North A Street, 317–962–5756). It contains exhibits of china, silver, textiles, and farm implements and replicas of a general store and blacksmith shop. The society also maintains an 1823 log house and the 1858 Italianate **Andrew Finley Scott House** (126 North Tenth Street, 317–962–5756), furnished with Victorian pieces.

LEVI COFFIN HOUSE

Six miles north of Richmond, the Levi Coffin House served as a major station on the Underground Railroad between 1839 and 1847. Levi and Catharine Coffin, Quakers from North Carolina, were important leaders in the antislavery movement, and assisted more than 2,000 escaped slaves on their flight to Canada. Coffin was a pork packer and merchant, and his store, Coffin & Parker, was a large Midwestern outlet for so-called free-labor goods— groceries and cotton items produced without the use of slave labor. The Coffins moved to Cincinnati in 1847, where they continued their activities in the free-labor goods movement and the Underground Railroad. Their 1839 house (115 North Main Street, Fountain City, 317–847–2432) contains period furnishings.

The Wright Brothers are identified with the Dayton, Ohio, area, but Wilbur Wright, the older brother, was born in Indiana in 1867. His birthplace, two miles north of Route 38 and the town of Millville on Wilbur Wright Road, has been restored and furnished to the 1860s. A life-size replica of the *Wright Flyer* is displayed.

INDIANAPOLIS

In 1821 a third and final site was selected for the state capital on the banks of the White River. There was little to recommend the spot, however, except its central location. Indianapolis, as the town was named, sat amid swampy woods on a portion of the White that was virtually unnavigable—particularly inauspicious in an era when river travel was a major means of moving goods and people.

Indianapolis's possession of governmental offices overcame this initial obstacle by luring businesses and in turn various means of overland transportation. In 1825, boosters convinced Congress to route the National Road through Indianapolis, and today ten highways lead into the city. The advent of railroads in the 1850s made Indianapolis both a governmental center and an agricultural, commercial, and manufacturing hub. Pork packing was an important nineteenth-century industry, and the early twentieth century brought auto manufacturers and other factories to the city.

A prosperous Indianapolis in 1854, thirty-three years after this central but inauspicious spot

As industry developed in the city so ensued labor activity. John L. Lewis established the United Mine Workers in Indianapolis, and labor organizer Eugene Debs spent a great deal of time in the city confronting railroad management on behalf of the American Railway Union. Around the turn of the century nine unions were headquartered in Indianapolis. This activity prompted a countervailing response from management. One of the leaders of the National Association of Manufacturers was an Indianapolitan, and the Associated Employers of Indianapolis was particularly successful in campaigning for open shops in the city. In 1919 the organization convinced the city council to prohibit labor picketing.

A significant economic and cultural force in the city for many years has been the pharmaceutical company established by Civil War veteran Colonel Eli Lilly in 1876. One of the first to produce penicillin and insulin in mass quantity, it was also the major supplier of the Salk polio vaccine in the 1950s. The Lilly Endowment is one of the largest philanthropic organizations in the country. The **Lilly Center** (893 South Delaware Street, 317–276–3512) exhibits materials pertaining to the company's history, the pharmaceutical

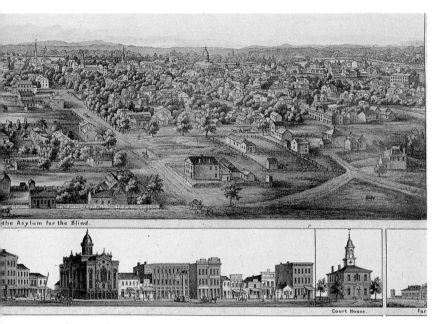

the Asylum for the Blind.

Court House.   Far

was chosen as the state capital.

industry, and early medicine. There is also a replica of the original
Lilly laboratory. The various pavilions of the **Indianapolis Museum of Art** (1200 West Thirty-eighth Street, 317–923–1331) sit on
the grounds of the 154-acre estate of J. K. Lilly, the grandson of
founder Eli. Also on the grounds are a botanical garden and the ca.
1914 **J. K. Lilly Mansion,** which houses the museum's decorative
arts collection.

Indianapolis's role as a transportation hub is neatly symbolized
in the city's original plan of wide boulevards radiating like spokes
from a small central circle. The scheme was designed by Alexander
Ralston, who had earlier assisted in Pierre Charles L'Enfant's plan
of Washington, DC. Known as **Monument Circle,** it is the focal
point of downtown Indianapolis and contains the 1901 Beaux-Arts
Soldiers' and Sailors' Monument, an obelisk surrounded by sculptures of historical and allegorical figures. The nearby **Christ
Church Cathedral** (125 Monument Circle, 317–636–4577), a Gothic Revival structure built in 1857, is the oldest church building in
continuous use in the city. Designed by William A. Tinsley, Christ
Church features Tiffany Studio windows dating from the 1900

renovation. The **Circle Theatre** (45 Monument Circle), with a facade that resembles a Greek temple and bas-relief interior motifs, was built in 1916 as a movie palace and now houses the Indianapolis Symphony Orchestra.

The **Indiana State Capitol** (West Washington Street, 317–233–5293) is a massive domed Renaissance Revival structure designed by Edwin May and Adolph Scherrer and built between 1878 and 1888. Located in the capitol complex, the **Indiana Historical Society** (315 West Ohio Street, 317–232–1882) and the **Indiana State Library and Historical Building** (140 North Senate Avenue, 317–232–3675) contain extensive collections of historical documents and periodic exhibits relating to the Old Northwest.

After a long period of neglect, the venerable **Union Station** (39 West Jackson Place, 317–267–0701), a Romanesque Revival structure built in 1888, has been renovated to accommodate restaurants and retail shops. The collection of commercial buildings and hotels surrounding Union Station is the historic Wholesale District developed during the Civil War and active to the 1930s.

Saint John Catholic Church and Rectory (121 South Capitol Avenue), the oldest Catholic church and parish in the city, is the work of Diedrich A. Bohlen, noted for church and institutional buildings throughout the state. It was started in 1867 and dedicated in 1871; the spires were added in 1893. The altars, shrines, pews, and pulpit of the Gothic Revival interior are intact.

The collections at the **Indiana State Museum** (202 North Alabama Street, 317–232–1637) deal with the cultural and natural history of Indiana. Exhibits of geology, history, popular culture, and works by Hoosier artists are housed in the 1910 Neoclassical Revival **Indianapolis City Hall**. The building's interior features a glass dome rotunda, murals, and elaborate marble inlay.

University Square (North Meridian and New York streets), used as a drilling ground during the Civil War, is today a lovely urban park in the midst of some of the city's finest public buildings. Just north is the **War Memorial Plaza and Indiana War Memorial** (431 North Meridian Street, 317–232–7615), housing a museum of military weapons and memorabilia ranging from the Battle of Tippecanoe to the Vietnam War. The **Ancient Accepted Scottish Rite Cathedral** (650 North Meridian Street, 317–262–3100), de-

OPPOSITE: *The Indiana War Memorial, part of a five-block complex of buildings and parks in downtown Indianapolis, contains a museum devoted to the role of Hoosiers in American military history from Tippecanoe to the present.*

signed by George Schreiber, is an opulent Tudor Gothic structure with a 212-foot tower that contains a fifty-four-bell carillon. The interior contains lavish carved woodwork, a massive crystal chandelier, and stained glass. The 1916 **Indianapolis–Marion County Public Library** (40 East Saint Clair Street) is a Neoclassical Revival structure noted for its entrance loggia supported by magnificent Doric columns. Designed by Philadelphia architect Paul Philippe Cret, it is ranked as one of the best Classical buildings in the country. The colorful ceiling of the great hall was restored in 1985.

The beloved Hoosier poet James Whitcomb Riley lived in Indianapolis's gracious **Lockerbie Square** neighborhood for the last twenty-three years of his life, with his longtime friends Major and Mrs. Charles L. Holstein. Lockerbie Street, lined with arching trees and flickering gaslights, prompted Riley's verse: "Such a dear little street it is, nestled away / From the noise of the city and heat of the day / In cool shady coverts of whispering trees."

The Holsteins's 1872 large brick Italianate home, now called the **James Whitcomb Riley House** (528 Lockerbie Street, 317–631–5885), contains carved woodwork, marble fireplaces, and Victorian furnishings belonging to Riley and the Holsteins. Many of the poet's papers, books, and personal items are on display. Riley died in 1916 and is buried in Crown Hill Cemetery.

Das Deutsche Haus–Athenaeum (401 East Michigan Street), is the near-north-side masterpiece of the Indianapolis architectural firm of Vonnegut and Bohn. (Principal designer Bernard Vonnegut was the grandfather of the famous Indianapolis-born author, Kurt Vonnegut, Jr.) Designed in the German Renaissance Revival style, the interior and exterior of this complex have changed very little since completion in 1898. Important architectural features include the massive slate roof, brick walls with limestone and terracotta details, art-glass leaded windows, ornate stairways and ceilings, the Kneipe bar and fireplace, a band shell, ballroom–concert hall, gymnasium, Biergarten, and Schlossgarten. The building, built as a physical education and cultural center, now houses business offices, a YMCA, and the American Cabaret Theater.

The **Morris-Butler House Museum** (1204 North Park Avenue, 317–636–5409) of mid-Victorian decorative arts is housed in the stately Second Empire structure designed by Indianapolis architect Diedrich A. Bohlen in 1864 for local businessman John Morris. Its opulent interior includes decorative moldings, stenciled ceilings, ornate chandeliers, and lavish Victorian furnishings.

Lockerbie Square, a residential district largely settled by German immigrants during the Civil War boom.

President Benjamin Harrison Home

Born in Ohio in 1833, Benjamin Harrison, a grandson of William Henry Harrison, came to Indianapolis as an adult to practice law. During the Civil War, Harrison led the Seventieth Indiana Regiment and retired as a brigadier general. He served in the U.S. Senate and, running on the Republican ticket, was elected president in 1888. After serving one term, Harrison returned to his law practice and the Italianate mansion he had built in Indianapolis in 1875. The house contains original furnishings, and the third-floor ballroom serves as a museum of Harrison memorabilia.

LOCATION: 1230 North Delaware Street. HOURS: February through December: 10–3:30 Monday–Saturday, 12:30–3:30 Sunday; call for January hours. FEE: Yes. TELEPHONE: 317–631–1898.

The Morris-Butler and Benjamin Harrison houses are within the **Old Northside Historic District** (Route 65, Sixteenth, Bellefontaine, and Pennsylvania streets), the most fashionable residential neighborhood in nineteenth-century Indianapolis. Just south is the 1873 **Kemper House** (1028 North Delaware Street, 317–639–4534), a small frame, Eclectic structure with Greek Revival and Second Empire elements. The house has been painted in what is probably its original five-color Victorian scheme. Elaborate decorative motifs on the exterior have earned it the name "Wedding Cake House." The house contains period furnishings and houses an office of the Historic Landmarks Foundation of Indiana. Earlier in the twentieth century, Indiana Avenue was a stronghold of jazz clubs. A remnant of that period is the Walker Building, now the **Madame Walker Urban Life Center** (617 Indiana Avenue, 317–236–2099). Madame C. J. Walker founded a beauty business in Indianapolis in 1910 that catered to the needs of black women. The 1927 Walker Building, designed by her daughter, A'Lelia Walker, is an Art Deco structure with African and Egyptian motifs. It housed the cosmetic company headquarters as well as a 1,300-seat vaudeville theater, ballroom, and restaurant, attractions which made it the center of Indianapolis's black community during the jazz era. The center sponsors arts and cultural events, including regular jazz concerts.

The **Lockfield Garden Apartments** (737 Lockfield Lane) were designed utilizing public-housing principles developed in the Bauhaus in Germany. Lockfield was one of the pioneer Modern-style buildings and one of the nation's first public-housing projects, constructed in 1935–1938.

Crown Hill Cemetery (entrance at 3402 Boulevard Place), with a commanding view of the region, was developed in 1863. One infamous Hoosier, John Dillinger, is buried here along with many prominent ones, including Benjamin Harrison, James Whitcomb Riley, Booth Tarkington, and Colonel Eli Lilly. Encompassing nearly 400 acres, Crown Hill is one of the largest cemeteries in the country, with several lovely High Victorian structures on the park-lined grounds. Particularly handsome are the arched Gothic gateway and the Romanesque Revival **waiting station** (317–925–3800), both designed by Indianapolis architect Adolf Scherrer. In the days of horse and buggy, the waiting station served as a place for mourners to congregate prior to graveside services. It is now restored and furnished with period pieces.

The **Indiana Medical History Museum** (3045 West Vermont Street, 317–635–7329) contains an extensive collection of medical implements and apparatus from the nineteenth and early twentieth centuries. Located on the grounds of the Central State Hospital, the museum is housed in the stately 1895 Old Pathology Building, designed by Adolf Scherrer. The amphitheater and laboratory retain original fixtures and equipment.

An early advertisement for the Indianapolis Motor Speedway, where the first Indianapolis 500 race was held in 1911.

The **Children's Museum of Indianapolis** (3000 North Meridan Street, 317–924–5431) contains many hands-on exhibits, and its turn-of-the-century **Dentzel Carousel**, still in use, is a designated National Historic Landmark.

Indianapolis Motor Speedway

The Indianapolis Motor Speedway is perhaps the most famous emblem of the city's preoccupation with overland transportation. It was originally built in 1909 as a testing ground for engines, brakes, lubricants, tires, and other automotive innovations. In 1911 the first Indianapolis 500 automobile race was held at the track, an international sporting event that now draws 400,000 spectators and prize money of many millions of dollars. One of the founders of the speedway was Carl Fisher, a prominent auto-parts manufacturer in Indianapolis who also pushed for road improvement in Indiana. His far-flung dealings—among other things Fisher developed 200 acres of oceanfront property in Florida that became Miami Beach—implied a lack of focus in the opinion of the other speedway founders, who sold the facility in 1927 to Eddie Rickenbacker, former Indianapolis race driver and World War I flying ace.

The Speedway's two-and-a-half-mile oval track encircles a large plot of land that includes a golf course and the **Hall of Fame Museum,** which contains many Indianapolis 500 winning cars as well as a collection of antique and classic passenger cars.

LOCATION: 4790 West Sixteenth Street. HOURS: *Museum:* 9–5 Daily. FEE: Yes. TELEPHONE: 317–484–6747.

Eiteljorg Museum of American Indians and Western Art

The Eiteljorg Museum, which has combined its collection with that of the Museum of Indian Heritage, focuses on the arts and crafts of North American Indians and on Western art and sculpture. The collection is strong in the artwork of Taos, New Mexico, painters, particularly the Taos Ten artists who were active in the early twentieth century. Native American art and artifacts from all sections of the country are on display, along with the works of Frederick Remington, Charles Russell, Albert Bierstadt, and others.

LOCATION: 500 West Washington Street. HOURS: 10–5 Tuesday–Saturday, 12–5 Sunday. FEE: Yes. TELEPHONE: 317–636–9378.

CONNER PRAIRIE

Conner Prairie is a living-history museum located just northeast of Indianapolis. It has been developed around the original home of William Conner, an influential fur trader who moved to this spot on the banks of the White River in 1802. Here he married a Delaware Indian woman named Mekinges and they had six children. Conner was an interpreter for the negotiators of the 1818 Treaty of Saint Mary's, Ohio, which effected the removal of the Delaware and other tribes from central Indiana to Missouri. Mekinges, the daughter of a chief, elected to move with the other Indians, bringing the children with her. Conner chose to stay. Eight months later he married Elizabeth Chapman, a white woman twenty years his junior, with whom he had ten children. In 1823 he built a Federal-style brick house on a bluff overlooking his property. The **Conner House** has been restored and furnished with period pieces, some original to the Conner family.

The **1836 Village** includes a number of residences and buildings arranged to portray a typical settlement of the period. Each is occupied by costumed guides who engage in normal daily work activities and explain aspects of life in early Indiana. The buildings include log cabins, several vernacular residences, a Greek Revival house, schoolhouse, general store, and blacksmith shop.

The **Pioneer Adventure Area** encourages visitors to participate in a variety of nineteenth-century chores (log splitting, soapmaking), crafts (quilting, weaving), and games (quoits), or observe special programs and demonstrations. The **Museum Center** has periodic exhibits relating to life in early-nineteenth-century America and Indiana.

LOCATION: 13400 Allisonville Road, four miles south of Noblesville. HOURS: May through October: 9:30–4:30 Tuesday–Saturday, 11:30–5 Sunday; April and November: 9:30–4:30 Wednesday–Saturday, 11:30–5 Sunday; December: candlelight tours, by reservation. FEE: Yes. TELEPHONE: 317–776–6000.

The **Indiana Transportation Museum** (325 Cicero Road, 317–773–6000) in nearby Noblesville has a collection of steam, diesel, and electric locomotives, railroad cars, including a dining car, Pullman sleeper car, and caboose, railroad equipment, and electric trolleys.

MOUNDS STATE PARK

Mounds State Park is located on the banks of the White River east of the city of Anderson. The park contains ten earthworks dating from approximately 2,000 years ago. The structures and artifacts taken from them indicate that the groupings were built by the Adena and later occupied by the Hopewell culture. For example, the largest earthwork, a circular embankment about 360 feet in diameter and 6 feet in height which dates to the Adena's occupation about 160 B.C., enclosed a central platform and small burial mound which was tied to the Hopewell at around A.D. 10–50. This is the only burial yet found, however. The area appears to have been used for ceremonial purposes, with some earthworks placed to accurately observe the equinoxes and solstices. Further survey work is underway.

LOCATION: 4306 Mounds Road, Anderson. HOURS: 7 A.M.–11 P.M. Daily. FEE: Yes. TELEPHONE: 317–642–6627.

N O R T H E R N   I N D I A N A

Indiana's northwest corner, which encompasses thirty miles of Lake Michigan shore, is known as the Calumet area, for the Grand and Little Calumet rivers. The region was formerly an expanse of huge sand dunes and wild rice swamps—terrain that was quite beautiful but rather inhospitable to early development, and this was the last part of Indiana to be settled. Once development began, however, the area changed rapidly, and today it is difficult to picture the undisturbed dunescapes. For over a hundred years Indiana's lakeshore has been heavily industrialized. The first to be successful was Detroit butcher George Hammond, who started a meat-packing plant in 1869 on the banks of the Grand Calumet, using ice from the river for refrigeration. By the late nineteenth century, the area was fast becoming an industrial outpost of Chicago, as financiers, feeling the crunch for land sites along Illinois's portion of Lake Michigan, began to develop steel mills and oil refineries amid the dunes.

GARY

Gary, the area's largest city, came into being when U.S. Steel purchased 9,000 acres of dunelands along the lake in 1905. The town was named for the company's chairman, Elbert H. Gary, and it attracted an influx of immigrant laborers. The **American Bridge Company** (1 North Bridge Street), on the town's western edge, was built in 1909 to manufacture structural steel for bridges and buildings. It is an excellent example of early-twentieth-century industrial architecture. The **Gary Land Company Building** (Fourth Avenue and Massachusetts Street in Gateway Park) has been restored and houses a small local-history museum and the offices of the historical society and the Gary Civic Symphony.

The **Hobart Historical Society** (706 East Fourth Street) in the Gary suburb of Hobart is housed in the 1915 Carnegie Library, an English Renaissance structure built of various colors of brick. The museum contains nineteenth-century clothing, linens, household items, and farm implements, a gallery of wheel-making and woodworking tools, and replicas of a blacksmith shop and print shop.

MICHIGAN CITY

Michigan City originated as a commercial port in the 1830s, was an important commercial fishery in the mid-1850s, and became a lakefront resort for Chicago residents at the turn of the century. Fronting Lake Michigan in Washington Park is the **Old Lighthouse Museum** (Heisman Harbor Road, 219–872–6133). The 1858 stone and clapboard structure contains lighthouse furnishings and implements, and exhibits of Michigan City history. The **Barker Mansion and Civic Center** (631 Washington Street, 219–873–1520) is an English manor house built in 1905 for railroad freight-car manufacturer John H. Barker. The lavish interior contains hand-carved woodwork, marble fireplaces, and original furnishings.

INDIANA DUNES

The fight to save the last remnants of Indiana's lakeshore dunes was one of the early conservation efforts in the country. Beginning in 1913, the Prairie Club of Chicago, including in its ranks Carl Sandburg and Jane Addams, began lobbying for preservation of the dunes. The first land purchase, made in 1927, became the 2,200-acre **Indiana Dunes State Park** (Route 49 north of Chesterton, 219–926–4520). In 1966 Congress authorized the formation of **Indiana Dunes National Lakeshore,** a 13,400-acre park divided into four units. The visitor center (Kemil Road and Route 12, Chesterton, 219–926–7561) provides maps and information about the area. The **Bailly Unit** (south of Route 12 at Mineral Springs)

Along the shore of Lake Michigan between Michigan City and Gary, Indiana Dunes National

contains two nineteenth-century homesteads. The **Bailly Homestead** was established on the banks of the Little Calumet River as a fur-trading post in 1822 by French Canadian Joseph Bailly, who lived here with his half-Ottawa wife until his death in 1835; she died here in 1866. The compound includes several restored structures, including the family's 1835 hewn-log house. The **Chellberg Farm** dates from the mid-1860s, when Anders and Johanna Kjellberg arrived here from Sweden. Three generations of the family, who anglicized their name to Chellberg, operated this subsistence farm, growing wheat, oats, and corn, keeping a dairy herd, and harvesting maple sugar. The extant structures include a mortise-and-tenon barn and a brick homestead.

SOUTH BEND

South Bend is an industrial city that sits on—and takes its name from—a meander of the Saint Joseph River. Robert Cavelier, sieur de La Salle, explored the area in 1679 with a party that included his

Lakeshore preserves dunes created from glacial deposits.

trusted lieutenant Henry de Tonti and the Catholic priest and historian Father Louis Hennepin. The explorers' portage between the Saint Joseph and the nearby Kankakee River secured for Europeans a new water route between the Saint Lawrence and Mississippi rivers. The Council Oak Tree in **Highland Cemetery** (2257 Portage Avenue) is where in 1681 La Salle negotiated an important treaty between the Miami and Illinois Indians that allied these tribes with the French and against the invading Iroquois. The French established a mission in the area in 1684 and Fort Saint Joseph in 1691, near what is now Niles, Michigan. They remained a potent influence in the Saint Joseph Valley for a hundred years.

In 1820 the fur trader Pierre Navarre established an American Fur Company post on the river's bend called Big Saint Joseph Station. He married a local Potawatomi woman and they raised ten children. Other traders settled in the area, and the village that grew up around these posts came to be called Southhold and later South Bend. The **Pierre Navarre Log Cabin,** the second that the trader built, stands on the banks of the Saint Joseph River just north of

On the University of Notre Dame campus, the 1875 Sacred Heart Church and the 1879 Administration Building.

downtown in Leeper Park. South Bend was laid out in 1830, and the Roman Catholic **University of Notre Dame** was established in South Bend in 1842.

In 1852, Henry and Clement Studebaker opened a blacksmith and wagon-building company in South Bend, and within twenty years, Studebaker Brothers was one of the world's largest manufacturers of wagons and buggies. The company produced automobiles from 1902 until 1963. Many of the wagons, carriages, and automobiles manufactured by the firm are in the **Studebaker National Museum** (120 South Saint Joseph Street and 525 South Main Street, 219–235–9714). A product of the Studebaker prosperity is preserved in **Tippecanoe Place** (620 West Washington Street, 219–234–9077), the opulent residence Clement Studebaker built in 1889. The Richardsonian Romanesque mansion now houses a restaurant.

Another of South Bend's prominent industrialists was Joseph D. Oliver, who expanded his father's plow-manufacturing business into the Oliver Plow Works. The **Joseph D. Oliver Mansion** (808 West Washington Avenue, 219–235–9664) is a large, stone Queen

Anne structure, which Joseph called Copshaholm after the Scottish village from which the Olivers emigrated. The thirty-eight room mansion, with original furnishings, adjoins 2.5 acres of gardens, a tea house, a carriage house, pergola, and fountain. The Oliver Mansion is a property of the Northern Indiana Historical Society, and is part of its **History Center** on the same site. In a museum, nine galleries show the development of the area from prehistory on. A home, ca. 1870, depicting the life of a typical worker's family, is also on the grounds. A Kidsfirst Children's Museum has interactive exhibits for children ages three to ten.

The twenty-acre **Gene Stratton Porter State Historic Site** (Route 9, 219–854–3790) sits on the banks of Sylvan Lake near **Rome City.** It encompasses the author-naturalist's second home, which she called the Cabin in Wildflower Woods, as well as her formal garden, orchard, and woodland trails. The rambling log structure, designed by Porter and built in 1914, contains original furnishings, memorabilia, and a number of her photographs.

AUBURN

Settled in 1836, Auburn is a small trade center in farm country. From 1900 until 1937, the town was noted for the production of automobiles, especially sleek and expensive models. The **Auburn-Cord-Duesenberg Museum** (1600 South Wayne Street, 219–925–1444) contains examples of these and many other antique and classic cars. It is housed in the original 1930 Auburn Automobile Company Administration Building.

FORT WAYNE

Many of the crucial events that led to the settlement of Indiana took place in the Upper Wabash Valley, a scenic stretch of the state that follows the Wabash River from Fort Wayne southwestward to Lafayette. Fort Wayne, in particular, is one of Indiana's most historic cities. Now a manufacturing center in the midst of farming and dairy country, Fort Wayne owes its early development to rivers. It lies near the Wabash and at the confluence of the Saint Marys and Saint Joseph, where they join to form the Maumee. This strategic location was at the hub of two important water highways: one leading east via the Maumee to Lake Erie, the other west by way of the Wabash to the Mississippi.

The Miami Indians had a large village near this confluence called Kekionga (the original site of the village is located near Edgewater Avenue in the Lakeside district of Fort Wayne). The Miami presence here in turn attracted French fur traders, who established a fortified trading post in the early 1700s. Fort Miami, as it was called, was rebuilt by the French in 1750 to stave off incursions by the British, an effort that failed in 1760 during the French and Indian War. The British never gained much authority in the Three Rivers area, because Kekionga remained a stronghold of Miami Indian resistance.

Throughout the American Revolution, the site was a lawless settlement called Miami Town and the portage was used by British and Americans alike. During the 1790s the United States, like the British, continued to have difficulties subduing the Indians, until General "Mad Anthony" Wayne finally defeated the influential and tenacious Miami chief Little Turtle in 1794 at the Battle of Fallen Timbers in present-day Ohio. General Wayne marched to Three Rivers and built a fort, naming it Fort Wayne. It was rebuilt several times, abandoned in 1819, and torn down in 1852.

Fort Wayne's industrial growth began with the opening of the Wabash and Erie Canal in the 1830s and surged with the arrival of the railroads in the mid-1850s. The city's turn-of-the-century optimism is perhaps best preserved in the 1900 **Allen County Courthouse** (715 South Calhoun Street, 219–449–7330), a domed limestone structure in the Renaissance Revival and Neoclassical Revival styles with a particularly lavish interior rotunda. Fort Wayne's agricultural legacy lies in **Johnny Appleseed Memorial Park** (Coliseum Boulevard, at Parnell Avenue, 219–427–6720), a nineteenth-century park that contains the grave of John Chapman, the itinerant nurseryman who lived the last twenty years of his life in the area, where he planted one of his biggest orchards.

The third and final Fort Wayne, built in 1815 under the direction of Major John Whistler (grandfather of James McNeil Whistler, the painter), was one of the most sophisticated of the wooden forts in North America. A replica of it known as **Historic Fort Wayne** (211 South Barr Street, 219–427–6003) stands near the original site. A stockade encloses numerous structures, including a hospital, a barracks, and officers' quarters. No interpretation is provided, but visitors may walk among the buildings.

OPPOSITE: *Horse-drawn carriages are still a common sight in northeastern Indiana, where many Amish farming communities maintain their traditions.*

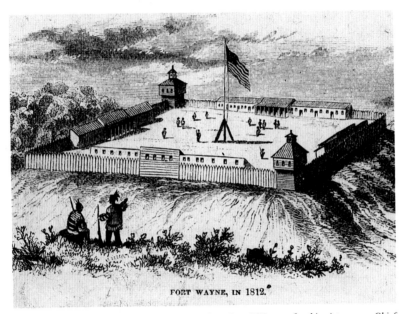

FORT WAYNE, IN 1812.

Fort Wayne in 1812, as built by General "Mad Anthony" Wayne after his victory over Chief Little Turtle.

The **Allen County–Fort Wayne Historical Society Museum** (302 East Berry Street, 219–426–2882) covers the frontier history of northeastern Indiana and the industrial growth of Fort Wayne after the opening of the Wabash and Erie Canal. Its collections include military artifacts from the 1790-to-1820 period, nineteenth- and twentieth-century clothing, Indian artifacts, glass, china, maps, and industrial implements. The museum is housed in the **Fort Wayne City Hall,** a distinctive Richardsonian Romanesque

The **Lincoln Museum** (200 East Berry, 219–455–3864) encompasses a major collection owned by Lincoln National Life Insurance and administered by its Lincoln National Foundation. Robert Todd Lincoln, son of the president, granted the company use of the Lincoln name. The collection includes personal and family items and memorabilia associated with Abraham Lincoln's election campaigns and assassination. Many original photographs are displayed, as well as the last portrait of Lincoln before his death. Visitors can fight a Civil War battle on a touch-screen computer.

Historic Fort Wayne, a replica of the 1815 fort built at this strategic site, is open for exploration and picnics.

HUNTINGTON

In 1832 Huntington was laid out on the Wabash and Erie Canal in the heart of the once-powerful Miami Nation, a remnant of which is preserved at the **Chief Richardville House and Miami Treaty Grounds** (Routes 24 and 9, two miles west of Huntington). The house was built on a fork of the Wabash River in 1833. Its owner, Chief Jean Baptiste Richardville (or Pechewa), was son of an important Miami matriarch, Tacumwah, and a Frenchman. He served as a chief of the Miami Indians from about 1815 until 1841. In 1831, because of increasing pressure from white settlement, he moved the tribal headquarters of the Miami Nation here from Kekionga. During this period Richardville helped negotiate a number of treaties between his tribe and the United States. An astute businessman, Richardville amassed considerable wealth in his lifetime. After his death, his son-in-law Francis LaFontaine (or Topeah) succeeded him as chief and served as primary negotiator when the last of the Miami were relocated to Kansas in 1846.

Nineteenth-century structures include the **Taylor–Zent House** (715 North Jefferson Street). The **Huntington County Historical Society Museum** is in the 1904 Courthouse. The **Dan Quayle Center and Museum** (815 Warren Street), in his hometown, has exhibits on Hoosier vice presidents: Schuyler Colfax, Thomas Hendricks, Charles Fairbanks, Thomas Marshall, and Quayle.

PERU

Peru is on the Wabash River near its confluence with the Mississinewa River. During the mid-nineteenth century it was a stop and turning basin on the Wabash and Erie Canal. The town is fondly remembered as the birthplace of the American composer Cole Porter, born in 1891. The family home (private) still stands at 102 East Third Street.

Prior to white settlement in the 1830s, the site was a Miami village. In 1812, a council of Indians met here and refused to join Tecumseh's confederacy. A wealthy and influential Miami Indian chief, François Godfroy, operated a trading post in the vicinity. He is buried near the old post in **Godfroy Cemetery** (three miles east of Peru on Route 124). The area was made famous by the story of Frances Slocum, a white woman who was captured in 1779 by Indians in Wilkes-Barre, Pennsylvania, when she was 5 years old. Her relatives found her some sixty years later living with her Miami husband among his tribe. She met with her white kin in Peru in 1837 but declined to return with them. The **Frances Slocum Grave and Monument** is at Mississinewa Reservoir, about ten miles southeast of Peru.

In 1883 local livery operator Ben Wallace acquired a circus that could not pay its stable fees. He embarked on a career of buying and selling circuses, of which the most famous was the Hagenbeck-Wallace Circus, established in 1908. He also set up winter quarters for a number of traveling circuses in Peru. The town was a haven for circus performers until the mid-1930s. The **Circus City Festival Museum** (154 North Broadway, 317–472–3918) contains costumes of famous performers, circus lithographs, trapezes and other circus paraphernalia, and furniture from the Ben Wallace Home. Each July Circus City stages circus performances and a circus parade. The **Miami County Historical Museum** (51 North Broadway, 317–473–9183) has exhibits pertaining to

Indian history, the Wabash and Erie Canal, and Peru's circus heritage. The museum is housed in the Senger Dry Goods Company Building.

LAFAYETTE

The city of Lafayette was founded on a plateau above the Wabash in 1825 by riverboat captain William Digby at the northernmost navigable point on the Wabash. He named it for the Revolutionary War general who served under George Washington. Lafayette is centered in an area of rich farmland, and today its economy turns on manufacturing and trade.

Here, too, a canal was vital. The Wabash and Erie Canal, which opened in 1843, extended the economic reach of Lafayette, and as canal traffic waned the city made the crucial transition to railroads. The nineteenth-century city is preserved in the **Downtown Lafayette Historic District** (Second, Ferry, Sixth, and South

Likenesses of General William Henry Harrison, the Marquis de Lafayette, and Shawnee statesman Tecumseh—three important figures in Tippecanoe County's history—decorate the pediment of the 1881 Tippecanoe County Courthouse.

streets), which includes the **Tippecanoe County Courthouse,** an exuberant blend of Gothic, Classical, Romanesque, and Renaissance styles built in the 1880s.

The **Tippecanoe County Historical Museum** (909 South Street, 317–742–8411) is housed in the Moses Fowler House. A wealthy Lafayette businessman, Fowler built his fine Gothic Revival house in 1851, basing its design on A. J. Downing's *Architecture of Country Houses*. The house contains period furnishings, relics from Fort Ouiatenon and the Battle of Tippecanoe, Indian artifacts, and nineteenth-century glassware, tools, clothing, and toys.

WEST LAFAYETTE

The **Indiana State Veterans Home Historic District** (two miles south of Route 65 on Route 43) preserves several of the original buildings of the institution established in 1895 to care for veterans of the Civil War. The 1899 Commandant's Residence contains furnishings of the commandants. **Purdue University,** founded in 1869, is another of the Midwest's major land-grant colleges, distinguished for its schools of agriculture and engineering.

Fort Ouiatenon Historical Park

Fort Ouiatenon (pronounced wee-AUGHT-e-non) was built by the French as part of their defensive strategy along the important Wabash-Maumee water highway. It was a thriving fur-trading post and village from 1717 until 1760, with a peak population of some 2,000 French, Indians, and persons of mixed heritage. The fort was across the Wabash from a large village of Wea Indians, one of the Miami bands. The Wea served as middlemen in a fur-trading network between the French and numerous tribes scattered on the prairies to the west.

After the French and Indian War, Fort Ouiatenon was garrisoned by British troops in an atmosphere of increasing Indian hostility. In 1763, the Ottawa chief Pontiac peacefully seized the fort as part of his ultimately unsuccessful effort to drive European intruders back over the Appalachian Mountains. Two years later at Fort Ouiatenon, Pontiac ended his war in negotiations with British Indian agent George Croghan by flinging his tomahawk to the ground, thus giving rise to the expression "bury the hatchet." Following Pontiac's uprising, Fort Ouiatenon fell into decline. In the 1780s the stockade was used by Indians as a base for raids into Kentucky until President George Washington ordered the destruction of Wabash villages in 1791.

Fort Ouiatenon Historical Park, a rustic twenty-acre expanse on the Wabash River, was established in the 1920s on what was then thought to be the site of the fort. (The actual site was subsequently located about a mile downriver and excavated by archaeogists in the 1970s.) A replica of a blockhouse contains a museum detailing the fort's history. Each fall, at the Feast of the Hunter's Moon, visitors sample food from hundreds of vendors; in a re-enactment, voyageurs arrive by canoe to trade with Indians.

LOCATION: South River Road. HOURS: *Park:* Dawn–Dusk Daily (in winter, weather permitting); *Blockhouse:* Mid-April through mid-October: 1–5 Saturday–Sunday. FEE: None. TELEPHONE: 317–463–2306.

TIPPECANOE BATTLEFIELD

The Battle of Tippecanoe, which took place on this site on November 7, 1811, was the bloody culmination of several years of unproductive discussions between the two most influential men in the Old Northwest, William Henry Harrison and the Shawnee chief Tecumseh. Their deliberations regarded the validity of the land concessions Harrison had obtained through various Indian treaties—debates that ultimately addressed the issue of who, Americans or Indians, were the rightful possessors of the vast territory north of the Ohio River.

Concerned about increased Indian hostility and feeling that he and his adversary were at an impasse, Harrison, then governor of Indiana Territory, mounted a campaign at Vincennes of about 1,000 U.S. infantrymen, Kentucky volunteers, and Indiana militia and marched toward Prophetstown near the confluence of the Wabash and Tippecanoe rivers. Prophetstown was a new village of Indians of numerous different tribes allied with Tecumseh and his charismatic brother, the Shawnee Prophet, or Tenskwatawa. For several years, Tecumseh had been trying to organize all Indians into a united front, while the Shawnee Prophet had been preaching a gospel of cultural renewal and temperance to the Indians.

Harrison had planned his attack to coincide with Tecumseh's absence from Prophetstown—the chief was in the South trying to recruit the Creek, Chickasaw, and other tribes to his federation. Harrison's troops camped on the edge of Prophetstown on the evening of November 6, and the Indians, estimated to number between 600 and 700, attacked before dawn the next day. After two hours of fighting, the Indians withdrew and the victory went to the Americans. Nonetheless many of Harrison's men were dead or wounded, and the battle failed to break Indian resistance. The Prophet suffered a considerable loss of prestige, and Tecumseh, abandoning his hopes of a united Indian front, soon allied himself with the British in the ensuing War of 1812. Memories of the battle were still strong three decades later: Harrison won the presidential election of 1840 using the slogan "Tippecanoe and Tyler too!" Harrison, while delivering the longest inauguration speech of any president, caught a cold that quickly worsened, and he died after just thirty days in office. The "Tyler" in the slogan was John Tyler of Virginia, who became the first vice president to succeed to the presidency upon the incumbent's death.

The park encompassing the Tippecanoe Battlefield is about a hundred acres of rugged, scenic woodland and marsh. The site of Harrison's camp is marked with a large obelisk; the park also has a nature center and hiking trails. The museum contains artifacts from the battle and literature from Harrison's 1840 presidential campaign.

LOCATION: Railroad Street, Battle Ground. HOURS: March through November: 10–5 Daily; December through February: 10–4 Daily. FEE: Yes. TELEPHONE: 317–567–2147.

KOKOMO

Kokomo, an industrial city founded in 1844, was named for an influential Miami chief. Its most prominent twentieth-century citizen was the inventor Elwood Haynes, the builder of the first commercially successful gasoline-powered car in America. Haynes test drove his first vehicle in Kokomo in 1894. The **Elwood Haynes Museum** (1915 South Webster Street, 317–456–7500), housed in a former home of the inventor, contains exhibits of Haynes's career, industrial products manufactured in Kokomo, and family memorabilia. The **Howard County Historical Museum** (1200 West Sycamore Street, 317–452–4314) is housed in the 1891 Sieberling Mansion, a rambling brick structure with Richardsonian Romanesque and Queen Anne elements. Monroe Sieberling was a magnate in the plate-glass and fiberboard industries. The museum contains exhibits pertaining to local inventions and manufacturing.

Limberlost Cottage, the large bungalow where the author and naturalist Gene Stratton Porter wrote novels and nature books.

LIMBERLOST STATE HISTORIC SITE

Limberlost was a vast expanse of forest and swampland near the town of Geneva. Though the wilderness was deemed a nuisance by most nineteenth-century settlers, it was a paradise for author and naturalist Gene Stratton Porter. In 1895 she and her druggist-banker husband, Charles Darwin Porter, built a house here named Limberlost Cabin, where they lived for eighteen years. Here she wrote several popular novels and nature books, including *Freckles* and *Girl of the Limberlost,* and studied the flora and fauna of the Limberlost swamp. She was also an excellent watercolorist and an early expert at nature photography. When the swamp was drained in 1913 the Porters retreated to another favorite haunt, Sylvan Lake near Rome City.

Limberlost Cabin, a large bungalow of log and frame construction, contains much of the original furnishings and memorabilia associated with the naturalist's life.

LOCATION: 200 Sixth Street, off Route 27, Geneva. HOURS: Mid-March through mid-December: 9–5 Tuesday–Saturday, 1–5 Sunday. FEE: None. TELEPHONE: 219–368–7428.

CHAPTER THREE

ILLINOIS

Illinois's grip on only sixty miles of Lake Michigan shoreline might make its status as a Great Lakes state dubious but for the fact that the preeminent city of Chicago is situated on that shore. The history of Chicago as both gateway to and hub of the western Great Lakes and Midwest requires its own chapter. Once the Erie Canal opened in 1825, Illinois tightened its economic and cultural ties with the Northeast via Chicago. Through that city the larger world, through the influx of immigrant Europeans, left its stamp on Illinois. At the other end of the state, Illinois leaned toward Southern mores and traditions, linked to them by the Mississippi River, which forms the state's western boundary, and the Ohio and Wabash, which form the eastern and southern. These major arteries between Illinois and New Orleans brought in settlers from Virginia, Kentucky, and Tennessee.

Illinois was at the center of trade, transportation, and communications in the middle of the expanding continent. It was also a stage for the conflicts that arise among merging cultures and social strata. Before 1860 the leading antagonists were antislavery Easterners, slaveholding French, and Southerners of various persuasions—some who denounced slavery and others who wished to perpetuate it.

While Illinois's waterways played a major role in its settlement and growth, just as important has been the vast prairie that covers most of the state. Early settlers from the heavily wooded South doubted the fertility of this treeless expanse and continued the back-breaking job of clearing the forests along Illinois's rivers. By the 1830s, however, enough farmers had discovered the prairie's potential to set off something like a land rush into Illinois's midsection. With the removal of the Indians after the Black Hawk War (1832), three events allowed farming in this area to rise above the subsistence level: John Deere's invention of the steel plow, the development of barbed wire, and the advent of the railroads, which brought goods to market in an area with no navigable rivers.

Cities such as Bloomington and Decatur sprouted on the prairie to serve the commercial and social needs of the farmers. To thrive they needed only two things: the title of county seat and a railroad line. New Salem, for example, was prosperous when Abraham Lincoln lived there as a young man, but went into rapid decline when it lost both title and train to nearby Petersburg.

Even in millennial terms, Illinois has been a cultural hub and crossroad. The fertile river valleys that cut through its prairies lured early peoples to waterways that provided both sustenance

An effigy bottle from the Cahokia Mounds in southern Illinois, representing a nursing mother, dates from A. D. 1200 to 1400.

and a means of transportation, permitting trade and communication with other populations. Evidence in the form of ceremonial mounds and village sites shows a major shift from hunting and gathering to a more sedentary life of farming. Later came immigrant tribes such as the Illinois (or Illiniwek), a loose association of several bands, including the Kaskaskia, Cahokia, and Peoria, who were present when the French first arrived in 1673. They

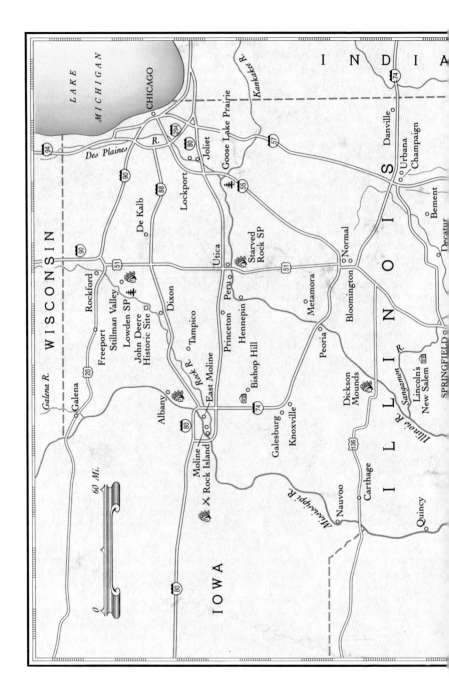

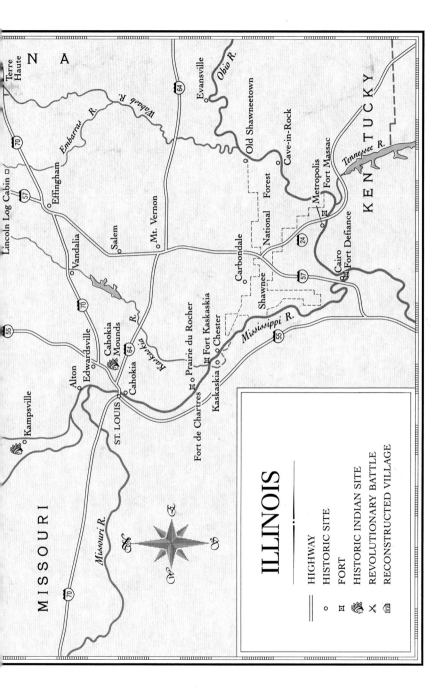

ILLINOIS

--- HIGHWAY
o HISTORIC SITE
Ⱶ FORT
🏵 HISTORIC INDIAN SITE
✕ REVOLUTIONARY BATTLE
🏛 RECONSTRUCTED VILLAGE

Forty-nine-year-old Abraham Lincoln in May 1858, several months before his series of debates with Stephen Douglas brought him to national attention.

developed close relationships with the French, but this alliance failed to stave off their decline, which was brought on by constant warfare with other native peoples such as the Mesquakie and Sauk as well as disease, alcoholism, factionalism, and the encroachment of white settlers. This once-thriving confederation, which numbered about 6,000 in 1700, had a population of only about a hundred by 1832, when they were removed to a reservation in Kansas.

The first recorded white visitors in the region were the French Jesuit priest Jacques Marquette and explorer Louis Jolliet, who in

1673 returned through the Illinois country via the Illinois and Des Plaines rivers from their landmark expedition through Wisconsin to the Mississippi River.

In his exploits in Illinois, the French explorer Robert Cavelier, sieur de la Salle, was a rival of Jolliet's and an adversary of the Jesuits. In 1680 La Salle, with his trusted companion, one-handed soldier Henri de Tonti, erected the first foreign fort on Illinois soil, Fort Crèvecoeur near present-day Peoria. Their later fortification, Fort Saint Louis at Starved Rock, near Utica, became an important gathering place for Illinois Indians seeking protection from invading Iroquois.

These French toeholds along the Illinois River did not last, chiefly because of harassment by local Mesquakie Indians. In 1699, however, successful French colonization commenced along the Mississippi River between the confluences of the Illinois and Ohio rivers. This region became a center of French culture on the new continent. Known as the "breadbasket of Louisiana," the area supplied foodstuffs to compatriots to the south. When the region was ceded to the British in 1763 after the French and Indian War, many of the French moved across the Mississippi to the fast-growing town of Saint Louis in territory held by Spain. However, the corridor retained its French atmosphere. The British were distracted on other fronts—first by wars with the Ottawa chief Pontiac and then by the Revolutionary War—and never established a substantial presence in the area.

The only action here during the Revolutionary War was the 1778 campaign of George Rogers Clark, who seized the French corridor, along with a vast area between the Mississippi and Ohio rivers, for the state of Virginia. Virginia in turn passed Illinois County, as it was called, to the Continental Congress in 1782, which was equally ill-equipped to govern this extended and unruly appendage. Only after the writing of the Northwest Ordinance in 1787 and the arrival of the territory's first governor, Arthur St. Clair, in 1790 was order re-established in the French corridor, where from 1763 anarchy and lawlessness had reigned.

As settlers began to trickle, then pour, into this old French stronghold, it became known as the American Bottom. Settlement was slow at first, largely because of Indian attacks and Britain's reluctance to give up its hold on the territory. One of America's major setbacks during the War of 1812 was the defeat and massacre in 1812 of some sixty soldiers and militia by the Potawatomi at Fort Dearborn, which stood adjacent to the nascent trading post of

Chicago. After the War of 1812, a series of Indian treaties eliminated the British influence and reduced the power of the Indians. By 1818 the federal government had title to most of Illinois, the territory achieved statehood, and settlement began in earnest. Many of the first settlers came from Virginia, Kentucky, and Tennessee, but by the 1830s, after the defeat of the Sauk-Fox chief Black Hawk, New Yorkers, New Englanders, and other Easterners began pouring into Illinois. These newcomers settled chiefly in Chicago or on the prairies, where many became prosperous farmers and livestock owners. With the opening of the Illinois and Michigan Canal in 1848 and the feverish laying of railroad track in the 1850s—by 1855 Illinois had two thousand miles of track, more than any other western state—Chicago emerged as a trading and transportation hub. And by the mid-nineteenth century, when its population passed the one million mark, Illinois was a thriving melting pot. Prosperous German farmers and tradesmen often settled in and around the smaller towns of Alton, Galena, Peoria, and Quincy. Irish laborers typically found jobs building the railroads, settling in towns through which the railroad passed. Scandinavians, such as the Swedish dissidents at Bishop Hill, tended toward rural areas.

The Compromise of 1818, written at the time of statehood, allowed the French to keep their slaves and permitted other settlers to keep indentured servants brought in during the territorial period. But the compromise prohibited the further introduction of slavery in the new state, with the exception of work on the salt springs near Shawneetown, where slavery was permitted until 1825. Illinois was the scene of skirmishes over the issue of slavery, one of the most violent being the murder of abolitionist editor Elijah Lovejoy at Alton in 1837.

Amid this atmosphere of conflict, Abraham Lincoln ran for the U.S. Senate against incumbent Stephen A. Douglas in 1858. In a series of seven debates held across Illinois, they confronted the major conflicts that slavery presented: "popular sovereignty" in the territories, states' rights, and the morality of slavery. Thousands of people came from miles around to hear Lincoln and Douglas; the debates were a national event as well, when for the first time journalists used the telegraph to wire stories of the campaign. Douglas defeated Lincoln for the Senate, but the favorable national attention Lincoln derived helped him win the presidency in 1860.

OPPOSITE: *A family farm near Verona in bucolic Grundy County.*

Illinois men volunteering to serve in the Civil War numbered 260,000, of whom 35,000 died. Among the volunteers was Ulysses S. Grant of Galena, who later became commander of the Union troops. Rock Island was used as a prison for Confederate captives during the war and thereafter became a military arsenal. At its strategic location at the confluence of the Ohio and Mississippi rivers, Cairo flourished during the Civil War as an army supply center and conduit for Union troops entering the South.

After the Civil War, the sharpest conflicts occurred between worker and employer, including the 1886 Haymarket riot and 1894 Pullman strike in Chicago. In 1861 striking miners in Illinois's extensive coal fields formed the nation's first organization of miners, which by 1890 had evolved into the United Mine Workers. The Union Miners Cemetery in Mount Olive in south-central Illinois contains the graves of participants in most of the early coal union events in the state.

The period of prosperity following the Civil War ended with the panic of 1873. This downturn in the economy exacerbated conflicts between labor and management and between farmers and both the middlemen buying their livestock and grain and the railroads carrying their produce. The former paid them too little, whereas the latter charged them too much. Illinois farmers participated in a wave of rural protest that swept across the Midwest and prompted the formation of new political parties such as the Grangers and Greenbackers.

In 1893 Chicago was the site of the World's Columbian Exposition, an event that brought the city to the attention of the world and infused the Midwest with a cosmopolitan air and a sense of optimism with which to greet the new century.

This chapter opens in northern Illinois, an area demarked by Route 80 on the south; part of it parallels the historic Illinois and Michigan Canal. Next is western Illinois, encompassing the land between the high bluffs of the Mississippi and the fertile Illinois River Valley. East-central Illinois comprises most of Illinois's prairies, including all the territory east of the Illinois River and north of Route 70. The chapter concludes with southern Illinois, where the first settlement in the region took place, a section lying south of Route 70 and bounded by the Mississippi and Ohio rivers.

NORTHERN ILLINOIS
GALENA

Galena, named after the Latin word for lead ore, has in recent years been restored to appear much as it did in the mid-nineteenth century, when it was a bustling mining, smelting, and steamboat town. In 1807 the U.S. Congress authorized the establishment of a federal mine district in this area, and with the advent of the steamboat in the 1820s, the lead boom was on. The first miners, who came from Missouri, Kentucky, Tennessee, and points south, lived in cabins, but as the townspeople grew wealthy, they built gracious, often grand, houses of brick and limestone on the valley precipices, while merchants constructed equally handsome businesses along Main Street. These residences remain picturesquely perched along the precipitous sides of the Galena River, some three miles upstream from that river's confluence with the Mississippi. The river was navigable into the town until deforestation caused erosion that in turn silted the river. During Galena's boom, which lasted until the late 1850s, 820 million pounds of lead were shipped from the local mines. The town declined rapidly as the lead mines were exhausted and railroads began to supersede steamboat travel. But Galena has preserved many of its early buildings, which include examples of Federal, Greek Revival, Gothic Revival, Second Empire, Italianate, and Queen Anne buildings.

Among the nineteenth-century commercial buildings and residences still standing on Main and Bench streets are the **Daniel A. Barrows House** (211 South Bench Street, 815–777–9129), an 1858 Italianate brick structure that contains the **Galena–Jo Daviess County History Museum.** Exhibits and artifacts pertain to the lead-mining and steamboating industries and to Grant and the Civil War, including Thomas Nast's painting *Peace in Union,* which depicts General Robert E. Lee surrendering to Grant.

An exhibit of the various architectural styles preserved in Galena is on display at the **Old Market House State Historic Site** (123 North Commerce Street, 815–777–3310). The building was city hall and public meeting place in the boom years. Beer is still made in the stone lagering cellar at the **City Brewery Museum** (418 Spring Street, 815–777–0354). The 1850 limestone Italianate building was a working brewery until 1881.

Galena was home to Ulysses S. Grant and his family before and after the Civil War and for a short time after his presidency. In 1860 he brought his wife, Julia, and their four children to a modest brick house that still stands at 121 High Street. Grant worked with his brothers at their father's leather goods store until the outbreak of the Civil War, when the West Point graduate and veteran of the Mexican War helped organize volunteers from the town and ultimately received a commission in the army. After the war, the citizens of Galena presented their hero with a house. The **U.S. Grant Home State Historic Site** (500 Bouthillier Street, 815–777–0248) is an Italianate structure built from 1859 to 1860. Situated on the east side of the river, the house has a commanding view of the western terraces and many of Galena's finest houses. It contains many original furnishings.

Galena welcomed its favorite son, Ulysses S. Grant, with a homecoming arch when he returned from a two-year round-the-world tour in 1879.

A grateful group of Galena citizens presented this Italianate house to victorious General Grant after the Civil War.

FREEPORT

Settled in 1835, following the Black Hawk War, Freeport was a stagecoach stop between Chicago and Galena, and its early economy was tied to the area's lead boom. The **Stephenson County Historical Museum** (1440 South Carroll Avenue, 815–232–8419) is housed in an 1857 Italianate brick residence furnished with period pieces. On the grounds are an arboretum with many trees planted by the original owners, a farm museum containing items from the 1850 to 1910 era, and a log cabin built by one of the many Irish immigrants who settled in the area in the 1840s and 1850s. The museum also contains material related to the second Lincoln-Douglas debate, held in Freeport on August 27, 1858.

ROCKFORD

Rockford was founded in 1834 by New Englanders at the site of a shallow ford on the Rock River. An influx of Swedish laborers arrived in the 1850s to build the Chicago Union Railroad, and successive arrivals of skilled immigrants helped turn Rockford into a manufacturing center. It is now the second-largest city in Illinois.

The Rockford **Midway Village and Museum Center** (6799 Guilford Road, 815–397–9112) is a fifty-three-acre complex containing twenty-four historical structures from the vicinity, including an 1800s jail and sheriff's office and a replica of Rockford's first hospital. Each contains period furnishings and exhibits pertaining to its history. Also of interest is the **Tinker Swiss Cottage** (411 Kent Street, 815–964–2424), a chaletlike structure built in 1865 and based on Swiss structures sketched by local industrialist Robert Hall Tinker. The **Erlander Home Museum** (404 South Third Street, 815–963–5559) houses the museum of the Swedish Historical Society.

STILLMAN VALLEY

Stillman Valley, fifteen miles south of Rockford, was the site of the first confrontation of the Black Hawk War, named after a Sauk-Fox Indian chief. On May 14, 1832, a scouting party of Illinois militia under Captain Isaiah Stillman attacked a group of Sauk, although the Indians were carrying a white flag. When the militia reached Chief Black Hawk's encampment on the Sycamore River, they were routed by the Indians. Called Stillman's Run, the battle so terrified the settlers that federal troops and state militias numbering 7,000 set out against an Indian force of perhaps 500 warriors. The half-starving band of Indians, which included women and children, led their pursuers through mosquito-infested swamps and dense thickets of the Rock River Valley into Wisconsin, where two final battles were fought. **Battleground Memorial Park** (815–645–2200) in Stillman Valley commemorates the battle with a granite monument. Twelve tombstones mark the graves of men killed in the battle.

To the southwest, **Lowden State Park** (815–732–6828) lies on the banks of the Rock River near the town of Oregon. The site was purchased in 1898 by Chicago art patron Wallace Heckman as an art colony for painters, writers, sculptors, and musicians. After

Sauk-Fox Chief Black Hawk and his son Whirling Thunder, painted by J. W. Jarvis in 1833, the year after they made an unsuccessful attempt to regain Indian homelands in western Illinois.

some fifty years the colony came to be called Eagle's Nest, and its guiding figure was sculptor Lorado Taft. It became a state park in 1945. Taft's paean to Heckman's patronage is a monumental concrete sculpture of an enrobed Indian chief that stands forty-eight feet and weights one hundred tons.

JOHN DEERE HISTORIC SITE

In 1837, working in his blacksmith shop in the Rock River Valley settlement of Grand Detour, former Vermonter John Deere successfully forged the first self-scouring steel plow, an invention that opened the Midwestern prairies to intensive farming. It was dubbed the "singing plow" for the sound the steel blade made shearing through the sod, and it soon replaced the pioneers' cast-iron plows, which were sluggish in turning the gummy prairie soil. In 1847 John Deere moved his thriving business to Moline.

A museum stands on the original site of the blacksmith shop and contains exhibits of tools and artifacts found there during archaeological digs. Also included are a replica of Deere's blacksmith shop and Deere's original home, a simple white frame structure built in 1836, which houses period furnishings.

LOCATION: 8393 South Main Street, Grand Detour. HOURS: April through October: 9–5 Daily. FEE: Yes. TELEPHONE: 815–652–4551.

DIXON

The Rock River community of Dixon, settled in 1830, served as Fort Dixon during the Black Hawk War. Abraham Lincoln was stationed here in the Illinois militia; a statue of the recruit is on Lincoln Statue Drive. In nearby Tampico is **Ronald Reagan's Birthplace** (111 South Main Street, 815–438–6175, by appointment), a six-room apartment above a bakery, where the fortieth president was born, February 6, 1911. A history society museum (119 South Main Street) has Reagan exhibits. In 1920 his family moved to Dixon. The **Ronald Reagan Boyhood Home** (816 South Hennepin Avenue, 815–288–3404), is a two-story frame house.

DE KALB

Founded in 1836 by New Englanders, De Kalb is a factory town on the Kishwaukee River. It was here in 1874 that Joseph Glidden produced and patented a highly effective type of barbed wire, a double-strand design called "the Winner." Glidden and his partner Isaac Ellwood were involved in a series of patent infringement suits with Jacob Haish, another local designer of barbed wire, which continued until the U.S. Supreme Court ruled in favor of the Glidden patent in 1891. The **Ellwood Mansion Museum** (509 North First Street, 815–756–4609), former home of Isaac Ellwood, is a Victorian brick mansion built in 1879. It contains period furnishings and costumes, barbed wire, and a collection of buggies.

The **Illinois and Michigan (I&M) Canal** was excavated—by hand—between 1836 and 1848 to eliminate the portage between the Chicago and Des Plaines rivers and to provide easy transit paralleling the unnavigable stretches of the Illinois River. Running ninety-six miles west from Chicago to present-day Peru, the canal bridged the divide between two great watersheds—the Saint Lawrence and the Mississippi—and so extended the reach of the Erie Canal, providing the first navigable passage from Lake Michigan to the Illinois, and in turn, the Mississippi River. Chicago's success as a trading and shipping hub was secured by the I&M, and numerous towns grew up along the canal's banks. The channelization of the Illinois River in 1933 spelled the end of the canal's usefulness. A map detailing the Illinois and Michigan Canal National Heritage Corridor, encompassing the towns and historic sites along the old I&M route, is available locally or through the Upper Illinois Valley Association (312–427–3688).

Well before the canal era, this system of rivers was a thorough-fare for French fur traders. Located in the town of **Romeoville,** the **Isle a la Cache Museum** (501 East Romeo Road, 815–889–1467) stands on an eighty-acre island in the Des Plaines River where fur traders may have stored furs and trade goods in the seventeenth and eighteenth centuries. The museum contains exhibits on Indi-ans of the area and life among the voyageurs during the fur-trading era.

LOCKPORT

Lockport was established in 1836 as headquarters for the I&M Canal. The **Illinois and Michigan Canal Museum** (803 South State Street, 815–838–5080) is housed in the original I&M Canal com-missioner's office, an 1837 frame structure with Greek Revival and Italianate elements. Maintained by the Will County Historical Soci-ety, it contains artifacts and exhibits on the canal's construction and operation. The society also operates the **Pioneer Settlement** (North Public Landing between Eighth and Ninth streets), an assemblage of fifteen nineteenth-century structures furnished with period arti-facts. The **Lockport Historic District** (between Seventh and Ele-venth streets and Canal and Washington streets) is a commercial area of some sixty buildings constructed between 1836 and 1896. Predominantly Greek Revival and Italianate in style, many were built of the distinctive cream-colored local limestone. The 1838 canal warehouse has been restored as the **Gaylord Building** (200 West Eighth Street), housing a restaurant, visitor center, and a gallery of the Illinois State Museum.

JOLIET

Founded in the 1830s, Joliet prospered with the opening of the I&M Canal. The town became an outlet for agricultural products and locally quarried limestone and a center for steel manufactur-ing. Of special interest is the **Rialto Square Theatre** (102 North Chicago Street, 815–726–7171), a gilded vaudeville palace built in 1926 and still a functioning performance hall.

GOOSE LAKE PRAIRIE STATE NATURAL AREA

This park near the I&M Canal town of Morris preserves a 1,500-acre swath of the stunning tall-grass prairie that once covered three-quarters of Illinois. It is the largest remnant prairie in the state. The park encompasses the site of **Jugtown,** an 1850s settlement named for the pottery its citizens made from local clay.

LOCATION: 5010 North Jugtown Road, Morris. HOURS: 10–4 Daily. FEE: None. TELEPHONE: 815–942–2899.

STARVED ROCK STATE PARK

Located on the south bank of the Illinois River one mile from Utica, the 3,000-acre Starved Rock State Park (815–667–4726) is rich in Indian heritage and scenic beauty. The **visitor center** (815–667–4906) has exhibits pertaining to the cultural and natural history of the region. The park takes its name from an impressive 130-foot sandstone butte. Atop this rock in about 1770, according to legend, a band of Illinois were trapped and eventually starved during a battle with the Ottawa, allied with the Potawatomi, to avenge the death of Chief Pontiac. Directly across the river on the north bank is the site of the large Illinois village of Kaskaskia, where in 1675 Jesuit missionary Jacques Marquette founded the first church in the region, Mission of the Immaculate Conception of the Blessed Virgin.

In 1682 to 1683, Robert Cavelier, sieur de la Salle, and Henri de Tonti built **Fort Saint Louis** on top of Starved Rock as part of a chain of forts intended to strengthen the French alliance with western Indian tribes. The area around the fort attracted an estimated 18,000 of the Illini Confederation seeking protection from invading Iroquois raids and further trade with the French. The Iroquois continued to press, and by 1692 the Illini Confederation had moved south toward Peoria for better and safer hunting areas. The fort burned down around 1721.

In nearby **Utica,** the **La Salle County Historical Society Museum** (Mill and Canal streets, 815–667–4861) is housed in an 1840s stone warehouse on the I&M Canal National Heritage Corridor. It contains Indian artifacts and pioneer furnishings.

OPPOSITE: *Joliet's magnificently restored Rialto Square Theatre, which seats nearly 2,000 people, is one of a handful of vaudeville movie palaces still operating in the United States.*

PRINCETON

Princeton, founded by settlers from Massachusetts in 1831, contains the **Owen Lovejoy Homestead** (East Peru Street, 815–879–9151), the residence of Congregational minister and antislavery politician Owen Lovejoy and an important station on the Underground Railroad. His brother, abolitionist editor Elijah P. Lovejoy, was killed by a proslavery mob in Alton. The two-story white frame house, built in 1838, contains period furnishings.

The metropolitan area straddling the Illinois-Iowa state line includes a cluster of cities around the confluence of the Rock and Mississippi rivers. Three are in Illinois—Rock Island, Moline, and East Moline. Their water power and shipping potential attracted industry in the nineteenth century, not the least of which was John Deere and Company, and for over a hundred years the area has been a major manufacturing center for farm implements.

Ten thousand years ago, Paleo-Indians were attracted to these river bluffs. Though not much evidence of their presence remains in the metropolitan area, the **Albany Mounds,** thirty miles north on Route 84, is one of the largest Hopewell Indian (300 B.C. to A.D. 400) sites in Illinois. It may contain as many as ninety mounds.

MOLINE

Set in a thousand acres of woodland overlooking the Rock River Valley, the 1964 **Deere and Company Administrative Center** (John Deere Road, 309–765–8000) is an impressive horizontal glass and steel structure, one of the masterpieces of architect Eero Saarinen. The product display building contains current and historical John Deere products and a large collage by Alexander Girard composed of some 2,000 agriculture-related objects from the period 1837 to 1918. The **Rock Island County Historical Society** (822 Eleventh Avenue, 309–764–8590), housed in the 1878 Victorian **Atkinson Mansion,** contains Indian artifacts, agricultural implements, and period furnishings, glassware, toys, and dolls. A research library is also on the premises.

ROCK ISLAND

Black Hawk State Historic Site (1510 Forty-sixth Avenue, 309–788–0177) is a 207-acre tract of rugged woodlands in the heart of the land once occupied by the area's dominant Indian tribes, the

Sauk and Mesquakie. Saukenuk, which stood adjacent to the site, was capital of the Sauk nation and, from around 1740 to about 1820, one of the largest Indian villages in North America. Saukenuk was the site of the westernmost battle of the Revolutionary War, when in 1780 American troops destroyed the village because of the Sauk's alliance with the British. Most of the Indians relocated across the Mississippi, but during the War of 1812 some 1,000 Sauk, Mesquakie, and Winnebago, under the command of Black Hawk and with 30 British troops, defeated about 400 American troops on September 14, 1814. The Sauk's resistance to American settlements culminated in the 1832 Black Hawk War. On the grounds the **Hauberg Indian Museum** depicts the life of the Sauk and Mesquakie during this tumultuous period in their history. It also contains displays from a later era when the site was one of America's earliest recreation parks. Called the Watch Tower, it operated from the 1880s to the 1920s, attracting as many as 15,000 people a day for concerts, vaudeville, and amusement rides.

The ca. 1862 **House on the Hill** (3052 Tenth Avenue, private) is a brick Victorian house built for lumber baron Frederick E. Weyerhaeuser. It is owned by Augustana College, which maintains the **Swenson Swedish Immigration Research Center** (309–794–7204), containing the country's largest collection of documents relating to Swedish immigration in the United States as well as artifacts and memorabilia.

ROCK ISLAND ARSENAL

Rock Island, not to be confused with the city of the same name, is a three-mile-long, 946-acre island in the Mississippi River. The arsenal on the island has produced equipment and supplies for the U.S. Army since the 1870s, and the government currently employs 1,750 people at its ordnance factory here. After the War of 1812, **Fort Armstrong** was built on the commanding bluffs on the west end of Rock Island to remind the Indians of the American claim to the frontier, and it was occupied from 1816 to 1836. A replica of a blockhouse stands at the original site. One of the oldest extant structures on the island is the 1833 Greek Revival **Colonel Davenport House.**

During the Civil War, work began on arsenal buildings, including numerous Italianate residences, stone workshops, and the **Clock Tower Building,** now offices for the army's Corps of Engineers. None of the buildings was completed during the war, however; the island was used as a prisoner-of-war camp. Over a period of twenty months, approximately 12,000 Confederate troops were confined on the island. Many prisoners died from smallpox, and some 2,000 soldiers are buried in the **Confederate Cemetery** at the center of the island. The **Arsenal Museum** (Building 60, 309–782–5021) displays the history of Rock Island and has an extensive collection of military firearms.

LOCATION: Rock Island. HOURS: 10–4 Daily. FEE: None. TELE-PHONE: 309–782–5013.

W E S T E R N   I L L I N O I S

BISHOP HILL

Bishop Hill Colony was founded in 1846 by Swedish religious dissenter Erik Jansson and his followers, who viewed their leader as the second Christ. Some 1,200 immigrants from Sweden joined the utopian village, but the murder of Jansson in 1850 marked the beginning of internal strife, and the colony disbanded in 1861.

The 1852 vernacular-style Bishop Hill Colony hotel—known as the Bjorklund Hotel after one of its early managers, Sven Bjorklund—continued operating until the 1920s.

Numerous original structures, predominantly in the Greek Revival style, remain at Bishop Hill. They include the 1852 **Bjorklund Hotel** and the 1848 **Colony Church,** which contains articles made or used by the Janssonists, including examples of their finely crafted furniture. The **Bishop Hill Heritage Museum,** housed in the 1854 **Steeple Building,** contains manuscripts and artifacts of the colony. Paintings of the communal village by folk artist Olof Krans, who spent his boyhood at Bishop Hill, are on exhibit.

LOCATION: Thirty miles northeast of Galesburg, off Route 34, Bishop Hill. HOURS: 9–5 Daily. FEE: None. TELEPHONE: 309–927–3345.

GALESBURG

Galesburg is an industrial city named for its founder, Presbyterian minister George Washington Gale, who came from New York with fifty families to found a college for training frontier theologians. Knox Manual Labor College, now **Knox College** (1 East South Street, 309–343–0112), opened in 1837. **Old Main** on the Knox College campus is a three-story brick Late Gothic Revival (Jacobethan Revival) structure built in 1857. On October 7, 1858, it was

Pulitzer Prize-winning poet and Lincoln biographer Carl Sandburg was born in this modest Galesburg house, now a state historic site.

the site of the fifth Lincoln-Douglas debate, attracting some 20,000, the largest crowd of the series. Old Main is within the **Galesburg Historic District** (Berrien, Clark, Pearl, and Sanborn streets), which includes numerous residential and commercial buildings in a range of nineteenth-century styles.

The **Carl Sandburg State Historic Site** (331 East Third Street, 309–342–2361) is a frame cottage in Galesburg's immigrant neighborhood where the author/poet was born in 1878. The house contains nineteenth-century furnishings and Sandburg publications and memorabilia. Sandburg's ashes lie beneath **Remembrance Rock** in the park behind the house.

NAUVOO

Nauvoo, a small commercial center for the outlying farm area, sits on a promontory of land formed by a bend in the Mississippi River. It was named Nauvoo, a Hebrew word meaning "beautiful place," by Joseph Smith, head of the Church of Jesus Christ of Latter-day Saints (commonly known as Mormons). Smith arrived here in 1839 with his followers after they had been driven from New York, Ohio, and Missouri. Mormons flocked to the area, and Nauvoo and

This sunstone was carved for the 1846 Nauvoo Temple, which was the largest structure west of Cincinnati and north of St. Louis. The carving is now in Nauvoo State Park.

Nauvoo, largely abandoned after Brigham Young led the Mormons west to Utah in 1846, has preserved many mid-nineteenth-century buildings from its Mormon period.

the surrounding territory had a population of some 12,000 during the 1840s. The Mormons' increasing political power, coupled with their religious practices and rapid growth, were viewed with alarm by many non-Mormons. Unrest and violence ensued, resulting in the murder of Joseph Smith and his brother Hyrum in 1844 in Carthage. In 1846 the majority of the Latter-day Saints followed Brigham Young to Utah, and by 1848 Nauvoo was virtually abandoned.

Since 1962 Nauvoo Restoration, Inc., has restored more than twenty homes, shops, and public buildings, most of which are open to the public. The **Nauvoo Historic District** encompasses many of the nineteenth-century structures built by the Mormons, including the **Brigham Young House**; the **Joseph Smith Homestead,** where Joseph and Hyrum are buried; and **Mansion House,** Smith's last residence. Greek Revival elements are common in the structures, as are distinctive Mormon motifs. The **L.D.S. Visitor Center** (Main and Young streets, 217–453–2237) and the **Joseph Smith Visitors Center** (149 Water Street, one block west of Route 96, 217–453–2246) offer tour information and exhibits including archaeological artifacts.

CARTHAGE

Carthage, a small trading and manufacturing center, was settled in 1833. On June 27, 1844, the Mormon leader Joseph Smith and his brother Hyrum were being held in the **Carthage Jail** (Walnut and North Fayette streets) on charges of treason and destroying a printing press when a lynch mob stormed the building and killed the two men. The two-story limestone structure, built in 1839, contains furnishings of the period. A **visitor center** (217–357–2989) offers information and tours. The **Carthage Courthouse Square Historic District** (Main, Adams, Wabash, and Madison streets) encompasses numerous nineteenth-century public and commercial buildings, including the 1907 **Hancock County Courthouse.** The **Carthage Alice Kibbee Museum** (118 North Scofield Street) has an extensive collection of Civil War and Indian artifacts, many relating to Hancock County.

QUINCY

This industrial city on the bluffs of the Mississippi was settled in 1822 and prospered during the steamboat era. Many German immigrants coming upriver made Quincy home, and the town was an important station on the Underground Railroad. The **Historical Society of Quincy and Adams County** (425 South Twelfth Street, 217–222–1835) is housed in the 1835 **John Wood Mansion,** a Greek Revival residence that was the home of the first settler in the area and a founder of the Republican party. On exhibit are items pertaining to the Lincoln assassination trial and to the Mormon era at Nauvoo. The **Downtown Quincy Historic District** (Hampshire, Jersey, Fourth, and Eighth streets) encompasses many nineteenth-century commercial structures as well as Quincy's main square, **Washington Park,** where the sixth Lincoln-Douglas debate was held on October 13, 1858. The **Gardner Museum of Architecture and Design** (332 Maine Street, 217–224–6873) is in the **Old Public Library,** an 1888 Richardsonian Romanesque building facing Washington Park. The museum contains historic photographs, drawings, exhibits, and artifacts of nineteenth- and twentieth-century Quincy buildings. **The Quincy Museum** (1601 Main Street, 217–224–7669) features American Indian artifacts and shell and fossil exhibits. The first floor recreates the 1890s.

OPPOSITE: *The Quincy Museum, housed in the 1891 Newcomb-Stillwell mansion, has a large collection of Indian artifacts from the region.*

In the town of **Kampsville** on the Illinois River, is the **Kampsville Archaeological Museum** (Route 100, 618–653–4316), part of an archaeological center involved in researching and preserving prehistoric sites in the lower Illinois and adjacent Mississippi river valleys. The museum maintains extensive collections of artifacts and exhibits showing the prehistory of west-central Illinois. A replica of a prehistoric Indian village is nearby.

DICKSON MOUNDS

This 162-acre preserve, set on a bluff near the Illinois and Spoon rivers, encompasses village and burial sites that demonstrate the evolving cultural patterns of prehistoric Indians in the fertile Illinois River Valley, especially between A.D. 900 and 1300. Over this time, the Indians shifted from dwelling in small, scattered settlements, such as the **Ogden-Fettie site,** where they sustained themselves by hunting and gathering, to living in fortified villages, as represented by the **Larson site,** where farming was the chief activity. The **Dickson Mounds,** for which the entire preserve is named, are burial mounds built about a thousand years ago in the middle of this cultural transition. The **Dickson Mounds Museum** contains exhibits of these cultures, and surveys, altogether, some 12,000 years of human history in the Illinois River Valley.

LOCATION: Forty miles southwest of Peoria, off Routes 97/78, between Lewistown and Havana. HOURS: 8:30–5 Daily. FEE: None. TELEPHONE: 309–547–3721.

EAST-CENTRAL ILLINOIS

PEORIA

The industrial city of Peoria grew where the Illinois River widens to form two large lakes. The city was incorporated in 1845, but its history extends well back into the seventeenth century when Louis Jolliet and Father Jacques Marquette explored the central Illinois River Valley. This area was also another focal point of activity for the indefatigable La Salle and his lieutenant Tonti. In 1680 they threw up a hasty stockade, calling it Fort Crèvecoeur, the first,

OPPOSITE: *The parlor of the 1837 John C. Flanagan Residence, the oldest house in Peoria. It was built by a wealthy Philadelphia lawyer who settled here in 1834, and has been refurnished with period pieces by the Peoria Historical Society.*

albeit short-lived, fort in the future state of Illinois. Departing to attend to other business, they left the structure with mutinous men who destroyed and abandoned it only a few months later. A replica stands in **Fort Crèvecoeur Park** (301 Lawnridge Drive, off Route 29, 309–694–3193) in the Peoria suburb of Creve Coeur. Every September, the park conducts an annual reenactment of a typical seventeenth-century trading rendezvous between the Indians and French fur traders.

The **Peoria Historical Society** (942 Northeast Glen Oak Avenue, 309–674–1921) is in the **John C. Flanagan House,** a 1837 brick structure with Federal and Italianate elements. It contains nineteenth-century furniture, china, toys, and textiles and includes a pioneer kitchen and antique-tool shop. The society also maintains the **Pettengill-Morron House** (1212 West Moss Avenue), an 1868 brick Second Empire residence with Queen Anne decorative motifs, furnished to the period. Additionally, from May through October, the historical society conducts bus and trolley tours throughout the city. An architectural tour and a tour of the brewing and distillery industry are among the options.

The **Peoria City Hall** (419 Fulton Street), built in 1897, is a massive stone structure in the Flemish Renaissance style. The **West Bluff Historic District** (Randolph, High, and Moss streets, east of Western Street) includes several hundred residential structures representing Greek Revival, Victorian, Prairie, and bungalow styles from the 1840s to the 1930s. Notable is Frank Lloyd Wright's Prairie-style **Francis W. Little House** (1505 West Moss Avenue), the first of several he designed for the family. The last of these was broken up, and a portion of it is housed in the Metropolitan Museum of Art in New York. The Central Illinois Landmarks Foundation (309–674–7121) conducts group tours of historic districts in Peoria by advance arrangement.

Fifteen miles north of Peoria in **Metamora** is the **Metamora Courthouse** (113 East Partridge Street, 309–367–4470), one of two extant courthouses in Illinois's historic Eighth Judicial Circuit. Abraham Lincoln traveled the 11,000-square-mile Eighth Circuit as a lawyer for over a decade. The 1845 Greek Revival building contains many original courtroom furnishings and pioneer articles of the period.

OPPOSITE: *An ornate Victorian house in Peoria's West Bluff Historic District.*

BLOOMINGTON–NORMAL

Bloomington and Normal are hubs of industry, commerce, and higher education lying in the heart of Illinois's fertile corn belt. Older and larger, Bloomington was founded in 1831. Illinois State University, established in 1857, was the nucleus for the town of Normal, so called because the school was originally a "normal" school for training teachers. The **Illinois State University Museum** (301 South Main Street, Normal, 309–438–5415) focuses on the history of Illinois from its geology and prehistoric cultures to the historic Indian tribes, the French colonial period, and the era of pioneer settlement.

In Bloomington, the 1872 **David Davis Mansion** (1000 East Monroe Street, 309–828–1084) was home to Eighth Circuit Court judge and Lincoln confidant David Davis. Davis engineered Lincoln's 1860 presidential campaign, and in turn Lincoln appointed Davis to the U.S. Supreme Court, where he served from 1862 to 1877. The yellow brick Second Empire structure, designed by French architect Alfred Picquenard, who immigrated to establish a practice in the Midwest, contains original Victorian furnishings.

Also in Bloomington, the **McLean County Historical Society** operates the **Old Courthouse Museum** (200 North Main Street, 309–827–0428) in the 1903 courthouse, a monumental Classical Revival structure. The "Encounter on the Prairie" exhibition interprets the diverse peoples who settled the county— Southerners, Yankees, African-Americans, Germans, and Irish. The museum arranges walking tours of the **Bloomington Central Business Historic District,** which includes many nineteenth-century commercial buildings. Several residential historic districts preserve examples of Queen Anne, Georgian Revival, Romanesque Revival, and California Mission styles.

CHAMPAIGN–URBANA

Like Bloomington and Normal, these twin cities grew up as industrial, commercial, and educational centers to serve the surrounding corn-belt farms. The first Europeans to settle in this flat, open country arrived from Champaign County, Ohio, in 1822. Urbana

OPPOSITE: *The 1845 Metamora Courthouse, constructed of locally made brick, is one of the last two extant courthouses in which Lincoln practiced law while on the Eighth Judicial Circuit.*

was incorporated in 1833 and Champaign in 1860. The **University of Illinois** was chartered in 1867. One of the oldest buildings on the university campus is **Altgeld Hall** (corner of Wright and John streets, Urbana). Built in 1896, it is a Richardsonian Romanesque structure with a 132-foot-tall tower.

The **Champaign County Historical Society** (709 West University Avenue, Champaign, 217–356–1010) is housed in a turn-of-the-century mansion that contains period furnishings, clothing, and items related to the settlement of the area. Also of interest is the **U.S. Post Office** (Randolph and Church streets), a Beaux-Arts building designed by James Knox Taylor and built in 1905.

The **Early American Museum and Garden** (Lake of the Woods Park, Mahomet, 217–586–2612) is part of the Champaign County Forest Preserve District eight miles west of Champaign–Urbana. Focusing on the period of 1820 to 1870, the museum's exhibits and room interiors present the architecture, trades and occupations, decorative arts, and domestic and agricultural lives of the area's settlers.

DANVILLE

Settlers were attracted to this area in the 1820s by nearby saline springs. One of Danville's most enterprising early citizens was Gurdon Hubbard, a fur trader who opened an Indian trading post in 1828 and packed goods by pony to and from Chicago. Hubbard's Trace became Route 1, State Street in Chicago.

The **Vermilion County Museum Society** (116 North Gilbert Street, 217–442–2922) occupies the house of William Fithian, a physician, state legislator, and friend of Abraham Lincoln. The 1855 brick Italianate house contains medical implements, a turn-of-the-century dental office, and Lincoln memorabilia.

In the spring of 1831, discouraged by the previous hard winter, Thomas and Sarah Lincoln were on their way back to Indiana when they decided instead to settle on the rolling prairies of Coles County, finally purchasing Goosenest Prairie Farm, near the banks of the Embarras River, in 1840. The original cabin was sent to the 1893 Columbian Exposition in Chicago and afterwards lost. In

OPPOSITE: *Inside the McLean County Courthouse in Bloomington a statue commemorates early entrepreneur Asahel Gridley, who made and lost several fortunes after he arrived in the area in 1831.*

1929 the structure was reconstructed and is now part of the **Lincoln Log Cabin State Historic Site** (eight miles south of Charleston, 217–345–6489). It is a large double-room log cabin furnished with typical pioneer items—the original structure accommodated eighteen family members in 1845, including Sarah's son and daughter and their spouses and children. Other buildings include a large log barn, corn crib, and root cellar. Thomas died in 1851, Sarah in 1869. They are buried in nearby **Shiloh Cemetery.**

BRYANT COTTAGE STATE HISTORIC SITE

Bryant Cottage was the site of a brief but important encounter between Abraham Lincoln and Stephen A. Douglas on the night of July 29, 1858. Some days earlier, as part of his campaign to win Douglas's seat in the U.S. Senate, Lincoln had challenged the incumbent to a series of debates to be held across Illinois. At the home of Douglas's friend, politician and businessman Francis. E. Bryant, Douglas and Lincoln settled upon an agenda for the seven debates that over the next three months would focus national attention on the issue of slavery. Built in 1856, the cottage is maintained in its original condition with original and period furnishings.

LOCATION: 146 East Wilson Street, Bement. HOURS: March through October: 9–5 Daily; Rest of year: 9–4 Daily. FEE: None. TELEPHONE: 217–678–8184.

DECATUR

Plotted in 1829 on the banks of the Sangamon River, Decatur became a trading center amid rich prairie farmland. It owes its prosperity in large measure to the soybean—the Archer-Daniels-Midland Company owns mammoth soybean-processing plants in the city. In 1858 Abraham Lincoln made his first political speech here in Lincoln Square, and it was here on May 9, 1860, that he received his first formal endorsement for president from the Illinois Republican Convention.

The **Macon County Museum Complex** (5580 North Fork Road, 217–422–4919) includes an 1855 log house and 1863 rural school. On display are photographs, tools, clothing, Victorian and early-twentieth-century mass-produced decorative arts, and farm and kitchen implements. The 1895 **Transfer House** (1 Central Park East) is an octagonal structure topped with a bandshell. Originally in Lincoln Square, it served as ticket office and transfer point for horse-drawn and electric trolleys and buses. The **James Millikin Homestead** (125 North Pine Street, 217–422–9003), built in 1876 by the founder of Millikin University, is a brick Second Empire mansion that has been completely restored.

Abraham Lincoln worked as a lawyer on the Eighth Circuit for more than a dozen years, and there are two sites near Decatur where he argued cases. The **Postville Courthouse State Historic Site** (914 Fifth Street, Lincoln, 217–732–8930) is a replica of the first county courthouse, which was constructed in 1839. The Federal-style frame structure contains period fixtures and exhibits pertaining to the circuit court system in Illinois. The **Mount Pulaski Courthouse State Historic Site** (Town Square, Mount Pulaski, 217–792–3919) preserves the original 1848 Greek Revival brick structure with period furnishings and the law books and gavel used by Judge David Davis when he held court here.

SPRINGFIELD

Springfield is situated amid rich, rolling farmlands just south of the Sangamon River. Several creeks feed into the river here, a propitious circumstance that attracted the area's first settlers in 1818. The town was incorporated in 1832 and quickly became a bustling prairie outpost. In 1837 members of the General Assembly, whose ranks included young lawyer Abraham Lincoln, voted to move the capital from Vandalia to Springfield, in part because of its location in the center of the state. That same year, Lincoln, who had been elected to the General Assembly in 1834, moved to the capital from nearby New Salem.

Springfield is the heartland of Lincolniana. It was here that the young politician courted Kentucky-bred Mary Todd, who had followed her two elder sisters to Illinois. (Another who vied for Mary Todd's attentions was Lincoln's political rival Stephen A. Douglas.) Abraham and Mary were married in 1842 and bought a home in Springfield two years later, the only one Lincoln ever owned and where the three youngest of their four sons were born. The eldest and only child to survive into adulthood, Robert, was born in 1843, followed by Edward (1846–1850), William (1850–1862), and Thomas (1853–1871).

With the nation divided over the issue of slavery, Lincoln was elected sixteenth president of the United States in 1860. When the president-elect left Springfield in 1861 for his inauguration in

Washington, DC, he made a farewell speech from the back of his train that included the prophetic remark, "I now leave, not knowing when, or whether ever, I may return." Following his assassination four years later, a special funeral train carried Lincoln's body to Springfield, pausing at each place where Lincoln had stopped to speak on his inaugural trip.

Lincoln Home National Historic Site

The neat frame house where Abraham and Mary Lincoln lived for sixteen years was built in 1839 and purchased by Lincoln from the Reverend Charles Dresser for $1,500. As Lincoln's political career prospered and his family grew, they added a second story to the structure. In 1860 the house was the center of a tumultuous public

Abraham Lincoln's Springfield house, now the Lincoln Home National Historic Site, is the only residence he ever owned. Three of his sons were born here.

celebration after Lincoln was nominated for president. The house contains period pieces, many original to the family. Lincoln's eldest son, Robert, donated the house to the state in 1887, and since 1972 it has been administered by the National Park Service. The Lincoln home is part of a four-block-square historic district of about a dozen homes dating to the mid-nineteenth century. The **Lincoln Home Visitor Center** (426 South Seventh Street) contains an exhibit of various other Lincoln sites in the area.

LOCATION: Eighth and Jackson streets. HOURS: 8:30–5 Daily; longer hours in summer. FEE: None. TELEPHONE: 217–492–4150.

Lincoln delivered his farewell address to Springfield from a train at the **Great Western Depot** (Monroe Street between Ninth and Tenth streets), which now contains restored waiting rooms and

A bedroom in the Lincoln home, refurnished with period artifacts and family pieces, features vividly colored wallpaper reproduced from the mid-nineteenth century original.

The restored courtroom that was Springfield's federal court from 1840 to 1855, on the first floor of the same building that housed Lincoln's law offices.

exhibits of Lincolniana. The **law offices** (Sixth and Adams streets, 217–785–7289) of Abraham Lincoln and his partner William Herndon are located in the surviving portion of a Greek Revival commercial block constructed between 1840 and 1841. The offices have been restored with period furnishings. Also located in the building is the old federal courtroom, until 1848 the only one in Illinois, in which Lincoln argued many cases. It has also been restored and furnished with period pieces.

Vachel Lindsay House

This handsome Greek Revival house next to the Governor's Mansion was the birthplace in 1879 of Vachel Lindsay, a major American poet known as the Prairie Troubadour. He brought his family to live in the homestead and died here in 1931. In 1906, 1908, and 1912, Lindsay undertook extensive walking tours across the United States, trading his poetry for food and lodging. The house was built in 1846, and one of its previous owners was merchant Clark Smith, whose wife, Ann, was Mary Todd Lincoln's sister.

LOCATION: 603 South Fifth Street. HOURS: Closed for restoration at time of publication. FEE: None. TELEPHONE: 217–785–7290.

Old State Capitol

The Old State Capitol was the seat of Illinois government from 1839 to 1876, when it became the Sangamon County Courthouse. Completed in 1853 by architect John Rague, it is a Greek Revival structure with a domed cupola and Doric porticos on the north and south sides. Stacked varicolored limestone created the distinctive striated pattern of the facade. Abraham Lincoln delivered his famous "House Divided" speech in the capitol in 1858, and his body lay in state here following his assassination.

Springfield's Old State Capitol was first occupied in 1839 but not completed until 1853. Lincoln used the governor's office when he was president-elect.

The interior of splendid spaces and fine proportions contains period furnishings, Lincolniana, and exhibits on nineteenth-century Illinois government. One of the original copies of the Gettysburg Address is on permanent display. It also houses the **Illinois Historical Library.**

LOCATION: Fifth and Adams streets. HOURS: 9–5 Daily. FEE: Yes. TELEPHONE: 217–785–7961.

The **Illinois State Museum** (Spring and Edwards streets, 217–782–7386) houses collections and exhibits pertaining to Illinois's natural history, prehistoric and historic Indians, and the decorative and fine arts. The brick Italianate **Governor's Mansion** (Fifth and Jackson streets, 217–782–6450) was built in 1855 and designed by John Murray Van Osdel. It contains many antiques and artifacts.

Dana-Thomas House State Historic Site

Built between 1902 and 1904, the Dana-Thomas House is one of the most elegant and best preserved of Frank Lloyd Wright's early Prairie-style structures, and one of the nation's most important buildings. Wright designed the house for Susan Lawrence Dana, a cosmopolitan woman of broad cultural and political interests. It was purchased in 1944 by Mr. and Mrs. Charles C. Thomas, who for thirty-seven years used the house as executive offices for their publishing company, until selling it to the state. Not fundamentally altered over the years, the house has been refurbished and contains more than a hundred pieces of the original white oak furniture designed by Wright as well as light fixtures, skylights, and a wealth of his characteristic art-glass doors, windows, and light panels.

LOCATION: 301 East Lawrence Avenue. HOURS: 9–4 Wednesday–Sunday. FEE: Yes. TELEPHONE: 217–782–6776.

Lincoln Tomb State Historic Site

When Abraham Lincoln was buried in Oak Ridge Cemetery on May 4, 1865, his remains rested in a series of temporary vaults, awaiting completion of a monument. Construction of the memorial began in 1869, and in October 1874 Lincoln's coffin was placed in a white marble sarcophagus in the center of the burial chamber, itself surmounted by a 117-foot granite obelisk. It and much of the

OPPOSITE: *The dome of the new Illinois State Capitol, built between 1868 and 1888, is 405 feet tall. It was designed by Chicago architect John C. Cochrane.*

statuary were designed by Vermont sculptor Larkin G. Mead. In addition, a large bust of Lincoln by Gutzon Borglum stands at the approach to the tomb, and in the foyer is a bronze model of Daniel Chester French's statue of the president in the Lincoln Memorial in Washington, DC. In 1876 an attempt was made to steal Lincoln's body and hold it for a $200,000 ransom. The conspirators were caught, convicted, and sentenced to prison. Lincoln's remains now lie sealed in a vault beneath the floor of the monument. His wife, Mary Todd, and three of his sons—Edward, William, and Thomas—are also interred in the monument. (His eldest son, Robert Todd, is buried in Arlington National Cemetery.)

LOCATION: Oak Ridge Cemetery, Monument Avenue. HOURS: 9–5 Daily. FEE: None. TELEPHONE: 217–782–2717.

ILLINOIS STATE CAPITOL

The Capitol, central building of the State Capitol Group, extends for more than three blocks on Second Street. Designed by the Chicago architect John C. Cochrane, it was constructed from 1868 to 1888, utilizing at least seven different kinds of marble and the murals, paintings, statuary, and a unique architectural design add to its beauty. The flagpole above the magnificent dome rises to 405 feet. Statues of Abraham Lincoln and Stephen A. Douglas are on the grounds. Tours are given daily from 9–3 (217–782–2099). **Edwards Place Historic Home and Gallery** (700 North Fourth Street, 217–523–2631), is the oldest (1833) house in town on its original site. As the hub of nineteenth century social and political life, it saw many renowned visitors, including Lincoln and Douglas.

LINCOLN'S NEW SALEM
STATE HISTORIC SITE

Abraham Lincoln arrived in New Salem in 1831 at the age of 22 and stayed for six years. It was in this thriving pioneer village on the banks of the Sangamon River that the future statesman gained experience in politics and law. Here Lincoln served in the state militia during the Black Hawk War, worked as postmaster, and ran for state office (he was elected to the General Assembly in 1834 after an unsuccessful try in 1832). New Salem fell into decline after nearby Petersburg was named county seat in 1839, and by the 1900s little remained at the village.

A growing interest in the life of Abraham Lincoln prompted the resurrection of the town, with much of the work done in the 1930s. The log houses of the twelve families that lived in New Salem in the 1830s have been reconstructed on original foundations, and the site also includes the Rutledge Tavern, a blacksmith shop, carding mill and wool house, and sawmill and gristmill. The Henry Onstot Cooper Shop is the only original New Salem structure. The buildings are appointed with period furnishings and implements, a number of which formerly belonged to New Salem residents, and a village museum exhibits artifacts. Guides in period clothing conduct historical demonstrations, and a replica of the 1830s steamboat *Talisman* plies the nearby Sangamon River hourly during the summer.

LOCATION: Route 97, twenty miles northwest of Springfield, near Petersburg. HOURS: April through October: 9–5 Daily; Rest of year: 8–4 Daily. FEE: None. TELEPHONE: 217–632–4000.

S O U T H E R N   I L L I N O I S

VANDALIA

Vandalia, on the west bank of the Kaskaskia River, came into being in 1819 when the first General Assembly of the new state of Illinois voted to move the capital here from Kaskaskia, and it served as such until 1839, when the seat of government was moved to Springfield. The **Vandalia Statehouse** (315 West Gallatin Street, 618–283–1161) was the third structure to serve as a capitol in Vandalia. Built hastily in 1836 in hopes of countering proponents of the move to Springfield, it is a white-painted brick structure with Greek Revival elements, containing furnishings of the period.

The 1840s Italianate **Little Brick House** (621 Saint Clair Street, 618–283–0024), now a museum, contains furniture, china, portraits, documents relating to early Vandalia history, and memorabilia of James Hall, a literary figure of the early West.

SALEM

Salem was a stop along the oldest stagecoach road in Illinois, which ran from Vincennes to Saint Louis. Incorporated in 1837, the town is site of the **William Jennings Bryan Museum** (408 South Broadway, 618–548–7791), an 1852 Greek Revival frame structure where the lawyer, orator, and would-be president was born.

ALTON

Built along the bluffs where the Mississippi River joins the Missouri, Alton is an industrial city that began as a steamboat and packing center. During the nineteenth century it was a rival of nearby Saint Louis. In 1837, the year it was incorporated, Alton gained notoriety when abolitionist minister and editor Elijah P. Lovejoy was murdered by a proslavery mob. A memorial to Lovejoy stands in the **Alton Cemetery.**

On October, 15, 1858, an estimated 6,000 people attended the seventh and last Lincoln-Douglas debate at the corner of Broadway and Market. During the Civil War, Illinois's first penitentiary was converted to a Confederate prisoner-of-war camp (William, Fourth, and Mill streets), where today only a few stones from one of the blockhouses remain. Many soldiers died during an outbreak of smallpox and are buried at the **Confederate Cemetery.** The **Alton Museum of History and Art** (2809 College Avenue, 618–462–2763) is housed in Loomis Hall of the Southern Illinois University Dental School, the oldest building used continuously for teaching (since 1842) in the state. The museum includes a re-created pilot house, Lovejoy's print shop, and Lincoln memorabilia.

High on river bluffs near Alton is a painting of the **Piasa,** a monster that figured in the legends of Indian tribes in the area. (The name means "the bird that devours men.") In 1673 Marquette and Jolliet noted a painting on the bluff of two reptilian figures with red eyes, beards, scaled bodies, and long tails. Quarrying operations destroyed the original in 1870. This modern rendering can be seen from Route 100 just northwest of Alton.

Just south of Alton, where the Wood River joins the Mississippi, Meriwether Lewis and William Clark camped with their expeditionary forces during the winter of 1803 to 1804. Here they prepared for their trek to the Pacific Ocean.

Incorporated in 1819, **Edwardsville** is one of the oldest cities in Illinois. Now a government center (county seat of Madison County), it depended in early years on farming and coal mining. The **Madison County Historical Society Museum** (715 North Main Street, 618–656–7562) is housed in the John S. Weir Residence, a brick structure built in 1836 that is one of the oldest extant houses in the area. It contains a reference library, period furnishings, and Indian and pioneer artifacts.

Several circular sun calendars—called woodhenges because of their similarity to Stonehenge—have been found at Cahokia Mounds, the site of the largest Indian city north of Mexico. The posts are modern replacements for the long-vanished originals erected a thousand years ago.

CAHOKIA MOUNDS

Cahokia Mounds is the site of the largest prehistoric Indian city north of Mexico. Covering six square miles, it was built on the fertile lands near the confluence of the Illinois, Missouri, and Mississippi rivers, an area favorable to trade and agriculture. An estimated 15,000 people of the Mississippian culture lived here between 1050 and 1250, with perhaps twice that number dwelling in nearby satellite villages. The Indians developed an elaborate agricultural system, with corn and squash as the principal crops. For unknown reasons, Cahokia's population began to decline around 1300, and the site was abandoned by 1500.

Of approximately 120 original mounds, 60 have been preserved. The Indians moved over 50 million cubic feet of earth to build the mounds, which were used primarily for ceremonial purposes. Most are platform mounds with sloping sides and flat tops, and the greatest of these—the largest prehistoric earthen work in

These stone discoidals or chunkey wheels, excavated at Cahokia Mounds, were used in a prehistoric game.

the New World—is Monks Mound, which covers fourteen acres and rises in four terraces to a height of 100 feet. Atop it stood a large ceremonial structure measuring 105 feet long, 48 feet wide, and 50 feet high. Several sun calendars called woodhenges have been excavated at Cahokia. They consist of large cedar posts set in a circular configuration similar to the boulder configuration at Stonehenge in England. The Cahokia Mounds Interpretive Center has prehistoric Indian artifacts and exhibits explaining the Cahokian culture.

LOCATION: One mile southwest of Collinsville, off Route 55. HOURS: 9–5 Daily. FEE: Yes. TELEPHONE: 618–346–5160.

The fifty-mile stretch of rich river bottomland and picturesque bluffs along the east bank of the Mississippi River contains some of the few vestiges of the French colonial period in the Upper Mississippi and Great Lakes area. Running from Cahokia south to Chester, the region was first settled by French Canadian missionaries hoping to convert the local Indians. In 1699 the Seminary of Foreign Missions established a church among the Indians at Cahokia, while the Jesuits opened their mission farther south in 1703 at the mouth of the Kaskaskia River. When this territory was ceded to the British in 1763 after the French and Indian War, many of the French simply picked up and moved across the Mississippi to Saint Louis.

CAHOKIA

Cahokia has been continuously occupied since the Seminarians arrived in 1699 and hence is the oldest community in Illinois. The restored **Church of the Holy Family** (120 East First Street) was built in 1799 in the typically French vertical-log style.

The **Cahokia Courthouse** (107 Elm Street, 618–332–1782), built in 1737, was the residence of Francois Saucier, son of the builder of Fort de Chartres. American administration of the area began in 1787, and from 1793 until 1814 the structure was used as a U.S. courthouse and center of political activity for the Northwest Territory. It is the oldest extant public building of European origin west of the Alleghenies and north of the Spanish colonies. Although moved and altered several times, it was restored on its original site in 1939. The courthouse is another example of *poteaux-sur-sole* construction, in which vertical timbers are secured to a sill log resting on a stone foundation.

In 1769 in Cahokia, Chief Pontiac, the Ottawa leader who had headed an alliance of Indian nations against the British in the aftermath of the French and Indian War, was killed by a member of the Peoria tribe of the Illinois. The vengeance of the Lake tribes for his death accelerated the decline of the Illinois Indians and their culture.

Located forty miles downriver from Cahokia, **Fort de Chartres** (Route 155, 618–284–7230) was built between 1753 and 1756, the last of several forts constructed by the French in the area in the 1700s. Two years after the 1763 Treaty of Paris, the French garrison at the fort surrendered to the British, who renamed it Fort Cavendish and occupied it until 1772. The powder magazine, the only original structure, has been restored, and the guardhouse, chapel, gateway, and other portions reconstructed. A visitor center includes exhibits of artifacts found in the fort area.

KASKASKIA

Historic Kaskaskia now lies underwater: Recurrent floods on the Mississippi in the 1800s buried both the site of the Jesuit mission founded in 1703 and the old town of Kaskaskia, which was a French bastion in the New World and Illinois's first capital from 1818 to 1820. These floods also caused the Mississippi to change course, creating a pocket of Illinois on the Missouri side of the river where present-day Kaskaskia stands.

The Garrison Hill Cemetery, near Fort Kaskaskia, contains some 3,800 early graves that were moved from their original location when threatened by Mississippi floodwaters.

Though nominally British after the French and Indian War, Kaskaskia was under the protection of local French militia when George Rogers Clark and his Long Knives, as his Kentucky and Virginia troops were called, occupied the town on July 4, 1778. They took the town by surprise without firing a shot, and the predominantly French citizenry happily greeted their liberation from Great Britain. Clark claimed this vast new territory for the state of Virginia, but the so-called Illinois County proved too difficult to govern from afar, and Virginia ceded the area to the Continental Congress in 1782.

In 1759, in the midst of the French and Indian War, the French inhabitants of Kaskaskia built **Fort Kaskaskia** (Fort Kaskaskia Road, five miles north of Chester, 618–859–3741) on a magnificent river bluff opposite their city to protect themselves against the British. The British never attacked, but the palisaded fort burned in 1766. The earthworks that supported the palisades are all that remain.

Just below stands the **Pierre Menard Home** (618–859–3031), built around 1802 by a successful French-Canadian businessman and politician. A frame structure with hipped roof built on stone

THE OHIO RIVER VALLEY

piers, it is the finest example of French colonial architecture in the central Mississippi River Valley. The house contains original furniture and artifacts as well as other period furnishings.

THE OHIO RIVER VALLEY

OLD SHAWNEETOWN

This riverfront town was plotted in 1810 by the federal government as a vantage from which to maintain its interests in the nearby salt springs. Located in the **Shawnee National Forest,** these saline springs were used by prehistoric Indians and, later, for the commercial processing of salt—the first important industry in Illinois.

In the early nineteenth century, Shawneetown was a gateway to the West. It served as a land office and chief banking center for the Illinois Territory, and it prospered from trade with the waves of settlers moving west via the Ohio River. After enduring countless floods, the town was moved to higher ground in the 1930s. The **First State Bank of Illinois** (Route 13), a Greek Revival brick and sandstone structure built in 1839, remains at its original site as proof of Shawneetown's commercial heyday.

CAVE-IN-ROCK STATE PARK

Cave-In-Rock State Park (New State Park Road, Cave-in-Rock, 618–289–4325), is named for a huge cavern set in the limestone bluff on the north bank of the Ohio River. A well-known landmark shown on many early maps, the cave was a hideout for river pirates who preyed on unsuspecting travelers coming down the Ohio River. After the mid-1830s, when the outlaws had been removed, the cave served as a shelter for settlers heading west.

LOCATION: New State Park Road, Cave-in-Rock. HOURS: 6 AM–10 PM Daily. FEE: None. TELEPHONE: 618–289–4325.

FORT MASSAC STATE PARK
AND HISTORIC SITE

Although strategically located on the north bank of the Ohio River, Fort Massac was destined to be on the periphery of momentous events. It was built by French soldiers from Fort de Chartres in 1757 during the French and Indian War, but only one skirmish with the Cherokee occurred. The fort's most active period was from 1794 until 1814, when U.S. soldiers rebuilt it to protect American military and commercial interests in the Ohio Valley from Indians, the Spanish, and the British. Portions of the American fort have been reconstructed, and a museum contains artifacts found during archaeological excavations.

LOCATION: Route 45, east of Metropolis. HOURS: 10–5 Daily. FEE: None. TELEPHONE: 618–524–9321.

CAIRO

The industrial city of Cairo was a center of river commerce during the nineteenth century, although its location at the confluence of the Ohio and Mississippi rivers made the town subject to regular flooding. In *Martin Chuzzlewit*, his novel set on the American frontier, Charles Dickens based the fictional town of Eden on his visit to Cairo in 1842. "There were not above a score of cabins," Dickens wrote, "in the whole (of Eden): half of these appeared untenanted; all were rotten and decayed. . . . A fetid vapor, hot and sickening as the breath of an oven, rose up from the earth, and hung on everything around; and as [Martin Chuzzlewit's] foot-prints sunk into the marshy ground, a black ooze started forth to blot them out."

Cairo began to grow after the Illinois Central Railroad arrived in 1855, but its heyday was during the Civil War. **Fort Defiance,** constructed in April 1861, shortly after the war broke out, served as the staging grounds for Ulysses S. Grant's invasion of the South in 1862. Over a million Union soldiers passed south through Cairo, and tens of thousands of Confederate soldiers were routed through the city to prisoner-of-war camps. **Mound City National Cemetery** (four miles north of Cairo) contains the graves of over 5,000 Confederate and Union soldiers. **Magnolia Manor** (2700 Washington Avenue, 618–734–0201), a brick Italianate house built in 1869 for milling and lumber merchant Charles Galigher, contains period furnishings and items related to local history and the Civil War. The 1869 **Old Customhouse** (Washington and Fourteenth streets) is a monumental stone structure in the High Victorian Italianate style, one of the largest nineteenth-century public buildings in the central Mississippi River Valley.

OPPOSITE: *A view of the Ohio River in the Shawnee National Forest, which spans southern Illinois from the Ohio River to the Mississippi.*

CHICAGO

OPPOSITE: *Chicago's Lake Shore Drive and Lincoln Park are legacies of Daniel H. Burnham's masterful 1909 city plan, which set aside large tracts of the Lake Michigan shoreline for parks.*

Chicago takes its name from *checagou,* the Indian word for the wild onions that once grew in marshlands here along the Lake Michigan shore. With a population of about 3 million, it is the third-largest city in the nation, but that statistic fails to convey a sense of Chicago's importance as a transportation and commercial hub or the richness of its urban fabric. Chicago occupies a strategic location at the mouth of the Chicago River, at the southern end of Lake Michigan, in the agricultural heartland of the nation. In the eighteenth and early nineteenth centuries, the growing town was a vital station on a major interior waterway: The Chicago River was a short portage from the Des Plaines River, which in turn joined with the Illinois and Mississippi rivers and ultimately the Gulf of Mexico. The city's history and development are closely linked to the evolution and proliferation of ever more sophisticated modes of transportation—canals, railroads, highways, and air traffic. As these systems supplanted the original fur-trade route, Chicago's reason for being became, and remains, unequivocal: It is a city positioned and designed to manufacture and trade goods and move those goods to all corners of the world.

Explorers Louis Jolliet and Father Jacques Marquette were the first recorded Europeans to pause on the Chicago lakeshore. En route to Green Bay in the late summer of 1673, they entered Lake Michigan from the Des Plaines and Chicago rivers on the last leg of their exploration of the Mississippi River. The following year Father Marquette embarked on an expedition to establish missions among the Illinois and Kaskaskia Indians when a severe bout of paratyphoid forced him to encamp during the winter of 1674–1675 at a site near where the Damen Avenue Bridge now crosses the South Branch of the Chicago River. He departed in early spring, but in May 1675 the peregrinating Jesuit, not fully recovered, died at the age of 38 near present-day Ludington, Michigan.

In the 1700s many tribes, including the Sauk, Mesquakie, and Potawatomi, lived in the vicinity of present-day Chicago. However, a hundred years passed after Marquette's visit before a non-Indian arrived to stay. Chicago's first trader and settler was Jean Baptiste Pointe du Sable, a Haitian of African and French descent who in the early 1770s established a thriving trading network along the southern tip of Lake Michigan and the Illinois River. In 1779 he built a cabin for his Indian wife and two children on the north bank of the Chicago River. It was the first permanent structure in Chicago. When du Sable sold this property in 1800 it included a gristmill, bakehouse, large cattle barn, and several other outbuildings.

The earliest known view of Chicago, from 1820, shows Fort Dearborn facing the house of the early settler John Kinzie across the Chicago River.

The du Sable holdings were bought in 1803 by John Kinzie, a trader and silversmith who, with his wife, Eleanor McKillip Kinzie, and four children, figures prominently in the early history of Chicago and the Northwest Territory. His son John H. Kinzie served as the Indian agent at Portage, Wisconsin. The Kinzies, who survived the Fort Dearborn massacre, occupied the du Sable compound off and on until 1827. After the elder Kinzie died in 1828, the house was used for various purposes before being demolished sometime in the 1830s. During that same time the Kinzie heirs entered the lucrative business of real estate by subdividing the family homestead and selling off lots. The site where the house once stood now lies under Pioneer Court, the main plaza of the Equitable Building, at 401 North Michigan Avenue.

In order to protect important trade routes from the British and their Indian allies and to strengthen the American presence on the frontier, the federal government built a series of forts in the early nineteenth century. These included Fort Dearborn, which overlooked the Chicago River at the present-day corner of East Wacker Drive and North Michigan Avenue. Completed in 1804, the small wilderness fort was the nucleus around which the town began, haltingly, to grow.

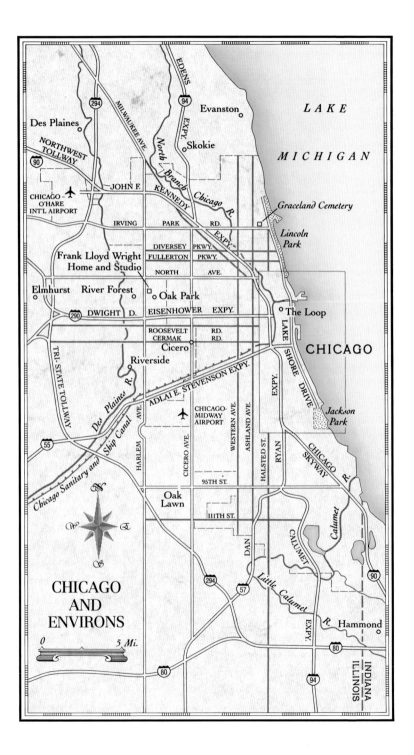

LAKE

MICHIGAN

294
Des Plaines

NORTHWEST
TOLLWAY
90

CHICAGO-
O'HARE
INT'L AIRPORT

EDENS EXPY.
94
Evanston
Skokie

MILWAUKEE AVE.
North Branch Chicago R.
JOHN F. KENNEDY EXPY.

Graceland Cemetery

IRVING   PARK   RD.
Lincoln
Park

DIVERSEY   PKWY.
FULLERTON   PKWY.
Frank Lloyd Wright
Home and Studio
NORTH   AVE.

Elmhurst   River Forest   Oak Park

The Loop

290
DWIGHT D.   EISENHOWER   EXPY.

CHICAGO

ROOSEVELT   RD.
CERMAK   RD.
Cicero

Riverside

LAKE SHORE DRIVE

TRI-STATE TOLLWAY
Des Plaines R.
ADLAI E. STEVENSON EXPY.

Jackson
Park

CHICAGO-
MIDWAY
AIRPORT
EXPY.

55

Chicago Sanitary and Ship Canal

HARLEM   AVE.
CICERO AVE.
WESTERN AVE.
ASHLAND AVE.
HALSTED ST.
RYAN
CHICAGO SKYWAY
CHICAGO R.

95TH ST.

Oak
Lawn

111TH ST.

DAN

Calumet
Calumet

90

294
57

Little Calumet R.
Hammond

CALUMET EXPY.

80

94

CHICAGO
AND
ENVIRONS

0   5 Mi.

80

INDIANA
ILLINOIS

CHICAGO LAKESHORE

NORTH AVE.

Lincoln Park

Chicago Historical Society

DIVISION ST.

0   1 Mi.

Newberry Library

Washington Square

Water Tower

Navy Pier

North Branch

Chicago R.

LA SALLE ST.

WACKER

THE LOOP

DR.

WASHINGTON ST.

Sears Tower

DWIGHT D.
EISENHOWER EXPY.

Art Institute of Chicago

Chicago Board of Trade

Hull House

Chicago Fire Academy

Grant Park

Field Museum of Natural History

ROOSEVELT   RD.

Branch Chicago R.

LAKE

LAKE

CERMAK   RD.

South

MICHIGAN

ADLAI E. STEVENSON EXPY.

ST.

EXPY.

ST.

AVE.

SHORE

Burnham Park

35TH

ST.

Douglas Tomb State Memorial

PERSHING

RYAN

MICHIGAN

RD.

AVE.

DRIVE

47TH

ST.

HALSTED

DAN

STATE

Kenwood Park

HYDE PARK

BLVD.

GARFIELD   BLVD.

Washington

GROVE

DuSable Museum

University of Chicago

Museum of Science and Industry

Park

PRAIRIE

Midway Plaisance Park

COTTAGE

Jackson Park

The Fort Dearborn massacre, one of several blows leveled against America by the British and their Indian allies during the early stages of the War of 1812, was a tragic setback. On August 15, 1812, obeying a command to abandon the fort, a group of about a hundred people, including fort commander Captain Nathan Heald, the garrison troops, Chicago militia, women, children, and a band of friendly Indians, evacuated the fort. Leading them was William Wells, who had been kidnapped and raised by the Miami Indians and later served as a scout under William Henry Harrison during the Ohio Indian Wars. Wells attempted to secure safe passage from the pro-British Indians; however, south of the fort, around present-day 18th Street and Calumet Avenue, the Indians attacked, killing about half of the group, including Wells, and burning down the fort.

After the massacre the village was quiescent, and for about a decade after Fort Dearborn reopened in 1816 Chicago was little more than a squatters' town. In 1830, however, it was chosen as the terminal for a canal connecting the Great Lakes with the Mississippi River and the Gulf of Mexico; this date marks a major turning point in the city's development. Chicago boomed. In 1833, when the federal government completed a harbor and the town was incorporated, its population was about 350. In 1848, when the Illinois and Michigan Canal was finished, Chicago's population had grown to 20,000.

In 1853 the first railroad, the Galena and Chicago Union, connected the bustling lakeshore port with the rich lead-mining city of Galena in northwestern Illinois. That railroad was followed by a succession of others, so that by the Civil War Chicago had replaced Saint Louis as the transportation hub of the West. The railroad network helped make Chicago the center of trade for agricultural commodities. With Cincinnati uncomfortably close to Civil War strife, meat packers took the railroad north to Chicago, which soon seized the distinction of being the meat-packing capital of the world, a title it held for a century.

By 1870 Chicago had a population of 300,000. The city's earliest settlers came mainly from the East Coast, but in the 1830s construction work on the Illinois and Michigan Canal lured Irish laborers. In the late 1840s and 1850s more Irish, induced to leave their country by overpopulation, poor crops, and the 1846 potato famine, immigrated to Chicago to work on the railroads. During the same period, unrest in the German states prompted a wave of immigrants from that region, primarily engineers, technicians, and other skilled professionals. Just as they had in Cincinnati, Indianapolis, Milwaukee, and many other smaller towns in the Great Lakes states, German immigrants left their stamp on Chicago; one of their legacies was helping to develop the labor movement. By World War I people of German descent represented 17 percent of Chicago's population, the city's largest ethnic group.

Between 1880 and 1920 a steady influx of immigrants from southern and eastern Europe joined the Chicago work force. Primarily from Poland, Italy, Bohemia, Lithuania, Greece, Serbia, Hungary, and Russia, these immigrants were typically consigned to low-paying jobs, substandard housing in crowded neighborhoods, marginal sanitation, and poor food. Upton Sinclair addressed their plight in his 1906 novel about the Chicago stockyards, *The Jungle,* while Jane Addams and Ellen Gates Starr founded Hull House to administer to the immigrants' needs and lobby for reform legislation. World War I marked the beginning of the northward migration of blacks from the rural South, attracted to Chicago and other large industrial cities by the relatively high wartime wages. By 1980 blacks constituted 40 percent of Chicago's population.

Much of the Great Lakes area suffered a severe drought in the summer and fall of 1871, and fires swept through the tinder-dry forests of the North Woods; the worst, the Peshtigo Fire, destroyed acres of timber around Green Bay. On the evening of October 8, 1871, the Great Chicago Fire broke out at DeKoven and Jefferson streets on the city's Southwest Side, supposedly begun by a cow kicking over a lantern in the O'Leary barn. The boomtown went up in flames. With a population of 334,000, the city was wildly overbuilt with flammable frame structures, and its fire department was woefully understaffed for the crisis at hand. A northeasterly wind stoked the fire, which fanned northward along the lakeshore and ravaged virtually every structure in its 2,000-acre swath. It burned until October 10, when rains checked its force and Lake Michigan halted its progress. Three hundred people were killed and 90,000 were left homeless; 18,000 buildings were destroyed.

Chicago's recovery in the aftermath of the fire was in many ways as stunning as the apocalypse itself. Chicagoans swung into action to rebuild their city with a level of optimism and energy that makes their efforts an oft-quoted parable of "can-do Americanism." Within a year, some $40 million worth of new structures stood in place of the fire-charred ruins. Miraculously, most of the city's stores of grain, lumber, and livestock and its manufacturing capacity were unscathed by the fire, a fortunate happenstance that aided in the city's rapid recovery.

The Great Fire created a blank space for real estate speculators and architects to shape and fill, and after 1871 Chicago's history provides an anthology of the theory and practice of architecture and city planning, the telling of which, even in modest detail, is beyond the scope of this book. In any case, the most impressive and visible legacy of the Great Fire is the skyscraper, a tall, steel-framed form making use of a mechanical elevator (the Otis passenger elevator was first used in 1857 in New York). Many of the engineering problems of the metal skeleton and floating foundation were resolved in Chicago, and it is fitting that the city can still claim the world's tallest building, the 109-story Sears Tower (233 South Wacker Drive). Many revered names in the annals of architecture are associated with the rebuilding and molding of Chicago after the Great Fire, including William Le Baron Jenney, Daniel Burnham, John Wellborn Root, Louis Sullivan, and Dankmar Adler. A draftsman in the firm of Adler and Sullivan, Frank Lloyd Wright, went on to become the most famous of Chicago's architects. Wright's career was prolific and long—he died at age 92—and he is most widely known for promulgating a distinctively American style of domestic architecture known as the Prairie Style. Wright's Prairie houses were ostensibly free of classical antecedents and devoid of frills; the architect was particularly scornful of Victorian excess.

This chapter begins on the city's lakefront and in the downtown area straddling the Chicago River before progressing northward through the Gold Coast neighborhood to Graceland Cemetery. It then proceeds to the Near West Side, once the heart of Chicago's manufacturing district and immigrant ghettos. Next is Chicago's South Side, an immense and historically diverse area where a handful of nineteenth-century mansions stand in the shadow of the world's largest housing projects. It concludes in the western suburbs of Oak Park and River Forest, where Frank Lloyd Wright lived for over twenty years.

OPPOSITE: *Chicago's Great Fire of 1871, which burned from October 8 to October 10, consumed some 18,000 buildings and left 90,000 people homeless. This view depicts the fire on October 9.*

THE LAKEFRONT

Chicago's Lake Shore Drive, one of the most impressive boulevards in the nation, skirts the Lake Michigan shore for 124 blocks—from Jackson Park at 67th Street on the south to Hollywood Avenue at the northern perimeter of Lincoln Park. The thoroughfare affords splendid views of the lake, its public beaches and parks, and the city's skyline. This urban scene is the most visible legacy of the 1909 Plan of Chicago, authored by Daniel H. Burnham with assistance from Edward H. Bennett. This ambitious scheme—to develop parks and public buildings and improve the city's infrastructure—grew out of the 1893 World's Columbian Exposition, for which Burnham served as chief of construction. With the Plan of Chicago, Burnham intended his beloved city to "outrival Paris." In the early twentieth century other cities around the world called upon Burnham (elsewhere in the Great Lakes he designed urban areas in Cleveland and Duluth), but it is Chicago that best reveals the magnitude of his energy and genius.

DOWNTOWN

Downtown Chicago is bisected east-west by the Chicago River, formerly a narrow stream that meandered through the lakeshore swamps, whose course has been greatly altered over the years. Used in the nineteenth century for raw sewage, the sluggish river contaminated drinking water and sent waves of dysentery, typhoid, and cholera through the city. In 1900 engineers cut the Sanitary and Ship Canal through the marsh to a point on the Illinois River that was lower than the mouth of the Chicago River. This reversed the river's gravitational flow, pulling in water from the lake, which increased the river's flushing capacity.

Downtown south of the Chicago River and east of the South Branch is called The Loop, a name probably derived from the elevated railroad built in the 1890s to encircle the business district. This is the heart of Chicago, containing the city's financial district and many of the architectural masterpieces that mark the evolution of the skyscraper.

OPPOSITE: *The Wrigley Building rises above the Chicago River—which, by way of the Sanitary & Ship Canal, the Des Plaines River, and the Illinois River, links Chicago to Saint Louis and the Mississippi River.*

CHICAGO ARCHITECTURE FOUNDATION

The foundation has recently occupied two historic buildings. Its previous home was the sixteen-story Monadnock Building (330 South Dearborn Street), the world's largest office building when built in 1891. The north half, by Burnham and Root, remains the tallest edifice with exterior wall-bearing masonry construction, which accounts for the six-foot-thick walls at its base. A steel frame supports the south half (1893), by Holabird and Roche.

The foundation now has space in the 1904 Railway Exchange Building, better known as the **Sante Fe Building** (224 South Michigan Avenue, 312–922–TOUR). Designed by Daniel Burnham, it was headquarters for several railroads in its early years. The foundation conducts regular walking tours of Chicago as well as bus and river trips. Some fifty special trips are also scheduled.

CHICAGO BOARD OF TRADE

From its commanding position on Jackson Boulevard, the Chicago Board of Trade looms like a temple over LaSalle Street, Chicago's financial district. Completed in 1930, the Art Deco structure was designed by Holabird and Root. (A Post-modern addition, echoing motifs of the Art Deco original, was added between 1979 and 1982.) Atop the forty-five-story building is a statue of Ceres, the Roman goddess of agriculture. The interior continues the Art Deco decor.

The Chicago Board of Trade was organized in 1848 to create a semblance of order out of the existing chaos of grain trading. At the time, farmers from across the Midwest poured into Chicago after harvest, going from merchant to merchant to seek the best price for their grain. The city's streets and riverways were jammed with loaded wagons and boats, and unsold grain was simply dumped in the lake as it spoiled. Prices fluctuated wildly, and because there were no standard weights per bushel or grades for grain, angry disputes often broke out between buyer and seller. Among its numerous accomplishments, the Board of Trade initiated standard grades for grain, set up methods of grain inspection, established procedures for warehousing and shipping commodities, and gathered and published trade statistics.

A visitors' gallery oversees the action in the separate circular trading pits, where wheat, soybeans, oats, and other commodities are bought and sold. On weekday mornings scheduled talks explain the gesticulations of the traders.

LOCATION: 141 West Jackson Boulevard. HOURS: 9–1:15 Monday–Friday. FEE: None. TELEPHONE: 312–435–3590.

Canyonlike LaSalle Street is lined with towering office buildings, government offices, and financial institutions. Two of historical note are the **Continental Illinois National Bank and Trust** and **The Rookery** (231 and 209 South LaSalle Street). Continental Illinois dates its origin to 1857 and claims to be Chicago's oldest bank. The 1924 structure was designed by Daniel Burnham's successor firm, Graham, Anderson, Probst, and White, along the lines of a Roman bathhouse with a huge banking floor flanked by majestic Ionic columns. The Rookery, designed by Burnham and Root, is an important precursor of the skyscraper. The exterior of the imposing granite-and-brick building is encrusted with terra-cotta ornamentation. It surrounds an atrium court intended to provide light to interior offices. Frank Lloyd Wright as well as Burnham and Root occupied office space in The Rookery; Wright was responsible for remodeling its lobby in 1905. It has been a prestigious address for financial firms, lawyers, and other businesses since it opened in 1888.

State Street was Chicago's first great retail shopping avenue and, while many of the opulent shops have moved north to the so-called Magnificent Mile, State Street remains a textbook of Chicago School structures designed by the city's leading architects. Two of the shrines of retail shopping—**Marshall Field** (111 North State Street) and **Carson Pirie Scott** (1 South State Street)—remain open for business. Designed by D. H. Burnham and Company and constructed between 1902 and 1914, Marshall Field occupies one city block. Carson Pirie Scott was designed by Louis Sullivan in 1899 with an addition in 1906 by D. H. Burnham and Company. Sullivan adorned the entryway and exterior of the lower two floors with elegant cast iron, above which are severe, rectilinear office floors. The store's upstairs horizontal windows offer excellent examples of the Chicago window (a fixed central pane flanked by

Some of Chicago's late-nineteenth- and early-twentieth-century buildings display elaborate decorative details, such as Louis Sullivan's fanciful cast-iron grillwork on the first two floors of

narrow double-hung windows), a device first used on Holabird and Roche's **Marquette Building** (140 South Dearborn Street). Another nearby architectural landmark is the **Reliance Building** (32 North State Street), designed by Charles B. Atwood of Burnham and Company and completed in 1895. With its steel skeleton, terracotta, and extensive use of glass, it is an early example of the Chicago School and precursor of twentieth-century glass-sheathed skyscrapers.

GRANT PARK

Grant Park extends along Lake Michigan and Michigan Avenue from Randolph Street on the north until merging with Burnham Park at Roosevelt Road. Proposed by the 1909 Plan of Chicago, it is the centerpiece of the parks along the Michigan lakefront. The 1926 **Buckingham Memorial Fountain** in the middle of the park and the 1908 statue of a seated **Abraham Lincoln,** the last work done by Augustus Saint-Gaudens, are landmarks.

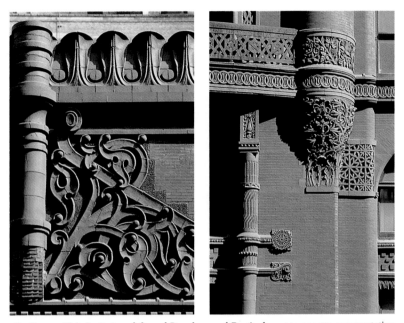

the Carson Pirie Scott store, left, and Burnham and Root's elegant terra cotta ornamentation from the Rookery, right.

Grant Park anchors four important cultural institutions, three of which are clustered toward the southern end of the park. These bear the names of influential nineteenth-century Chicago entrepreneurs and provide imposing reminders of the philanthropic spirit that helped realize the 1909 Plan of Chicago. The **Adler Planetarium** (1300 South Lake Shore Drive, 312–322–7827) was funded by Max Adler, a former vice president of Sears Roebuck and Company. In addition to the planetarium itself, the building contains a fine collection of early astronomical and navigation instruments. The **John G. Shedd Aquarium** (1200 South Lake Shore Drive, 312–939–2438), the world's largest, is named for its donor, a former chairman of the board of Marshall Field and Company. On exhibit are extensive collections of live marine and freshwater animals. The **Field Museum of Natural History** (Lake Shore Drive and Roosevelt Road, 312–922–9410) was built with funds given by Marshall Field I, founder of the retail stores that bear his name. The mammoth Classical Revival building was designed by D. H. Burnham and Company and Graham, Anderson,

Probst, and White and was constructed between 1915 and 1920. Among its vast collections is an excellent ethnological exhibit on American Indians. Around these museums is the site of the 1933–1934 Century of Progress exposition.

The fourth of the Grant Park museums, the **Art Institute of Chicago** (Michigan Avenue and Adams Street, 312–443–3600), stands at the park's western edge. The museum's original wing, facing Michigan Avenue, is Beaux-Arts in style and was designed by Shepley, Rutan, and Coolidge in 1893. The Art Institute takes special interest in Chicago's architectural history and has a permanent installation of architectural fragments from Chicago buildings that have been demolished. The Art Institute reconstructed the Trading Room of the 1894 **Stock Exchange Building** (which formerly stood at 30 North LaSalle Street), with its lavish interior, "a masterpiece of architectural form and color," providing a priceless example of the ornamental style of Louis Sullivan. Sullivan collaborated with expert colorist Louis J. Millet on the intricate stencil patterns that cover the walls and ceiling. In the garden fronting the new wing stands the Stock Exchange Building's entryway, a handsome arch of stone and terra-cotta.

Facing Grant Park on the west side of Michigan Avenue are many significant turn-of-the-century structures. Of these perhaps the most important, and surely the most beloved, is Adler and Sullivan's **Auditorium Building and Theatre** (430 South Michigan Avenue). The 1889 building combined office space with a hotel and theater and during its heyday was a social and cultural center of the city. The theater is renowned for its acoustics, Adler's contribution, and its exquisitely detailed interior ornamentation, the work of Sullivan. In 1946 Roosevelt University purchased the Auditorium Building (it had gone bankrupt during the Great Depression) and renovated the former office and hotel spaces for use as a downtown campus. The theater, which faces East Congress Parkway, has been restored and is in use. The university also maintains a small exhibit of Adler and Sullivan memorabilia in the former hotel lobby.

OPPOSITE: *The reflecting pool in Grant Park mirrors buildings from two eras of Chicago architecture: the preserved facade of Louis Sullivan's Chicago Stock Exchange (1894) and Edward Durrell Stone's Standard Oil Building (1974).* OVERLEAF: *Georges Seurat's* Sunday Afternoon on the Island of La Grande Jatte *(detail), one of the highlights of the Art Institute of Chicago's collection.*

N E A R   N O R T H   S I D E

The downtown area north of the Chicago River is generally referred to as the Near North Side. This district, now a commercial and retail stronghold, began its rise to glory in the 1920s with the opening of the Michigan Avenue Bridge and subsequent construction of the glistening white terra-cotta **Wrigley Building** (400 North Michigan Avenue), a Graham, Anderson, Probst, and White project completed in 1921, and **Tribune Tower** (435 North Michigan Avenue), the Gothic Revival skyscraper designed by Raymond Hood and John Howells and constructed in 1925. It is here that Michigan Avenue takes on the name **Magnificent Mile,** an appellation confirmed by the presence on the avenue of several upscale retail institutions.

Navy Pier (600 East Grand Avenue), which juts out 3,040 feet into Lake Michigan, was completed in 1916 as a part of Burnham's Plan of Chicago. The east promenade affords splendid views of the lake and skyline, and four structures on the pier—the domed Auditorium and the Shelter, Recreation, and Terminal buildings—are now used for special events and festivals.

The Great Fire of 1871, coupled with socioeconomic changes in Chicago's first fashionable enclave along Prairie Avenue on the Near South Side, spurred the elite to migrate to the Near North Side, where they could live in proximity to businesses in the commercial district just to the south. The neighborhood roster included such prominent Chicago names as the Leiters (dry goods), McCormicks (reapers), and Ryersons (steel), who built mansions in the popular Victorian style. One survivor is the 1883 **Samuel M. Nickerson House** (40 East Erie Street, private), a baronial three-story mansion built of now-darkened gray limestone.

WATER TOWER AND PUMPING STATION

The many-turreted Gothic spire of the Water Tower, once artfully concealing a 138-foot-tall standpipe, and the adjacent Pumping Station are cherished landmarks in Chicago. The fanciful limestone structures were designed by W. W. Boyington and completed in 1869, and they were among the few buildings in the Near North

OPPOSITE: *The Water Tower, designed by W. W. Boyington.*

Side to survive the Great Fire. While the Water Tower no longer stores water (it houses a visitor information center of the Chicago Office of Tourism), the Pumping Station has been in use since the 1871 fire.

LOCATION: Chicago and Michigan avenues. HOURS: *Information Center:* 9–5 Daily. FEE: None. TELEPHONE: 312–744–2400.

Facing Chicago's oldest park, the small Washington Square, is the Romanesque Revival **Newberry Library** (60 West Walton Street, 312–255–3510). The granite structure, built in 1893 and designed by Henry Ives Cobb, holds a reference library with emphasis on history and the humanities.

T H E   G O L D   C O A S T

Along with the Near North Side, the Gold Coast (North Avenue, Lake Michigan, and Oak and Clark streets) developed in the late nineteenth century as an enclave for affluent Chicagoans, a role it still plays. A sense of the neighborhood's elegance is preserved in the townhouses along narrow, tree-lined Astor Street between Division Street and North Avenue. The spare and symmetrical **Charnley House** (1365 North Astor Street, 312–573–1365) stands in conspicuous contrast to its more ornate nineteenth-century townhouse neighbors. Built in 1892 as a residence, it is a masterpiece of early modern design. Now headquarters of the Society of Architectural Historians, it was originally commissioned from the offices of Adler and Sullivan, although Frank Lloyd Wright, then a young draftsman, claimed credit for the actual design.

On adjacent corners of State Parkway and Burton Place stand two historic Gold Coast mansions. The 1902 **Madlener House** (4 West Burton Place, private) was designed by Richard E. Schmidt and Hugh M. G. Garden with elegant detailing; in the garden is a collection of fragments from buildings designed by Louis Sullivan. The 1893 **Patterson-McCormick Mansion** (20 East Burton Place, private) was designed by Stanford White of the New York firm of McKim, Mead & White. The orange brick-and-terra-cotta residence was built as a wedding present for Mrs. Robert Patterson, whose father was editor of the *Chicago Tribune*. Facing Lincoln Park on the north edge of the Gold Coast stands the **Roman Catholic Archbishop's Residence** (1555 North State Parkway), built in 1880 and noted for its nineteen chimneys.

CHICAGO HISTORICAL SOCIETY

Located at the south end of Lincoln Park, this long-standing Chicago institution was founded in 1856. The Society's Georgian-style structure, which was recently renovated and expanded, was built in 1932 to designs by Graham, Anderson, Probst, and White. The collections on the Civil War, Lincoln, folk and decorative arts, and costumes are supplemented by permanent exhibits on Fort Dearborn and the events leading up to the Fort Dearborn massacre, pioneer life in Illinois, economic and social development of Chicago, and the 1933–1934 Century of Progress Exhibition. The museum also houses a collection of first printings of important American documents, including a rare broadside of the Declaration of Independence and the first official printing of the Bill of Rights.

LOCATION: Clark Street at North Avenue. HOURS: 9:30–4:30 Monday–Saturday, 12–5 Sunday. FEE: Yes. TELEPHONE: 312–642–4600.

LINCOLN PARK

A long, narrow expanse of land embracing about five miles of the Lake Michigan shore, Lincoln Park is over 1,200 acres in size and the largest park in Chicago. The south end was formerly a municipal cemetery, the graves of which were moved to make way for the park. One family objected to the disruption and won a lawsuit to leave the Ira Couch Mausoleum in place. The tomb, overgrown with shrubbery, can be seen just to the north of the Chicago Historical Society. To the east of the Society stands an 1887 bronze statue of Abraham Lincoln by Augustus Saint-Gaudens.

Lincoln Park is embellished with thirty or so statues of such historic personages as Beethoven, Shakespeare, and John Peter Altgeld, the outspoken Illinois governor who pardoned three of the men convicted after the Haymarket Riot and unsuccessfully opposed the intervention of federal troops during the American Railway Union strikes. The fine **Lincoln Park Zoo** (2200 North Cannon Drive, 312–742–2000), begun in 1868 and billed as America's oldest zoo, contains many imaginative structures. More than one thousand different mammals, birds, and reptiles are at home here. A children's zoo, a sea lion pool, and a replica of a farm are among the other exhibits. Present-day Fullerton Parkway, which cuts across the southern portion of Lincoln Park. marks the northern limits of the Great Chicago Fire.

NEAR NORTHWEST SIDE

The Near Northwest Side, which is composed of the neighborhoods of West Town, Wicker Park, and Logan Square, was a stronghold of Polish, German, and Scandinavian working-class immigrants during the nineteenth and early twentieth centuries. Cutting diagonally northwest to southeast through the area is Milwaukee Avenue, a busy commercial strip that now supports many Hispanic enterprises. The **Polish Museum of America** (984 North Milwaukee Avenue, 312–384–3352), possibly the largest ethnic museum in the country, displays military memorabilia, religious artifacts, costumes, folk art, and other articles relevant to Polish culture. The area has a particularly rich concentration of beautiful churches, including **Saint Mary of the Angels** (Hermitage and Cortland streets), a Roman Catholic church reminiscent of Saint Peter's in Rome. The 1,800-seat church, constructed between 1911 and 1920, is an exceptional example of Roman Renaissance architecture. It was designed by Worthmann and Steinbach, who also did the **Saint Nicholas Ukrainian Catholic Cathedral** (Oakley Boulevard and Rice Street). Richly ornamented with mosaics and iconography, it was fashioned after the Basilica of Saint Sophia in Kiev and dedicated in 1915. **Saint Stanislaus Kostka** (1351 West Evergreen Avenue), a neo-Renaissance structure designed by Patrick Charles Keely, was completed in 1881. The **Holy Trinity Roman Catholic Church** (Noble and Division streets) served another Polish congregation that formed in the mid-1870s. Designed by Oleszewski and Krieg, the neo-Baroque structure was completed in 1906. **Holy Trinity Orthodox Cathedral** (Leavitt Street and Haddon Avenue), a Russian Orthodox church designed by Louis Sullivan and completed in 1903, is an intimate stucco structure with the architect's trademark geometric trim around eaves, doors, and windows and richly stenciled polychrome interiors.

One of the most cherished landmarks on Chicago's North Side is **Wrigley Field** (Clark and Addison streets). Built in 1914 to house the Chicago Whales franchise of the now-defunct Federal League, it has been the home of the Chicago Cubs since 1916 and is one of the country's last classic ballparks—that is, it lacks a dome and synthetic turf.

OPPOSITE: *Holy Trinity Orthodox Cathedral, designed by Louis Sullivan, has the traditional appearance of a Russian church but displays many of that architect's distinctive decorative flourishes.*

Many of the magnates of early Chicago rest at **Graceland Cemetery** (North Clark Street and West Irving Park Road), their remains appropriately memorialized with an impressive array of monuments and statuary. The slate includes such names as Armour, Field, Glessner, Palmer, Pullman, Ryerson, and Wacker. Also buried here are the great architects Louis Sullivan, Daniel Burnham, John Root, and Ludwig Mies van der Rohe. Of the various shrines, the 1890 Getty Tomb is the most stunning. Designed by Sullivan at the peak of his career, the door and window arches and the intricate ornamentation on the bronze fixtures and incised in the stone are typical of the architect's work.

NEAR WEST SIDE

The Near West Side lies across the South Branch of the Chicago River just west of downtown. Its boundaries are roughly Lake Street on the north, Canal Street on the east, Roosevelt Road on the south, and Damen Avenue on the west. During the nineteenth century this district was distinguished by its sweatshops, which employed prodigious numbers of Jewish, Italian, Greek, and other immigrant laborers from the nearby ghettos. The ethnic neighborhoods have largely been displaced and the area is now a commercial and institutional district. Remaining are numerous ethnic churches, including **Old Saint Patrick's Church** (700 West Adams Street), a massive Romanesque Revival cathedral erected in the mid-1850s by a congregation of working-class Irish, and **Holy Family Catholic Church** (Roosevelt Road and May Street), a Gothic Revival cathedral built in 1857 as a "church of all nations."

JANE ADDAMS' HULL HOUSE MUSEUM

Desperately poor, uneducated, not fluent in English, overworked, and underpaid, the inhabitants of the immigrant enclaves on the Near West Side suffered from a litany of ills and abuses. To deal with these woes, Jane Addams and Ellen Gates Starr pioneered the concept of the settlement house, a haven that provided immigrants with infant and child care, recreational facilities, and language and citizenship classes. Founded in 1889, the Hull House group were also active in the areas of sanitation, infant mortality, child labor,

OPPOSITE: *Saint Stanislaus Kostka Church, built to serve Polish immigrants, had the world's largest Roman Catholic congregation in the late 1890s.*

Jane Addams, right, campaigning for women's suffrage in 1912. She won the Nobel Peace Prize in 1931 for her many humanitarian crusades.

and fair labor practices. Jane Addams, who won the Nobel Peace Prize in 1931, lived and worked here until her death in 1935.

The Hull Mansion and Dining Hall are the only extant buildings of the original thirteen-building complex, much of which was removed in the 1960s to make way for the University of Illinois at Chicago campus. Built in 1856, the mansion barely escaped the Great Fire, which started just a few blocks to the east. When Addams and Starr took over the then-dilapidated old mansion, they retained the name of its original owner, Charles J. Hull, an early Chicago real estate dealer. The first floor of the house contains period furnishings, while the nearby Dining Hall contains an exhibit describing the nearby ethnic neighborhoods. The museum is operated by the University of Illinois.

LOCATION: 800 South Halstead Street. HOURS: 10–4 Monday–Friday, 12–5 Sunday. FEE: None. TELEPHONE: 312–413–5353.

One of the historic, and most volatile, confrontations in the nineteenth-century struggle to achieve the eight-hour workday occurred at **Haymarket Square** (Desplaines and Randolph streets)—the Haymarket Riot. During the spring of 1886 Chicago was seething with unrest as thousands of workers, at the urging of the newly organized American Federation of Labor, agitated for an eight-hour workday. On May 4, 1886, a band of 180 policemen, led by the antilabor officer Captain John "Black Jack" Bonfield, moved to break up a workers' meeting in the square when a bomb was thrown into police ranks and panic ensued. Seven policemen and at least two civilians were killed, and many were injured. The bomb thrower was never identified, but during a trial of questionable fairness eight alleged anarchists were convicted; four were hanged, three were eventually pardoned, and one committed suicide.

The Near West Side was also where the Great Chicago Fire broke out in 1871. The **Chicago Fire Academy** (558 West DeKoven Street, 312–744–4730), a modern fire-engine-red brick building, stands on the historic site of the O'Leary barn, where the fire allegedly began. In marked contrast to the immigrant ghettos of the Near West Side, the **Jackson Boulevard Historic District** (1500 block of West Jackson Boulevard, between Laflin Street and Ashland Avenue) represents the wealthy residential neighborhoods that grew up in the late nineteenth century around then-popular **Union Park** (Washington Boulevard and Ashland Avenue). Although urban renewal projects in the 1960s razed most of these areas, the Victorian townhouses on the 1500 block of Jackson Boulevard were among the few nineteenth-century structures left untouched, and many have been rehabilitated. The **First Baptist Congregational Church** (Washington Boulevard and Ashland Avenue) was built in 1869 amid this affluent community to serve a strongly antislavery congregation.

NEAR SOUTH SIDE

Historically an assortment of disparate commercial and residential enclaves, the Near South Side is roughly defined by Roosevelt Road on the north, Lake Michigan on the east, 35th Street on the south, and the South Branch of the Chicago River, Federal and Clark streets on the west. The premier nineteenth-century neighborhood from just after the Great Fire until the turn of the century was the **Prairie Avenue Historic District** (Prairie Avenue between 18th and 21st streets). A vestige can be seen in several houses along Prairie Avenue and in two that are maintained as house museums.

JOHN J. GLESSNER HOUSE

This magnificent house was one of the last works by Boston architect Henry Hobson Richardson, who died before the project was completed, and the only one of the three Chicago structures he

Glessner House, designed by Henry Hobson Richardson, presents a fortresslike facade to Prairie Avenue.

designed that is extant. Commissioned in 1885 by John J. Glessner, a founder of International Harvester, the house was completed in 1887 and became a gathering place for Chicago's elite. Although many Prairie Avenue residents migrated north of the river at the turn of the century, Frances and John Glessner continued to live here until their deaths in the 1930s.

Richardson's design emphasizes privacy. The severe facade, of rusticated granite, is delicate in its details, with a few small windows along with a trademark Richardsonian arched doorway. The audacious floor plan looks inward—many of the principal rooms open onto a serene interior courtyard. Although when the house was completed neighbors resented the intrusion of what they called a "fortress" insensitively placed on elegant Prairie Avenue, it is now thought to be one of Richardson's masterpieces, and its influence on a number of architects of the emerging Chicago School has made it one of the most important houses of its period. Most of the furnishings are in the Arts and Crafts style. The wallpaper is also notable.

LOCATION: 1800 South Prairie Avenue. HOURS: 12–4 Wednesday–Sunday; Guided tours begin at 1, 2, and 3. FEE: Yes. TELEPHONE: 312–326–1480.

HENRY B. CLARKE HOUSE

Built in 1836 or thereabouts—no one is quite sure—this Greek Revival residence is also known as the Widow Clarke House. It is the oldest extant structure in the city, dating from the era when Chicago was rapidly emerging from a rough-and-tumble frontier village to a booming metropolis. Hearing of opportunities in the town, New Yorker Clarke came to Chicago in 1835, bought land along the south shore of Lake Michigan, and prospered in real estate ventures, banking, and the wholesale hardware business.

Henry and Caroline Clarke used the traditional timber-frame method of construction for their house, which has survived Chicago's fires and has been moved twice. When the Clarkes built their home, which originally stood just to the north at present-day 16th Street and Michigan Avenue, it sat on the prairie over a mile south of the nearest house.

The Henry B. Clarke House, Chicago's oldest surviving building, was built by a pioneer couple who, after a year in a log cabin, wanted a house like the ones they had left in New York State.

Before the house was completed, the Panic of 1837 greatly reduced Clarke's means, and to make ends meet he turned to farming, dairying, hunting, and clerking, which provided a comfortable if not lavish life for the Clarkes and their six children through the 1840s. In 1849, Henry Clarke died during a cholera epidemic that swept the city. Before her death in 1860, the widow Clarke provided for her family by subdividing and selling twenty acres of family land, which also enabled her to complete the house interiors and erect a stylish Italianate cupola. The Clarke offspring lived in the house until 1872. The house has been restored to its appearance in the 1850s, and it contains furnishings of the time.

> LOCATION: Access is from the John J. Glessner House, 1800 Prairie Avenue; tours begin from the Glessner House. HOURS: Tours begin at 12, 1, and 2 Wednesday–Sunday. FEE: Yes; a combination tour with Glessner House is available. TELEPHONE: 312–326–1480.

Notable privately owned mansions in the Prairie Avenue District include the 1890 Chateauesque-style **Kimball House** (1801 South Prairie Avenue), designed by Solon S. Beman; the 1886 Romanesque **Coleman House** (1811 Prairie Avenue); and the ca. 1870 Italianate **Keith House** (1900 South Prairie Avenue).

Two blocks west of Prairie Avenue stands the **Second Presbyterian Church** (1936 South Michigan Avenue), the place of worship for many of the neighborhood's nineteenth-century millionaires. A splendid Chicago landmark, the Gothic Revival structure was designed by the famed nineteenth-century church architect James Renwick and constructed between 1872 and 1874. Louis Millet and Louis Comfort Tiffany were among the artists responsible for the stained-glass windows.

A variety of events conspired to make the environs of Prairie Avenue undesirable for its wealthy inhabitants, who by the mid-1890s were being lured by real estate magnate Potter Palmer to the Near North Side. Prairie Avenue was becoming a warehouse district as retail businesses crowded out such facilities within The Loop. With the advent of the automobile, car dealerships were attracted to the broad boulevard of South Michigan Avenue, which in the early twentieth century became "Automobile Row." At the same time, city law enforcement was nudging vice out of The Loop, whose criminal participants simply took up business in the Near South Side.

Union Stock Yards opened in 1865. By consolidating first the stock pens and then the meat-packing facilities around nine converging railroads in the mid-1870s, the stockyards thrust Chicago forward as the meat-packing capital of the world, a title it held for more than a century. The stockyards and so-called Packingtown spread out over more than 600 acres, covering an area from 35th Street and Pershing Road on the north to Halsted Street on the east, 47th Street on the south, and Ashland and Western avenues on the west. As the architectural historian John Zukowsky writes, Union Stock Yards "virtually functioned as a city within a city, providing housing, hotels, restaurants, and exchange. Its pens could hold 20,000 cattle, 75,000 hogs, and 20,000 sheep. In 1871 the meatpackers processed more than 500,000 cattle and some 2,400,000 hogs. . . ." Eastern European immigrants, and after World War I, blacks, provided the bulk of the labor force. By World War I the stockyards and meat-packing plants employed some 40,000 workers.

Another landmark church on the Near South Side is the 1890 **Pilgrim Baptist Church** (Indiana Avenue and 33rd Street), which first served as Temple K.A.M. The massive stone structure was designed by Dankmar Adler (whose father served as the first rabbi) and Louis Sullivan.

Overlooking Lake Michigan, the **Douglas Tomb State Memorial** (35th Street and Lake Park Avenue) stands on ground that was once part of Oakenwald, the estate of Stephen A. Douglas, the indefatigable Illinois politician, lawyer, and land speculator. Douglas was an avid proponent of development along Chicago's south shore. He owned land in the Lake Calumet area and promoted it as the industrial area that it eventually became. In 1852 he purchased seventy acres and planned a residential subdivision in the area where his memorial now stands.

Several buildings designed by a master of modern architecture can be found on the **Illinois Institute of Technology** campus (South State Street from 31st to 35th streets), where Ludwig Mies van der Rohe, one of the International Style's greatest practitioners, was director of the department of architecture from 1939 to 1959. Mies buildings of particular note here include the 1946 Alumni Memorial Building, the 1952 Chapel, and, especially, the 1956 Crown Hall, home of the school's department of architecture. **Comiskey Park** (333 West 35th Street) is home to the Chicago White Sox baseball team.

S   O   U   T   H   S   I   D   E

This area of Chicago embraces the affluent, tree-shaded neighborhoods where many of the city's prominent people have lived, including Louis Sullivan, brothers-in-law Julius Rosenwald and Max Adler, both of Sears and Roebuck, the clothier Joseph Schaffner, and Enrico Fermi, the Nobel laureate physicist whose work led to the development of atomic fission. This area also includes the site of the 1893 World's Columbian Exposition, the great international fair that turned the eyes of the world on Chicago.

Kenwood (East 48th Street, Dorchester and Blackstone avenues, East Hyde Park Boulevard, and Ellis Avenue) began as a middle- and upper-middle-class suburb in the late 1850s, and by the turn of the century it had become the most fashionable neighborhood on the South Side. Its variety of nineteenth- and early-twentieth-century residences range in style from neo-Georgian, Jacobethan, Queen Anne, and Italianate to Prairie School and Shingle Style. Several were designed by Frank Lloyd Wright, including two of the so-called moonlighting houses he designed on the side while working for Adler and Sullivan, which led to his dismissal from the firm. These houses are at 4858 and 4852 South Kenwood Avenue.

Hyde Park (Hyde Park Boulevard, Lake Michigan, Midway Plaisance, and Cottage Grove Avenue) was established in the 1850s by Paul Cornell, a tireless young lawyer from New York who envisioned an affluent suburb on the order of Hyde Park on the Hudson River in his home state. To a large extent he achieved his aim. Cornell arranged for commuter transportation on the Illinois Central Railroad and fathered the South Side's impressive park system. Largely through his lobbying, park commissioners began acquiring land in 1869 amid the dunes and marshes and hired two prominent landscape architects, Frederick Law Olmsted and Calvert Vaux, to design the reserves now known as Washington and Jackson parks.

Two events in the late nineteenth century spurred growth in Hyde Park and Kenwood. At Daniel Burnham's urging, Jackson Park was selected as the site of the 1893 World's Columbian Exposition, and in 1892 the **University of Chicago** (5801 South Ellis Avenue, 773–702–8374) opened on land in Hyde Park donated by Marshall Field. Founded by the Baptist Church and funded with a $600,000 endowment from John D. Rockefeller, the university

The Classical buildings at Chicago's 1893 World's Columbian Exposition, in Jackson Park, helped to establish the Beaux-Arts style as the standard for the era's public buildings.

took its lead from the Gothic portions of Oxford and Cambridge in England. The result, an imposing and unexpected Gothic look on the prairie, was achieved by the university's first architect, Henry Ives Cobb, whose works on campus include **Cobb Gate** and **Hull Court** (1000 block of East 57th Street), **Snell Hall** (5709 South Ellis Avenue), **Cobb Hall** (5811 South Ellis Avenue), and the **Quadrangle** (57th and 59th streets between South Ellis and University avenues). Another of the great Gothic-inspired buildings on campus is **Mandel Hall** (1131 East 57th Street), a 1903 Shepley, Rutan, and Coolidge–designed building generally based on Crosby Place in England. On a more modern note, Henry Moore's 1967 sculpture *Nuclear Energy* (South Ellis Avenue between 56th and 57th streets) stands near the spot where Enrico Fermi's team of scientists accomplished the first self-sustaining, controlled nuclear chain reaction on December 2, 1942.

The university's first president, William Rainey Harper, established a tradition of academic excellence by raiding prominent faculties from other established institutions. Hyde Park became home to many of these faculty members, who put the distinctive stamp of the intelligentsia on the neighborhood. Hyde Park, as one historian writes, "came to be dominated by people who were economically conservative, liberal on social issues, and politically independent." Together with Kenwood it has been home to more than forty Nobel laureates.

Hyde Park churches include the Gothic **Rockefeller Memorial Chapel** (5850 South Woodlawn Avenue), the Victorian **United Church of Hyde Park** (1448 East 53rd Street), and **K.A.M. Isaiah Israel Temple** (1100 East Hyde Park Boulevard), a 1924 Byzantine tile-and-stone structure designed by Alfred S. Alschuler. K.A.M. Isaiah Israel was formed in 1847 and is the oldest Jewish congregation in the Midwest. The history of the congregation and artifacts and memorabilia are on exhibit at the temple in the **Morton B. Weiss Museum of Judaica** (773–924–1234).

ROBIE HOUSE

One of the seminal works of twentieth-century domestic architecture, the Robie House is the most famous residence in Hyde Park. Frank Lloyd Wright designed this consummate Prairie house for Frederick C. Robie; it was built between 1908 and 1910. Shocking for its time, it is a spare brick structure with a hooded, private look that is achieved by high walls and extended eaves. With the interior, Wright did away with the nineteenth-century concept of separate rooms, creating spaces that flow into one another. Achieving harmony with nature was a recurring theme in Wright's work, and had there been much nature nearby, this tenet would have been beautifully manifested in the large expanses of windows and French doors paned with art glass designed by Wright, which lead the eye out-of-doors. The Robie House is now owned by the University of Chicago and contains originals or reproductions of the furnishings Wright designed for the house.

LOCATION: 5757 South Woodlawn Avenue. HOURS: Tours at noon Monday–Saturday. FEE: Yes. TELEPHONE: 773–702–8374.

Frank Lloyd Wright's Robie House, considered the finest example of the Prairie-style house, sits far from the prairie on a narrow city lot near the University of Chicago.

MUSEUM OF SCIENCE AND INDUSTRY

The Museum of Science and Industry overlooks a tranquil lagoon in Jackson Park. Twentieth-century visitors to Chicago can begin to imagine the spectacle of the 1893 World's Columbian Exposition by inspecting this mammoth Greek Revival structure, which served as the fair's Palace of Fine Arts. Daniel Burnham was the chief of construction for the fair, and his firm, D. H. Burnham and Company, designed this building, drawing inspiration from the Acropolis at Athens. After the exposition and until 1920 the building housed the Field Museum of Natural History. Following a period of neglect, Sears Roebuck mogul Julius Rosenwald underwrote restoration of the building and the installation of the Museum of Science and Industry. The museum's exhibits, many of them interactive, explain and illustrate the principles of science and technology. Among the objects on display are early automobiles and airplanes and a captured German U505 submarine. LOCATION: 57th Street and Lake Shore Drive. HOURS: June through August: 9:30–5:30 Daily; September through May: 9:40–4 Monday–Friday, 9:30–5:30 Saturday–Sunday. FEE: Yes. TELEPHONE: 773–684–1414.

Located in Washington Park, the **Du Sable Museum of African-American History** (740 East 56th Place, 773–947–0600) is named for Chicago's first permanent citizen, Jean Baptiste Pointe du Sable. It features rotating exhibits of cultural artifacts from Africa, the Caribbean, and the United States, with special emphasis on the history and life-styles of blacks in the Midwest.

PULLMAN

The historic structures remaining in the company town of Pullman are a poignant reminder of the paternalism of railroad car magnate George Pullman. An early conglomerate, monopoly, and multinational corporation, the Pullman Palace Car Company manufactured and leased railroad cars to the railroads, provided them with sleeping-car porters and dining-car waiters, and supplied Italy, England, and France with sleeping cars as well.

In 1880 Pullman began building a "model town" for his workers, selecting the architect Solon S. Beman and landscape engineer Nathan F. Barrett to design the community. Their efforts yielded a fine nineteenth-century town plan and a handsome array of structures. It is sometimes said, however, that Pullman was less inspired by humane considerations than by the practical concerns of isolating his laborers from the growing influence of labor organizers in the inner city of Chicago. Removed from these "evil influences," 11,000 workers in Pullman rented their homes and were never permitted to purchase them.

An undercurrent of dissatisfaction with this arrangement reached a head after the Panic of 1893. Pullman laid off several thousand workers and slashed the wages of remaining laborers without a commensurate reduction in rent and city services. In the spring of 1894 a committee of workers presented a list of grievances to Pullman, whereupon three were fired. On May 11, 1894, almost the entire Pullman work force walked off the job.

At the urging of a delegation of Pullman workers, the American Railway Union, an industry-wide union organized by Eugene Debs, agreed to refuse to move trains equipped with Pullman cars, and the Pullman strike evolved into a tense nationwide boycott. In July, at the behest of President Grover Cleveland but against the wishes of Illinois governor John Peter Altgeld, 14,000 federal troops broke the strike and arrested Eugene Debs. It was not until after Pullman's death in 1897 and an order of the Supreme Court of Illinois in 1907 that the town of Pullman was sold to its citizens. Scores of buildings remain in Pullman. Among the most prominent are the **Administration Building and Clock Tower** (East 111th Street and South Cottage Grove Avenue), an immense red brick Victorian structure that housed the corporate offices of the Pullman Palace Car Company, and the **Florence Hotel** (East 111th Street and South Cottage Grove Avenue), a grand Victorian structure named for Pullman's favorite daughter.

All Pullman workers were required to board their horses at the **Pullman Stables** (East 112th Street and South Cottage Grove Avenue), a profitable enterprise that also cut down on clean-up. **Greenstone Church** (East 112th Street and South Saint Lawrence Avenue), which Pullman attended, is a Gothic Revival structure. The **row houses** on the 11100 block of Champlain were designed by Beman, and the **Bay Entrance Row Houses** (11400 block of Champlain), named for their bay entries, are among the most attractive of Beman's designs in Pullman.

SUBURBAN CHICAGO

Adjacent to Chicago's northern border is its oldest and largest suburb, **Evanston,** which stretches for three and a half miles along the Lake Michigan shore. Evanston is named to honor John Evans, one of the founders of **Northwestern University,** which was established there in 1851. The city is proud of its many fine late nineteenth and early twentieth century houses and has two extensive historic districts, the **Evanston Ridge Historic District** and the **Evanston Lakeshore Historic District.**

OAK PARK AND RIVER FOREST

The residential suburbs of Oak Park and River Forest, lying some ten miles west of the Loop, are famous for possessing the world's largest concentration of structures—twenty-five in Oak Park, six in River Forest—designed by Frank Lloyd Wright. Wright moved to Oak Park in 1887 and remained for more than twenty years. It was here that he began his architectural career, married his first wife, Catherine Tobin, fathered six children, designed homes for friends who encouraged his experimentations, and commenced an affair with a neighbor, Mamah Borthwick Cheney, for whom he had designed a house and with whom he ultimately fled Oak Park. In the nurturing environs of Oak Park and River Forest, the young Wright developed many of the tenets of the Prairie School while acting out, to the chagrin of some of his neighbors, his characteristically high passions.

The **Oak Park Visitor Center** (158 North Forest Avenue, 312–848–1500) provides information on walking tours of the area,

Frank Lloyd Wright's Fricke House in Oak Park, built in 1901.

offers guided tours of Unity Temple and the Frank Lloyd Wright Home and Studio, and sells an array of books, maps, and guides.

Unity Temple

Completed in 1909, Frank Lloyd Wright's Unity Temple is a landmark in ecclesiastical architecture. The simple, boxlike sanctuary lacks the florid historical references that were common in turn-of-the-century church design, and the interior, with its stagelike pulpit surrounded on three sides by pews, is notable for its lack of ornamentation. The building is further distinguished by its poured-concrete construction, which served to keep the cost of building it within a $45,000 budget. The temple, still serving as an active Unitarian Universalist church, is open for tours.

LOCATION: 875 Lake Street. HOURS: Guided Tours at 1, 2, and 3 Saturday–Sunday. Memorial Day through Labor Day: 10–5 Monday–Friday; Rest of year: 1–4 Monday–Friday. FEE: Yes. TELEPHONE: 708–383–8873.

Frank Lloyd Wright Home and Studio

Wright designed and constantly remodeled his Oak Park residence and studio between 1889 and 1898. He designed the original Shingle Style cottage for his bride Catherine when he was 22 years old. The house changed and grew along with the family, at the same time becoming a laboratory for Wright's early explorations in furniture design, indirect lighting, and integrated heating. One of the most delightful rooms, added in 1895, was the children's playroom, an airy and spacious retreat with skylights and an impressive barrel-vaulted ceiling. Wright lived and worked at the Oak Park compound until 1909. In 1911 he established Taliesin, a new home and studio near his birthplace in Wisconsin. In that same year he extensively remodeled the Oak Park house as rental property and the studio as living space for Catherine and the children. Restoration work has returned the house and studio to their 1909 configuration; they contain original and reproduction furnishings.

LOCATION: 951 Chicago Avenue. HOURS: 11–3 Monday–Friday, 11–4 Saturday–Sunday. FEE: Yes. TELEPHONE: 708–848–1976.

OVERLEAF: *Wright added this playroom for his six children to his Oak Park residence in 1895.*

C H A P T E R   F I V E

MICHIGAN

OPPOSITE: *Hartwick Pines State Park, which contains a replica of a nineteenth-century logging camp and the only remaining virgin pine forest in a state that was once covered with them.*

Michigan is composed of two landmasses—the Upper Peninsula and the Lower Peninsula—separated by the five-mile-wide Straits of Mackinac (pronounced MACK-i-naw). Four of the five Great Lakes surround the state: Superior on the north, Michigan on the west, and Huron and Erie on the east. Together they give Michigan some 3,000 miles of shoreline. The Upper Peninsula lay in the main path of French exploration in the seventeenth century and became a hub of their fur-trading empire in the eighteenth. In the nineteenth and twentieth centuries its abundant deposits of iron and copper fueled the state's economy and helped underwrite the budding automotive industry in and around Detroit. Remote even by today's standards, the Upper Peninsula nonetheless figures richly in Michigan history. The mitten-shaped Lower Peninsula is laced with river systems feeding into Lakes Michigan, Huron, and Erie. Only the Saint Joseph River in the southwestern corner of the state provided passage to the mighty Mississippi, but many others—such as the Saginaw, Muskegon, and Grand—served as highways into the interior for French fur traders. During the nineteenth-century lumber era these rivers carried millions of logs to booming sawmill towns.

Modern Michigan can pinpoint its beginnings at present-day Sault Sainte Marie, on the north shore of the Upper Peninsula. In search of a northwest passage, French explorers Étienne Brulé in 1618 and Jean Nicolet in 1634 portaged there, where rapids are formed by Lake Superior's twenty-foot descent into Lake Huron. In 1668 the explorer-priest Father Jacques Marquette founded the first permanent settlement in Michigan on the same spot. In 1671 he moved to the south shore of the Upper Peninsula and established the second permanent settlement—Mission Saint Ignace—at the Straits of Mackinac. Marquette's explorations had been inspired by religious fervor, but the next major imprint on Michigan was motivated by secular concerns. Antoine de la Mothe Cadillac, commandant of the fort associated with Mission Saint Ignace, was also a shrewd businessman. His first objective was to stave off British encroachment in France's fur empire; his second was to limit the power of the Jesuits, who were trying to enlist the French crown in their efforts to shelter the Indians from the corrupting influence of the fur traders. Cadillac shifted the center of activity out of their immediate field of vision—from the Straits of Mackinac to another strategic strait, the river between Lakes Saint Clair and Erie, where he founded Detroit in 1701. Throughout the eigh-

An Ojibwa Indian encampment at Sault Sainte Marie, where the Saint Marys River joins Lake Superior to Lake Huron, painted by Paul Kane in 1845.

teenth century, Frenchmen of lesser fame established riverside fur-trading posts that became the nuclei of many Michigan towns.

During the French and Indian War, the Revolutionary War, and the War of 1812, the French settlements—the fortifications at the Straits of Mackinac and Detroit and Fort Saint Joseph at present-day Niles—were of great strategic importance. The succession of power at each site was relatively bloodless except when the warring Europeans enlisted the Indians in their cause. The most notorious raiding parties were organized by Henry Hamilton, the British lieutenant governor at Detroit during the Revolutionary War. Pontiac's War in 1763 was a fierce attempt by the Ottawa chief and his Indian followers to drive back the encroachments of the British. The Indians captured Forts Michilimackinac and Saint Joseph and laid siege to Detroit for five months before the British were able to quell them. Soon, however, the Indians aligned themselves with the British against the American settlers because Great Britain's New World policies, like those of France, discouraged permanent settlement in the vast northwestern forests.

WISCONSIN

LAKE

MICHIGAN

MILWAUKEE

ILLINOIS

Ludington

Pere Marquette R.

Manistee

National Forest

Muskegon R.

Whitehall

Muskegon

Grand Haven

Holland

Kalamazoo R.

Douglas

South Haven

Kalamazoo

Benton Harbor

94

Warren Woods Natural Area

Niles

90

80

South Bend

INDIANA

31

10

96

31

SOUTHERN
MICHIGAN

	HIGHWAY
o	HISTORIC SITE
	HISTORIC INDIAN SITE
	RECONSTRUCTED VILLAGE
	PARK

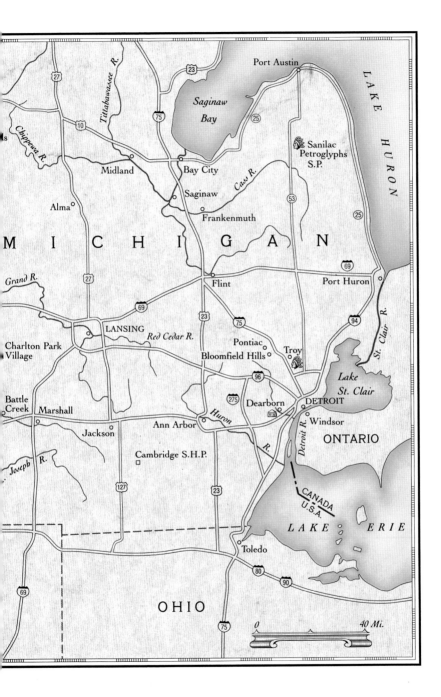

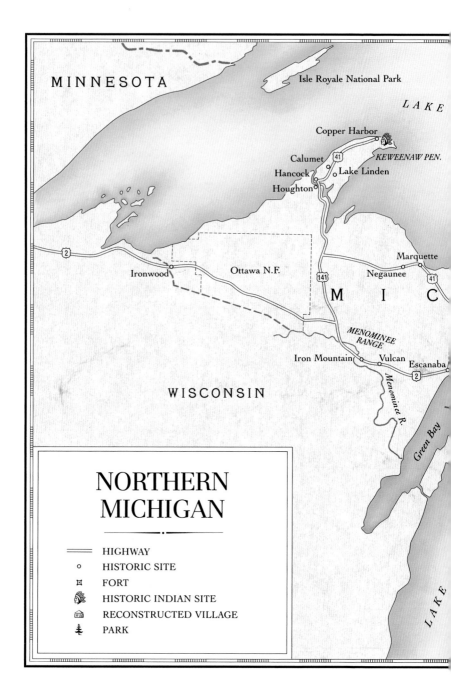

MINNESOTA

Isle Royale National Park

LAKE

Copper Harbor

Calumet   41   *KEWEENAW PEN.*

Hancock   Lake Linden

Houghton

Ottawa N.F.   141   Marquette

Ironwood   Negaunee   41

2

M   I   C

MENOMINEE RANGE

Iron Mountain   Vulcan   Escanaba

2

Menominee R.

WISCONSIN

Green Bay

NORTHERN MICHIGAN

—— HIGHWAY
○ HISTORIC SITE
⌐ FORT
 HISTORIC INDIAN SITE
 RECONSTRUCTED VILLAGE
 PARK

LAKE

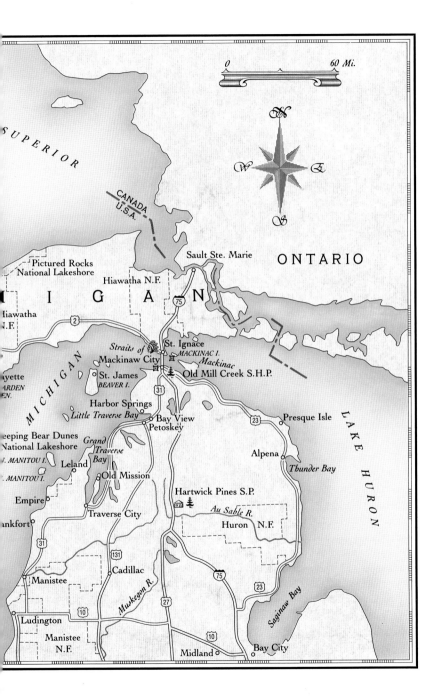

0   60 Mi.

N

W   E

S

L A K E   S U P E R I O R

CANADA
U.S.A.

Sault Ste. Marie

ONTARIO

Pictured Rocks
National Lakeshore

Hiawatha N.F.

M I C H I G A N

75

Hiawatha
N.F.

2

Straits of
Mackinaw City

St. Ignace
MACKINAC I.
Mackinac
Old Mill Creek S.H.P.

ayette
*ARDEN
EN.*

St. James
BEAVER I.

31

Harbor Springs
Little Traverse Bay

Bay View
Petoskey

23

Presque Isle

L A K E   H U R O N

eeping Bear Dunes
National Lakeshore
. MANITOU I.
. MANITOU I.

*Grand
Traverse
Bay*

Leland

Old Mission

Alpena

Thunder Bay

Empire

Traverse City

Hartwick Pines S.P.

Au Sable R.

Huron   N.F.

ankfort

131

Cadillac

Muskegon R.

75

23

Saginaw Bay

Manistee

10

27

Ludington

Manistee
N.F.

10

Midland

Bay City

From the 1600s until the mid-1800s several tribes predominated in Michigan's two peninsulas. The Ojibwa occupied most of the Upper Peninsula and the eastern portion of the Lower, the Ottawa lived in the western part of the Lower Peninsula, and the Potawatomi were found in its southern regions. The Huron, fleeing the Iroquois to the east, settled at the Straits of Mackinac and subsequently around Detroit. The Indians got along with French, who traded much and settled little; not so well with the British, who settled more and traded less; and scarcely at all with the Americans, who settled. Some Americans made notes upon the life they were destroying: Henry R. Schoolcraft, an American who served as Indian agent among the Ojibwa at Sault Sainte Marie and on Mackinac Island, was fascinated with Indian legends and culture and recorded many of the Indian customs. But Indian ways were largely incompatible with those of white settlers. The architect of their removal in Michigan was Lewis Cass, who served as governor from 1813 to 1831. He negotiated the 1819 Treaty of Saginaw, whereby Indians relinquished the eastern half of the Lower Peninsula, and the 1821 Treaty of Chicago, which gave the southwestern portion of the Lower Peninsula to Michigan. Treaties in 1836 and 1842 gave the federal government title to the remaining lands.

Cass inherited a territory with an image problem and no infrastructure. In the northeastern states Michigan was thought of as an impenetrable swamp. While that description was somewhat undeserved, Michigan Territory was nevertheless a roadless wilderness far removed from the Ohio River—which at the time was the main avenue of settlement—with huge expanses of interior removed even from the shores of the Great Lakes. In 1820 Cass made a three-month-long, 5,000-mile tour of inspection, and largely through his efforts Detroit was linked by road to Saint Joseph on Lake Michigan and to Chicago by the 1830s. During this period, two other events made Michigan eminently more appealing to settlers. In 1818, *Walk-in-the-Water,* a steamship from Buffalo, New York, docked at Detroit, heralding the advent of steamship travel on the Great Lakes. In 1825 the Erie Canal opened. The easier route west, combined with liberal land policies, overcame settlers' suspicions, and the territory's population tripled between 1820 and 1830 and increased sevenfold over the next ten years.

With ample inhabitants Michigan applied for statehood in 1834, but the so-called Toledo War had to be settled before the state could be admitted. This dispute pitted Ohio against Michigan in a fight over a strip of land around Lake Erie that included the prosperous port of Toledo. The settlement gave Ohio possession of the Toledo Strip, while Michigan reluctantly accepted the Upper Peninsula as compensation. The boon of that trade became apparent some years later when vast quantities of iron and copper were discovered in the Upper Peninsula. Michigan's application for statehood called for another compromise—between the Northern and Southern states. Under the terms of the 1787 Northwest Ordinance, Michigan entered the Union as a free state. To appease the slave-owners of the South, Congress granted Arkansas's entry as a slave state and Michigan joined the Union in 1837.

Michigan was once covered almost entirely by forests, with hardwoods in the southern Lower Peninsula giving way to conifers in the northern part. For 150 years these forests supplied the fur trade with beaver and other fur-bearing animals, but as the beaver disappeared in the 1830s the trees themselves became the raw materials of a burgeoning lumber industry. In Michigan it got its first toehold in the Saginaw Valley in the mid-1830s, but the Big Cut, as it came to be called, spread rapidly through the pinelands of the Lower Peninsula. Lumbering dominated the lower half of Michigan for over fifty years, and by 1900 there were fifty-two sawmills in the vicinity of Muskegon, which called itself "the lumber queen of the world." At Cheboygan there was a heap of sawdust almost a mile wide and forty feet high. Timber fed the thriving furniture factories and the carriage industry, and it provided jobs to the tide of immigrants entering Michigan in the mid-nineteenth century. The first were Germans, followed by Dutch and Irish. Successive waves of Swedes, Norwegians, Finns, Italians, and Canadians worked in the lumber camps and in the copper and iron mines of the Upper Peninsula. The mines went into full swing in 1855 with the opening of the Soo Locks, which made navigable the treacherous rapids at Sault Sainte Marie.

By the turn of the century much of the pine forests had been depleted, and Michigan's economy went into rapid decline. But it was soon saved by the birth of the automotive industry in the triangle formed by Lansing, Flint, and Detroit. Detroit eventually emerged as the leader of the industry, in Michigan and the nation. There had been a healthy carriage industry in southeastern Michigan, particularly in Flint and Detroit, which provided expertise and

OVERLEAF: *Pictured Rocks National Lakeshore runs along the south shore of Lake Superior.*

capital for the new industry. Men like Henry Ford, R. E. Olds, and William C. Durant supplied the genius and energy to bring about an industrial and social transformation of America. A new school of industrial architecture emerged to meet the needs of the industry. Blacks migrated from the rural South to fill jobs, provoking racial tensions in the urban North. Labor was organized into the United Auto Workers. The auto industry's rise paralleled that of the oil industry, establishing a firm footing for the later growth of aeronautics in the state.

Much of Michigan's history revolves around this transition from fur trading to lumbering and mining to auto manufacturing, but there were other livelihoods being made as well. Commercial fishing was an important aspect of the coastal economy up until the 1930s. Wheat, corn, and dairy farmers planted the deforested land across the Lower Peninsula. Along Lake Michigan, where water temperature moderates the climate, the cleared lands proved suitable for orchards, especially of cherries and apples, which remain a part of the coastal landscape today. The saline wells that underlie much of the eastern Lower Peninsula made Michigan a major producer of salt. At the turn of the century these wells became the focus of the nascent chemical industry, as extraction processes made possible the production of commercial quantities of chlorine, bromine, and other substances.

Beginning in the late nineteenth century with the advent of luxury steamship travel on the Great Lakes, the many scenic charms of Michigan soon became apparent to the larger world. The beautiful dunescapes of Lake Michigan began to attract tourists, and Mackinac Island became a summer haven for wealthy families from Chicago and Detroit. In the northwestern corner of the Lower Peninsula, Bay View was the site of a large Methodist encampment, while nearby Petoskey gained a following among hay-fever sufferers. Michigan's hospitable climes have inspired countless artists and writers, the most famous of whom, Ernest Hemingway, spent summers as a youth on Walloon Lake near Petoskey. In 1900 L. Frank Baum wrote *The Wizard of Oz* in a summer cabin in Macatawa on Lake Michigan.

No original structures remain in Michigan from the French era for two reasons: The seventeenth-century French method of vertical-log construction was relatively impermanent (the logs rotted at ground level), and in 1805 Detroit, a center of French culture for a hundred years, burned to the ground. But visitors can

During the last third of the nineteenth century, Michigan produced more lumber than any other state. Here, the beginning of a log drive on the Muskegon River in the 1890s.

glean at least a sense of the French impact on Michigan at the numerous historic sites in the Straits of Mackinac. Cities throughout the Lower Peninsula preserve the mansions of lumber barons built at the height of the Victorian age. Lavish entertainment halls were a standard fixture in booming lumber towns, and some neighborhood historic districts preserve the modest houses of sawmill workers. Railroads, which grew in tandem with the lumber industry, determined the course of development of many towns. Automobile production called for factories and corporate complexes the likes of which industrial and entrepreneurial America had never imagined, and Detroit became the center of this emerging architecture. Albert Kahn designed most of the factories and company headquarters as well as the mansions of Detroit's affluent industrialists.

This chapter begins with the state capital, Lansing. It then turns up the Lake Michigan shoreline to jump across the Straits of Mackinac to the remote wilderness of the Upper Peninsula. The towns along the shore of Lake Huron are visited next, concluding with the state's largest city, Detroit.

SOUTHWESTERN MICHIGAN
LANSING

Situated at the confluence of the Grand and Red Cedar rivers, Lansing is the capital of Michigan and an industrial and trade center. Its smaller satellite city, **East Lansing,** is the home of Michigan State University, the country's first land-grant college. When the state constitution designated that the capital be moved from Detroit in 1847 numerous towns in lower Michigan vied for the honor. Legislators haggled for months before selecting Lansing, a decision that seems to have been highly arbitrary. The new capital was little more than a wilderness settlement inhabited by a few pioneers from Lansing, New York, but government spurred business, and in 1857 Michigan Agricultural College was opened. Nonetheless, the town was held back by a poor transportation system and did not develop industrially until the railroad arrived in 1871. In that same year the legislature appropriated funds to construct a third state house. Completed in 1879, the **Michigan State Capitol** (Capitol and Michigan avenues, 517–335–1483), a Second Renaissance Revival structure designed by Elijah E. Myers, dominates the downtown skyline.

Lansing's industrial boom coincided with the rise of automotive pioneer Ransom E. Olds, one of the designers of the internal combustion engine. Olds's Lansing factory was the nation's largest car producer in the early 1900s. During that same period Lansing was also a major producer of agricultural implements and gasoline engines. Oldsmobiles are still manufactured here. The **R. E. Olds Museum** (240 Museum Drive, 517–372–0422) exhibits automobiles built in Lansing, including the Reo, Star, Durant, and the first Oldsmobile, built in 1897. A variety of nonmotorized vehicles, such as bicycles, wagons, and carts, and exhibits explaining Olds's contribution to the industry are also on display. The **Michigan Historical Museum** (717 West Allegan Street, 517–373–0515) traces the state's history in a series of dioramas illustrating the European arrival in America, farm life, a mine, and a sawmill. The history of manufacturing in Michigan is also documented.

The **Turner-Dodge House and Park** (100 East North Street, 517–483–4220) is an estate expanded at the turn of the century by prominent Lansing businessman and politician Frank L. Dodge. The Greek Classical Revival exterior of the house incorporated walls of an existing structure built in 1858 for early settler and

The Michigan State Capitol, Lansing.

merchant James Turner. The interior is Georgian Revival. The nearby **North Lansing Historic Commercial District** (East Grand River Avenue and Turner Street) contains numerous nineteenth-century structures in the Italianate and Romanesque Revival styles.

MARSHALL

Many of Michigan's towns, especially on the Lake Michigan side, were formed on rivers that provided an outlet to the lake. Situated on the banks of the Kalamazoo River and Rice Creek, Marshall is a charming and well-preserved town founded in 1830 by New Yorker Sidney Ketchum and named by him for Chief Justice John Marshall. Two of Marshall's early settlers were instrumental in establishing a system of public schools for Michigan.

The railroad arrived in 1844, and with it came railroad yards and a switching station. Marshall's economy boomed, but labor concerns grew with it. In 1863 the country's first railroad union was organized in Marshall. Called the Brotherhood of the Foot-board, it is now the Brotherhood of Locomotive Engineers. When the railroad shops were relocated to nearby Jackson in 1872, Marshall fell into economic quiescence.

In the 1830s, when the legislature in Detroit contemplated moving the capital, Marshall campaigned hard for the designation. So confident was Senator James Wright Gordon, who lived in town, that he built a governor's mansion. When Lansing was selected Gordon moved into the house himself. Still referred to as **Governor's Mansion** (612 South Marshall Street), the Greek Revival frame structure has a delicate interior wooden staircase. The **Adam Crosswhite Monument** (at the intersection of East Michigan Avenue, Lincoln Street, and East Drive) marks the site of the cabin of a fugitive slave from Kentucky. Crosswhite and his family had lived in Marshall for several years when, in 1847, a representative of their former master attempted to reclaim them. A crowd of townspeople gathered at the cabin to prevent the arrest; instead, the Southerner was himself arrested for assault and housebreaking and sent home empty-handed, while the Crosswhites were spirited off to Canada. The affair did not end there: the rebuffed slaveowner sued and was eventually awarded $1,926 for the loss of his property. In 1850, in response to this and similar events, Congress passed the Fugitive Slave Act, which imposed harsh penalties on anyone who aided a runaway.

Many other fine nineteenth-century houses are scattered throughout Marshall. The **National House Inn** (Michigan Avenue and Sycamore Street), built in 1835, is the oldest brick building in town and still serves as an inn. The octagonal **Pendleton-Alexander House** (218 South Eagle Street, private) was built in 1856 and is unusual among such houses for its decorative trim, which was added in 1875. Other notable private houses include the 1871 Gothic Revival **Simmons House** (325 Forest Street); the Italian Villa-style **Karstaedt-William Wallace Cook House** (603 North Kalamazoo Avenue), built in 1869 with round-headed windows and an ornate cupola (the Classical verandah was added in 1897); and the imposing Greek Revival **Hays House** (303 North Kalamazoo Avenue), constructed ca. 1838 of local sandstone. The **Marshall Historical Society,** headquartered in the Honolulu House, conducts an annual historic homes tour each September.

Honolulu House

This exotic residence was built in 1860 by Abner Pratt, a U.S. consul to Hawaii in the 1850s who had been forced to return to the

OPPOSITE: *The singular Honolulu House is one of many distinguished houses in Marshall, which preserves a wide variety of nineteenth-century architectural styles.*

United States because of his wife's illness. So enamored was he of his former home in Honolulu that he built something like it in Michigan. Constructed of sandstone with board and batten siding, the house has a distinctive central tower and a long gallery supported by fancifully bracketed columns. The interior contains extensive woodwork, a curved stair, trompe l'oeil murals, and 1860s period furnishings. The Marshall Historical Society also maintains exhibits in the house of nineteenth-century Midwestern artifacts and other items pertaining to the early settlement of the town.

LOCATION: 107 North Kalamazoo Street. HOURS: May through October: 12–5 Daily. FEE: Yes. TELEPHONE: 800–877–5163.

BATTLE CREEK

Battle Creek, at the confluence of the Kalamazoo and Battle Creek rivers, is best known as a producer of breakfast cereal. The city and the river take their name from an 1825 skirmish between an Indian and a land surveyor. Established in 1831 by a New Yorker, Battle Creek was incorporated in 1859, when the town was a stop on the Underground Railroad and a Republican stronghold.

In 1855 a small religious group moved their printing press from Rochester, New York, to Battle Creek. Eight years later, this group was organized officially as a denomination called Seventh-Day Adventists. Battle Creek was their world headquarters until 1903. To promote their ideas of temperance and health, the Seventh-Day Adventists opened the first of their sanitaria in Battle Creek in 1866. Called the Western Health Reform Institute and later the Battle Creek Sanitarium, it became the cradle of the cereal industry. Sanitarium superintendent from 1876, Dr. John Harvey Kellogg, and his brother W. K. Kellogg, the business manager, were interested in the healthful properties of grains and nuts and developed a flaking process for grain that was perfected in 1894. W. K. Kellogg was more intent than his brother on marketing and advertising, and in 1906 he formed his own enterprise, the Battle Creek Toasted Corn Flake Company, which eventually became the Kellogg Company. (One of the sanitarium's patients, C. W. Post, developed his own line of cereal products based on foods he was served there.) The **Battle Creek Sanitarium** buildings (74 North Washington Avenue), now used for federal offices, are Neoclassical Revival in style.

The 1886 **Kimball House Museum** (196 Northeast Capital Avenue, 616–966–2496) is a Queen Anne residence that displays period furnishings, household effects, and items related to Battle Creek's health and medical history. Home of the Historical Society of Battle Creek, it also displays some rare personal effects of Sojourner Truth, the black abolitionist and women's rights advocate, who lived in Battle Creek from 1867 until her death in 1883.

NILES

Niles occupies the site of a major convergence of land and water routes used by the Indians. This point attracted French explorers, fur traders, and missionaries as well, and in the 1680s the Jesuits established a mission in the area. The French built **Fort Saint Joseph** (historical marker at Fort and Bond streets) in 1691, from which they pursued their fur-trading interests. The British took over the fort in 1761, but with the outbreak of Pontiac's Rebellion in 1763, Indians seized and held it for two years. During the Revolutionary War it was not garrisoned, although it remained a strategic outpost for Indian relations. In 1781 a group of anti-British Indians and French from Saint Louis, Missouri, with Spanish authorization, captured the fort. The Spanish flag flew for one day before the fort was looted and burned. Later Spanish claims for territory in the Great Lakes area were based on this incident.

British traders continued to work in the area well after the Treaty of Paris, much to the displeasure of American interests. The conflict was resolved with the War of 1812.

The **Fort Saint Joseph Museum** (508 East Main Street, 616–683–4702) contains an extensive inventory of artifacts recovered from the fort and an important collection of nineteenth-century Dakota Indian garments and artwork, including autobiographical pictographs by Sitting Bull and Rain in the Face. The museum is housed in the outbuildings of the Chapin House, a Queen Anne structure that contains the offices of the Niles City Hall. Niles retains a wealth of residences, churches, and commercial structures in a range of nineteenth-century styles.

Some twenty miles west of Niles near Three Oaks is the **Warren Woods Natural Area** (616–426–4013). On the Galien River near Lake Michigan, this preserve encompasses a 311-acre stand of virgin beech, oak, and maple and offers visitors a glimpse of the vast hardwood forest that once covered southern Michigan.

LAKE   MICHIGAN   SHORE

SOUTH HAVEN

Situated at the mouth of the Black River, South Haven is a small industrial and fruit-processing center in Michigan's orchard country. South Haven was a sawmill and shipbuilding town in the nineteenth century. Like many of the villages along the southern shores of Lake Michigan, it has beautiful stretches of beach that began attracting vacationers out of Chicago in the 1880s. The **Lake Michigan Maritime Museum** (Dyckman Avenue at the Black River Bridge, 616–637–8078) interprets the area's shipbuilding era and exhibits a variety of Great Lakes vessels.

Moored in the Kalamazoo River in **Douglas,** the SS *Keewatin* (Blue Star Highway and Union Street, 616–857–2107) is a 1907 Canadian luxury steamship that plied the Great Lakes from Georgian Bay to Thunder Bay until the 1960s. Now a marine museum, it boasts handsome interiors and elegant fixtures that recall the red-carpet era of cruise travel on the Great Lakes.

HOLLAND

Holland was settled in 1847 by Dutch who had immigrated for religious reasons and to escape the potato famine. More Hollanders followed, establishing satellite villages such as **Zeeland, Overisel,** and **Vriesland.** Now a small agricultural and manufacturing center—and the country's major producer of wooden shoes—Holland thrived on woodworking, furniture, and tourism in the nineteenth century, though the town was practically destroyed by forest fires in 1871.

The leader of Holland's founding group was the Reverend Albertus Van Raalte, and the most distinctive structure that dates to the era of his guidance is the 1856 Greek Revival **Pillar Christian Reformed Church** (Ninth Street and College Avenue). The **Holland Museum** (31 West Tenth Street, 616–392–9084), in a 1914 restored Classical Revival (Post Office) building, features Dutch heritage and local history. Dutch decorative arts, including pewter, delft pottery, and copper furniture, are exhibited.

OPPOSITE: *"Big Red," built in 1907, marks Holland Harbor on Lake Michigan.*

GRAND RAPIDS

The second largest city in Michigan, Grand Rapids is a manufacturing and trade center located thirty miles east of Lake Michigan on the Grand River. During the nineteenth century the west bank of the river was home to the Ottawa Indians, whose presence attracted Baptist missionaries in 1825. In 1826, Louis and Sophie Campau established a fur-trading post on the east bank of the river beside the rapids for which the town is named.

Campau foresaw that the rapids could provide power for mills and that the site would be at the head of navigation for boats plying upstream from Lake Michigan. In 1831 he bought a tract of land on the east bank that became the heart of Grand Rapids. Within ten years steamboats were making regular trips upriver from Grand Haven, and by the mid-1850s Grand Rapids was a booming sawmill town. The rapids also powered one of the early hydroelectric plants in the Midwest, which began service in 1881. With easy access to the raw materials, several Grand Rapids entrepreneurs

The diverse architecture of Grand Rapids' Heritage Hill Historic District includes, left, Frank Lloyd Wright's Prairie-style Meyer-May House and, right, the Voigt House with its Corinthian columns.

The church in Charlton Park Village, built in another town in 1885 and moved here in 1972.

turned to furniture manufacturing. In 1876 three Grand Rapids companies displayed lavish examples of their work at the Philadelphia Centennial Exposition and received nationwide acclaim.

The **Heritage Hill Historic District** (Michigan and Union Avenues, Pleasant Street, and Lafayette Avenue), situated just east of downtown, was the city's most fashionable residential area by the 1890s. Preserving a range of architectural styles, the neighborhood is a mix of baronial mansions, including the 1895 **Voigt House** (115 College Avenue SE, 616–456–4600), the immense brick Victorian home of German immigrant Carl Gustav Voigt. Modeled after a French chateau, it contains carved woodwork, parquet floors, stained-glass windows, and period furnishings. Also in Heritage Hill is the **Meyer-May House** (450 Madison Avenue SE, 616–246–4821), a Frank Lloyd Wright Prairie-style structure built in 1908. Much of the furniture was designed by Wright for the house, and the leaded-glass ceiling windows are particularly fine.

The **Gerald Ford Museum** (303 Pearl Street, 616–451–9263) traces the life and career of the former president and displays gifts from other heads of state and bicentennial gifts—including a large collection of handmade quilts—from all over the country. The museum also features a model of the White House and an exact replica of the Oval Office. The **Public Museum of Grand Rapids** (272 Pearl Street NW, 616–456–3977) maintains numerous exhibits pertaining to local history and nature. Its collections include nineteenth- and early-twentieth-century American furniture, decorative arts from 1830 to the present, Indian artifacts, and prehistoric Hopewell Indian items.

The largest site of Hopewell culture in Michigan is the **Norton Indian Mounds** (Indian Mounds Drive, off Route 196), a group of twelve mounds located on the east bank of the Grand River. Built about 2,000 years ago, the mounds contain a number of burials, with artifacts from other regions of the country. Materials excavated from the site are on display at the public museum.

In **Hastings,** about midway between Battle Creek and Grand Rapids, the 300-acre **Charlton Park Village** (2545 South Charlton Park Road, 616–945–3775) is an assemblage of about twenty nineteenth-century structures from the vicinity. Among them are the **Bristol Inn,** an 1852 Federal-style stagecoach stop; the Gothic Revival 1885 **Carlton Center Church;** and the vernacular 1869 **Lee School,** a rural one-room schoolhouse. Demonstrations of nineteenth-century crafts are conducted throughout the village.

MUSKEGON

The largest city on the eastern shore of Lake Michigan, Muskegon is located at the mouth of the Muskegon River. In the 1600s the French encountered marshes and dunes here, but the upper reaches of the Muskegon flowed through a narrow, densely forested valley. The river thus gave them easy access to hunting grounds, and for 100 years the French traded with the Indians in the valley. The era of white settlement began after an 1836 treaty with the Indians secured most of the land north of the Grand River, and intense lumbering of the pine forests commenced. The first sawmill on Muskegon Lake began operation in 1837, and Muskegon grew to be the largest of the lumber towns on the lake. The backbone of the industry was immigrant labor, supplied mainly from Norway, Sweden, Ireland, Scotland, Germany, and French Canada. With the destruction of the pinelands by 1900, the lumber industry waned. The last mill in Muskegon closed in 1910.

Muskegon's boomtown era is preserved in the **Muskegon Historic District** (Muskegon, Webster, and Clay avenues between Second and Sixth streets), which includes several opulent mansions of the lumber barons and examples of the public works they underwrote. The grandiose Queen Anne **Hackley and Hume houses** (West Webster Avenue and Sixth Street, 616–722–7578), built in the late 1880s by millionaire lumberman Charles Hackley and his business partner Thomas Hume, contain Victorian furnishings. The nearby **Fire Barn Museum** (510 West Clay, 616–722–2600) is a replica of an 1874 volunteer fire company with exhibits of nineteenth-century equipment. The **John Torrent House** (Third Street and Webster Avenue, private) is a grand stone structure built in 1892 by another of Muskegon's lumber barons. Across the street is the 1888 **Hackley Public Library** (Third Street and Webster Avenue). Named for its benefactor, it is an imposing Richardsonian Romanesque structure of pink granite. The **Muskegon County Museum** (430 West Clay Avenue, 616–722–0278) contains exhibits pertaining to the fur-trading era and the lumber industry.

South of Muskegon in **Grand Haven,** the **Tri-Cities Museum** (1 North Harbor Drive, 616–842–0700), housed in the 1870 Grand Trunk Depot, contains Victorian period rooms and exhibits pertaining to the fur trade, shipping and the Coast Guard, logging, and agriculture.

In nearby **Whitehall,** north of Muskegon, the **White River Light Station and Maritime Museum** (6199 Murray Road, 616–894–8265) preserves the 1875 lighthouse at the head of White Lake. It contains photographs, paintings, and artifacts relating to Great Lakes shipping and lighthouse history.

LUDINGTON

At the mouth of the Pere Marquette River, Ludington is named for Milwaukee lumberman James Ludington, who helped stimulate the town's economy after the 1850s depression. It was known for its salt wells in the 1800s. Numerous nineteenth-century homes remain in Ludington, including the Victorian mansion of lumberman James Foley (702 East Ludington Avenue, private). The

Mason County Historical Society's **White Pine Village** (1687 South Lakeshore Drive, 616–843–4808) is a reconstruction of a nineteenth-century pioneer settlement that overlooks Lake Michigan three miles south of Ludington. The complex has twenty buildings gathered from the area, including logging and maritime museums and the **Rose Hawley Museum,** which exhibits Indian artifacts, farming and lumbering tools, Victorian furnishings, and household implements. The buildings are clustered around the first **Mason County Courthouse,** which stands on its original site. The vernacular frame structure, which became the first county seat in 1855, was built in 1849. Other buildings include the 1850 log cabin of a French trapper, a replica of a rural church, and an 1880s farmstead. Each contains period furnishings, many of them original.

The peripatetic Jesuit priest Jacques Marquette, who was one of the preeminent characters in the early history of the Great Lakes, died and was buried somewhere along the eastern shore of Lake Michigan on May 18, 1675. Although the exact location of the grave is disputed by the Jesuits, descriptive notes of the place point to either Ludington or **Frankfort,** some sixty miles north. Both cities have historical markers.

MANISTEE

Manistee is another of the Lake Michigan villages that grew up around the mouth of a river, in this case the Little Manistee. The nineteenth-century lumber and salt-mining town attracted many immigrant workers, and Manistee preserves this heritage with a number of ethnic churches. **Guardian Angels Church** (5th and Sycamore streets) is a massive structure with Gothic and Romanesque elements built by Irish and German Catholics in 1889, and **Our Savior's Evangelical Lutheran Church** (302 Walnut Street) is a simple frame building constructed between 1868 and 1870 to serve primarily Danish immigrants. Manistee's lumber barons attended the 1892 **First Congregational Church** (412 4th Street), a Romanesque-style structure designed by prominent Chicago architect William LeBaron Jenney.

The **Manistee County Historical Museum** (425 River Street, 616–723–5531) is housed in the 1883 A. H. Lyman Drugstore and contains all of the original fixtures. Exhibits focus on the town's Victorian period and lumber industry.

Sand dunes at Sleeping Bear Dunes National Lakeshore, formed atop glacial deposits that are 11,000 years old. Some of the dunes rise to a height of 460 feet.

Route 22 north of Manistee hugs the Lake Michigan shore, runs past **Frankfort,** where the **Father Marquette Historical Marker** stands at the waterfront next to the Coast Guard Station, passes the handsome 1858 **Point Betsie Lighthouse,** and enters the spectacular **Sleeping Bear Dunes National Lakeshore.** This federally operated park also includes **North and South Manitou Islands,** accessible by ferry. In the village of **Empire,** the **Lakeshore Visitor Center** (9922 Front Street, 616–326–5134) contains exhibits on maritime and natural history. The park maintains the **Sleeping Bear Point Coast Guard Station Museum** (off Route 209, one-half mile west of Glen Haven), with exhibits on the U.S. Life Saving Service, the Coast Guard, and shipping and shipwrecks in Lake Michigan. The dunes take their name from an Ojibwa legend that assigned animal names to the distinctive land forms: One of the large mainland dunes represented a sleeping mother bear, while the Manitou Islands were her two cubs.

LELAND

Lumbering, iron smelting, and commercial fishing were the nineteenth-century mainstays of Leland, which was founded in 1853. On the waterfront, where the Leland River flows into the lake, **Fishtown** preserves a sampling of weathered fishermen's shanties built from the turn of the century until the 1930s. The **Leelanau Historical Museum** (203 East Cedar Street, 616–256–7475), housed in the 1901 brick County Jail House, interprets the history of the settlement and development of Leelanau County through artifacts, photographs, and paintings. At the tip of the Leelanau Peninsula is the **Grand Traverse Lighthouse,** established in 1852. The present structure, a combination house and light, was built in 1864 and is one of the oldest lights on the Great Lakes.

TRAVERSE CITY

Traverse City is situated on the Boardman River at the south end of Grand Traverse Bay. Settlement began in the late 1840s, but the town's boom era commenced in the 1850s when three Chicago businessmen—Perry Hannah, Albert Lay, and James Morgan—founded the lumber company that would dominate the town's economy until the turn of the century.

The red brick **City Opera House** (112½ East Front Street, 616–941–8082), built in 1891 at the end of the lumber boom, has Palladian and Richardsonian Romanesque elements and an elaborate interior, which has remained virtually intact. Among the many nineteenth-century structures in the Central Neighborhood District is the **Perry Hannah House** (305 Sixth Street, private), a three-story frame Queen Anne mansion completed in 1893. The vernacular residence at 502 Fifth Street (private), built in 1900, is representative of sawmill workers' housing.

On the waterfront in Clinch Park, the **Con Foster Museum** (616–922–4905) traces the geological formation of the region and the history of human activity in the region from prehistoric Indians through European exploration and American development of the lumber and maritime-related industries and agriculture.

In a glorious digression, Route 37 travels northward up the beautiful Old Mission Peninsula through the cherry orchards and vineyards that are a distinctive part of the local economy. At the tip of the peninsula is the village of **Old Mission,** and one mile south of

it is the **Old Mission Church,** a replica of the original structure
built in 1839 by the Reverend Peter Dougherty, the energetic Presbyterian missionary who worked among the Ojibwa and Ottawa
Indians in this part of Michigan. Inside are interpretive exhibits.

BEAVER ISLAND

Although isolated from the mainland, Beaver Island has a rich
past. Prehistoric Indians built mounds here, Ojibwa and Ottawa
Indians lived on the island, and French and American fur traders
encamped here. The American Fur Trading Company established
a post in 1831, and commercial fishing was another thriving nineteenth-century industry. The only settlement on the island is Saint
James, which is primarily a tourist town.

Beginning in 1847 a group of some 2,600 Mormons who had
splintered from the dissolving community at Nauvoo, Illinois, settled on Beaver Island. They crowned their charismatic leader,
James J. Strang, king and hoped that the island's remoteness would
shield them from societal criticism. Their plan was thwarted by
local fishermen, who did not care to share their fishing grounds
and who quickly grew impatient with the Mormons' abstinence
from liquor and their benevolent treatment of the Indians. The
Mormons' nine-year stay on the island was marked by hostile conflict with their neighbors and bitter internal strife, culminating in
the murder of Strang in 1856 by two of his followers. The Mormons were forcibly removed from the island by a mob. Later
settlement was by Irish immigrants fleeing the potato famine.

In **Saint James,** the Beaver Island Historical Society maintains
the **Mormon Print Shop** (Main and Forest streets, 616–448–2254),
which exhibits material relevant to the Indian, Mormon, and Irish
eras. The society also administers the **Marine and Harbor Museum**
(Main Street, 616–448–2254), which documents fishing and lumbering activities and general history of the Beaver archipelago.

PETOSKEY

Petoskey was settled in the 1870s after the Ojibwa-Ottawa Reservation, established in 1836, was closed by the federal government and
its lands made available for purchase. The town takes its name
from Ignatius Pe-to-se-ga, an Ojibwa who had owned much of the
land in the vicinity. In the nineteenth century, lumbering was the
main activity, augmented by quarrying and tourism. The **Little**

Traverse Historical Museum (1 Waterfront Park, 616–347–2620), housed in an 1892 Richardsonian Romanesque railroad depot, contains exhibits of Indian artifacts, local history, and memorabilia pertaining to Ernest Hemingway, who summered in the area, and to Civil War historian Bruce Catton, who was born in Petoskey. Hemingway's boyhood summer cottage, **Windemere** (private), is located on Walloon Lake, south of town.

HARBOR SPRINGS

Harbor Springs is a summer resort overlooking Little Traverse Bay. The area from here to **Cross Village** is rich in Ojibwa and Ottawa lore and in missionary history and affords spectacular views of Lake Michigan. The **Chief Andrew J. Blackbird Museum** (368 East Main Street, 616–526–7731) contains a small collection of Indian artifacts, tools, and clothing, primarily of the Ottawa. It is housed in the 1868 residence of Ottawa historian Chief Blackbird, who wrote several books on Indian language and legends.

S T R A I T S   O F   M A C K I N A C

MACKINAW CITY

Mackinaw City lies at the northern tip of Michigan's Lower Peninsula overlooking the Straits of Mackinac, the narrows connecting Lakes Michigan and Huron, and one of the most historically significant places in the Great Lakes. Countless Indians passed through the straits, and in the seventeenth century many members of the Ojibwa, Huron, and Ottawa tribes, fleeing the hostile Iroquois to the east, settled on the nearby shores. They were followed by French explorers, missionaries, and fur traders. The fortified posts the French maintained on the straits were the nexus of the fur trade in the Northwest for almost a hundred years. The first permanent settler arrived in Mackinaw City in 1870, when lumbering was the chief industry.

Fort Michilimackinac and Mackinac Maritime Park

In about 1715 the French decided to built a fort on the south shore of the straits, after a fifteen-year military hiatus in the area. In the 1680s they had built Fort de Buade at Saint Ignace on the north

OPPOSITE: *A small steeple marks the Church of Sainte Anne in Fort Michilimackinac, a reconstruction of the fort established by the French to protect their fur traders in the early 1700s.*

shore, but that fortification was abandoned in 1698, its troops moving southward to present-day Detroit. Fort Michilimackinac, constructed to strengthen Indian alliances and to halt the inroads of the British, was center of French fur trade for some fifty years. In 1755, during the early years of the French and Indian War, Charles Langlade, who was half Ottawa, assembled a war party of Indians at Fort Michilimackinac that successfully routed British general Edward Braddock at far-off Fort Duquesne near present-day Pittsburgh. After the war, Langlade ventured west to found Green Bay, the first permanent settlement in Wisconsin. The British took over Fort Michilimackinac in 1761 amid increasing unrest among the Indians who had been strongly allied with the French. Their dissatisfaction led to Pontiac's War in 1763, when a band of local Ojibwa, ostensibly engaged in a game of lacrosse at the fort's gates, stormed the stronghold, killing or capturing most of the occupants. The British reoccupied the fort a year later, and in the face of increasing American settlement of the West, were able to forge alliances with the Indians. During the Revolutionary War the fort was used to assemble Indian war parties targeted at American outposts. Fearful, however, that the position was too vulnerable to American attack, the British abandoned it in 1779 and commenced building Fort Mackinac on Mackinac Island.

The reconstructed palisade at Fort Michilimackinac encloses numerous structures, including the Commanding Officer's House, a British Trader's House, a French Trader's House, and the Church of Sainte Anne. The Soldier's Barracks houses a museum where costumed guides explain the fort's history and give craft and military demonstrations.

Adjacent to the fort, the **Mackinac Maritime Park** contains an array of marine-related exhibits including the *Welcome,* a replica of the sloop used in 1779 to carry material from Fort Michilimackinac to Mackinac Island for construction of the new fort, and the 1891 Shay steam yacht, designed by local inventor Ephraim Shay. The **Old Mackinac Point Lighthouse** contains a museum that explains the history of early boating in the straits area.

LOCATION: Route 75, beneath the south approach of the Mackinac Bridge. HOURS: Mid-June through Labor Day: 9–6 Daily; mid-May through mid-June and Labor Day through mid-October: Hours vary. FEE: Yes. TELEPHONE: 616–436–5563.

Three miles south is the **Mill Creek State Historic Park** (Route 23, 616–436–7301), the excavated site of a sawmill and settlement that was active from the 1780s until the 1830s. The park includes a museum explaining the archaeological investigations and a reconstructed water-powered sawmill that has log-sawing demonstrations.

MACKINAC ISLAND

Mackinac Island, a limestone hump arising from Lake Huron, is deserving of its Indian name, Michilimackinac—the great turtle. This beautiful island, at the strategic bottleneck between Lakes Huron and Michigan, has served as a burial ground for prehistoric Indians, a fortress and fur-trading post for the British and Americans, a supply center for nineteenth-century fishing and lumbering industries, and, since the mid-1800s, as a summer resort. The dominant structure on Mackinac Island and a splendid remnant from the days of luxury steamboat travel on the Great Lakes is the **Grand Hotel,** perched on a high bluff overlooking the straits. The gargantuan white frame structure, whose verandah is 660 feet long, opened in 1887 and is still in operation.

Mackinac Island State Park

Abandoning Fort Michilimackinac on the mainland, the British moved to fortresslike Mackinac Island in 1780–1781. They built **Fort Mackinac** of stone, setting it on a promontory overlooking the harbor. The 1783 Treaty of Paris concluding the Revolutionary War awarded the island to the United States, but for more than a decade the British continued to occupy the fort and conduct fur-trading business with Indians. The British did evacuate in 1796 with the signing of the Jay Treaty. Nonetheless, their reluctance to relinquish their former western holdings helped precipitate the War of 1812. Early in the war a band of some thousand British soldiers, fur trappers, and Indians took Fort Mackinac from an unprepared American force of fifty. The fort did not revert to the United States until the war was over. It was garrisoned until 1895.

The restored fort contains structures such as the officer's stone quarters and the stone ramparts that date from the early British occupation. The other buildings, including the post commandant's house, the soldiers' barracks, and the post headquarters, were built during the period of American occupation. Each contains interpretive exhibits and period furnishings. Soldiers attired in the garb of the Twenty-third Infantry regularly fire cannon and muskets.

The state park maintains several other sites in the vicinity of Fort Mackinac, including the **Mission Church** (Huron Street), built in 1830 for the community and for workers and teachers at the school for Indian children. The **Indian Dormitory** (Huron Street), a large, three-story white frame building, was constructed under the terms of the 1836 Treaty of Washington with the Ojibwa. It was designed by the Indian agent Henry R. Schoolcraft and used to board Indians who came to the island to conduct business with the agency. Appointed with period furnishings, it contains a museum of Great Lakes Indian artifacts and exhibits pertaining to the Indian legends gathered by Schoolcraft and later adapted by Henry Wadsworth Longfellow in the poem *Hiawatha*.

The **Beaumont Memorial** (Market Street) contains exhibits explaining the work of Dr. William Beaumont, the Army surgeon who in the 1820s made landmark observations of the human digestive system by examining over a long period of time the stomach of Alexis St. Martin, a *voyageur* who had suffered a gunshot wound in the abdomen. (St. Martin was shot in the American Fur Company store which is now restored as part of the Stuart House Museum.)

The unrestored **Fort Holmes** is on the highest point of the island, with a fine view of the straits. It was built by the British in 1814 in anticipation of an American attack during the War of 1812. The original earthen walls of the fort are visible. The **Mackinac Island State Park Visitor Center,** on Huron Street near the boat docks, contains information about the various historic sites.

LOCATION: Mackinac Island. HOURS: *Fort Mackinac:* Mid-June through Labor Day: 9–6 Daily; Hours vary in spring and fall. *Other sites:* Mid-June through Labor Day: 11–5 Daily. FEE: Yes. TELEPHONE: 906–847–3328.

Within a few years of the War of 1812, John Jacob Astor set up the Great Lakes headquarters for the American Fur Trading Company on Mackinac Island, which dominated the island's economy for about fifteen years. The 1817 **Stuart House** (Market Street), built as the residence of company agent Robert Stuart, is now a museum displaying Indian artifacts, American Fur Trading Company records, furs, pelts, trade items, artifacts of the War of 1812, and period rooms. Adjacent is the **Old County Courthouse,** the county seat from 1839 to 1882 and now the city hall.

OPPOSITE: *A ward in the Fort Mackinac hospital, which has been restored to its 1880s appearance.*

The 1887 Grand Hotel on Mackinac Island in Lake Huron has retained its nineteenth-century air. No automobiles are allowed on the island. OPPOSITE: *The hotel's 660-foot-long porch.*

Mackinac Island, which is five miles from Saint Ignace and eight miles from Mackinaw City, is accessible by ferry from both towns, but no motorized vehicles are allowed on the island.

SAINT IGNACE

Saint Ignace, a small lumber and fishing town during the nineteenth century, dates to 1671, when Father Jacques Marquette and a group of Huron refugees fleeing from the Iroquois built a mission here named for Saint Ignatius of Loyola, the founder of the Jesuit order. Two years later Marquette embarked from Saint Ignace with Louis Jolliet on their seminal journey down the Mississippi River. In 1675, while ministering to the Iroquois, Marquette died somewhere along the eastern shore of Lake Michigan, trying to return to Saint Ignace. Two years later a band of native hunters who had known him retrieved his remains and reburied them under his Saint Ignace chapel.

A late-nineteenth-century studio portrait of Ojibwa Chief David Shoppenagons with his wife and one daughter, now in the collection of the Museum of Ojibwa Culture.

Marquette Mission Park and Museum of Ojibwa Culture

Situated on the site of the 1671 Huron village, this site includes a Huron longhouse and garden typical of the Indian lifestyle. An adjacent century-old monument marks what many believe to be Father Marquette's original burial spot. The Museum of Ojibwa

Culture, housed in a Victorian church building, interprets the culture of the Ojibwa people, the original inhabitants of the Upper Great Lakes, and addresses the French, Jesuit, Huron, and Ottawa presence in the area.

LOCATION: 500 North Street. HOURS: Memorial Day through Labor day: 10–8 Monday–Saturday; 12–8 Sunday; Rest of September through October 20: 1–5 Daily. FEE: Yes. TELEPHONE: 906–643–9161.

The **Father Marquette Memorial** (720 Church Street in Straits State Park, 906–643–9394) is a modern monument overlooking the Straits of Mackinac. The **museum** exhibits memorabilia from the Jesuit era and explains the history of Marquette's exploration of the Mississippi River and his missionary work among the Indians.

In the 1680s the French built **Fort de Buade,** just south of the Jesuit mission. By the 1690s the population of Saint Ignace was thriving, and the village's ruling factions sparred. The Jesuits and Commander Antoine de la Mothe Cadillac were at odds over the Jesuits' belief that the fur trade was corrupting the Indians. In 1701 Cadillac, along with many of the Huron—the middlemen of the fur trade in the area—moved south and founded Detroit. The Jesuits abandoned their depopulated mission in 1705. The **Fort de Buade Museum** (334 North State Street, 906–643–6622) displays a private collection of Indian artifacts, paintings of Great Lakes Indians, and antique guns.

THE UPPER PENINSULA

Michigan's Upper Peninsula has more in common with Wisconsin's Chequamegon Bay and the arrowhead-shaped wedge of northeastern Minnesota than it does with the lower part of the state. This area's history is distinct and indelible in large measure because the three regions embrace Lake Superior, the largest body of fresh water in the world. Holding 10 percent of the earth's supply of fresh surface water, Lake Superior is 350 miles long, more than 150 miles wide, and over 1,000 feet deep in places. Its water is bone-chilling in all seasons, and it is infamous for its storms.

For 300 years, Lake Superior has been the main avenue of development and commerce for the region. Before that, Indians used it for travel and the copper trade, but it seems probable that their canoes were too vulnerable for them to risk exploring it extensively. Via Lake Superior, French explorers and missionaries penetrated westward in the seventeenth century and vast numbers

An Indian burial ground at L'Anse, in Michigan's Upper Peninsula.

of pelts were transported from the interior to Montreal throughout the eighteenth and early nineteenth centuries. With the demise of the fur trade came the rise of copper and iron-ore mining and to a lesser extent logging and commercial fishing. Today the area, noted for its beauty and remoteness, is promoting tourism.

French explorers and *voyageurs* portaged around the mile-long series of rapids at Sault Sainte Marie where Lake Superior joins Huron, but the rocks and rills were a hindrance to full-scale commercial shipping in Lake Superior. Engineers overcame this obstacle when they constructed the Soo Locks, which opened in 1855. The Soo Locks provided the wheat lands of the Dakotas with distant markets and linked the iron-ore fields of Michigan and Minnesota with the coal mines of Ohio and Pennsylvania, beginning the booming steel industry in the Cuyahoga and Mahoning valleys of Ohio. Inland ports sprang up, and the shipping of these grains and raw materials gave rise to a network of railroads across the nation's midriff, while the nascent steel industry fueled the manufacturing of automobiles in and around Detroit. Almost overnight, the landscape, complexion, and pace of the Great Lakes region changed: Cities burgeoned, smoke-belching factories sprouted along rivers and lakeshores, immigrant laborers poured in to build the canals and railroads and man the factories, and the self-made Midwestern millionaire emerged on the scene. Even though the exploitation of its raw materials helped bring about this transformation, the Lake Superior country has remained relatively remote and thinly populated.

An interesting array of vernacular structures are scattered throughout the Lake Superior country, and these attest to the resourcefulness of the hearty immigrants who were laborers in the iron-ore industry or who eked out livings as commercial fishermen or subsistence farmers. In the Upper Peninsula, these include the iron-smelting village of Fayette and the Finnish fishing village near Calumet on the Keweenaw Peninsula. The Lake Superior area is distinctive architecturally, however, because of the assortment of engineering feats associated with the mining and shipping industries, structural realizations of the ingenuity required to extract raw materials from the earth and ship them to all corners of the world.

SAULT SAINTE MARIE

Sault Sainte Marie stands on the south bank of the Saint Marys River across from its Canadian counterpart, Sault Sainte Marie, Ontario. Over about a mile, the Saint Marys River, which connects Lake Superior with Lake Huron, drops some twenty-one feet, a gradient that forced *voyageurs* to portage here. Numerous notable French explorers passed this way—Etienne Brulé in 1618, Jean Nicolet in 1634, and Pierre Esprit Radisson and Médard Chouart des Groseilliers in 1658—and in 1668 Jesuit priest Jacques Marquette founded Mission Sainte Marie at the Ojibwa village of Bawating, which overlooked the rapids.

Dating its origins from this mission, Sault Sainte Marie is the oldest permanent community in Michigan. In 1671, during a dramatic pageant at Bawating, French representatives laid claim to interior North America on behalf of Louis XIV while members of some fourteen Indian tribes looked on. In the face of assaults from the Iroquois, many of the Indians fled south to forts at Michilimackinac and Detroit by the eighteenth century. For ten years (1751 to 1762), the French maintained Fort Repentigny here, but it burned to the ground in the same year, 1763, that France lost its New World possessions to the British.

Although technically the British ceded the area in the Treaty of Paris in 1783 and Jay's Treaty in 1796, they did not stop interfering with American settlement until they were defeated in the War of 1812. In 1823 Lewis Cass, Michigan's territorial governor, appointed Henry Rowe Schoolcraft to be the Indian agent at Sault Sainte Marie, and Schoolcraft became the first American to study in detail the cultural life of Michigan Indians, particularly the Ojibwa. The **Schoolcraft House and Indian Agency** (Water Street, private), built in 1827, is one of the oldest extant buildings in Michigan, as is the nearby **John Johnston House** (Water Street, private), a log and clapboard house built in 1815 and altered in 1822. Johnston was a prominent fur trader and merchant in the area, as well as the father-in-law of Schoolcraft, who also occupied this house during his tenure at Sault Sainte Marie. In 1822 the U.S. Army built Fort Brady to protect American interests at this critical river passage. A second Fort Brady was built in 1893 on a location better suited to guard the Soo Locks; it was deactivated in 1944. Several buildings from the **New Fort Brady** still stand on the campus of Lake Superior State College (Easterday Avenue).

The discovery of massive quantities of iron ore along the shores of Lake Superior in the mid-nineteenth century provided the impetus for a shipping passage through the rapids on the Saint Marys River. In 1855 a canal and lock were built at Sault Sainte Marie. The opening of the Soo Locks stimulated mining in the Upper Peninsula and the Iron Range of Minnesota, which in turn gave rise to a host of industries, including the manufacturing of steel in Cleveland and Youngstown and of automobiles in and around Detroit. The Soo Locks also opened the door for grain shipments from the rich wheat lands of western Minnesota and the Dakotas. In 1881 the U.S. Army Corps of Engineers took over operation of the locks, which have been rebuilt several times. The corps maintains the **Saint Marys Falls Canal Visitor Center** (West Portage Avenue, 906–632–3311), which contains a working lock model, pictorial displays of old locks, and three observation decks overlooking the MacArthur Lock (one of the four in the system) that provide close-range views of ships in transit.

SS Valley Camp and Marine Museum

The SS *Valley Camp* is a 550-foot Great Lakes freighter that has been converted into a marine museum and aquarium. The pilothouse, captain and crew quarters, and engine room are appointed with appropriate furnishings and fixtures, while the ship's huge holds contain displays of shipwrecks, famous mariners, and Great

Lakes history. The museum also operates the nearby Tower of History, a 210-foot observation tower that affords a panoramic view of the Soo Locks and Sault Sainte Marie.

LOCATION: *SS Valley Camp:* Johnston and Water streets, five blocks east of Soo Locks. *Tower of History:* Portage Avenue, three blocks east of Soo Locks. HOURS: Mid-May through June: 10–6 Daily; July through August: 9–9 Daily; September through mid-October: 10–6 Daily. FEE: Yes. TELEPHONE: 906–632–3658.

MARQUETTE

Marquette, perched amid rocky bluffs on the south shore of Lake Superior, has for many years been a major shipper of Upper Peninsula iron ore. Visitors can watch huge Great Lakes freighters being loaded at the city's historic ore docks. In 1841, Michigan's first state geologist, Douglass Houghton, confirmed reports of iron ore in the area, and in 1844 U.S. deputy surveyor William A. Burt discovered rich veins of the mineral near present-day Negaunee, where in 1846 the Jackson Mining Company initiated the first iron-ore mining in Michigan.

The **Marquette County Historical Society Museum** (213 North Front Street, 906–226–3571) has a variety of exhibits that explain the history of mining, shipping, lumbering, and railroads in the area. It also has collections of Ojibwa artifacts, glass, silver, toys, and costumes. The society also maintains the 1858 **John Burt House** (220 Craig Street), a simple structure built of sandstone from the nearby Burt Brothers quarry. It contains furnishings typical of a pioneer workman. The **Marquette Maritime Museum** (Lakeshore Drive and East Ridge Street, 906–226–2006), housed in the 1890 Richardsonian Romanesque Waterworks Building, displays vintage small watercraft, underwater diving gear, and documentary photographs of Great Lakes shipping.

Located between Marquette and Negaunee in the heart of the Marquette Iron Range, the **Michigan Iron Industry Museum** (73 Forge Road, three miles east of Negaunee, 906–475–7857) overlooks the Carp River on the site where the Jackson Iron Company operated a forge from 1848 to 1855. On display are mining tools and equipment and photographs and memorabilia of mine workers and their families.

FAYETTE HISTORIC STATE PARK

Set on the natural harbor of Big Bay de Noc against a backdrop of stunning white limestone cliffs, Fayette was a thriving iron-smelting village in the mid-nineteenth century. In 1867 a blast furnace was opened here with iron ore from the Marquette Range transported via railroad to Escanaba, thence by boat to Fayette, with a ready supply of lime and charcoal (made from the nearby hardwood timber) providing the other necessary ingredients for the smelting process. By the late nineteenth century, the nearby source of charcoal had been depleted, and the newer coke-fired blast furnaces in northeastern Ohio were producing more and better iron. Fayette's furnace closed in 1891, and it became a ghost town. Its numerous structures, which have been preserved as the Fayette Historic State Park, include portions of the blast furnace, a rebuilt charcoal kiln, a hotel, opera house, and numerous homes. A self-guided walking tour provides views of the cliffs and Lake Michigan.

LOCATION: Seventeen miles south of Route 2 on Route 183, on the Garden Peninsula. HOURS: June through Labor Day: 9–7 Daily; Day after Labor Day through mid-October: 9–5 Daily. FEE: Yes. TELEPHONE: 906–644–2603.

IRON MOUNTAIN

Iron Mountain lies in the heart of the Menominee Iron Range, the second of the three Upper Peninsula iron-ore belts to be developed. It was white pine that attracted settlers to this area in the mid-nineteenth century, but mining soon supplanted lumber-related activities. Mining began here in 1877 after the completion of a railroad to Escanaba, the Lake Michigan shipping point for iron ore. The highest grade of ore had been mined out by the early twentieth century, when mines in this area began to close.

Although the Iron Mountain area was rich in iron ore, it proved difficult to mine as much of it lay in swampy land. Cave-ins were regular occurrences, and it was necessary to pump water out of the mines. The Chapin Mine District, located on the south end of town, preserves various structures associated with the mine, including the **Cornish Pump and Mining Museum** (Kent Street and Carpenter Avenue, 906–774–1086). The immense pump—its

OPPOSITE: *Ruins of an iron smelter in Fayette, the site of the prosperous Jackson Iron Company from 1867 to 1891 and now a ghost town.*

flywheel is forty feet in diameter—was constructed to extract water from the Chapin Mine (from 1880 to 1932 roughly 25 million tons of iron ore were taken from this mine). The museum contains mining equipment and information on area mines. The **Menominee Range Historical Museum** (300 East Ludington Street, 906–774–4276) has exhibits on Indian culture, the fur trade, lumbering, and mining. Also displayed are replicas of a general store, pioneer kitchen, Victorian parlor, one-room school, doctor's office, and other nineteenth-century rooms containing period furnishings, clothing, and tools.

Ten miles east of Iron Mountain in **Vulcan** is the **Iron Mountain Iron Mine** (Route 2, 906–563–8077). Active from 1877 to 1945, it produced over 22 million tons of ore. Train tours travel underground through 2,600 feet of tunnels and caverns as guides explain the geology of the mine and demonstrate nineteenth- and twentieth-century mining technologies.

IRON COUNTY MUSEUM

Deep in the North Woods is the Iron County Museum, a pioneer village of nineteenth- and early-twentieth-century structures. Dominating the settlement are the headframe and enginehouse from the Caspian Mine. Other buildings include a two-story log house built around 1890, several log homesteads, barns, and sheds, a logging camp cookhouse, schoolhouse, blacksmith shop, and the 1892 Chicago Northwest railroad depot. Many contain period furnishings. Underground ore cars and mining equipment are on display, and there are exhibits of pioneer life.

LOCATION: Route 424 off Route 2, near Caspian. HOURS: June through August: 9–5 Monday–Saturday, 1–5 Sunday; May and September: 10–4 Monday–Saturday, 1–4 Sunday. FEE: Yes. TELEPHONE: 906–265–2617.

HOUGHTON AND HANCOCK

The twin towns of Houghton and Hancock lie on a narrow arm of Portage Lake midway up the crooked finger of Keweenaw Peninsula. In 1873 a canal bisected the peninsula via the lake, following a route used by Indians and *voyageurs,* and shortened shipping time

OPPOSITE: *An abandoned ironworkers' dormitory is one of the many structures left in Fayette Historic State Park.*

around the peninsula. These small industrial towns developed around copper mining, the major activity here from the mid-nineteenth century until the end of World War I.

The mines attracted scores of immigrant laborers, including the Cornish, who were noted for their mining skills, and Finns, who founded **Suomi College** (601 Quincy Street, 906–482–5300) in Hancock in 1896, which remains the only college founded by Finns in the country. The Richardsonian Romanesque **Old Main,** on the campus, was built in 1900 of local red sandstone and is typical of many nineteenth-century buildings on the Keweenaw Peninsula. **Michigan Technological University** (Route 41), founded in Houghton in 1885 to train mining engineers, geologists, and metallurgists, has the **A. E. Seaman Mineralogical Museum** (Electrical Energy Resources Center, 906–487–2572), which displays a large collection of minerals, lapidary specimens, and examples of native copper, silver, and iron ores from the Upper Peninsula.

One of the most productive copper zones in the area was the Pewabic lode, and the largest operation to exploit these deposits was the Quincy Mining Company. Of the one billion pounds of copper ore taken from the lode over about a hundred years, this company extracted some 930 million pounds. The **Quincy Mine No. 2 Shaft House** (Route 41 north of Hancock, 906–482–5569) towers over the Portage Ship Canal. Nearby is the **Norbert Hoist**— the world's largest steam hoist, which heaved ten-ton loads of copper ore from depths of 9,200 feet. Installed in 1920, it weighs 1.7 million pounds and is sixty feet high.

ISLE ROYALE NATIONAL PARK

Forty miles off the Keweenaw Peninsula, Isle Royale National Park preserves a forty-five-mile-long island in northwest Lake Superior. The rugged island is ridged by cliffs and covered with spruce and balsam forest, and its irregular shoreline is notched with beautiful fiordlike bays. Prehistoric Indians fashioned tools from the copper they found here and, later, the Hudson's Bay Company operated a fur-trading post from this domain of the Ojibwa. As part of an effort to secure copper-rich lands in the Lake Superior region, the federal government obtained Isle Royale from the Indians in 1842, and copper was mined sporadically until 1883.

OPPOSITE: *The Quincy Mine No. 2 Shaft House, where a cable wound around a thirty-foot drum lifted loads of copper ore from the mine.*

Several nineteenth-century structures have been preserved, including the 1855 **Rock Harbor Lighthouse.** The **museum,** on Mott Island, contains prehistoric artifacts, Indian baskets, photographs, shipwreck items, and nineteenth-century copper-mining tools.

LOCATION: *Mainland office:* 800 East Lakeshore Drive, Houghton, MI 49931. *Island headquarters:* Mott Island. The park is accessible by ferry from Houghton (a six-hour trip) and Copper Harbor (four hours) in Michigan and Grand Portage in Minnesota. HOURS: Mid-April through October: Daily. FEE: For ferry only. TELEPHONE: *Houghton:* 906–482–0984.

In **Lake Linden,** at the head of Torch Lake, the **Houghton County Historical Society Museum Complex** (Route 26, 906–296–4121) preserves a Victorian frame church, one-room school house, railroad depot, firehouse, and the mill office of the Calumet and Hecla Mining Company, which contains a variety of nineteenth-century collections and exhibits. Nearby at the mouth of the Traverse River is the **Big Traverse Bay Historic District,** a rare example of an early-twentieth-century ethnic fishing village. Finnish lumbermen and miners settled in the area late in the nineteenth century and many became commercial fishermen. The village is composed of vernacular frame houses, Finnish saunas, net-drying racks, and shingled fishing buildings.

CALUMET

Calumet, another of the string of villages that sprang up along the spine of the Keweenaw Peninsula during the copper boom, was the company town of one of the largest and longest-running operations on the peninsula, the Calumet and Hecla Mine, founded in 1871 and operated until 1968.

The **Calumet and Hecla Industrial District** (Calumet Avenue, Red Jacket Road, Sixth Street, and Mine Street) preserves various industrial structures, including the machine shop, blacksmith shop, roundhouse, and boiler house, of the mining company. The brick and native sandstone structures of the downtown district display a variety of copper, terra cotta, and sandstone decorative motifs on their facades. Two such adorned examples are the **Calumet Theater** (340 Sixth Street, 906–337–2610), an eclectic opera house built in 1900, and the **Calumet Fire Station,** across the street, a Richardsonian Romanesque structure completed in 1899. Both are used today as performance halls.

Coppertown U.S.A. (109 Red Jacket Road, 906–337–4354) displays tools and machinery from the Calumet and Hecla Mining Company, photographs documenting daily operations of the company, and memorabilia of immigrant mine workers.

COPPER HARBOR

Copper Harbor, once the chief port of the copper-mining district, perches on the tip of the Keweenaw Peninsula, where it commands spectacular views of Lake Superior and the forest-covered ridges of the Keweenaw Mountains.

Fort Wilkins Historic Complex

Fort Wilkins was built in 1844 in anticipation of conflicts between newly arrived copper miners and the Ojibwa, long-standing residents who had recently ceded their lands to the federal government. Trouble never materialized, however, and the fort was garrisoned for only two years before its troops were withdrawn to fight in the Mexican War. It was used again after the Civil War, from 1867 to 1870, for recuperating Union veterans. Virtually unaltered over the years, the fort consists of a log stockade surrounding sixteen structures, most of log construction with clapboard siding. The buildings contain period furnishings and exhibits pertaining to the history of the area and guides in 1870s costume interpret life at the frontier outpost.

LOCATION: Fort Wilkins State Park, Route 41. HOURS: Mid-May through mid-October: 8–Dusk Daily. FEE: Yes. TELEPHONE: 906–289–4215.

Fort Wilkins State Park also encompasses the **Copper Harbor Lighthouse,** situated on a bluff overlooking the town and Lake Superior. One of the oldest light stations on the lake, it was first built in 1848 and rebuilt in 1866.

Another former copper-mining operation open to the public is the **Delaware Mine** (twelve miles south of Copper Harbor on Route 41, 906–289–4688). The tour includes a walk through the mine and the ruins of the buildings associated with it. Also on the grounds is a prehistoric mining pit.

EASTERN   MICHIGAN

ALPENA

Tucked away on Thunder Bay, Alpena was settled in the 1850s as a lumber and shingle mill town. The bay has a long history of shipping disasters because of its many rocky shoals and islands. **Thunder Bay Underwater Preserve** (800–4–ALPENA) is an area containing some eighty shipwrecks—from a wooden schooner that sank in the 1860s to a 550-foot steel steamer that went down in 1966—that can be visited by scuba divers. Information is available from the Alpena Area Chamber of Commerce (517–354–4181).

The **Jesse Besser Museum** (491 Johnson Street, 517–356–2202) maintains collections of nineteenth- and twentieth-century furnishings and decorative arts, lithographs, artifacts of Great Lakes copper culture Indians, agricultural equipment, and lumbering implements. Among the nineteenth-century structures on the grounds are an 1890 log building and an 1896 schoolhouse.

Twenty-three miles north of Alpena, the **Old Presque Isle Lighthouse and Museum** (5295 Grand Lake Road, Presque Isle, 517–595–2059) commands a striking view of Lake Huron and the forested shore. The lighthouse was in service from 1840 until 1870 during which time Presque Harbor was a thriving port. The restored keeper's cottage contains maritime items, lighthouse memorabilia, and period furnishings.

BAY CITY

An industrial, trade, and tourist center, Bay City lies at the mouth of the Saginaw River. The first permanent settlers in the area of Saginaw Bay were two French Canadian fur traders, Joseph and Medor Tromble (their name has long been spelled Trombley), brothers who built a trading post and residence on Saginaw's east bank in 1836. The **Trombley House,** a handsome, frame Greek Revival structure, has since been moved to the west bank of Bay City (901 John F. Kennedy Drive). To exploit the rich timber in the Saginaw Valley, the first sawmill was built in 1836, and by the 1860s the area had emerged as one of the nation's lumber capitals. A nineteenth-century observer characterized a local sawmill, described in the late 1860s as the largest in the world, as "one of the sights of the valley, a monster of the woods with more sets of teeth than a wholesale dentist. . . ."

Bay City's **city hall** (301 Washington Avenue) is an impressive Richardsonian Romanesque structure built in 1897 during the peak of the lumber era, and the **Center Avenue Historical District** preserves the Victorian mansions of the nineteenth-century lumber barons. With the depletion of Michigan lumber and the placement of a tariff on Canadian timber, Bay City slipped into decline at the turn of the century. The **Historical Museum of Bay County** (321 Washington Avenue, 517–893–5733) contains costumes, maps, photographs, and artifacts relating to the history of the area.

Visitors interested in Great Lakes aboriginal history will find the state's only known Indian rock carvings off the beaten path in the middle of Michigan's "thumb." **Sanilac Petroglyphs State Historic Park** (four miles east of Route 53, 517–373–3559) is some forty miles east of Bay City between the small towns of Cass City and Ubly. The sandstone outcrops contain over a hundred carvings of human figures, hands, and feet; game animals and their tracks; birds; and geometric designs that are thought to date to the Late Woodland period (A.D. 800).

SAGINAW

Louis Campau established a fur-trading post on the banks of the Saginaw River in 1816. Because of his familiarity with the Indians, Campau was enlisted by territorial governor Lewis Cass to help negotiate the 1819 Treaty of Saginaw. Campau moved on to found Grand Rapids in 1826. Along with Bay City, Saginaw grew into a major lumber town. The **Historical Society of Saginaw County** (500 Federal Avenue, 517–752–2861), housed in the 1898 Castle Station, has exhibits on lumbering and the fur trade.

MIDLAND

West of Saginaw Bay, at the confluence of the Tittabawassee and Chippewa rivers, amid the deep forests and abundant streams that made the area prized by Indians, Midland grew up around fur-trading posts. The city was incorporated in 1856 and became another nineteenth-century lumber town destined for decline with the depletion of the timber. But in 1891 the town's fortunes took a turn for the better when Herbert H. Dow founded the Midland Chemical Company, now Dow Chemical. Extensive brine wells underlie central Michigan, and by perfecting an electrolytic process Dow was able to extract commercial quantities of useful chemicals, such as bromine, from the salt solution. This discovery led to the early success of the company, which now produces a vast array of chemicals, plastics, and pharmaceuticals.

In the early twentieth century, petroleum was discovered in association with the brine wells, and the subsequent development added to Midland's affluence. Midland retains the air of a well-organized and prosperous company town. Architect Alden B. Dow, youngest son of Herbert and Grace Dow and a student of Frank Lloyd Wright, designed many of the structures in the city. The **Midland County Historical Society** building (1801 West Saint Andrews Drive, 517–835–7401) contains glass, silver, textiles, and other artifacts of early Midland history. The **Benjamin Bradley House** (3200 Cook Road, 517–835–7401) is a Gothic Revival structure built in 1874 for a wealthy Midland businessman.

The sixty-acre **Dow Gardens** (Eastman Road and West Saint Andrews Drive, 517–631–2677) preserve many of the plantings tended by Herbert Dow, who was a horticulturist as well as a chemist. The gardens surround the original Dow homestead, a handsome 1899 green frame vernacular structure.

Situated at the confluence of the Pine and Chippewa rivers, the 1,200-acre **Chippewa Nature Center** (400 South Badour Road, 517–631–0830) explains the human history of the area in its **Man, Time, and Environment Museum** through exhibits of Indian artifacts and nineteenth-century pioneer tools, among others. Also on the grounds are an 1880s log schoolhouse and an 1870s furnished farmstead, which includes a maple-sugar house and log barn.

HARTWICK PINES STATE PARK AND LOGGING MUSEUMS

About a hundred miles north of Midland, Hartwick Pines State Park and Logging Museums is near the town of Grayling in the finger portion of Michigan's mitten. This is the heart of the state's historic logging region, and the museums' exhibits explain the dealings of the lumber barons and the life of the loggers who lived in the remote camps. A logging camp exhibit in a stand of virgin pine features a bunkhouse, blacksmith shop, and mess hall. LOCATION: Route 93, north of Grayling and Route 75. HOURS: *Park:* 8 A.M.–10 P.M. Daily. *Visitor Center:* Memorial Day through Labor Day: 9–7 Daily; Labor Day through late May: 9–4 Tuesday–Sunday. *Museum:* As Visitor Center, except closed November through April. FEE: Yes. TELE-PHONE: 517–548–7068.

FRANKENMUTH

Frankenmuth, on the Cass River, was settled in 1845 by German immigrants from Franconia in Bavaria. Long known for its beer and wine, Frankenmuth still supports two breweries, of which the **Frankenmuth Brewery** is the oldest in the state, and wineries still buy grapes from local vineyards. The **Frankenmuth Historical Museum** (613 South Main Street, 517–652–9701), housed in the 1905 Kern Hotel, contains exhibits of regional ethnic artifacts.

FLINT

Flint is closely tied with the automotive industry, particularly with General Motors, which was organized in 1908 by Flint's millionaire carriage maker, William C. Durant. The first settler, in 1819, was fur trader Jacob Smith. The town was incorporated in 1855 and began to prosper during the lumber era, with local sawmills providing the raw materials for a growing number of cart and carriage manufacturers. By the late 1890s Flint was one of the nation's largest producers of carriages, giving it a competitive edge in the nascent years of the automotive industry.

The Buick Motor Company came to Flint in 1903. A year later, when Buick began having financial troubles, Durant was hired to help promote their product. In 1905 Durant convinced Charles Stewart Mott to move his Weston-Mott Axle Company from Utica, New York, and in 1908 Durant masterminded the formation of General Motors—a company that can be considered the country's first conglomerate. General Motors initially included Buick, Cadillac, and Olds, and by 1910 it controlled some thirty companies. The automotive industry attracted immigrant labor and blacks from the South, and Flint became a city of immense, clamoring auto-assembly factories. Automobile assembly and parts manufacturing remain the chief industries.

A finished car body is skidded down a wooden ramp onto a chassis, and a Model T rolls off the assembly line at the Ford Motor Company Highland Park Plant in 1913.

The 1896 **Durant-Dort Carriage Company Office** (315 West Water Street) was headquarters for Flint's largest carriage manufacturer, which was operated by William Durant and his early automotive partner, J. Dallas Dort. Within the **Carriage Town Historic District** (Flint River, Fifth Avenue, and Begole and Saginaw streets) are many of the homes of early automotive magnates, including the 1890 **Charles W. Nash House** (307 Mason Street, 810–234–5117), the Queen Anne–style home of the founder of Nash Motor Company. The 1859 Italianate **Robert Whaley House** (624 East Kearsley Street, 810–235–6841) was the home of the Flint banker who financed Durant and Dort's first carriage venture in 1886. It is furnished according to the period.

Alfred P. Sloan Museum

Named for the president of General Motors in the 1920s and 1930s, the museum contains a collection of antique and experimental automobiles, including a 1902 Flint Roadster and a 1904 reproduction of the first Buick. There are also exhibits of early Flint history, including two Victorian period rooms.

LOCATION: 1221 East Kearsley Street. HOURS: 10–5 Monday–Friday, 12–5 Saturday–Sunday. FEE: Yes. TELEPHONE: 810–760–1181.

In the early years of the twentieth century, the industrial boom was providing jobs, but municipalities were hard pressed to provide adequate housing. Tar-paper shacks and tents often served as dwellings for factory families. The **Civic Park Historic District** in northwest Flint is a housing development begun by General Motors shortly after World War I in response to a critical housing shortage.

The **Fisher Body Plant Number 1** (4300 South Saginaw) and **Fisher Body Plant Number 2** (201 North Chevrolet Avenue) give an impressive glimpse of the proportions of automobile-assembly factories. The plants are also significant in the history of American labor relations. The year 1936 marked the rise of the United Auto Workers, and in Flint a strike began at the Fisher Body Plant Number 1 on December 30, 1936. The first large-scale sit-down strike in Michigan, it quickly spread to Fisher Body Plant Number 2, and ultimately to the Chevrolet Plant. Over the course of several weeks auto workers clashed with police, and the National Guard was called in. The strike was settled six weeks later, on February 11.

PORT HURON

Port Huron is an industrial and tourist center at the head of the Saint Clair River, where it flows south out of Lake Huron. The dashing Montreal fur trader Daniel Greysolon, sieur Duluth (for whom Duluth, Minnesota, is named), built **Fort Saint Joseph** at this strategic point in 1686, but it was occupied for only two years. In 1790 a Frenchman from nearby Detroit established a colony here. During the War of 1812, Americans built **Fort Gratiot** at the mouth of Lake Huron to stave off advances of Britain's naval forces and to contain their Indian allies. Some of the original earthworks remain, along with a plaque at Scott and Mansfield streets.

Thomas A. Edison spent his boyhood in Port Huron. Artifacts excavated from the sites of Fort Gratiot, the Edison home, and a local Woodland Indian village are on display at the **Port Huron Museum of Arts and History** (1115 Sixth Street, 810–982–0891). Exhibits include materials salvaged from Great Lakes ships, a reconstructed pilot house from a Great Lakes freighter, and portions of the skeleton of a woolly mammoth found in the area. An original 1850s log house with period furnishings is on the grounds.

D E T R O I T

Detroit is the largest city in Michigan and the tenth largest in the
country. Within the Great Lakes area it is second in size only to
Chicago. Bounded on the east by Canada, the city sits on the
Detroit River, which connects Lake Erie with Lake Saint Clair,
which in turn is linked to Lake Huron by the Saint Clair River.
Detroit's name is synonymous with the automotive industry.

On July 24, 1701, Antoine de la Mothe Cadillac, with an
entourage of some hundred French soldiers and artisans and an
equal number of Indians, encamped on a bluff overlooking the
strait between Lake Saint Clair and Lake Erie. Cadillac was concerned about the growing British threat to the French fur-trading
empire and gained the consent of Louis XIV to establish a fur-
trading post at this site to protect the waterways. Cadillac and his
men erected Fort Pontchartrain du Detroit, Pontchartrain being
one of Louis XIV's ministers, and Detroit French for "the strait."

*An aquatint of the Detroit waterfront done by W. J. Bennett in 1836, after the opening of the
Erie Canal had transformed the frontier town into a metropolitan port (detail).*

The fur-trading outpost grew steadily until the outbreak of the French and Indian War in 1754. Although no fighting occurred, at the end of the war Detroit surrendered to Major Robert Rogers, commander of Fort Michilimackinac. Many of Detroit's French inhabitants departed for Saint Louis, to be replaced by an influx of Dutch, Scottish, and New England merchants, and despite its remoteness, Detroit emerged a very cosmopolitan town.

The Indians were less sanguine about the change of Europeans in their midst and about the trading practices of the British and French. In 1763, under the leadership of the Ottawa chief Pontiac, a bloody war was fought against European incursions, as tribes rose across the Northwest and into Pennsylvania. Many forts fell to the Indians, and they laid siege to Detroit for five months but were never successful in capturing it, nor were they able to take Fort Pitt in Pennsylvania. (It was at Fort Pitt that the Indians were given blankets infected with smallpox virus, which set off an epidemic among several tribes, an early example of the use of germ warfare to achieve genocide.) Pontiac's War ground to a halt with the onset of winter, increasing defections among his ranks, and, finally, with the refusal of many French to join the cause.

The British inherited warehouses full of furs at Detroit, and the fur trade flourished under their thirty-year rule. With the coming of the Revolutionary War, the civil officer at Detroit, Lieutenant Governor Henry Hamilton, organized Indian parties that embarked on lightning raids across Ohio, Kentucky, and Pennsylvania. His policy of paying the Indians for scalps earned him the designation "Hair Buyer," though scalps were taken on both sides.

The British clung to their western outposts for more than a decade after the Revolutionary War, finally leaving Detroit in 1796 under the terms of the Jay Treaty. A year before, the Treaty of Green Ville in Ohio had included terms for the Indians to cede their land in the environs of Detroit. American dominion of the city began in earnest, and in 1805 Detroit was named capital of Michigan Territory—the same year that it burned to the ground. Beginning with a clean slate, Judge Augustus Woodward, one of the administrators of the new territory, laid out the city along classical French lines like those of L'Enfant for Washington, DC.

The governor of Michigan Territory, General William Hull, did not take steps to defend Detroit from the British in 1812, even though he was well aware that hostilities were imminent, and he surrendered the city in August without a fight. After Oliver Hazard Perry's Lake Erie victory and several successes of his own, William Henry Harrison reoccupied the city a year later and established General Lewis Cass as military governor at Detroit. In the next twenty years, Cass negotiated virtually all the Indian treaties that transferred Michigan lands into American hands.

Fifty years of intermittent warfare, a cholera epidemic, and the decline of the fur trade had left Detroit in a sorry state. Furthermore, the town was far removed from the main wave of settlement that was occurring along the Ohio River. But a new pathway to the West opened in 1825 with the completion of the Erie Canal, which made travel time from Detroit to New York one-tenth of what it had been. New Englanders and New Yorkers began pouring into the city, while flour, grain, fish, and other commodities began making their way to markets in the Northeast. Detroit was changing from backwater town to busy metropolis. The decline of the fur trade in the 1830s paralleled a rise in the logging industry. With a ready source of lumber, Detroit emerged as a major shipbuilding center, and carpenter shops began turning out furniture, carriages, and other wood products. Mining in the Upper Peninsula, beginning in the 1840s, initiated copper and iron smelting in the city. Detroit also developed into an important railroad center in the 1840s and 1850s, with financier James F. Joy resurrecting the defunct state-owned railroad. Joy's Michigan Central became a crucial link between New York and Chicago, and the manufacturing of railway cars and bicycles became significant industries.

In the 1890s, many inventors and engineers in America were closely following automotive advances being made in France and Germany. And with the economic downturn of 1893 behind them, millionaires who had made their money in lumbering, railroads, and mining began backing the auto inventors. Detroit became the stage for much of the wheeling and dealing. In 1896 Detroiter Henry Ford, an Edison Electric Company engineer who spent his spare time experimenting with engines, drove his first motorized quadricycle nine miles, from Detroit to the family farmstead in Dearborn. A cast of ingenious Americans were ahead of him, but Ford's 1896 accomplishment is emblematic of the turn-of-the-century advances that would bring about nationwide upheavals in transportation, labor relations, and many other aspects of life.

The new auto factories in Detroit were manned mainly by immigrant laborers, many of whom had worked on the railroads or as "shanty boys" in the now declining lumber industry. Beginning in the 1840s, Germans had arrived in Detroit, followed by Irish (1845–1850), and finally Poles (mid–1870s), who became the city's largest ethnic group. The city's proximity to Canada had made it a major stop on the Underground Railroad before the Civil War, and a growing number of freed blacks had made their homes in Detroit. The nineteenth-century waves of immigrants were followed by others in the twentieth century.

Although the grandeur of Augustus Woodward's original city plan has been obliterated over the years, a vestige of it remains at the semicircular **Grand Circus Park,** where a number of thoroughfares converge. One of these spokes is Griswold Street, along which tower some of the early Detroit high-rises, including two by Daniel Burnham, the 1909 **Ford Building** (615 Griswold Street) and the 1910 **Dime Building** (719 Griswold Street). The 1886 **Bagley Memorial Fountain** (Woodward and Monroe avenues) is a granite pavilion with carved lion's-head fountains. It was designed by Henry Hobson Richardson and is the only work by the architect in the state. The **Old Mariner's Church** (170 East Jefferson Avenue) was established in the 1840s, when Detroit was a maritime city. The 1849 Gothic Revival structure remains an active Episcopal parish.

The **Museum of African–American History** (315 East Warren Avenue, 313–494–5800) was begun in a private home by Dr. Charles Wright in 1965. When it opened in a new location in 1997 it was acclaimed as the premier museum of black history in the United States. Exhibits trace the travails of American blacks as well as their many contributions to society. A model slave ship contains forty life-size figures of slaves, each modeled on a Detroit resident. The complex includes a theater, classrooms, and a library.

Pewabic Pottery (10125 East Jefferson Avenue, 313–822–0954) is a 1907 Arts and Crafts structure built for noted ceramicist Mary Chase Perry Stratton, whose glazed tiles became an important architectural element in buildings in the 1920s. A museum displays some of Stratton's ceramic work, drawings, and writing.

Albert Kahn, born in Westphalia, Germany, in 1869, was the son of an itinerant rabbi who immigrated to America in 1880. Beginning as a child apprentice in a Detroit architectural firm, Kahn went on to command a multimillion-dollar firm of his own, and his career was intertwined with virtually all of Detroit's automotive industrialists. Kahn designed their giant factories, which became models of industrial architecture, as well as their mansions,

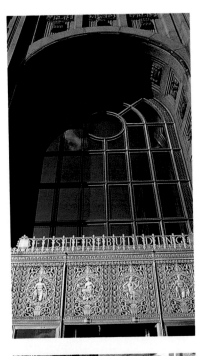

A delicate brass screen, above left, on Albert Kahn's 1928 Fisher Building in Detroit's New Center. The 1929 Guardian Building, above right, is decorated with colorful local Pewabic tiles. Its stepped roofline, left, echoes the stepped arches surrounding its lower windows. OVERLEAF: A detail from Diego Rivera's fresco cycle Detroit Industry, in the Detroit Institute of Arts. The murals record Rivera's fascination with Henry Ford's River Rouge Industrial Complex.

which were baronial. While many of his residences have been demolished, two that remain are the Edsel and Eleanor Ford House and George Booth's Cranbrook House. His landmark factories included the 1902 Packard plant, the 1914 Ford Highland Park plant, the 1917 Ford River Rouge plant, and the 1937 Chrysler Half Ton Truck facility. Most have either been torn down, abandoned, or greatly altered.

Two extant examples of his corporate architecture, and two of his finest works, stand facing each other on West Grand Boulevard between 2nd Avenue and Cass Street. They are the 1922 **General Motors Building** and the 1928 **Fisher Building.** When it was completed, the General Motors Building was the country's largest corporate office complex.

DETROIT INSTITUTE OF ARTS

The institute displays one of the most comprehensive art collections in the country, with works from ancient times to the modern era from around the world. Its holdings in American art are strong, particularly the collection of eighteenth- to early twentieth-century paintings. The artists represented here include John Singleton Copley, Benjamin West, Charles Willson Peale and other Peales, Frederic E. Church, James McNeill Whistler, and William Merritt Chase. The institute also has important collections of American silver, sculpture, and eighteenth-century furniture. An entire room is filled with a monumental, 27-panel mural by Diego Rivera depicting Detroit industry, based on the Ford Motor Company's River Rouge plant. The mural, which portrays the mechanization of life in a manner that is not always flattering, shows the industrial process from the removal of minerals from the earth to the creation of finished products.

LOCATION: 5200 Woodward Avenue. HOURS: 11–4 Wednesday–Friday, 11–5 Saturday–Sunday. FEE: Yes. TELEPHONE: 313–833–7900.

Across the street from the Institute, the **Detroit Public Library** (5201 Woodward Avenue, 313–833–1000) is housed in a Renaissance Revival Building designed by Cass Gilbert and completed in 1921. The building is adorned with remarkable sets of murals: a mosaic mural over the Cass entrance by Millard Sheets, depicting with allegorical figures the services of a library; allegorical murals by Edwin Blashfield around the Grand Stairway; historical murals by Gary Melchers in the exhibit hall; and the large "Spirit of Transportation" mural by John S. Coppin, also in the exhibit hall.

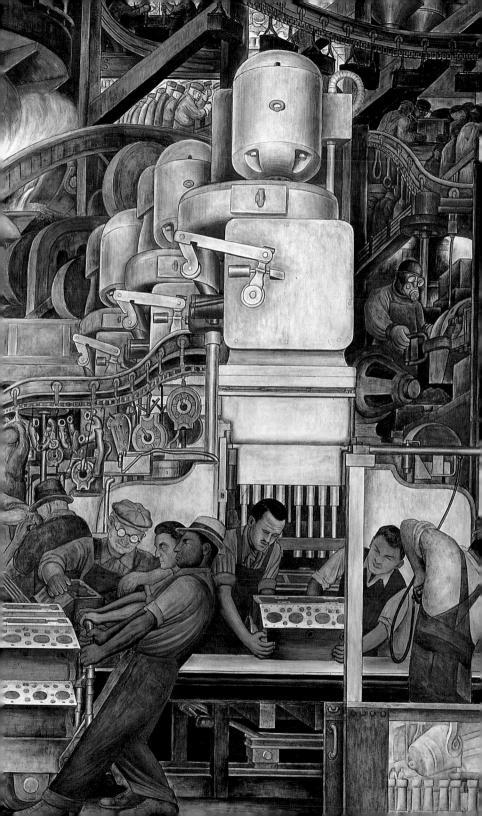

EASTERN FARMERS MARKET

Just northeast of the interchange of the Fisher and Chrysler freeways is the **Eastern Farmers Market** (Russell Street), first established as a hay and wood market in 1870. **Shed Number 2,** the oldest extant building, is a Victorian brick structure built in 1892. The **Detroit Historical Museum** (5401 Woodward Avenue, 313–833–1805) displays nineteenth-century period rooms, costumes, decorative arts, tools, and transportation and automotive items.

BELLE ISLE

In 1879 the city purchased this 1,000-acre island in the Detroit River and opened it as a public park, originally planned by Frederick Law Olmsted. It contains several structures designed by Albert Kahn, including the **Whitcomb Conservatory,** the **Aquarium,** and the **Livingstone Lighthouse.** Also on Belle Isle, the **Dossin Great Lakes Museum** (100 Strand, 313–267–6440) displays scale models of historic ships, including the 1679 *Griffon,* the first sailboat on the Great Lakes, and the 1818 *Walk-in-the-Water,* the first steamboat on the Great Lakes. It also exhibits nautical paintings and photographs, antique navigational instruments, and shipbuilding tools. One section of the museum houses the restored lounge of the 1912 luxury steamer *City of Detroit III*.

Overlooking the Detroit River and Belle Isle, the **Fisher Mansion** (383 Lenox Avenue, 313–331–6740) is one of several palatial estates of automotive magnates in the area. The rambling Spanish Eclectic structure was built in 1927 for Lawrence Fisher, a founder of Fisher Body Works. The opulent interior includes stone and marble work, hand-carved paneling, parquet floors, stained glass, and an array of furniture styles.

D E T R O I T   E N V I R O N S

During the French period the scenic shores of Lake Saint Clair were partitioned into ribbon farms, narrow strips of land that extended back a mile or so from the lake frontage. In the 1840s wealthy Detroit industrialists started building summer retreats along the lakeshore, taking up full-time residence with the advent of the automobile. The shore is divided into a series of villages that include **Grosse Pointe Park, Grosse Pointe, Grosse Pointe Farms** (the oldest of the communities, incorporated in 1879), **Grosse Pointe Woods,** and **Grosse Pointe Shores.**

EDSEL & ELEANOR FORD HOUSE

Overlooking Lake Saint Clair, the Edsel & Eleanor Ford House was the home of Henry Ford's only child and his wife and four children. Albert Kahn designed the compound of buildings to resemble the architecture of the Cotswolds in England. The mansion, completed in 1929, contains many interior fixtures from English estates. The original furnishings include eighteenth-century French pieces, four complete Art Deco rooms, and a collection of Old Master and Impressionist paintings. The tree-lined avenues and gardens were planned by the Fords with architect Jens Jensen.

LOCATION: 1100 Lake Shore Road, Grosse Pointe Shores. HOURS: April through December: Tours 12–4 Daily; January through March: Tours 1–4 Daily. FEE: Yes. TELEPHONE: 313–884–4222.

HISTORIC FORT WAYNE

Fort Wayne was built in the 1840s in response to border tensions between the United States and Canada, at a bend in the river downstream from Detroit. Captain Montgomery Meigs, later quartermaster general for the Union during the Civil War, drew up the preliminary plans. Named for General Anthony Wayne, the fort was completed in 1850 but not garrisoned until 1861, when it served as an inspection post and instruction camp.

An infantry detachment remained at the fort throughout the Civil War and from 1870 until the turn of the century. With its many dress parades, formal reviews, and military band concerts, Fort Wayne's most important nineteenth-century function was as a lively social center for Detroit. During World Wars I and II and up until the 1960s, when all military personnel were removed, the fort served variously as a motor supply depot, detention camp, induction center, military police battalion, and guided-missile repair site.

The twenty-two-foot scarp enclosing the fort was constructed in 1864 and has been restored, as have numerous structures within the compound. The 1848 limestone Georgian-style barracks

houses a museum of Detroit military history. The 1880 Victorian Post Commander's Residence contains period furnishings reflecting the lifestyle of a high-ranking post officer. Dating from the Spanish-American War period, the 1889 post guardhouse contains prison cells and an exercise yard. Because of budgetary reasons, Historic Fort Wayne was closed in the late 1990s, and no date for reopening had been announced. The **Great Lakes Indian Museum,** which had exhibited a variety of artifacts tracing the history of Michigan Indians from prehistoric times to the present, was housed in the 1906 married officers' quarters, and it was also closed. Adjacent is a 900-year-old **Indian burial ground.**

Also on the site, and open, the **Tuskegee Airmen Museum** has memorabilia of the first black aviation unit in World War II.

LOCATION: 6325 West Jefferson Avenue, in Detroit. TELEPHONE: *Historic Fort Wayne: 313–833–1805; Tuskegee Airmen Museum: 313–843–8849.*

DEARBORN

Dearborn lies on the River Rouge, the banks of which were subdivided into French ribbon farms in the eighteenth century. American settlers arrived in the area after the War of 1812, and several townships sprang up. Dearborn was a stop on the Chicago Road (today's Michigan Avenue) and later on the Michigan Central Railroad, guaranteeing it prosperity.

Another boost to the town's economy was the U.S. arsenal, a military facility built between 1822 and 1837 and active until 1875. Two extant structures from the arsenal are operated as museums by the **City of Dearborn Historical Museum** (915 Brady Street, 313–565–3000). The **commandant's quarters** (21950 Michigan Avenue), built in 1833, is a blend of Georgian, Federal, and Greek Revival styles. It contains exhibits depicting the arsenal era as well as period furnishings, Indian artifacts, costumes, and decorative arts. The **McFadden-Ross House** (915 Brady Street), originally the arsenal's powder magazine, was built in 1839.

OPPOSITE: *The Edsel & Eleanor Ford House, above, designed by the versatile Albert Kahn and completed in 1929. It incorporates many English architectural elements, including an early seventeenth-century stairway from Lyvedon Manor in Northamptonshire, which was placed in the entrance hall, below.*

The evolution of the automobile is one of the major themes explored at the twelve-acre Henry Ford Museum, whose collection of more than one million objects also includes entire railroad

Dearborn's biggest boom was induced by Henry Ford, who had been born and raised on a nearby farm. In 1915 Ford purchased 2,000 acres along the River Rouge for a vertically integrated superfactory. (At the time this land lay within the city of Fordson, which merged with Dearborn in 1928.) Completed in 1917, the River Rouge plant was a huge complex of assembly-line factories, coke ovens, and blast furnaces. Millions of Model Ts and Ford tractors were assembled here in the 1920s.

Eschewing and eschewed by most members of Detroit society, Henry Ford cloistered himself on his estate in Dearborn. He also chose Dearborn as the site of his museum, which he began planning in the 1920s.

Henry Ford Museum and Greenfield Village

The collections at this complex reflect their founder's profound interest in American ingenuity and his belief in America as a land of opportunity. They also preserve Ford's nostalgic remembrances

trains, airplanes, steam engines, printing presses, and farm machinery. The adjacent Green-field Village contains more than eighty historic buildings moved to the site.

of the rural, unmechanized America that he helped to change. Together the Henry Ford Museum and Greenfield Village form the largest indoor-outdoor museum in the country. The museum's facade is a facsimile of Philadelphia's Independence Hall; inside it contains some twelve acres of exhibits. The major theme of the museum is the American transition from a rural agricultural society to an urban, industrial one, including the cultural changes the car caused in the twentieth century. There is an exhibit of the machines that sparked the industrial revolution and displays of agricultural equipment, everyday home appliances, lighting devices, and communications-related equipment. Also displayed is a large collection of American furniture and decorative arts from the seventeenth to the twentieth centuries.

Adjacent to the museum is the eighty-one-acre Greenfield Village, an outdoor assemblage of historic structures. There are a village green typical of an early American town; several streets lined with historic homes that date from the seventeenth to the nineteenth centuries; a turn-of-the-century family arcade called

Suwanee Park; a cluster of nineteenth- and twentieth-century mills, and workshops; and a working nineteenth-century farm. In the 1920s Henry Ford began gathering together the structures where several of America's most famous inventors and luminaries had worked, lived, or were born, and it is these historic buildings for which Greenfield Village is best known. Thomas Edison's laboratory from Menlo Park, New Jersey, is included, as is the Sarah Jordan Boardinghouse, which stood across the street from Edison's lab. Home to several of Edison's employees, this residence was one of the first houses in America to be equipped with incandescent lighting. There are also Orville and Wilbur Wright's home and bicycle shop from Dayton, Ohio, where they built their first airplane; the 1840 Logan County Courthouse from Illinois, where Abraham Lincoln practiced law; the Noah Webster Home from New Haven, Connecticut, where the lexicographer worked on his first dictionary; the nineteenth-century Ohio farmhouse where tire magnate Harvey Firestone was born; and Henry Ford's birthplace, an 1860 white frame structure built by his father, William. The structures contain period furnishings, and craftspeople in period garb conduct demonstrations throughout Greenfield Village. Visitors can ride on a steamboat, a steam railroad, or in a Model T, or take a narrated tour in a horse-drawn carriage.

LOCATION: 20900 Oakwood Boulevard. HOURS: 9–5 Daily. FEE: Yes. TELEPHONE: 313–271–1620.

Fair Lane

Now located on the University of Michigan's Dearborn campus, Fair Lane was built in 1914 for Henry and Clara Ford on the River Rouge. Set amid extensive gardens, the rambling limestone structure with Prairie-style elements was designed by W. H. Van Tine and is furnished to the 1920s period. The powerhouse, which is still functional, supplied the estate with energy and was connected to the house by a 300-foot tunnel. The grounds were planned by landscape architect Jens Jensen. Clara Ford's extensive plantings at one time required the attention of twenty full-time gardeners. One of her rose gardens has been restored.

LOCATION: 4901 Evergreen Road. HOURS: April through December: 10–3 Monday–Saturday, 1–4:30 Sunday; Rest of year: Tour at 1 Monday–Friday, 1–4:30 Sunday. FEE: Yes. TELEPHONE: 313–593–5590.

In Troy the **Troy Museum and Historical Village** (60 West Wattles Road, 810–524–3570) preserves several nineteenth-century structures around a village green, including an 1820s log cabin, and an 1832 Greek Revival farmhouse, all with period furnishings. The museum, housed in a replica of a Dutch Colonial tavern, displays agricultural equipment, pioneer tools, and household items.

In **Rochester,** on the campus of Oakland University, **Meadow Brook Hall** (810–370–3140) is the lavish 100-room English Tudor style mansion of Alfred and Matilda Dodge Wilson. Matilda was the widow of auto magnate John Dodge. Completed in 1929, the house is profusely decorated with carved wood and ornamental plaster. Many original furnishings and art objects collected by the Wilsons are displayed. The two-story ballroom features carved gargoyles and stained glass.

Alfred and Matilda Dodge Wilson's Tudor-inspired Meadow Brook Hall, designed by William Kapp, has forty-two individually designed chimneys.

CRANBROOK HOUSE AND GARDENS

Located twenty-five miles northwest of Detroit in Bloomfield Hills, the Cranbrook House and Gardens is the former estate of George Gough Booth and Ellen Scripps Booth and their five children. A largely self-educated Canadian, Booth came to Detroit when he was 17 with his parents and nine siblings. He took an early interest in art, design, and architecture and for a while was a salesman and designer for an ornamental ironworks company. In Detroit he married Ellen Scripps, the daughter of the owner of the *Detroit Evening News*. Booth became publisher of that newspaper and a founder of the Booth newspaper chain. The Booths had far-ranging interests in art, education, family life, and philanthropy that led them to form the 325-acre **Cranbrook Educational Community** in the 1920s. This cultural center includes the Cranbrook Academy of Art and Cranbrook Institute of Science. Many of the buildings were designed by architect Eliel Saarinen in the early 1940s.

The Booth estate lies on forty acres of land within the Cranbrook Educational Community. Designed by Albert Kahn, the English manor house was built in 1908. The Booths were patrons of the Arts and Crafts movement in America, and the mansion contains many examples of furniture, pottery, woodcarving, and ironwork in that style as well as an eclectic assortment of European and Oriental furnishings and decorative arts. All the furnishings and effects in the house are original. The grounds include extensive plantings of trees, an array of gardens, outdoor sculpture, a Greek theater, and a reflecting pool.

LOCATION: 380 Lone Pine Road, Bloomfield Hills. HOURS: *House:* May through September: Tours at 11 and 1 Thursday. *Gardens:* May through August: 10–5 Monday–Saturday, 11–5 Sunday; September: 1–3 Daily; October: 11–3 Saturday–Sunday. FEE: Yes. TELEPHONE: 810–645–3149.

ANN ARBOR

On the banks of the Huron River, Ann Arbor is a trade center set amid orchard country and the home of the University of Michigan. The first settlers were two land speculators who arrived along the well-wooded stream in 1824 and began selling lots. They apparently christened their new town for their wives, both named Ann. The river provided ample mill sites, and within five years Ann Arbor had a population of a thousand. Ann Arbor was the scene of the political negotiations that resolved the so-called Toledo War, the boundary dispute between Ohio and Michigan that was concluded by giving Michigan the Upper Peninsula and Ohio the Toledo Bay area. This solution allowed Michigan to achieve statehood in 1837.

The 1853 **Kempf House** (312 South Division Street, 313–994–4898) is a white frame Greek Revival structure. Originally built for a prominent university official, it was later the home of musician Reuben Kempf and was a lively social center. The house contains Kempf's restored music studio, Victorian furnishings and decorative arts, and exhibits of nineteenth-century domestic life.

The **Ann Arbor Central Fire Station** (219 Huron Street, 313–995–5439), a charming Victorian brick structure built in 1883, now contains the **Ann Arbor Hands-On Museum.** It features participa-

The Univeristy of Michigan's Angell Hall, designed by Albert Kahn and completed in 1924, was named for a former president, James B. Angell. Eight Doric columns extend along the front of the building, which is 480 feet long.

tory science exhibits, as well as displays of artifacts found in the building, old photographs of the structure, and nineteenth-century firefighting equipment.

The **University of Michigan** occupies more than 1,300 acres. Structures of interest include the **School of Music** building designed by Eero Saarinen, the Gothic buildings of the **Law Quadrangle,** and the **Burton Memorial Tower.** The tower's fifty-five-bell Baird Carillon has bells ranging in weight from twenty-one pounds to twelve tons. The **William L. Clements Library** has collections of Americana, original manuscripts, maps, and rare books. The **Exhibit Museum of Natural History** encompasses a planetarium, dinosaurs and other fossils, and displays on biology, anthropology, and astronomy.

WALKER TAVERN AND CAMBRIDGE STATE HISTORIC PARK

Thirty-five miles southwest of Ann Arbor, the Walker Tavern sits amid a scenic area known as the Irish Hills. Built in 1832, the tavern was a busy inn and hostelry at the crossroads of the Detroit-Chicago Road (now Route 12) and the Monroe Pike (now Route 50). It contains 1840s period furnishings. The visitor center displays artifacts from Michigan's stagecoach era, and a reconstructed nineteenth-century barn houses old maps and a wheelwright shop.

LOCATION: Junction of Routes 12 and 50. HOURS: June through August: 11:30–4 Wednesday–Sunday. FEE: None. TELEPHONE: 517–467-4414.

MONROE

Monroe, at the mouth of the River Raisin, began as a French settlement in 1784 and was known as Frenchtown until 1817. The river and the town figured prominently in the War of 1812: The village surrendered on August 17, 1812, the day after Detroit fell to the British, but five months later American forces retook the outpost from a band of Canadians and Potawatomi Indians. The British, augmented by more Canadian soldiers and Indians, counterattacked and forced the American army to retreat. Half of the 400 American soldiers were killed and most of the remaining captured. Another 500 Kentucky militiamen, fighting successfully on a nearby front, nonetheless surrendered on the understanding that the wounded Americans would be protected. The British failed to uphold these terms, withdrawing quickly to tend to their own casualties and leaving the unarmed and wounded Americans to be massacred by Indians. The **River Raisin Battlefield Visitor Center** (1403 East Elm Street, 313–243–7137) has exhibits. By the 1820s Monroe had become a shipping center and port of entry for New Englanders pouring into the Midwest. The 1834 **Saint Mary Catholic Church** (10 West Elm Avenue) is the oldest Catholic church on the Lower Peninsula. Monroe was the boyhood home of General George Armstrong Custer, who lived here at the home of his stepsister until he was 16. In 1864 he returned briefly from the Civil War battlefront to marry his childhood sweetheart, Elizabeth Bacon, in the **First Presbyterian Church** (Washington and First streets). After the war he served mainly on the Western frontier and was killed in 1876 at the Battle of Little Bighorn in Montana. The **Custer Statue** (Monroe Street and Elm Avenue) was erected in 1910 to commemorate his role in the Gettysburg campaign. The **Monroe County Library** (3700 South Custer Road, 313–241–5277) issues permits to see Custer memorabilia at another branch. The **Monroe County Historical Museum** (126 South Monroe Street, 313–243–7137) stands on the site of the Judge Bacon residence, where Elizabeth Bacon grew up. (She wrote three highly popular books about her life with Custer, including the famous *Boots and Saddles* (1885), which did much to mythologize the controversial Indian fighter.) The museum contains exhibits about the Indians of the region, relics from the War of 1812, Custer memorabilia, pioneer tools and craftwork, and Victorian furnishings. Self-guided tour maps of the River Raisin Battle and massacre sites are also available. In addition, the museum also operates the **Navarre Anderson Trading Post and Country Store** (North Custer and Raisinville roads, 313–243–7137). One of Michigan's oldest extant structures, the trading post dates from 1789, when it was constructed by French settler Eutreau Navarre. It contains period furnishings and trade goods. The brick country store, built ca. 1860 as a schoolhouse, exhibits a collection of early twentieth-century store items.

WISCONSIN

OPPOSITE: *The allegorical frieze above the main door of Milwaukee's restored Grain Exchange shows Agriculture, at left, and Industry, at right, offering their bounty to two goddesses contemplating an early tickertape machine.*

Wisconsin lies in the large crook formed by Lake Superior and Lake Michigan, and it is bounded on the west by the Saint Croix and Mississippi rivers. Its interior is crisscrossed with many other navigable rivers and streams, of which the most significant historically is the Fox-Wisconsin riverway. Wisconsin's two earliest European settlements, Green Bay and Prairie du Chien, formed at the terminals of this waterway. And it was on the Fox-Wisconsin riverway that in 1673 Jesuit priest Jacques Marquette and explorer Louis Jolliet canoed in relative ease—there is only one portage on this route—to the Mississippi River. This discovery marked a turning point in the history of the continent, for on the heels of Marquette and Jolliet followed explorers, fur traders, missionaries, miners, loggers, and finally permanent European settlers. Equally important, their find established an inland link between the Saint Lawrence River and the Gulf of Mexico.

While roughly 80 percent of present-day Wisconsin was covered in forest in the 1700s, geological events had provided enough open spaces—deltas, savannahs, and alluvial terraces—to settle, and these often had convenient access to, and commanding views of, major confluences. Starting with Father Claude Allouez, Europeans established Green Bay along the banks of the broad Fox River. Agents of New York fur trader John Jacob Astor built their houses on 10,000-year-old Indian mounds overlooking the Mississippi at Prairie du Chien. Bayfield on Chequamegon Bay was built on a natural deep-water port with a view of the beautiful Apostle Islands. Sturgeon Bay grew up around the narrow isthmus, and expedient portage point, on the Door Peninsula. Milwaukee required a lot of Yankee—and German—ingenuity to settle, built as it was in a tamarack swamp.

Successive waves of newcomers were attracted by a landscape of overwhelming natural abundance, rich in fur-bearing animals, timber, fish, and fertile farmland, that had been already found fertile by many Native Americans. Seven nations—the Menominee, Ottawa, Ojibwa, Mesquakie, Winnebago, Potawatomi, and Sauk—were living in the vicinity of Green Bay during the main era of French occupation from 1720 to 1761. Wisconsin's current Indian population of some 25,000 people encompasses a greater variety of tribal provenances than any other state east of the Mississippi: three linguistic stocks, six broad tribal affiliations, and twelve distinct Indian societies.

An early view of a Menominee village in Wisconsin, published in France in 1838. PAGES
346–347: Southwestern Wisconsin's rolling terrain contains many small farms.

Because of genuine compatibility of trading interests the
French and, to a lesser extent, the British lived in relative accord
with the Indians. But the Americans were intent on owning land—
a concept foreign to Indians. The United States entered into a
series of treaties with the various Wisconsin tribes, all with the
intent of removing the Indians from the territory outright or
consolidating them onto portions of their ancestral lands.

There were local conflicts throughout the region, and two
battles were fought at Prairie du Chien during the War of 1812
between Americans and Indian tribes allied with the British. The
defeat of Chief Black Hawk in 1832, however, was the last Indian
conflict to take place on Wisconsin soil. Settlers from the East
began to pour into the area, while Southerners, as well as the
Cornish, continued to work the lead mines around Mineral Point
that had been developed much earlier by the Indians and French.
Though the American lead-mining boom was brief compared to
the long-standing fur trade, it explains why virtually uninhabited

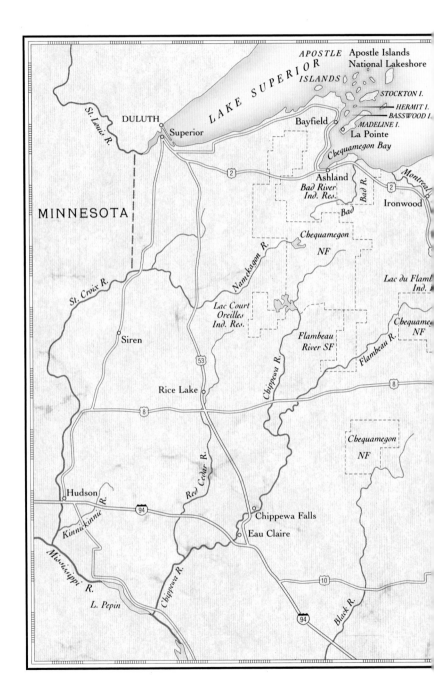

APOSTLE Apostle Islands
ISLANDS National Lakeshore

LAKE SUPERIOR

STOCKTON I.
HERMIT I.
BASSWOOD I.
MADELINE I.

St. Louis R.

DULUTH

Superior

Bayfield

La Pointe

Chequamegon Bay

Montreal

MINNESOTA

2

Ashland

Bad River
Ind. Res.

Bad R.

Bad

Ironwood

Chequamegon
NF

Lac du Flam
Ind.

Namekagon R.

St. Croix R.

Lac Court
Oreilles
Ind. Res.

Chequame
NF

Siren

53

Flambeau
River SF

Chippewa R.

Flambeau R.

8

Rice Lake

8

Chequamegon
NF

Red Cedar R.

Hudson

94

Kinnickinnic R.

Chippewa Falls

Eau Claire

Mississippi R.

10

L. Pepin

Chippewa R.

94

Black R.

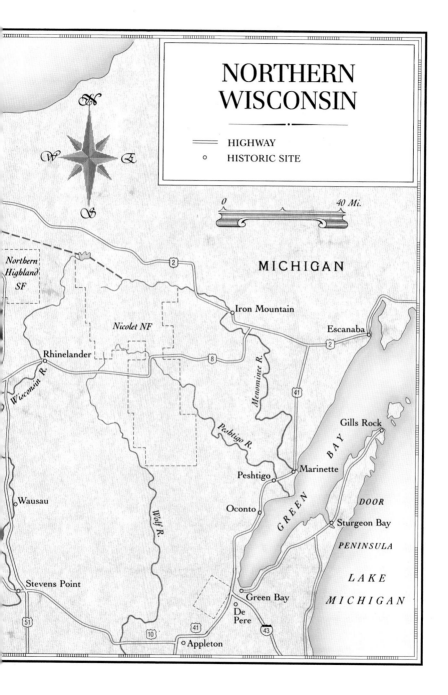

NORTHERN WISCONSIN

HIGHWAY

○ HISTORIC SITE

0 — 40 Mi.

N
W E
S

MICHIGAN

Northern
Highland
SF

2

Iron Mountain

Nicolet NF

Escanaba

2

Rhinelander

8

Menominee R.

41

Wisconsin R.

Peshtigo R.

Gills Rock

BAY

Peshtigo

Marinette

DOOR

Wausau

Oconto

GREEN

Sturgeon Bay

PENINSULA

Wolf R.

LAKE

Stevens Point

MICHIGAN

51

Green Bay

De
Pere

41

10

43

Appleton

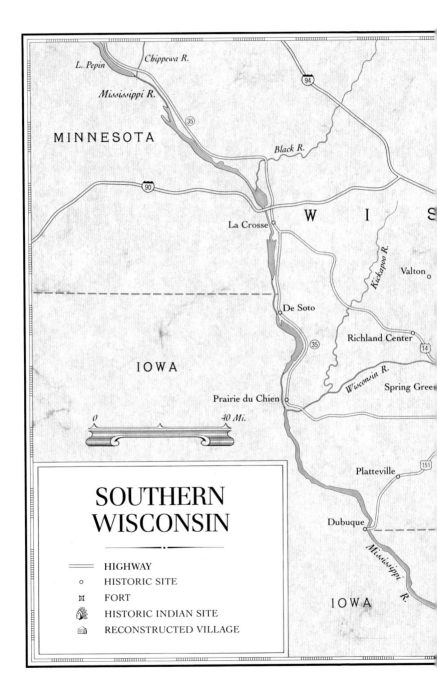

L. Pepin

Chippewa R.

Mississippi R.

MINNESOTA

Black R.

WIS

Kickapoo R.

Valton

La Crosse

De Soto

Richland Center

IOWA

Wisconsin R.

Spring Green

Prairie du Chien

0   40 Mi.

Platteville

SOUTHERN WISCONSIN

Dubuque

Mississippi R.

IOWA

═══ HIGHWAY
○   HISTORIC SITE
Ħ   FORT
🪶   HISTORIC INDIAN SITE
🏠   RECONSTRUCTED VILLAGE

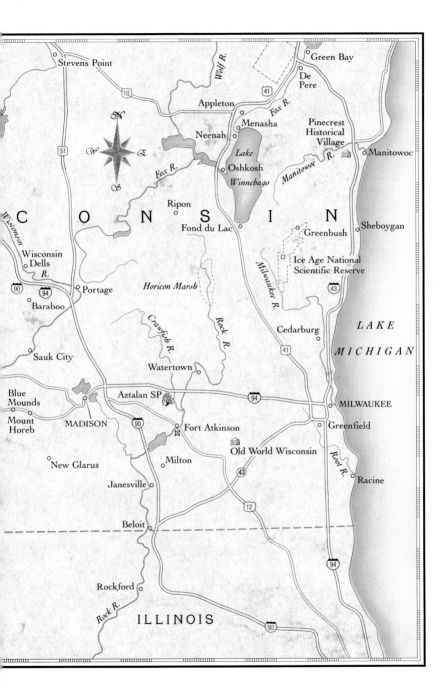

land in this area was selected as capital of the new territory. With lead mining and land speculation its main economic preoccupations, Wisconsin was admitted to the Union in 1848.

Corn and wheat became the next sources of wealth. During the last half of the nineteenth century, and concurrent with the wheat-growing era, the lumbering of white and red pine was going full tilt in Wisconsin's North Woods. The coming of the railroads allowed for the logging of ever more remote stands of forest. As trees were felled, farmers planted the cleared land with wheat.

Having early exhausted many of its natural resources, Wisconsin shaped some of the country's leading conservationists. In 1849 John Muir's family immigrated from Scotland, settling in the rocky hills of south-central Wisconsin. At Muir's urging, his brother set aside a portion of the farm as a sanctuary in 1865, the first in the state. Later Muir founded the Sierra Club and helped to preserve Yosemite and the Grand Canyon.

This chapter begins in the northeast corner of the state, where the era of French fur trading centered in Green Bay was followed by intense logging of the pine forests north of the bay. This section also includes the scenic Door Peninsula and the lakeshore city of Manitowoc, as well as the paper-mill towns that grew up around the state's largest lake, Lake Winnebago. The chapter then moves to southeastern Wisconsin. This section covers the remains of an ancient Indian city at Aztalan, the state's largest historical museum at Old World Wisconsin, mill towns in the beautiful Rock River Valley, and Milwaukee and the other industrial port cities along Lake Michigan. The third section deals with southwestern Wisconsin, a region that is often called the Driftless Area because its ancient geology was never buried by glaciers. Here we encounter the venerable old fur-trading town of Prairie du Chien along the banks of the Mississippi, the lead-mining era of Mineral Point, the final battles of the Black Hawk War, the birthplace of Ringling Brothers Circus, and the gracious state capital at Madison. The final section covers the northwestern portion of the state, including the river valleys of the Chippewa and Saint Croix, an area whose history was shaped by the fur trade and logging industry, as well as Superior, the splendid Apostle Islands, and the towns on Chequamegon Bay, all on Lake Superior.

OPPOSITE: *Widespread logging throughout Wisconsin cleared the terrain for wheat farming, which in turn gave way to dairy farming after cinch bugs destroyed the wheat crop.*

NORTHEASTERN WISCONSIN

PESHTIGO

On the night of October 8, 1871, at the same time that Chicago was burning to the ground, an immense fire swept across 2,400 square miles of drought-stricken forest in northeastern Wisconsin, cutting a swath around Green Bay and up the Door Peninsula. It was the greatest forest fire disaster in American history. Approximately a thousand people were killed, most of them in or near the sawmill town of Peshtigo. The disaster led to improved methods of fire protection in government and the lumbering industry.

The **Peshtigo Fire Museum** (400 Oconto Avenue, 715–582–3244), housed in the first church built in the town after the fire, contains documents and artifacts pertaining to the conflagration as well as a period kitchen, schoolroom, drugstore, and blacksmith shop. Adjoining the museum is the **Peshtigo Fire Cemetery,** where victims of the disaster are interred, including 350 unidentified persons buried in a mass grave.

In the vicinity of Peshtigo, the **Marinette County Historical Museum** (Route 41 on Stephenson Island, 715–732–0831) in Marinette, and the **Beyer Home Museum and Annex of Oconto County Historical Society** (917 Park Avenue, 414–834–3860) in Oconto have excellent exhibits of northeastern Wisconsin history, focusing on the Late Archaic (3000 to 1000 B.C.) Indians of northern Wisconsin, who were distinguished for the making of copper implements, and on the logging industry in the area. The 1868 Beyer Home also has a display of antique vehicles.

GREEN BAY

The river flowing into this long, narrow bay provided a natural passage into the interior for natives, missionaries, and explorers. The first white man to come here, in 1634, was the French explorer Jean Nicolet, sent by Samuel de Champlain to find a route to China. Much to the astonishment of the Indians, he embarked wearing a damask robe, meant to impress the mandarins he hoped to encounter. In 1669 the French Jesuit Claude Allouez arrived at the mouth of this river, now called the Fox, to open a mission for the numerous tribes of Indians living in the region. It was a hub of exchange between Indians and French until it closed in 1728.

The French called the area La Baye Verte, for the greenish cast of the water at certain seasons. Its interior access helped it become a major fur-trading post. The Sauk and Mesquakie, who provoked hostilities with the newcomers, were routed by 1731 and were soon replaced by the Potawatomi and Menominee, who were more interested in trading with the Europeans. Green Bay became Wisconsin's first permanent settlement with the arrival in 1745 of the fierce and patriarchal Charles de Langlade, known as the "Father of Wisconsin." The area passed to England after the French and Indian War, and then to the United States following the Revolution. After the War of 1812 the United States sought in earnest to secure the Northwest. In 1816 Fort Howard was established on the west bank of the Fox River, and the American Fur Company, under the command of its shrewd general manager, Ramsay Crooks, soon overpowered the local traders.

The Black Hawk War in 1832 prompted construction of the Military Road between Green Bay and Prairie du Chien. This highway, roughly following the Fox-Wisconsin waterway, encouraged interior settlement in the Wisconsin Territory and was the progenitor of the overland transportation system that finally supplanted river travel.

The 1910 **Brown County Courthouse** (100 South Jefferson Street), a large dressed-stone Beaux Arts structure, is perhaps the most handsome public building in the county.

Heritage Hill State Park

Overlooking the Fox River, this forty-eight-acre historical park contains several of Wisconsin's most important historic structures, including the **Roi-Porlier-Tank Cottage,** one of the oldest extant buildings in Wisconsin and home to several prominent Green Bay families. It is a rare example of French-style architecture in the Great Lakes, its central portion built by the French method of vertical log construction, or *poteaux-et-pièces-en-coullisant.* A 1762 French fur trader's cabin, built of huge cedar logs in a horizontal method of French construction called *pièce-sur-pièce,* contains pelts of beaver, otter, and fox and the items the Indians received in exchange for the furs, such as blankets and tobacco.

Green Bay's Heritage Hill State Park represents the development of northeastern Wisconsin with twenty-two historic structures, including a 1762 fur trader's cabin, opposite.

The **Henry S. Baird Law Office,** the oldest law office west of the Great Lakes, is also on the site. The simple Greek Revival structure was built in 1831 and used between 1837 and 1865 by Baird, an attorney who was active in territorial and Green Bay politics. Other structures in the park include the 1834 **Fort Howard Hospital** and **Fort Howard Company Barracks Kitchen,** an 1870s **Door County Belgian Farmstead,** an 1881 **Victorian bandstand,** the 1897 **DeWitt Blacksmith Shop,** and a replica of a **Catholic bark chapel** used by early Jesuit missionaries.

LOCATION: 2640 South Webster Avenue. HOURS: Memorial Day through Labor Day: 10–4:30 Tuesday–Saturday, 12–4:30 Sunday; 12–4:30 September weekends. FEE: Yes. TELEPHONE: 414–448–5150.

The large, modern **Neville Public Museum of Brown County** (210 Museum Place, 414–448–4460) contains extensive natural-history and cultural exhibits running from Wisconsin's Ice Age to the present. It has collections of anthropology, archaeology, geology, and mineralogy, and historical negatives and photographs. Among its many Green Bay relics is the sacramental chalice presented by

French commandant Nicolas Perrot to the Mission Xavier in 1686. The silver chalice, buried when the mission was burned by Indians in 1687, was accidentally rediscovered in 1802.

Hazelwood is a distinguished Greek Revival house overlooking the Fox River, built in 1837 for Yankee entrepreneur Morgan L. Martin and his wife, Elizabeth. Martin was instrumental in drafting the state constitution and guiding Wisconsin to statehood in 1848. The house contains many original furnishings and numerous nineteenth-century paintings, including an 1856 portrait of the Martins' children done by the English painters Samuel M. Brookes and Thomas H. Stevenson.

The small white frame building known as **White Pillars** (403 North Broadway, De Pere, 414–336–3877) overlooks the De Pere rapids on the Fox River, site of Saint Francis Xavier Mission. Built in 1836, it served many functions—a land company, casket factory, store, lawyer's office—and housed Wisconsin's first bank, set up by speculators gambling on rapid expansion in the area with the construction of a dam at the rapids in 1836. It contains artifacts pertaining to local history, including a large photographic collection.

The Menominee Indians ceded some of their land in the 1820s to the uprooted Oneida Indians, who were once part of the Iroquois Confederacy living in the vicinity of New York state. West of Green Bay, in the suburb of De Pere, is the **Oneida Nation Museum** (886 EE Road, 414–869–2768), the largest repository of Oneida history and artifacts. It contains clothing, ceremonial garb, and tools. On the grounds is a reconstructed Oneida bark longhouse within a stockaded village.

DOOR PENINSULA

The 85-mile-long Door Peninsula juts into Lake Michigan, forming the thumb of Wisconsin, and includes 250 miles of shoreline on Lake Michigan and Green Bay. It takes its name from the dangerous channel at the tip of the peninsula called by the French Porte des Morts, or Death's Door. A scenic area of rocky coves and small fishing villages reminiscent of the New England coast, it has numerous cherry, apple, plum, and pear orchards.

Sturgeon Bay, the largest community in Door County, is located on an isthmus. Early travelers in the area, including Father Jacques Marquette and Father Claude Allouez in the 1670s, portaged here to avoid the time-consuming and often dangerous 100-mile trip around the peninsula's tip. In 1878 construction was completed on a canal to facilitate travel across the isthmus and its expansion in 1882 to accommodate commercial navigation prodded growth in Sturgeon Bay.

The **Door County Maritime Museum** (101 Florida Street, 414–743–6246) is housed in the former Roen Steamship Company building. The museum displays artifacts detailing the area's maritime heritage, including ship building and commercial fishing, as well as maritime commerce and transportation. A branch of the museum, in Gills Rock (414–854–1844), at the tip of the peninsula, includes the Cana Island Lighthouse among its facilities.

The **Door County Historical Museum** (Fourth and Michigan streets, 414–743–5809) houses more than 5,000 artifacts and exhibits. One wing resembles a turn-of-the-century fire station, complete with a bell tower, fireman's pole, and several antique fire trucks. Another wing contains a shipbuilding exhibit, an old-time grocery store, a doctor's office, a dressmaker's shop, and a music store complete with old phonographs.

On Rock Island, accessible by ferry from Washington Island, are several buildings constructed by entrepreneur Chester H. Thordarson to recall his Icelandic heritage.

Perched on cliffs above Green Bay is **The Clearing** (Garret Bay Road, in Ellison Bay, 414–854–4088), the summer home and school of landscape architect Jens Jensen. He used indigenous plants and materials in designing landscapes. One-week courses ("clearing the mind") are offered in the arts, nature, and humanities.

Tiny **Rock Island** lies across the Porte des Morts Strait. Reputedly, Wisconsin's first white visitor, the French explorer Jean Nicolet, stopped here in 1634. The island contains many sites associated with various Great Lakes Indians and with the French exploration and fur-trading era, including the massive stone **Viking Hall,** built by Icelandic-born entrepreneur and inventor Chester H. Thordarson when he owned the island between 1910 and 1945. It now houses nature and photographic exhibits. Also on the island is the **Potawatomi Lighthouse,** the first light station in Wisconsin, built in 1837. The current structure was erected in 1858 after the original was washed away. Most of the island is now **Rock Island State Park** (414–847–2235).

MANITOWOC

Manitowoc, situated at the mouth of the Manitowoc River where the river enters Lake Michigan, was known in the nineteenth century as the Clipper City for the superior schooners its shipyards produced. Submarines and landing craft were manufactured here until the advent of bulk carriers in the 1960s when shipbuilding declined because the Manitowoc River was not large enough to accommodate the launching of such huge vessels. The **Wisconsin Maritime Museum** (75 Maritime Drive, 414–684–0218) records over a hundred years of Great Lakes maritime history from early sailing ships to World War II submarines and displays salvage artifacts from sunken ships, models of Great Lakes vessels, historical manuscripts, and 20,000 photographs of Great Lakes maritime activity. There is a full-scale reproduction of the midship section of the nineteenth-century schooner *The Clipper City,* and the 1943 submarine USS *Cobia* is moored next to the museum.

Five miles west of Manitowoc is **Pinecrest Historical Village** (924 Pinecrest Lane, 414–684–5110), more than twenty historic buildings—log cabins, a schoolhouse, general store, bank, machine shed, sawmill, and train depot among them—which have been furnished to depict life in the area around 1900.

OPPOSITE: *Chester H. Thordarson's Viking Hall on Rock Island now contains nature and photographic exhibits.*

LAKE WINNEBAGO AREA

At 215 square miles, Lake Winnebago is the largest body of water in Wisconsin. Fed and drained by the Fox River, it was an important portion of the Fox-Wisconsin riverway, the region's early transportation system. In 1670 Father Claude Allouez said mass to the Indians near present-day Oshkosh. By the 1830s farmers were moving into the area, coming upstream on the Fox River from Green Bay to work the rich agricultural lands that ring the lake.

Neenah and **Menasha** are twin cities lying on opposite sides of the channel that drains Lake Winnebago into the north-flowing Fox River. Immigrant factory workers settled in Menasha and built small neat cottages, while Neenah was home to wealthy landowners and financiers who lived in large mansions. On the island in the middle of the channel is the **Doty Cabin** (414–751–4614). Land speculator and politician James Duane Doty made this rustic log cabin, which he called the Grand Loggery, his permanent home in 1845 after his term as Wisconsin's second territorial governor.

Edwin H. Galloway purchased an 1847 Fond du Lac house in 1868 and remodeled it into this thirty-room Italianate mansion.

Fond du Lac, at the south end of Lake Winnebago, flourished in the mid-nineteenth century as a sawmill town and as an important hub for overland traffic. The **Galloway House and Village** (336 Old Pioneer Road, 414–922–6390), operated by the Fond du Lac County Historical Society, features an ornate 1847 Victorian mansion with carved woodwork, stenciled ceilings, and original furnishings. Other nineteenth-century structures on the site include a one-room school, courthouse and law office, print shop, blacksmith shop, and gristmill.

Greenbush was the main overland stop between Fond du Lac and Sheboygan. In 1851 Sylvanus Wade and his son-in-law Charles Robinson built a gracious three-story inn here to serve passersby. Now the **Old Wade House and Wesley W. Jung Carriage Museum** (W7747 Plank Road, off of Route 23, 414–526–3271), it preserves the history of tavern life and overland transportation in Wisconsin prior to the coming of the railroads. The interior, which includes a taproom and ballroom, is furnished with items typical of the period, many original to the inn. Also on the premises is a blacksmith shop and the restored home of Charles Robinson, **Butternut House,** named for the sumptuous butternut woodwork in the interior. The carriage museum contains 100 restored wagons, buggies, buckboards, phaetons, and other carriage types from the period 1870 to 1915, many made in nearby Sheboygan.

In 1844 **Ripon** (twenty miles west of Fond du Lac) was home to a brief experiment in socialized agriculture when followers of socialist François-Marie-Charles Fourier started a farm which they called Ceresco, for Ceres, the Roman goddess of agriculture. They disbanded in 1850 when the tide of settlement increased the value of their land. The town was also a stronghold of abolitionism. On March 20, 1854, Alvan Earle Bovay of Ripon called a meeting of antislavery members of various political parties to organize a single unified party. They met in response to the recent passage in Congress of the slavery-expanding Kansas-Nebraska Act. This gathering, which met in the **Little White Schoolhouse** (303 Blackburn Street, 414–748–4730), was one of the first—if not the first— grassroots coalitions that led to the formation of the national Republican Party in 1856 in Pittsburgh. The Greek Revival schoolhouse was moved to its present site in the 1950s. It is now a museum with Republican presidential memorabilia, pioneer tools, and furnishings. The **Ripon Historical Society** (508 Watson Street, 414–748–5354) maintains archives, costumes, and manuscripts pertaining to local history.

Aztalan was the site of a ca. 1075–1300 Middle Mississippian stockaded village, the only such

SOUTHEASTERN WISCONSIN

HORICON MARSH

Fifty miles northwest of Milwaukee is the largest freshwater cattail marsh in the United States, the 32,000-acre Horicon Marsh. A retreat for hunters, trappers, fishermen, and naturalists, it is perhaps best known for the 200,000 Canada geese that linger to feed in the marsh every spring and fall.

Horicon is an extinct glacial lake. At the close of the Wisconsin Ice Age, the basin filled with glacial meltwater. This large, shallow lake slowly filled with sediment, and as the glacial moraine that held back the water eroded, the lake drained, leaving behind this marsh. Since the arrival of European settlers, its history has mirrored conflicting ideas of land use. Its restoration as a refuge is a case study in the evolution of a conservation ethic and of wildlife management techniques.

site in Wisconsin. Several truncated mounds and stockaded sections have been restored.

In 1846 settlers dammed the marsh, changing it back into a lake. Lawsuits forced the removal of the dam in 1869, after which the area reverted to marsh. For several decades recreational and commercial hunting were the primary activities. In the early 1900s, a drainage project was attempted to convert the marsh to farmland. In the 1920s conservationists organized to restore the marsh to make it hospitable to wildlife through land acquisition and the building of a dam to reflood the area. By 1941 the federal government had bought the remainder of the marsh to establish a national wildlife refuge.

Today the northern two-thirds is administered by the U.S. Fish and Wildlife Service (414–387–2658), the southern third by the Wisconsin Department of Natural Resources as a state wildlife area. This area is also part of the **Ice Age National Scientific Reserve** (1210 North Palmatory Street, 414–387–7860) and offers nature interpretation programs.

The Wisconsin Glaciation, spanning a period from about 100,000 to 10,000 years ago, was a time when massive ice sheets advanced and retreated across northern North America. Since the Wisconsin landscape carries the most dramatic reminders of this period on the continent, the National Park Service, the Wisconsin Department of Natural Resources, and private organizations have established parks and an extensive system of trails across the state where drumlins (elongated hills), kames (conical mounds), eskers (serpentine ridges), and other vestiges of the glaciers can be seen. The Ice Age National Scenic Trail, when complete, will be a 1,000-mile hiking trail that follows the terminal moraine of the Wisconsin Glaciation. Approximately half of the trail is finished.

AZTALAN STATE PARK

Aztalan is an ancient Indian settlement on the banks of the Crawfish River, now within the confines of a state park. The Middle Mississippian group, who were active between A.D. 800 and 1500, just prior to historic contact, occupied Aztalan from 1075 to 1300, making it the northernmost Middle Mississippian site yet discovered and the only one representative of this group in Wisconsin.

The largest structure at Aztalan is a two-level truncated pyramid forty feet wide and twenty-five feet high. The flat top provided a site for a wooden palisaded residence or temple. The people who settled here probably migrated north from Cahokia, the large Middle Mississippian city in Illinois. They were farmers who also hunted, fished, and gathered mussels in the nearby river.

LOCATION: Off Route 89 via Routes B and Q southwest of Watertown. HOURS: April 15 through October: 7–Dusk Daily. FEE: None. TELEPHONE: 414–648–8774.

WATERTOWN

Watertown was founded in the 1830s by a group of New Englanders to take advantage of a particularly steep gradient in the Rock River; the river drops twenty feet in two miles. Beginning in the 1850s, the town became an intellectual center for German students and professionals escaping political upheaval. Its best-known and most outspoken citizens were Carl and Margarethe Meyer Schurz. He was an abolitionist and supporter of the new Republican Party. After serving in the Civil War, Schurz became an

OPPOSITE: *Watertown's fifty-seven-room Octagon House contains original family furnishings. The miniature version in the foreground was built for a local parade.*

influential politician and writer who promoted high moral standards in government and civil service reform, helping to lead both the Liberal Republican Party and the Mugwumps. Margarethe Schurz introduced the Froebelian method of teaching young children to the United States and in 1856 organized the first kindergarten in America. The building where she taught was moved from downtown Watertown to the grounds of the **Octagon House** (919 Charles Street, 414–261–2796). The interior, a living room used as a classroom, is filled with period furniture and mannequins portraying a kindergarten class in progress.

The Octagon House itself was built in 1854 by John Richards, who came to Watertown from Massachusetts in 1837. It is a very large five-story brick structure, perhaps the largest family residence in pre–Civil War Wisconsin, with Italianate decorative elements and a two-story wraparound verandah. The interior contains original furnishings from the Richards family and a splendid cantilevered hanging spiral staircase rising from the first floor to the cupola, or lantern, atop the house—the home has a commanding view of the Rock River and the dam where Richards operated a gristmill, linseed oil mill, and sawmill.

FORT ATKINSON

Fort Atkinson was named for General Henry Atkinson, who in 1832 threw up a hasty stockade here at the confluence of the Rock and Bark rivers, while in pursuit of Chief Black Hawk. The town was home to the influential editor and politician William Dempster Hoard, who in the 1870s launched the dairy industry in Wisconsin in an effort to wean farmers away from the soil-depleting practice of growing wheat. He organized the Wisconsin Dairyman's Association and published the widely read *Hoard's Dairyman*. The **Hoard Historical Museum and Dairy Shrine** (407 Merchants Avenue, 414–563–7769) has exhibits and artifacts relating to the dairy industry, local Indian history, and the events surrounding the Black Hawk War. A remnant of the area's ancient history is preserved in the **Panther Intaglio Effigy** (Route 106 at the western edge of Fort Atkinson). Rather than being heaped earth, this effigy mound is incised in the ground. It is a shallow excavation 125 feet long and 35 feet wide thought to resemble a panther. Dating from about A.D. 1000, it is one of only two surviving.

MILTON HOUSE

The town of Milton was a stopover on the road from Chicago to Madison. In 1844 Joseph Goodrich built Milton House as a stagecoach inn. The hexagonal building was constructed of concrete, making it an early example of the rediscovery of concrete, first used by the Romans, as a building material. Orson Squire Fowler credited Goodrich with introducing the idea to him—and through him to the nation. Now a museum, the house contains nineteenth-century pioneer items, Civil War artifacts, period costumes, and tools. On the grounds are the Goodrich family's 1837 log cabin, livery stable, buggy shed, country store, and blacksmith shop. Goodrich was an abolitionist, and the tunnel connecting the inn to the family's log cabin is thought to have harbored slaves escaping to Canada.

LOCATION: 18 South Janesville Street. HOURS: Memorial Day weekend through Labor Day: 10–5 Daily; May and September through mid-October: 10–5 Saturday–Sunday. FEE: Yes. TELEPHONE: 608–868–7772.

JANESVILLE

Janesville was named for the peripatetic Henry F. Janes, who arrived here in 1836 and founded other Janesvilles in Iowa and Minnesota before heading to the Pacific Coast. Janesville grew from a ferry crossing and stagecoach stop to an industrial city in the 1920s. The **Tallman House** (440 North Jackson Street, 608–752–4519) is an opulent Italian villa built by W. M. Tallman, a New York–born attorney and ardent abolitionist who made his fortune as a perfume maker and land speculator. In 1855 he was in a financial position to build one of America's most impressive examples of the style. The mansion had running water, indoor privies, and central heat. Tallman's home was on the Underground Railroad, and Abraham Lincoln visited here on a campaign swing through Wisconsin in 1859. The house now contains nineteenth-century decorative arts and furnishings, the George Kemp Tallman weapons collection, and the Tallman ethnological collection. On the grounds are the original horse barn and the 1842 Greek Revival Stone House, moved to the site. The Tallman House is operated by the **Rock County Historical Society** (10 South High Street, 608–756–4509), which maintains a museum of local history at its headquarters.

OLD WORLD WISCONSIN

Thirty-five miles southwest of Milwaukee is Old World Wisconsin, a 576-acre outdoor museum displaying the homes, farms, churches, business places, and other structures constructed by the major ethnic groups that settled Wisconsin in the nineteenth century. The State Historical Society relocated fifty historic pioneer buildings from around Wisconsin and arranged them to depict the folkways of these cultures at different periods in the state's development. Special events and demonstrations by costumed guides focus on important aspects of life in Wisconsin from the early nineteenth to the early twentieth century.

A Crossroads Village reflects the Yankee influence in Wisconsin, including the Harmony Town Hall, an 1876 frame building used for local government meetings, an institution introduced by Yankee settlers. The German Area consists of three farmsteads originally located in parts of southeastern Wisconsin. The Schulz

Immigrant lifestyles are reflected in the nineteenth-century structures at Old World Wisconsin, including a school used by Norwegian settlers on Lake Superior before 1914 and, opposite, a restored bedroom from a German farm.

Farm area portrays grain farming techniques in the 1860s; the Koepsell Farm demonstrates horse-powered dairy farming in the 1880s. The Schulz and Koepsell houses are fine examples of German *fachwerk* (half-timber) construction. The Norwegian Area has two farmsteads and a school, which have been gathered from throughout Wisconsin. The Fossebrekke Farm area is a subsistence-level pioneer farm dependent on wheat growing and trapping in the 1840s. In contrast is the Kavaale Farm, which demonstrates a prosperous, well-established, diversified farm of the 1860s. It includes a corncrib, two barns, granary, and summer kitchen. There are also Danish and Finnish areas.

LOCATION: Route 67, 1.5 miles south of Eagle. HOURS: May–June and September–October: 10–4 Monday–Friday, 10–5 Saturday–Sunday; July–August: 10–5 Daily. FEE: Yes. TELEPHONE: 414–594–6300.

BELOIT

Like many towns in the Midwest, Beloit was settled by a group of townspeople relocating virtually in toto from a New England community. In 1837 the New England Emigrating Company brought many citizens from Colebrook, New Hampshire, who quickly left a cultured and refined stamp on the little Rock River community. In 1846 seven Yale graduates founded **Beloit College,** hence its nickname "Yale of the West." The **Logan Museum** (608–363–2677) on campus, founded in 1892, houses Paleolithic artifacts as well as an extensive Native American collection.

The **Hanchett-Bartlett Homestead** (2149 Saint Lawrence Avenue, 608–365–7835) is operated by the Beloit Historical Society. A pioneer Yankee contractor and builder of dams, James Hanchett came to Beloit in 1840 and built dams in Indiana, Illinois, and Wisconsin, including the first dam across the Rock River at Beloit in 1844. Using locally quarried limestone, he built this house in 1857 for his wife and ten children. The house was constructed in a transitional Greek Revival–Italianate style and has been restored to its period colors. On the grounds are the original stone barn and smokehouse and a restored rural schoolhouse. The **First Congregational Church** (801 Bushnell Street, 608–362–4821), built by noted area architect Lucas Bradley in 1859, is a brick structure with Greek Revival elements.

CEDARBURG

This German and Irish mill town, now a suburb of Milwaukee, grew up in the 1840s along the banks of fast-flowing Cedar Creek. Many of the immigrants' homes and businesses, built of Niagara limestone from local quarries, are still standing along Washington Avenue, the town's main street. The 1855 **Cedarburg gristmill** (N58 W6181 Columbia Road), an immense five-story structure, is one of the finest extant mills in the Midwest. Area residents gathered in this fortresslike building during the 1862 Dakota uprising. The **Cedarburg Woolen Mill** (N70 W6340 Bridge Road) was built during the Civil War. The Cedarburg Chamber of Commerce (W63 N645 Washington Avenue, 414–377–9620) publishes a self-guided walking tour of buildings.

MILWAUKEE

Milwaukee grew up around three rivers—the Milwaukee, Menomonee, and Kinnickinnic—that converged in marshland and a tamarack swamp fronting Lake Michigan. The swamp has long been filled, and the lakefront merges almost imperceptibly with what used to be distinct high bluffs ringing the marshland. A **plaque** on the Marc Plaza Hotel (corner of Wisconsin Avenue and Fifth Street) commemorates a Potawatomie village, situated by a wild rice swamp, that existed on the site until the Indians were evacuated in 1838. Other Indians living in the vicinity when the first French traders arrived included Sauk, Mesquakie, Ojibwa, Winnebago, Ottawa, and Menominee.

An 1833 treaty with the Indians in Chicago and one signed in Washington in 1831 opened this area to white speculators and settlers. After 1835 Milwaukee was in the midst of a land and building boom. Three men began purchasing land, and three competitive, often fractious towns rose: Juneautown, between the lake and Milwaukee River, was formed by French-Canadian fur trader Solomon Juneau, who had been in the area since 1818. Byron Kilbourn, born in New England and raised in Ohio, developed Kilbourntown west of the Milwaukee River. George H. Walker of Virginia purchased the area south of the Kinnickinnic. Of the three, only Walker's Point retains a number of original structures.

The first brewers in Milwaukee were Welsh, but the type of ale they made did not have a great appeal. It was the Germans, in the 1840s, who introduced lager with good keeping qualities and who went on to develop Pabst, Blatz, Schlitz, and Miller, the mammoth breweries for which Milwaukee became renowned. Miller Brewing Company conducts tours of its facilities, which includes the **Caves Museum** (4251 West State Street, 414–931–2337), a cavern buried deep in a hillside with forty-four-inch-thick brick and limestone walls. Brewers took advantage of the bluffs ringing Milwaukee by excavating caverns in them to provide naturally cooled chambers for aging beer. Antique bottles, copper's tools, old advertisements, and a miniature reproduction of the original Frederick Miller Plank Road Brewery are on display. The **Pabst Brewery** (414–223–3709) also conducts tours.

By 1910 three-fourths of Milwaukee's inhabitants were immigrants or had at least one foreign-born parent. While 20 percent of the population spoke German, many other ethnic groups were arriving to work in the rolling mills, meat-packing plants, and tanneries. Milwaukee's ethnic diversity is reflected in its impressive number of churches, a fact that can be noted by counting its spires and domes. One of the most beautiful is **Saint Josaphat Basilica** (West Lincoln Avenue at South Sixth Street), the first Polish basilica in North America. The ornate style of this Neo-Renaissance structure, designed in 1897 by Erhard Brielmaier, belies its frugal history. It was built largely by its working-class Polish parishioners of materials salvaged from the old Chicago main post office. With its towering French Gothic spires, the Roman Catholic **Church of the Gesu** (1145 West Wisconsin Avenue, 414–288–7101) on the Marquette University campus is another imposing structure. Its exceptional pipe organ was brought from the Studebaker Theater in Chicago.

The **Pabst Theater** (144 East Wells Street, 414–286–3665) was built on this site in 1895 when Frederick Pabst's opera house burned. Pabst called his brewery architect Otto Strack into service to design this Victorian Baroque theater, which is noted for its superb acoustics. Next door is the **Milwaukee City Hall** (200 East Wells Street), designed in 1893 by H. C. Koch in the German Renaissance Revival style. The problems of building massive structures in a swamp are typified by this hefty baronial edifice, which is stabilized by 25,000 cedar piles.

OPPOSITE: *Computerized instrument panels now control the otherwise traditional brewing process at Milwaukee's Miller Brewing Company.*

Nº 2
BREW KETTLE
CAP. 500 BBLS.

Among the businesses on Michigan Street between Water and Broadway are the **Mitchell Building** and **Mackie Building** (207 and 225 East Michigan Street). These flamboyant, heavily encrusted Victorian structures were designed by Milwaukee's most prolific architect, Edward Townsend Mix, in 1876 and 1879, respectively, at the behest of Alexander Mitchell. Mitchell, a Scotsman who came to Milwaukee in 1839, was a leading figure in the grain trade, railroads, banking, and insurance. The **Grain Exchange Room** (414–272–6230) on the second floor of the Mackie Building is an opulent remnant of Milwaukee's heyday as a wheat-trading center. It was here that the concept of the trading pit was developed.

Milwaukee Public Museum

This large museum has extensive exhibits of both natural history and human history, including displays of an East Indian bazaar, a Melanesian ceremonial house, a Moorish courtyard, and ocean life. On the local level, it has a life-size diorama depicting the outpost of fur trader and Milwaukee developer Solomon Juneau and the city's many ethnic neighborhoods.

LOCATION: 800 West Wells Street. HOURS: 9–5 Daily. FEE: Yes. TELEPHONE: 414–278–2702.

Milwaukee County Historical Center

The Milwaukee County Historical Center is housed in the former Second Ward Bank, a handsome Beaux-Arts building situated on a triangular lot. In addition to displays of an early twentieth-century bank, pharmacy, and cooper's shop, its collections include a research library, county archives and records, naturalization papers, fire equipment, brewery materials, transportation items, costumes, and decorative arts. The center lies in the heart of what was the main German shopping area of Milwaukee.

LOCATION: 910 Old World Third Street. HOURS: 9:30–5 Monday–Friday, 10–5 Saturday, 1–5 Sunday. FEE: None. TELEPHONE: 414–273–8288.

OPPOSITE: *An octagonal medallion in the floor of the restored Grain Exchange commemorates the first commodities trading pit.*

Pabst Mansion

The west end of Wisconsin Avenue, known as Grand Avenue in the nineteenth century, was once lined with stately elms and the mansions of Milwaukee's prosperous entrepreneurs and industrialists. Remnants of Victorian houses can be seen behind storefront facades. One of the few remaining intact is this exotic Flemish Renaissance Revival mansion, home in the later years of his life to German-born beer tycoon Frederick Pabst. Pabst came to Milwaukee at the age of 24, a successful Great Lakes steamship captain, where he was befriended by brewer Phillip Best. He bought shares in Best's Empire Brewery and married Best's eldest daughter, Maria. Pabst was 54 when he engaged Milwaukee architect George Bowman Ferry to design this lavish thirty-seven-room home of tan pressed brick with elaborate terra cotta ornamentation. The interior contains opulent rooms designed in styles popular among the wealthy of the time, include a parlor and dining room in the French Rococo Revival style.

LOCATION: 2000 West Wisconsin Avenue. HOURS: 10–3:30 Monday–Saturday, 12–3:30 Sunday. Guided tours take about one hour. FEE: Yes. TELEPHONE: 414–931–0808.

The furnishings in the Pabst Mansion dining room include an original chandelier built to use kerosene, gas, or electricity.

The 1892 Pabst Mansion. The small pavilion at right was first erected in the Agriculture Building of the 1893 Chicago World's Columbian Exposition to display Pabst Brewery products.

Charles Allis Museum

This handsome Jacobethan house was built in 1909 by Charles Allis, son of Edward P. Allis, the founder of what later became the Allis-Chalmers Corporation, manufacturer of farm implements. The house is appointed with original furnishings and displays Allis's personal collection of paintings and decorative arts, ranging from Chinese, Korean, and Japanese art objects to French and American nineteenth-century painting and seventeenth- and eighteenth-century French furniture.

LOCATION: 1801 North Prospect Avenue. HOURS: 1–5 Wednesday–Sunday and 7–9 Wednesday evenings. FEE: None. TELEPHONE: 414–278–8295.

The **Villa Terrace Decorative Arts Museum** (2220 North Terrace Avenue, 414–271–3656) is a 1922 Mediterranean-style villa that houses the Milwaukee Art Museum collection of decorative arts, period furnishings, and porcelain.

GREENDALE

Greendale was one of three planned greenbelt communities in the United States to be built in the 1930s as part of the Resettlement Administration. Rexford Guy Tugwell, head of this federal agency, dreamed of implementing a network of "garden towns" in suburban areas across the country.

Before it was a greenbelt town, Greendale was a farming area containing limestone quarries. In the last half of the nineteenth century the limestone was processed in kilns to produce lime. **Trimborn Farm Park** (8881 West Grange Avenue, 414–332–7275) preserves the lime kilns of Prussian immigrant Werner Trimborn, which he operated here with his sons from 1847 until 1900, when the emphasis shifted over to dairy farming. Two barns, a Greek Revival farmhouse, and a granary recall this era.

RACINE

Another town that took root after the Black Hawk War, Racine was founded by Massachusetts-born Gilbert Knapp in 1834 on the Michigan lakeshore at the mouth of the Root River. Racine burgeoned during the wheat-growing era, and its reputation as a major producer of agricultural implements was established in 1844 when the J. I. Case Company began manufacturing threshing machines. The **Case Headquarters Building** (700 State Street, 414–636–7818), built in 1904, is in Northside Racine, the neighborhood north of the Root River originally settled by the town's immigrant labor population. The **Erie Street cottages** (Erie Street and Goold to Yout streets) are examples of the modest homes built between the 1860s and 1900 for the German and middle-European workers that settled in Racine. They are constructed of the cream brick so distinctive of Wisconsin's lakeshore cities. The **Racine Heritage Museum** (701 South Main Street, 414–636–3926) contains local-history exhibits and archives and collections of glass, firearms, costumes, and historic photographs.

Racine is also home to the **SC Johnson Wax Administration Center** (1525 Howe Street, 414–260–2154), and **Wingspread** (33 East Four Mile Road, 414–681–3322), both designed by Frank Lloyd Wright. In 1886 Samuel Curtis Johnson bought out his

OPPOSITE: *The living room at Wingspread, the house Frank Lloyd Wright designed for Herbert F. Johnson, Jr., in Racine. The ladder next to the chimney leads to a belvedere on the roof.*

Frank Lloyd Wright, at center, with Herbert F. Johnson, Jr., at right, on the Johnson Wax Company construction site. OPPOSITE: *The completed headquarters building.*

employer's parquet floor business, where he had been a salesman for several years, but the centerpiece of his growing enterprise would become the wax he formulated to polish those floors. In 1936 the company commissioned Frank Lloyd Wright to design its headquarters and research center. The interior of the main administrative area—a large open expanse punctuated with graceful flower-stem columns—is a landmark in modern workplace design.

Wright designed Wingspread in 1937 as a residence for Herbert F. Johnson, Jr., grandson of Samuel. This is one of Wright's Prairie Style houses, an octagon from which sprout four wings pointing in the cardinal directions. Wingspread, now owned by the Johnson Foundation, is an educational conference center open by appointment.

SOUTHWESTERN WISCONSIN

PRAIRIE DU CHIEN

Prairie du Chien, the second-oldest settlement in Wisconsin, was for 10,000 years a natural gathering place for Indians, predominantly the Mesquakie, Sauk, and Winnebago when the French began to arrive. Built on broad terraces near the confluence of the Mississippi and Wisconsin rivers, it is named for a Mesquakie chief whose name translates as "dog," *chien* in French.

Marquette and Jolliet discovered the Mississippi River near here in 1673, and in 1685 Nicolas Perrot scouted the area for its fur-trading potential. For the next 150 years, until 1840, Prairie du Chien was a major interior fur-trading post. In 1826 Hercules Dousman arrived in Prairie du Chien as an agent for John Jacob Astor's American Fur Company. He went on to achieve wealth from land speculation and investments in the lumber industry and railroads and, in 1843, he built a sprawling brick home for his bride atop an Indian ceremonial mound on the banks of the Mississippi. Upon Dousman's death in 1868, she razed it and built a more modern and stylish Victorian mansion, designed by Milwaukee architect Edward Townsend Mix. **Villa Louis** (521 North Villa Louis Road, 608–326–2721) contains furnishings and decorative arts that reflect Victorian life on the Midwestern frontier. On the grounds is the **Fur Trade Museum,** housed in an 1854 stone structure on the site of previous American Fur Company warehouses.

Two forts also stood on the site of Villa Louis. Fort Shelby, built in 1814, was seized by the British and burned in the aftermath of the War of 1812. Fort Crawford was built in 1816 on the same site, but flooding prompted a move to higher ground in 1829. It was abandoned in 1856. The fort's military hospital has been restored as the **Fort Crawford Medical Museum** (717 South Beaumont Road, 608–326–6960). In this hospital Dr. William Beaumont continued his landmark experiments on digestion, begun in 1822 at Fort Mackinac in Michigan. The museum is a repository of Wisconsin medical history, with displays of a nineteenth-century doctor's office, dentist office, and pharmacy, as well as medical artifacts.

PLATTEVILLE

Platteville lies in the hills of Wisconsin's lead mining area. The **Mining Museum** (385 East Main Street, 608–348–3301) traces the history of lead and zinc mining and includes a tour of the 1845 Bevans lead mine. Associated with it is the **Rollo Jamison Museum,** which includes household furnishings, farm implements, and musical instruments from the local historian's personal collection.

MINERAL POINT

The territory around Mineral Point was extracted from the Potawatomi, Ojibwa, Ottawa, and Winnebago Indians by the 1829 Treaty of Prairie du Chien. The French and the Indians had long been mining lead from these hills, but, by the 1830s, Mineral Point was a boom town, settled by Southern prospectors in the late 1820s and then by Cornish miners in 1832. Many of the miners lived in hillside dugouts called "badger holes" where they remained over the winter, unlike other miners who only worked seasonally. Consequently Wisconsin came to be known as the Badger State.

Pendarvis, at Mineral Point, preserves six Cornish miners' cottages, resembling the houses the miners had left behind in Cornwall, England.

The lead boom in the 1830s made Mineral Point a center of economic and political activity, and it was here that in 1836 the Territory of Wisconsin came into being. Mineral Point was also known as Shake Rag for the main street in town. From here the Cornish wives would wave dish towels to call their men home for dinner. **Pendarvis** (114 Shake Rag Street, 608–987–2122), named after a village in Cornwall, is a collection of restored limestone and log cottages built by the Cornish miners who came to Mineral Point in the 1830s. After lead prices fell in 1847, some of the miners became farmers, while others followed the Gold Rush to California. The houses contain nineteenth-century furnishings, mining tools, and equipment.

Several buildings associated with Frank Lloyd Wright can be seen just south of **Spring Green.** In 1902 Wright designed a private school complex for his aunts, Jane and Nell Lloyd Jones, in a lovely valley of the Wisconsin River, an area settled by Wright's family in the 1850s. Since 1932, the **Hillside Home School** (608–588–7900) has served as headquarters for the Taliesin Fellowship, now known as the Frank Lloyd Wright School of Architecture, an atelier for architectural students.

The Hillside Home School, originally a progressive boarding school founded by Frank Lloyd Wright's aunts, was remodeled in 1954 and is now used by the Taliesin Fellowship. OPPO-SITE: *Wright named his Spring Green house Taliesin—literally "Shining Brow"—after a legendary Welsh poet.*

This remote valley became a semipermanent retreat for the Chicago-based architect in 1911, when, somewhat to the shock of local residents, he built a home here for Mamah Borthwick Cheney, the recently divorced wife of a former neighbor and client. Called **Taliesin,** the house has a commanding view of the river. Taliesin has had a phoenixlike history, having been damaged by several fires, one of which was set by a crazed servant who first, outraged by Wright and Mamah's unorthodox relationship, murdered Mamah, her children, and several employees. Wright settled at Taliesin permanently in the 1930s with his fourth wife, Olgivanna Milanoff. A memorial to Wright is located nearby in the cemetery of the **Unity Chapel,** designed in 1886 by Joseph L. Silsbee for the Lloyd Jones family. Taliesin is not open to the public but can be easily seen from Highway 23. A nearby restaurant called **The Spring Green** was also designed by Wright. About two miles south of Taliesin is the 1956 **Wyoming Valley Grammar School.**

Wright was born in 1867 some twenty miles up the road in **Richland Center.** In 1915 he designed the **A. D. German Warehouse** (300 South Church Street, 608–647–6205), a red brick monolithic structure topped with an elegant concrete frieze reminiscent of Mayan motifs. An interior grid of concrete columns provides structural support, eliminating the need for interior walls and allowing a large uninterrupted interior space. Inside is an art gallery and a museum of Wright memorabilia.

BATTLE OF WISCONSIN HEIGHTS

Just southeast of Sauk City on Route 12, a State Historical Marker designates the site of a battle in the Black Hawk War fought on July 21, 1832. The previous April, about a thousand Sauk and Mesquakie, under the leadership of Chief Black Hawk, attempted a peaceful return to their ancestral village near present Rock Island, Illinois to plant a corn crop. Some 3,000 militia (including Abraham Lincoln) and several hundred federal troops (including Jefferson Davis) drove them from Illinois in an episode that was more a sporadic massacre than a battle. Informed by a Winnebago spy of Black Hawk's flight into Wisconsin, frontier fighter Colonel Henry Dodge and his troops pursued the retreating Indians across the site of present-day Madison to this point near Sauk City, where the Indian warriors stood their ground and fought until nightfall. The women and children escaped across the Wisconsin River and by daybreak the warriors had also fled.

BATTLE OF BAD AXE

The final confrontation of the Black Hawk War occurred some eighty miles to the west on August 2, 1832, where the Bad Axe River flows into the Mississippi. The site, two-and-a-half miles north of De Soto on Route 35, is designated with a marker. Colonel Dodge had combined forces with General Henry Atkinson and his federal troops, and the Indians were forced onto mudflats and islands in the Mississippi by soldiers on land and aboard an armed steamboat in the river. Many drowned trying to escape across the Mississippi, and as one writer described it, the Indians fell like "grass before the scythe."

BARABOO

Harness maker August Rüngeling, having simplified his name to Ringling, arrived in Baraboo in 1855. By 1884 son Albert, a juggler and tightrope walker, had organized his own circus, using four brothers for various acts and his wife, Louise, as snake charmer. Baraboo was the winter quarters for Ringling Brothers Circus until 1918, when it merged with the Barnum and Bailey circus. The Beaux-Arts **Al Ringling Opera House** (136 Fourth Avenue) was built by Albert in 1915 as a gift to the city. It is now a movie theater. The **Circus World Museum** (426 Water Street, 608–356–8341) maintains extensive collections of circus artifacts, programs, route books, business records, lithographs, and negatives, and there are over a hundred circus wagons on display. The museum gives live circus performances, antique circus music and calliope concerts, parades, and other demonstrations.

Well off the beaten path, in the 1897 building of the Modern Woodmen of America, is the **Painted Forest Folk Art Museum** (eight miles southwest of Wonowoc in Valton, 608–983–2352). The walls and ceiling are covered with a fine folk-art mural depicting the initiation rites of the fraternal organization and community life in Valton at the turn of the century, painted in 1899 by Ernest Hupeden, a German immigrant and itinerant artist. It is operated by the Historical Society of the Upper Baraboo Valley.

WISCONSIN DELLS

In 1931 the town of Kilbourn changed its name to Wisconsin Dells in hopes of attracting visitors to the Wisconsin River, where it cuts through canyons of castellated rock. H. H. Bennett, an important

Part of H. H. Bennett's photographic studio in Wisconsin Dells is maintained by his descendants as a museum. Publication of Bennett's striking photographs, opposite, lured tourists to the town in the late nineteenth century.

nineteenth-century landscape photographer, from 1865 until his death in 1908 recorded southwestern Wisconsin landscapes, Winnebago Indians, raftsmen moving lumber down the Wisconsin River, and urban life in Milwaukee and Chicago. A prolific producer of the then-popular stereoscopic photographs, he was also an early experimenter with stop-action photography, devising a camera with a rubber-band-operated shutter. Members of his family are still associated with a museum in the **H. H. Bennett Studio** (215 Broadway, 608–253–2261), which displays early photographic equipment and houses a collection of Bennett's work.

The **Dells County Historical Society** (737 Broadway, 608–254–8129) displays a letter from Abraham Lincoln commending General Joseph Bailey for his extraordinary services during the Civil War. Bailey was a founder of Kilbourn and a self-taught engineer who served with the Fourth Wisconsin Cavalry. In the spring of 1864 when the water level of the Red River in Louisiana dropped suddenly, Bailey persuaded General Nathanial Banks that he could build a dam to allow Admiral Porter's fleet of gunboats to float freely. Despite the skepticism of army engineers, lumberjacks from Wisconsin and Maine completed the dam in eleven days, reportedly saving the Union $2 million and shortening the Civil War by as much as two years.

The **Spring Grove Cemetery** (Route 23) is the site of a memorial to Belle Boyd, a Confederate spy during the Civil War who was renowned for her exploits during Stonewall Jackson's Valley Campaign. The information she gained led to the defeat of Federal troops at Port Republic, and Jackson made her an honorary aide on his staff. After the war, she traveled the country lecturing; she died in Wisconsin Dells in 1900.

PORTAGE

In the nineteenth century this town was a major point on the Fox-Wisconsin waterway between Green Bay and Prairie du Chien. Here the Fox River flows within a mile and a half of the Wisconsin River, requiring an overland haul. This portage was well trod by the Indians, but the first recorded Europeans to cross it were Marquette and Joliet. Carrying two birch bark canoes, they made their last overland haul before encountering the Mississippi River on June 17, 1673. In 1828 the U.S. Army built Fort Winnebago on a hill overlooking the portage point, primarily to protect lead miners in southwestern Wisconsin from Indian provocations. Lieutenant Jefferson Davis served here after graduating from West Point, and the fort was occupied until 1845. The restored **Fort Winnebago Surgeon's Quarters** (Route 33, two miles east of Portage, 608–742–2949), all that remains of the garrison, was originally the log home of François LeRoi, who from 1812 to about 1824 ran a business assisting boats over the portage.

In 1832 John Harris Kinzie, Indian agent to the Winnebago Indians, built the **Indian Agency House** (Agency House Road, 608–742–6362), at a cost of $3,500. Quite genteel for its time and circumstance, the two-story frame structure was a social center for Fort Winnebago. Kinzie's wife, Juliette, recorded life at this remote outpost in the book *Wau-Bun*. The house is furnished with antiques and decorative arts of the American Empire period. The road to the house parallels the Portage Canal, constructed between 1838 and 1876, which finally connected the rivers and eliminated the portage.

MADISON

The capital of Wisconsin has grown up around four lakes—two large, Mendota and Monona, and two small, Waubesa and Wingra. Once covered in impenetrable thickets, the city was thought uninhabitable by early settlers. However, the perspicacious politician and land speculator James Duane Doty began buying up land around the lakes in the 1830s and in 1836 convinced members of the legislature at the then-capital of Belmont to move the seat of government to the Four Lakes area. At the time no white settlers inhabited the region. In 1849 wealthy Milwaukeean Leonard Farwell arrived and began instigating various improvements, including damming a portion of Lake Mendota and building a gristmill. The University of Wisconsin was established here in 1848 with the coming of statehood.

Despite advances, in the 1850s Madison remained a city within a dense thicket on the sparsely settled frontier. It began to grow with the coming of the Civil War, when the state fairgrounds were converted to a training camp for recruits. Camp Randall, as it was called, was the largest in Wisconsin, training 70,000 of the 91,000 Civil War soldiers from the state. **Camp Randall Memorial Park,** on the original site of the camp (now part of the University of Wisconsin campus), contains numerous statues, plaques, and markers commemorating the Civil War camp.

The **Wisconsin State Capitol** (Capitol Square, 608–266–0382), a white granite structure in the Classical Revival style, dominates the narrow isthmus between Lakes Mendota and Monona. Built between 1906 and 1917 by George B. Post & Sons, it has a commanding view of the city and surrounding lakes. The interior is dominated by the rotunda encircled by massive Corinthian columns executed in rose Numidian marble and green Tinos marble. Four panels of glass mosaics symbolizing liberty and justice, made with some 400,000 pieces of glass, adorn the pendentives around the dome. The **Wisconsin Veterans Museum** (30 Mifflin Street, 608–267–1799) honors state citizens who served in America's wars. Dioramas create combat environments, including the Battle of the Bulge and New Guinea in World War II. Aircraft include a Sopwith Camel from World War I and a helicopter from the Vietnam War. Models of ships are also on display.

Nearby on Capitol Square, the **State Historical Museum** (30 North Carroll Street, 608–264–6555) focuses on the history of Wisconsin Indians from prehistoric times into the twentieth century. Life-size dioramas depict the modes of Indian life, including a replica of a dwelling at the ancient city of Aztalan. The important treaties that the United States entered into with Wisconsin Indians between 1825 and 1848 are described in another exhibit area. The

The Wisconsin State Capitol, erected in 1917 in the Beaux Arts style, has four wings of equal size to accommodate the chambers of the executive branch, judiciary, senate, and house.

administrative offices of the **State Historical Society of Wisconsin** (816 State Street) were designed in 1896 by George Bowman Ferry and Alfred Clas in the Second Renaissance Revival style.

The Georgian Revival **Richard T. Ely House** (205 North Prospect Avenue) was built in 1896 for Ely, a noted and controversial economist and professor at the University of Wisconsin in the 1890s. The Greek Revival **Old Spring Tavern** (3706 Nakoma Road, private) was built in 1854 on the Madison–Monroe stagecoach road to the lead-mining region to the southwest.

The many prehistoric effigy mounds in and around Madison include the **Burrows Park Effigy Mound and Campsite,** which contains a Woodland-period campsite and an effigy mound in the shape of a straight-winged bird; the **Farwell's Point Mound Group,** which contains thirteen conical mounds, four linear mounds, two panther effigy mounds, and one bird effigy mound; and the **Mendota State Hospital Mound Group,** with three large bird effigy mounds, two conical mounds, two panther effigy mounds, two bear effigy mounds, and one deer effigy mound.

The dome of the capitol—designed by the New York architects George B. Post & Sons—is the second highest in the United States.

While the towns on the Lake Michigan shore owe their prosperity to Central and Eastern European immigrant labor, the region south of Madison became home to Norwegian and Swiss immigrants, attracted to the rugged terrain vaguely reminiscent of their homelands. **Blue Mounds** (fifteen miles west of Madison on Route 18), named for a 1,700-foot conical hill nearby, lies in the heart of Norwegian settlement in Wisconsin. **Little Norway** (between Blue Mounds and Mt. Horeb, 608–437–8211), the restored 1856 homestead of Norwegian immigrant Osten Haugen, contains Norwegian and pioneer artifacts and the replica, built in 1885, of a twelfth-century Norwegian church. It was used as an exhibition building at the Columbian Exposition in Chicago in 1893.

A group of immigrants from Glarus, Switzerland, founded the town of New Glarus in 1845. The **Swiss Village Museum** (612 Seventh Avenue, 608–527–2317) commemorates the lives and skills of these immigrants through collections of their tools and artifacts, plus replicas of a log church and log cabin, a cheese factory, printshop, blacksmith shop, school, and country store.

NORTHWESTERN WISCONSIN

EAU CLAIRE

After the fur trade had diminished and the government had negotiated treaties to land rights, it was the white pine growing in the Chippewa Valley that lured settlers to this area in the 1820s. Before the area was logged out in the 1890s, over twenty sawmills were in operation in Eau Claire. Competing interests quarreled frequently over the placement of dams and booms on the Chippewa River, since these structures impeded the floating of logs.

The **Chippewa Valley Museum** in Eau Claire (Carson Park Drive, 715–834–7871) covers the Woodland Indian culture, the fur trade, logging, and the industrial growth of the valley through exhibits of small towns and farm life, including an operating switchboard, silos, and threshers. Other displays explore topics such as women's work on farms, river use and abuse, and area architecture. Next to the museum is the 1860 **Lars Anderson log house** and the one-room **Sunnyview school.**

Lunch time in a logging camp near Eau Claire, a city that had more than twenty sawmills before the region was logged out in the 1890s.

The 1884 William Phipps House in Hudson, one of many houses on Third Street that reflect the town's late-nineteenth-century prosperity from lumbering and industry.

SAINT CROIX RIVER VALLEY

With its deep gorges and tree-covered ridges, the Saint Croix River Valley is noted for its beauty. In the town of **Hudson,** named after the city on the Hudson River, is the **Octagon House** (1004 Third Street, 715–386–2654), the museum of the Saint Croix Historical Society. The two-story frame and stucco octagonal structure, with an octagonal cupola, was built in 1855 for county judge John S. Moffat. The house contains period furniture, books, tools, clothing, and a doll collection. On the grounds are a nineteenth-century blacksmith shop, carriage house, and garden house.

South of **Saint Croix Falls,** the **Ice Age Interpretive Center at Interstate Park** (Route 35, 715–483–3747) explains the Wisconsin glaciation with exhibits and a film. The park includes an extremely beautiful section of the river called the Dalles of the Saint Croix. When the river was used to float logs to market, the Dalles held the world's largest logjam—as much as 150 million board feet of lumber would stack up for three miles upstream.

The **Burnett County Historical Society** in **Siren** (8500 County Road U, 715–866–8890) operates the **North West Company and XY Company Wintering Posts** at that location. Replicas of the fur-trading wintering outposts are seven miles northwest of Webster on the banks of the Yellow River. The site dates from the early 1800s and shows two competing fur companies. The British North West Company site originally contained three structures surrounded by a ten-foot-high stockade with bastions. Just ninety feet away, its upstart rival, the Montreal-based XY Company, conducted business in a single unfortified cabin. Guides in period costume interpret the site, and there is a replica of an Ojibwa Indian village on the grounds.

BAYFIELD

Set on a natural deep-water harbor, Bayfield is a quaint Victorian village overlooking beautiful Chequamegon Bay and the Apostle Islands. Minnesota financier Henry M. Rice selected the deep-water harbor site with the hopes of developing a commercial port to rival Chicago. The town was laid out in 1856, and Rice christened it after British naval officer Henry Bayfield, who charted Lake Superior in the 1820s.

The lumber industry began in earnest in 1869 with the opening of the Little Daisy sawmill. Commercial fishing was established by 1870. Another important resource in the area was brownstone. Quarrying began in 1868, and Bayfield stone was used for buildings in Chicago, Milwaukee, and throughout the Midwest. With its balmy summers and beautiful vistas, Bayfield at the same time gained a reputation as a fine resort.

Bayfield's early development blossomed from about 1880 to 1910, although several factors prevented it from becoming the giant port of Henry Rice's dreams: The lumbermen exhausted the timber supply; Ashland won the railroad connecting Chequamegon Bay with southern Wisconsin; Duluth gained an edge as a commercial port because of its proximity to the rich iron ranges and Western wheat fields; architectural styles using steel and concrete ended the demand for brownstone as a building material; and commercial fishing began to decline because of uncontrolled harvesting and pollution of the spawning grounds by sawmills.

OPPOSITE: *Bayfield, which nineteenth-century developer Henry M. Rice hoped would rival Chicago as a port, is today a popular Lake Superior resort.*

The **Old Bayfield County Courthouse** (Washington Avenue between Fourth and Fifth streets, 715–779–3397), a monumental 1884 brownstone, typifies late-nineteenth-century public architecture, combining Classical Revival and Romanesque Revival elements. Now renovated, it serves as the **Apostle Islands National Lakeshore Visitor Center.** Also of interest is the commodious Queen Anne **Allen C. Fuller House** (301 Rittenhouse Avenue), one of several Victorian mansions in Bayfield. A Civil War general, Fuller built it in 1890 as a hay fever retreat. It is now an inn.

Just south of town on the banks of Pike Creek is the handsome brownstone **State Fish Hatchery** (715–779–5430), begun by Captain R. D. Pike in 1877 in response to the rapidly declining fish populations in Lake Superior. In 1895 he donated it to the state.

APOSTLE ISLANDS NATIONAL LAKESHORE

This spectacular federal preserve encompasses twenty-one of the Apostle Islands and a strip of lakefront on the northwestern Bayfield Peninsula. Nomadic prehistoric Indians foraged on the islands and netted fish along their shores. Later the islands supported logging and fishing camps and brownstone quarries.

During the nineteenth century six **lighthouses** were built on the Apostles to guide ships through or around the islands. Now fully automated, four of the six are open to the public in summer, staffed by guides who explain the history of each structure and the lightkeeper's routine. Abandoned brownstone pits can be seen on **Stockton, Hermit, and Basswood islands,** where quarry workers cut the brownstone into three-by-three-by-six-foot blocks. An old commercial **fishing camp** has been preserved on **Manitou Island.**

The twenty-one islands that are under the jurisdiction of the Apostle Islands National Lakeshore are not accessible by automobile. The **visitor center** (Washington Avenue, Bayfield, 715–779–3397) provides information on sightseeing excursions.

Madeline Island

Madeline Island is the largest of the Apostle Islands and the only one that is not part of the National Lakeshore. The village of **La Pointe** has a small year-round population, but the island is primarily a summer community. From April through December (when the lake is not frozen), the Madeline Island Ferry Line (715–747–2051) runs hourly between Bayfield and La Pointe.

Although the historical record is not clear, Ojibwa Indians apparently lived on Madeline Island from 1680 until their removal to nearby reservations in 1854. The Ojibwa name for the island, Moningwunakauning, is the term for yellow-shafted flicker, a bird abundant here, especially during migration. In 1693 the French established the first trading post on the island. Abandoned in 1698 because of a glut in the fur market, it was reactivated in 1718 under the name of Fort La Pointe and operated by a series of French explorer-entrepreneurs, including Louis Denis, sieur de la Ronde and Joseph Gaultier, chevalier de La Vérendrye. After the French and Indian War, the North West Company began to dominate the fur trade in the Chequamegon Bay area.

Permanent European settlement on the island dates from 1793, when Michel Cadotte was appointed the North West Company factor. The previous year he had married Equaysayway, daughter of the Ojibwa chief White Crane. She was given the Christian name Madeline, and the island was in turn named for her by her father. In 1816 John Jacob Astor's American Fur Company took over the fur-trading post and, in 1818, two New England brothers, Lyman and Truman Warren, arrived on the island, married Cadotte's daughters, and became involved in the fur trade as well as commercial fishing and various educational and religious activities. The American Fur Company dominated the island economy until 1847.

In 1831 Presbyterian minister Sherman Hall, an emissary of the American Board of Commissioners for Foreign Missions, established a school among the Indians. His labors aroused the interest of the peripatetic Austrian-born priest Father Frederic Baraga, who erected a Catholic mission on Madeline Island in 1835. In response, Hall built a church for his charges in 1839, one of the first Protestant churches in Wisconsin. In 1854 the Treaty of La Pointe called for the removal of the Ojibwa from Madeline Island to nearby reservations that reflected these religious factions—Red Cliff Indian Reservation on Bayfield Peninsula formed for the Catholic Ojibwa, while the Bad River Reservation east of Ashland comprised the Protestant group.

The **Madeline Island Historical Museum** (Colonel Woods Avenue, 715–747–2415), on the site of the American Fur Company post, is housed in four historic log structures, including a fur company warehouse. It contains Indian crafts and artifacts, mis-

sionary-related documents, fur-trade exhibits, memorabilia related to frontier life at La Pointe, and a Fresnel lens from the Raspberry Island lighthouse.

The **Indian Burial Ground** (south of the Madeline Island Marina and Yacht Club) contains several Ojibwa graves as well as those of pioneers who embraced the Catholic faith. Distinctive miniature houses reflect the Ojibwa tradition of providing shelter for the spirits of the deceased, although their architectural style is distinctly Anglo-Saxon. Chief Buffalo, who during the 1854 treaty negotiations fought to retain Ojibwa reservation lands, is buried here, as is Michel Cadotte and many of his descendants.

SUPERIOR

The Victorian **Fairlawn Mansion and Museum** (906 Harbor View Parkway East, 715–394–5712) overlooks Lake Superior. Built by lumber and mining baron Martin Pattison, it now houses the collections of the Douglas County Historical Society, including ca. 1890 furniture and furnishings, Chippewa crafts, the David Barry collection of Sioux portraits, and regional industrial artifacts.

East on Route 13, about 1.5 miles, is the SS *Meteor* (715–394–7716), which is docked on **Barker's Island.** Ships of this type, called whaleback carriers, modernized bulk cargo transport on the Great Lakes. The steel-hulled tankers were designed at the turn of the century by Duluth shipbuilder Alexander McDougall, and most of them were assembled in the twin ports. The freighter's pilot house, galley, and engine room, which contain original fittings and exhibits of maritime artifacts, can be toured.

During the nineteenth and early twentieth centuries, immigrants, especially of Scandinavian descent, were an important part of the labor force and instrumental in organizing the People's Cooperative Society, a workers' organization that maintained a grocery store, a service station, and credit union for its associates. Superior, in particular, was known nationwide as a stronghold of the cooperative movement, many of whose ranks were members of the Communist party. With the outbreak of the Russian Revolution, a few of Superior's cooperative followers migrated to Russia. The **Tyomies Building** (7th and Tower streets), now in a state of disrepair, is a Romanesque Revival structure that served as the center of Superior's cooperative movement.

OPPOSITE: *Sand Island Lighthouse, one of six built to guide ships in and around the Apostle Islands.*

MINNESOTA

OPPOSITE: *Restored officers' quarters at Minnesota's Fort Snelling, established as a wilderness outpost to safeguard the American frontier after the War of 1812.*

People tend to think of Minnesota as the "Land of 10,000 Lakes." While these countless bodies of water provide fascinating clues to the area's Ice Age past, it is Lake Superior and the state's assortment of meandering rivers that have shaped Minnesota's more recent history and—except for a few straight lines and right angles along its borders with Iowa and South Dakota—the state itself. Because Minnesota's terrain is slightly convex, its rivers drain into three different water systems. The Rainy and Pigeon rivers, in the north, flow via Lake Superior into the Atlantic Ocean. The Red River, which forms part of the state's western boundary, drains into Hudson Bay and thence to the Arctic Ocean. The Minnesota River, which cuts west to east across the southern third of the state, and the Saint Croix, which forms part of the Wisconsin-Minnesota border, both feed the Mississippi, which flows south to the Gulf of Mexico.

Each of these waterways, paths for exploration and trade, was important to the state's cultural and economic development. In the mid-1800s the Saint Croix Valley was the center of the lumber industry, which, along with the earlier-established fur trade, brought permanent white settlement of the Minnesota country. In 1823 the arrival at Fort Snelling of the *Virginia*—the first steamboat to ply the upper Mississippi, bound from Saint Louis—marked the ascendancy of that mighty river as the nation's first interior artery of commerce. A short distance upstream, Saint Anthony Falls provided the water power to make Minneapolis a giant in the flour-milling industry, while just downstream flat terraces breaking the line of limestone bluffs below a set of rapids provided excellent landing sites for the port city of Saint Paul. Wheat from the fertile Red River Valley helped the milling and shipping industries grow. The Minnesota Valley was the backdrop for the 1862 Dakota Conflict, the last major confrontation between Indians and white settlers in the Great Lakes area. Finally, Lake Superior, via the port of Duluth, provided an outlet for wheat grown in Minnesota and points west and for iron ore mined in the nearby Vermilion, Mesabi, and Cuyuna ranges. This northeastern part of the state is known as the Arrowhead region for its triangular shape.

Ten thousand years before white settlement, prehistoric Indians fished in these rivers and chose beautiful vantages along the banks and bluffs for their ceremonial and burial mounds. Historic Indians used the rivers not only as a source of food but also for transportation, communication, trade, and warfare. When the

Fort Snelling guarded the confluence of the Mississippi and Minnesota rivers, as shown in this 1844 view painted by John Casper Wild.

French began to penetrate lands west of Lake Superior in the late seventeenth century—via its rivers, of course—the Dakota (Sioux) Indians were the dominant tribe in the forested lake region, with the Ojibwa (Chippewa) living along the fringes in the areas that are now Wisconsin and Canada. Various factors, including French trade policies with the Cree of Canada, caused friction between the two tribes that resulted in prolonged war. The Ojibwa, armed with French guns, proved the superior force and drove the Dakota out of the forest and onto the plains surrounding the Minnesota River Valley. Skirmishes between the two tribes continued well into the nineteenth century and were a constant deterrent to French exploration and missionary work.

The first of the French expeditions into Minnesota country was led by Daniel Greysolon, sieur Duluth, in 1679–1680. Hoping to make peace between the Ojibwa and Dakota and to find the Pacific Ocean, he explored the western shores of Lake Superior and the environs of Mille Lacs. In the same year a party of French explorers, organized by Robert Cavelier, sieur de La Salle, was captured by the Dakota Indians. Duluth was able to arrange for their eventual release, but during their captivity Louis Hennepin, a Franciscan friar who was a member of the party, was shown the

N D

Fergus Falls

Brainerd

⊞ Fort Ripley

Little Falls

Sauk Centre

St. Cloud

Cold Spring

Bois des Sioux R.

94

71

10

29

75

Lake Traverse

Chippewa R.

Mississippi R.

Elk R.

N. Fork Crow R.

Big Stone Lake

Lac Qui Parle Lake

SOUTH DAKOTA

Lac Qui Parle S.P.

Montevideo
Pioneer Village

MINNESOTA

212

S. Fork Crow R.

212

Upper Sioux Agency

Minnesota R.

Yellow Medicine R.

Birch Coulee Park

Le Sueur

Ottawa Township

Lower Sioux Agency

Fort Ridgely

Traverse des Sioux S.P.

Cottonwood R.

New Ulm

St. Peter

Clevela

14

14

Jeffers Petroglyphs

Mankato

Pipestone N.M.

Blue Earth R.

75

Luverne

90

Fairmont

Sioux Falls

29

Des Moines R.

71

I O W

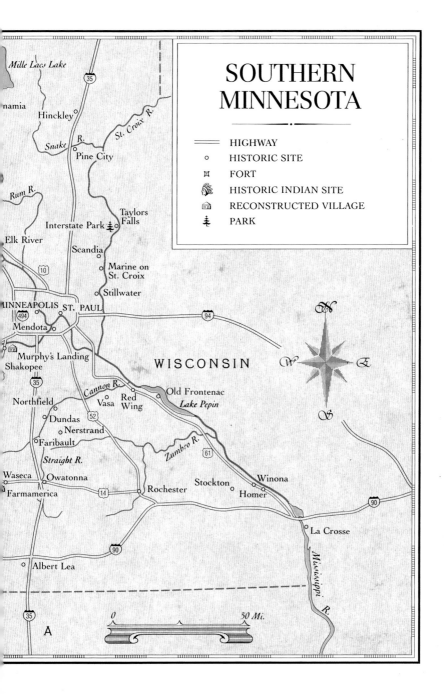

SOUTHERN MINNESOTA

═══	HIGHWAY
○	HISTORIC SITE
⊞	FORT
🪶	HISTORIC INDIAN SITE
🏛	RECONSTRUCTED VILLAGE
🌲	PARK

Mille Lacs Lake

namia

Hinckley

Snake R.

St. Croix R.

Pine City

Rum R.

Taylors Falls

Interstate Park

Elk River

Scandia

MINNEAPOLIS ST. PAUL

Mendota

Marine on St. Croix

Stillwater

Murphy's Landing

Shakopee

WISCONSIN

Cannon R.

Northfield

Vasa Red Wing

Old Frontenac

Lake Pepin

Dundas

Nerstrand

Faribault

Straight R.

Zumbro R.

Waseca Owatonna

Farmamerica

Stockton

Winona

Rochester

Homer

La Crosse

Albert Lea

Mississippi R.

0   50 Mi.

A

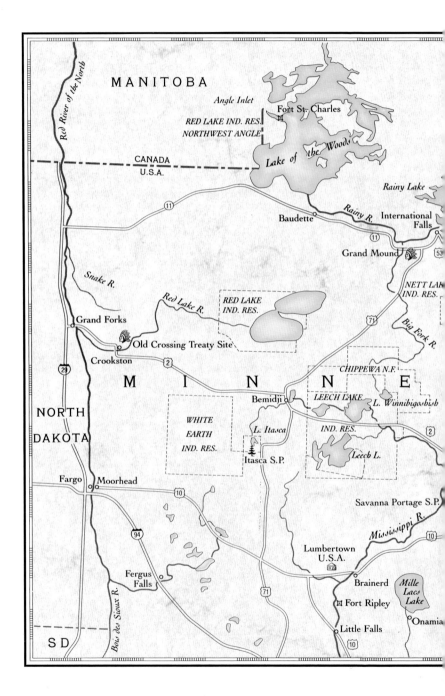

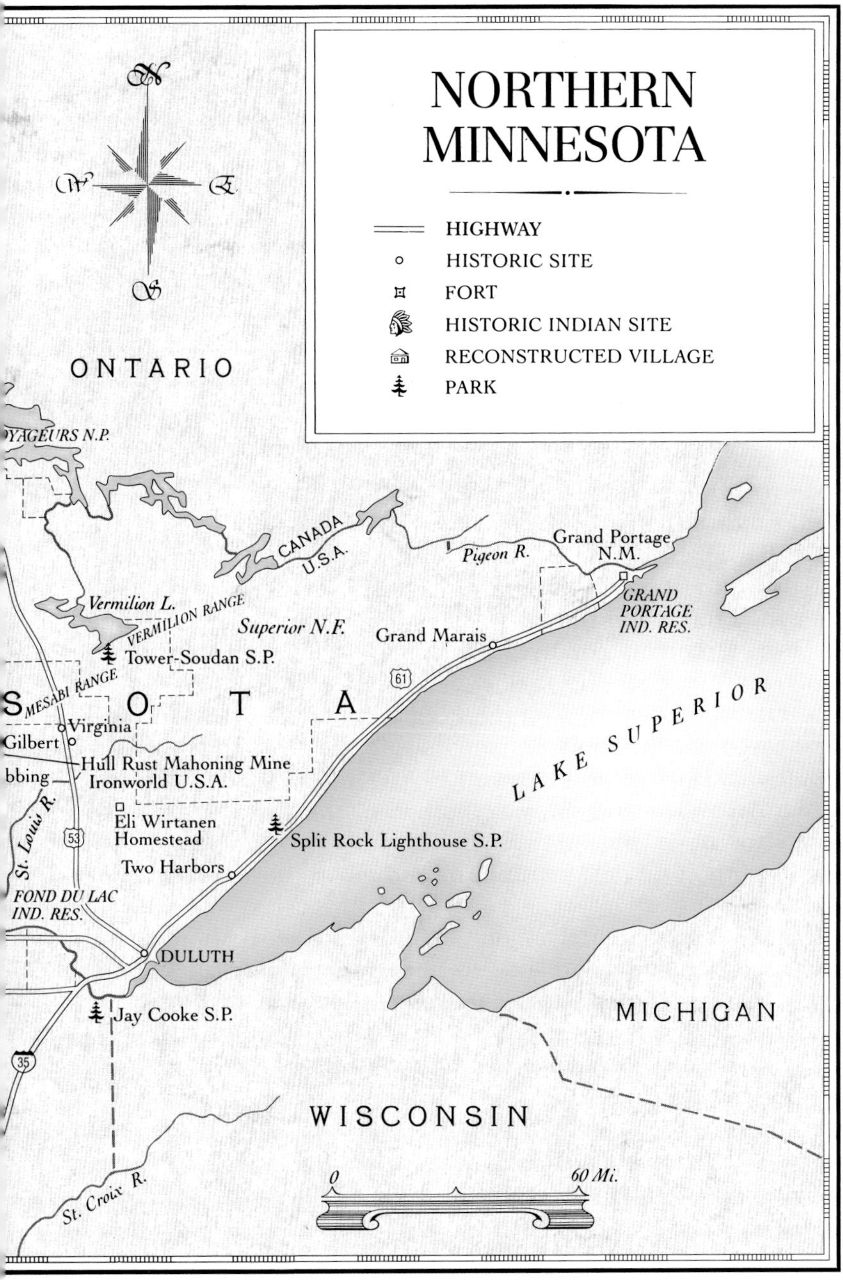
NORTHERN
MINNESOTA
HIGHWAY
HISTORIC SITE
FORT
HISTORIC INDIAN SITE
RECONSTRUCTED VILLAGE
PARK
ONTARIO
CANADA
U.S.A.
Pigeon R.
Grand Portage N.M.
GRAND PORTAGE IND. RES.
Vermilion L.
VERMILION RANGE
Superior N.F.
Grand Marais
Tower-Soudan S.P.
MESABI RANGE
61
S O T A
Virginia
Gilbert
Hull Rust Mahoning Mine
Ironworld U.S.A.
LAKE SUPERIOR
St. Louis R.
Eli Wirtanen Homestead
53
Split Rock Lighthouse S.P.
Two Harbors
FOND DU LAC IND. RES.
DULUTH
Jay Cooke S.P.
MICHIGAN
35
WISCONSIN
0
60 Mi.
St. Croix R.

impressive cascades on the Mississippi River that he named Saint Anthony Falls. Hennepin's adventures, as recounted (and ornamented) in his 1683 *Description de la Louisiane,* did a great deal to popularize the New World in Europe. In 1689, standing on the shores of Lake Pepin at present-day Red Wing, trader Nicolas Perrot officially claimed the upper Mississippi for Louis XIV. Other important French explorations included Pierre Charles Le Sueur's 1700 expedition to the Minnesota River to look for copper (the bluish earth that so intrigued the explorer turned out to be clay) and the exploits of Pierre Gaultier de Varennes, sieur de La Vérendrye, and his sons along the Rainy River and Lake of the Woods in the 1730s and 1740s. The French built a scattering of forts—usually short-lived—and fur posts, but they never established the firm presence here that they did along the Mississippi River in southern Illinois, Missouri, and Louisiana.

France ceded the lands west of the Mississippi to Spain in 1763, but Spanish influence on this far-flung territory was nominal. By contrast the British, who acquired the lands east of the river after the French and Indian War in 1763, were much more influential in Minnesota country. The English continued the French explorers' quest for the Pacific, or at least a Northwest Passage. The English also carried on the French fur trade, with the Montreal-based North West Company having the largest influence in Minnesota. During the 1780s and 1790s Grand Portage, at the tip of the Arrowhead region, was the hub of the North West Company's fur trade, but in 1803 the company grudgingly accepted that its outpost sat on American soil and moved north to Thunder Bay.

The Louisiana Purchase of 1803 placed western Minnesota in American hands but did little to budge the British fur traders. Their tenacity, combined with the Indians' loyalty, prompted the United States to assert its sovereignty over the region. In 1805 Captain Zebulon Pike embarked on a mission to find a site for a fort on the upper Mississippi, which would serve to discourage British fur traders and win the allegiance of the Indians. Pike selected the commanding bluffs at the confluence of the Mississippi and Minnesota rivers and acquired the land from the local Dakota. Established in 1819, Fort Snelling provided a safe haven for trade and commerce and attracted the influential leaders who would extract the land from the Indians and steer the territory toward statehood.

Treaty negotiations with the Indians began in 1825 and were largely complete by 1863. The Treaty of 1825 at Prairie du Chien in Wisconsin established the boundaries between the Ojibwa and Dakota lands in Minnesota and thus set the stage for the federal government to acquire those properties. The Ojibwa in the Arrowhead region ceded their land with treaties in 1837 and 1854 (further land was ceded in 1866, after iron was discovered on the Lake Vermilion Reservation), while the Ojibwa in northwestern Minnesota sold their lands in the Red River Valley in 1863. These treaties led to the establishment of seven Ojibwa reservations in the state.

The four bands of Dakota Indians were pressed into treaties in 1851, a direct result of the influx of white settlers after Minnesota became a territory in 1849. These treaties were transacted at two different places—Traverse des Sioux and Pilot Knob—in order to dilute the power of the Dakota chiefs. The Dakota ceded all their lands in Minnesota, and two reservations, comprising a strip 150 miles long by 10 miles wide, were established along the Minnesota River. The reservations were reduced by half in 1858. Seeds of distrust planted during these treaty negotiations led to the Dakota Conflict of 1862, which the federal government used as an excuse to abrogate the 1851 treaties and force the Dakota out of Minnesota. In ensuing years a few Dakota returned to the Minnesota River Valley, where their descendants still live.

Minnesota was very lightly settled prior to the Civil War and was distant from the main theaters of the conflict. Nonetheless the state provided some 24,000 soldiers, who fought in many decisive battles, the best known being the First Minnesota Regiment's heroic charge at Gettysburg on July 2, 1863. Minnesota was also incidentally involved in one of the disputes that led up to the war: Dred Scott, slave of a physician at Fort Snelling in the 1830s, later sued for his freedom on the grounds that he had lived in free territory at the fort. The Supreme Court denied the claim in 1857, in a famous decision mixing racist propaganda and tortuous legal reasoning that denied blacks citizenship and prevented Congress from excluding slaves from territories. The case was the high-water mark of the antebellum slavocracy.

It was predominantly New Englanders, New Yorkers, and Pennsylvanians—together with a few (but important) French families such as the Faribaults—who sought territorial status for Min-

OVERLEAF: *Rolling farmland, typical of central Minnesota.*

nesota and then guided it to statehood in 1858. Many were attaining their wealth in the lumber industry in the Saint Croix Valley, in the flour mills of Minneapolis, and in shipping and railroads in Saint Paul; the history of nineteenth-century Minnesota is a classic account of the link between entrepreneurship and politics. Immigrants, mainly German and Scandinavian, were attracted to Minnesota by the prospect of farming their own land and by ample jobs in lumbering, milling, and railroad building.

This chapter covers all of Minnesota, beginning in the northern portion of the state with the Northwest Angle and the Arrowhead region, then moving to central Minnesota, a region that includes the original settlements in the Saint Croix Valley and the vast pine forests that fed the lumber industry. Next is Minneapolis and Saint Paul, a metropolitan area of more than two million people that grew from Fort Snelling and the fur-trading village of Mendota. From there the chapter turns west to the Minnesota River Valley and concludes with southern Minnesota, which encompasses both Indian sites on the western prairie and nineteenth-century river towns along the Mississippi.

NORTHERN MINNESOTA

THE NORTHWEST ANGLE
AND LAKE OF THE WOODS

The Northwest Angle is a sparsely populated 132-square-mile plot of land isolated from the lower forty-eight states by Canada and Lake of the Woods. The sprawling, shallow (average depth, twenty-six feet) lake is a remnant of the huge glacial Lake Agassiz, which covered much of the Dakotas and northern Minnesota 10,000 years ago. Geographic confusion at the signing of the 1783 Treaty of Paris led to long disputes between Canada and the United States as to the exact boundary between the two countries in this important fur-trading region. By 1821 the Canadian companies began to abandon their posts, but it took the Webster-Ashburton Treaty of 1842 to establish the boundary. At **Northwest Point,** near Angle Inlet, are the ruins of a nineteenth-century Canadian village built to ensure Canadian interests in the area.

Fur trader Pierre Gaultier de Varennes, sieur de La Vérendrye—a great French explorer who with his sons helped open the
West—established Fort Saint Charles in 1732. The outpost was an
important hub from which La Vérendrye established trading posts
between Lake Superior and Lake Winnipeg, while his sons, search-
ing for the Northwest Passage in 1742, may have penetrated as far
as the eastern slopes of the Rocky Mountains, farther west than any
other European explorers at the time. In 1736 Vérendrye's eldest
son and nineteen other Frenchmen were killed near the fort by
Dakota angered by French trade with the Cree of Canada. The
massacre heightened Ojibwa hostility toward the Dakota and led to
increased warfare between the two tribes, which continued into the
nineteenth century. **Fort Saint Charles** was occupied until the
1750s, longer than any other French fort on Minnesota soil. A
replica of the fort now stands on **Magnusen Island.** (Because the
water level of Lake of the Woods has risen, the fort site is now
detached from the mainland.) **Lake of the Woods County Museum**
(8th Avenue Southeast, 218–634–1200), in **Baudette,** contains exhibits of local Indian tribes, the commercial fishing and
logging industries, and early agriculture.

GRAND MOUND

West of International Falls is the largest surviving prehistoric earth
structure in the upper Midwest. Measuring 136 feet by 98 feet and
25 feet high, Grand Mound is one of five mounds lying in deep
forest at the junction of the Big Fork and Rainy rivers. Various
cultures visited or occupied the area beginning about 5000 B.C.,
coming to fish the large sturgeon in the rivers. The mounds, which
were apparently used for burial purposes, were built by people of
what we call the Laurel Culture, hunter-gatherers who flourished
here from about 500 B.C. to A.D. 800. For the next 600 years the
area was occupied by people of the so-called Blackduck Culture,
who may have evolved from the Laurel group, although the con-
nection between the two remains unclear. An interpretive center
operated by the Minnesota Historical Society offers programs and
exhibits explaining the archaeological history of the site.

LOCATION: Route 11, 17 miles west of International Falls. HOURS: May
through Labor Day: 10–5 Monday–Saturday, 12–5 Sunday; Rest of
September through October: 10–4 Saturday, 12–4 Sunday. FEE: Yes.
TELEPHONE: 218–285–3332.

INTERNATIONAL FALLS

International Falls is a small industrial center on the south bank of the Rainy River, which forms the boundary between Canada and the United States. La Vérendrye's son and nephew built a fort here in 1731, but the area was not settled until the early 1900s, when a paper mill began to use the water power of the Koochiching Falls. The **Koochiching County Historical Society Museum** (214 Sixth Avenue, 218–283–4316) contains exhibits of the prehistory and natural history of the area, Indian artifacts, agricultural equipment, and logging-industry items, including a scale model of a sawmill that operated on the Little Fork River from 1914 to 1934. **Voyageurs National Park,** which is east of International Falls, has its headquarters in town (Route 53, 218–283–9821). The park, established in 1975, preserves 217,000 acres of forest and waterways once traveled by fur trappers.

DULUTH

Known as the Twin Ports, Duluth and its Wisconsin counterpart, Superior, share the westernmost tip of Lake Superior where the Saint Louis River snakes its way into the lake—Duluth on the granite terraces that characterize the rocky north shore, and Superior on the flat river delta. After the Soo Locks opened at Sault Ste. Marie in 1855, the cities grew as ports for the shipment of grain, iron ore, coal, and lumber.

Duluth is named for the dashing French trader Daniel Greysolon, sieur Duluth, who explored the western Lake Superior country in 1679. French fur traders established a seasonal outpost here beginning in the 1750s, a century before the city was permanently settled. Around it grew a small village of Indians, missionaries, and fur-trade operatives.

The city's history has been punctuated by a series of boom-and-bust cycles since its incorporation in the same year as the panic of 1857. The outlook improved in 1870 when it became the northern terminus of financier Jay Cooke's Lake Superior and Mississippi Railroad, connecting Saint Paul with the Great Lakes. Another major downturn followed when Cooke went bankrupt during the nationwide panic of 1873. Recovering within a decade, Duluth emerged as a grain-shipping rival of Chicago, and the opening of the Vermilion Range in 1884 and the Mesabi Range in 1891 secured its role as a major shipper of iron ore.

Duluth's Aerial Lift Bridge accommodates the large ships that call at this westernmost Great Lakes port.

Canal Park Marine Museum

This museum, operated by the U.S. Army Corps of Engineers, relates the history of shipping in the Twin Ports and exhibits a ship's pilothouse, engine room, and crew quarters, as well as illustrations and models of Great Lakes vessels and displays of ship damage caused by the 1905 and 1975 storms on Lake Superior. Canal Park is located beneath the 230-foot-high **Aerial Lift Bridge,** an impressive engineering feat built in 1905 and reconstructed in 1929–1930. Spanning the Duluth Ship Channel, it rises 135 feet to allow the passage of ships into Superior Bay. The bridge connects Duluth with Minnesota Point, a narrow, six-and-a-half-mile-long sand spit that acts as a natural breakwater between Lake Superior and Saint Louis and Superior bays.

LOCATION: Canal Park Drive at the Duluth Ship Channel. HOURS: April through May and September through mid-December: 10–4:30 Sunday–Thursday, 10–6 Friday–Saturday; June through August: 10–9 Daily; mid-December through March: 10–4:30 Friday–Sunday. FEE: None. TELEPHONE: 218–727–2497.

The Depot: Saint Louis County Heritage and Art Center

Designed by the Boston firm of Peabody and Stearns, with distinctive towers capped with conical roofs, the rambling chateauesque Duluth Union Depot served as the city's train station from 1892 until 1969. The brownstone structure now houses a variety of exhibits, including the **Lake Superior Museum of Transportation,** which has an extensive collection of trains and heavy equipment. On display are the first engine used on the Northern Pacific Railroad, a steam-powered wrecking crane, snow plows, cabooses, and a McGiffert log loader, as well as photographic exhibits documenting the importance of rail transportation to the growth of Duluth. **Depot Square** is an assembly of three-quarter-size replicas of turn-of-the-century Duluth commercial buildings. A vintage trolley runs past a meat and fish market, fire department, barber shop, bank, tent and awning company, and other stores.

The **Saint Louis County Historical Society Museum** displays many exhibits in the Depot, including a fine collection of Indian portraits by nineteenth-century American landscape and portrait artist Eastman Johnson. There are also exhibits of Ojibwa beadwork, clothing, and tools, nineteenth-century furnishings and costumes, and the shipping, lumber, and mining industries.

LOCATION: 506 West Michigan Street. HOURS: Mid-May through mid-October: 10–5 Daily; mid-October through mid-May: 10–5 Monday–Saturday, 1–5 Sunday. FEE: Yes. TELEPHONE: 218–727–8025.

Set amid dramatic cliffs and with its face to Lake Superior, Duluth is Minnesota's most picturesque city, and, with San Francisco, one of the two most beautifully sited cities in America. It was also the only municipality in the state to embrace the tenets of the City Beautiful Movement in the early part of this century. The **Duluth Civic Center** (West 1st Street between West Fourth and Sixth avenues) was planned at the turn of the century by Chicago architect Daniel Burnham. Its centerpiece is the 1909 Beaux Arts **Saint Louis County Courthouse,** also designed by Burnham. Other Beaux Arts structures on the plaza include the 1928 **City Hall** and 1930 **Federal Building.** Saint Paul architect Cass Gilbert designed the **Soldiers and Sailors' Monument** in 1921.

Superior Street, running northeast from downtown along the lake, cuts through the heart of the city's oldest affluent neighborhood, graced with many mansions built during the boom years by its wealthy and ebullient residents. The 1912 **Kitchi Gammi Club** (831 East Superior Street, private), founded by Duluth's wealthy in 1883, is a handsome Jacobean Revival building designed by the New York firm of Cram, Goodhue, and Ferguson. Kitchi Gammi is the Ojibwa name for Lake Superior. The **Traphagen House** (1511 East Superior Street, private) is a venerable Richardsonian Romanesque residence built in 1892 by prominent Duluth architect Oliver Traphagen with his partner, Francis Fitzpatrick. The 1902 **Crosby House** (2029 East Superior Street, private) is a brownstone bungalow built to mansion proportions by George H. Crosby, millionaire mine promoter who helped develop the Mesabi Range. It reflects the influences of H. H. Richardson, Louis Sullivan, the British Arts and Crafts movement, and the Art Nouveau style. The balcony entrance is dominated by an impressive carved stone lion's head.

Fronting Lake Superior is **Glensheen** (3300 London Road, 218–724–8864), the Jacobean mansion and estate of Duluth millionaire Chester A. Congdon. Completed in 1908, the massive red-brick structure was designed by Saint Paul architect Clarence Johnston. The furnishings, custom-designed for the house, range from Georgian to the Mission and Art Nouveau styles.

As French explorers and *voyageurs* began to penetrate the western Lake Superior country in the seventeenth century, they learned from the Indians of the area's vast network of rivers and lakes. One of the most important highways during the fur-trading era was the Saint Louis River, which with the Savanna River connected Lake Superior with the Mississippi. Portions of two portages on the route can be seen in state parks in the Duluth area. In **Jay Cooke State Park** (500 Route 210 East, 218–384–4610), the Grand Portage of the Saint Louis traverses some of the most rugged and beautiful country in northern Minnesota. This seven-mile portage was a narrow, crooked path along the boulder-strewn banks of the Saint Louis River that avoided a series of perilous rapids. Sixty miles west of Duluth is **Savanna Portage State Park** (Route 14, off Route 36, ten miles east of Route 65, 218–426–3271), where the six-mile Savanna Portage connected the Savanna River with Big Sandy Lake and the Mississippi River. The portage, which went through a mosquito-infested swamp, was the *voyageurs'* most dreaded carrying place in the Northwest.

Route 61, one of the most spectacular drives in the Great Lakes region, skirts the cliffs of Lake Superior's north shore from Duluth to Grand Portage. The area's history and economy are linked to the fur trade, iron-ore mining and shipping, commercial fisheries, and logging. The importance of these industries is emphasized in the exhibits of the **Lake County Historical Society and Railroad Museum** (Waterfront Drive and South Avenue, 218–834–4898) in **Two Harbors**. In **Grand Marais**, the **Cook County Museum** (Broadway) highlights commercial fishing and logging. It is housed in an 1896 lighthouse keeper's residence.

SPLIT ROCK LIGHTHOUSE AND HISTORY CENTER

Situated on a dramatic cliff overlooking Lake Superior, Split Rock Lighthouse was completed in 1910 to guide vessels along the treacherous north shore of the lake and into Two Harbors, an important shipping point for Minnesota iron ore. The lighthouse was built largely in response to a devastating November gale that struck Lake Superior in 1905, wreaking havoc on the booming iron-ore industry. It was in service for some sixty years. The compound includes a brick light tower, a fog-signal building, three keepers' dwellings, and the history center with exhibits on Lake Superior navigation, shipwrecks, and commercial fishing.

LOCATION: 2010 Route 61, 18 miles northeast of Two Harbors. HOURS: *Lighthouse Station:* 9–5 Daily; *Park:* 8 A.M.–10 P.M. Daily. FEE: Yes. TELEPHONE: 218–226–6377

GRAND PORTAGE NATIONAL MONUMENT

Located at the northeasternmost tip of Minnesota, the Grand Portage National Monument is a free adaptation of the North West Company fur-trading headquarters, which was built in the late eighteenth century to guard the important interior trade route on the Pigeon River. Two hundred years ago, this far-flung site was a major hub of the fur trade; from here the North West Company

OPPOSITE: *Split Rock Lighthouse, the tallest lighthouse in the United States, was built after a storm disabled eighteen ships on Lake Superior in November 1905.*

controlled a vast empire that stretched between both oceans. North West Company founders Benjamin and Joseph Frobisher, Simon McTavish, and James and John McGill came to Grand Portage from Montreal each summer to count their returns and distribute stock earnings. At the same time traders from widely scattered interior posts came to exchange pelts for trade goods and supplies and *voyageurs* arrived to receive their wages. By July Grand Portage's population swelled to a thousand or more. The 1783 Treaty of Paris, concluding the Revolutionary War, awarded the area south of the Pigeon River to the United States, and in 1803 the North West Company reluctantly decamped northward to Thunder Bay, where they established Fort William.

The reconstructed post stands near the head of the nine-mile Grand Portage Trail, which bypasses the unnavigable falls and rapids on the Pigeon River. At the terminus of the portage is the site of a former depot called Fort Charlotte, where furs from interior posts were temporarily stored during overland hauls to the stockade at Grand Portage. The portage trail, which has been restored, crosses the reservation of the Grand Portage Band of the Ojibwa. A stockade of vertical cedar pickets surrounds the trading post, a compound dominated by the Great Hall, the large building where fur-trade business was conducted and summer evening entertainment occurred. Meals were prepared in the kitchen to the rear of the Great Hall; both now contain fur-trade exhibits and period furnishings and fixtures. Outside the stockade the canoe warehouse, used originally to store fur and trade goods, now houses fur-trade artifacts, including replicas of the two types of birchbark canoes manned by the *voyageurs,* a large thirty-six-foot lake canoe used on the trip between Montreal and Grand Portage and a slimmer twenty-four-foot vessel designed to navigate the narrow, often rapid inland waterways. Guides in period costumes interpret the history of the site and an annual rendezvous reenacts the yearly assembly of the North West Company.

LOCATION: Route 61, 36 miles northeast of Grand Marais. *Main headquarters:* Old Coast Guard Building, 315 South Broadway, Grand Marais. HOURS: Mid-May through mid-October: 8–5 Daily. FEE: Yes. TELEPHONE: 218–387–2788.

OPPOSITE: *The Great Hall within the stockade at Grand Portage National Monument, a reconstructed North West Company fur trading depot five miles from the Canadian border.*

Although well off the beaten track, the **Eli Wirtanen Home** (west of Route 4, 218–733–7580) preserves an increasingly rare example of Finnish culture and rural architecture. The bachelor Eli Wirtanen homesteaded his property in 1904 and lived there until the 1950s. Typical of Finns in rural northern Minnesota, he worked at a variety of jobs (mainly in area lumber camps) and was a subsistence farmer. The farm is a cluster of small structures—most built by Wirtanen—including a square-hewed log house, privy, root cellar, horse barn, and a classic smoke sauna. The forty-acre farmstead, maintained by the Saint Louis County Historical Society, is approximately forty miles north of Duluth.

THE ARROWHEAD REGION

The Arrowhead region—the northeastern wedge of Minnesota above Lake Superior—is also often called the Iron Range in reference to the massive iron-ore deposits in the area. This remote province is noted for its harsh winters and for its scenic beauty, especially in autumn. Ridged with low, rugged hills, pocked with bogs and swamps, and blanketed with vast evergreen-aspen forests, it is sparsely populated, and what towns there are owe their origins and fluctuating prosperity to the mining of iron ore. Within this region are two massive and distinct deposits of iron ore: the Vermilion Range, where mining operations began in 1884, and the Mesabi Range, which was opened in 1891. (A third, the Cuyuna Iron Range, discovered in 1904, is located about a hundred miles west of Duluth near Aitkin.) Iron ore was discovered in the Vermilion and Mesabi ranges in the 1860s but was of little interest to prospectors who were intent on finding gold. Two of the first people to recognize the potential were Duluth banker George Stone and Philadelphia financier Charlemagne Tower, who with others formed the Minnesota Iron Mining Company in 1882.

SOUDAN UNDERGROUND MINE
STATE PARK

In 1884, the Minnesota Iron Mining Company shipped its first ore from the Vermilion Range's Soudan Mine (then the Breitung Mine), near present-day Tower, to the Lake Superior port of Two Harbors. Deep shafts had to be excavated to extract the ore in the Vermilion Range and, despite the high grade of its iron ore, the range is no longer being worked because extraction methods proved too expensive. The Soudan Mine shut down operations in 1962, but its underground workings are preserved in this park, along with several mining structures—engine house, crusher house, drill shop, and headframe—and an elevator that travels down a 2,400-foot shaft to one of the mine's last working areas.

LOCATION: Off Route 169, Soudan. HOURS: Memorial Day through Labor Day: 10–4 Daily. FEE: Yes. TELEPHONE: 218–753–2245.

Three miles north of Hoyt Lakes is the **Longyear Drill Site** (218–749–3150), where in 1890 mining engineer E. J. Longyear first used a diamond drill to take a core sample in a search for iron-ore deposits. His method revolutionized the exploration of iron ore and other minerals and also became useful for taking test borings for large construction projects. Representative diamond drill equipment—including a Sullivan Model H drill, Cameron #3 water pump, churn buck, and vertical steam boiler—have been reassembled on the original site, which is maintained by the Iron Range Historical Society in nearby **Gilbert.**

Northeast of Soudan in **Ely** is an entry point for canoe trips through the **Boundary Waters Canoe Area,** a three-thousand-square mile preserve of forest and waterways that looks much as it did when French fur trappers plied this region in the eighteenth and nineteenth centuries. Information about the Boundary Waters, which is part of the Superior National Forest, can be obtained at the Superior National Forest Information Center (1600 East Sheridan Street (218–365–7681).

HULL RUST MAHONING MINE

In the Mesabi Iron Range on the outskirts of Hibbing, the Hull Rust Mahoning Mine resembles a man-made Grand Canyon. Three and one-half miles long and one and one-half miles wide, and some six hundred feet deep, it is the world's largest open-pit iron-ore mine. The water depth is 368 feet. Although the late twentieth century saw a decline in the American steel industry, taconite was still being mined near Hibbing in 1997 by the Hull Rust mine owners. The big pit can be viewed from the Central Mine Observation Station; a bus tour of the taconite mine may be taken.

LOCATION: East.Third Avenue, 2 miles north of Hibbing. HOURS: Late June through late August: 9–7 Daily. FEE: Yes, for bus trip. TELEPHONE: 218–262–4166.

Hibbing, plotted in 1893, has shifted over the years to allow mining operations to probe the rich iron-ore deposits on which it was originally built. The 1920s bus line established to carry passengers between the new section of town and the old, depopulated section later grew into Greyhound Bus Lines. Of interest is **Hibbing High School** (800 East 21st Street, 218–263–3675), a mammoth Jacobethan structure built between 1920 and 1923 to replace a school torn down to make way for iron-ore excavations. Mining operators provided most of the capital and they did not skimp.

In the midst of the Mesabi Iron Range is **Ironworld Discovery Center** (Route 169, Chisholm, 218–254-3321), featuring the 36-foot Iron Man Memorial. A railroad skirts the edge of the Glen Open-Pit Iron Mine. The **Minnesota Museum of Mining** (Route 169, Chisholm, 218–254–5543) has an Old Town Chisholm exhibit.

FOREST HISTORY CENTER

This history center depicts and interprets the logging industry when it was at its height, at the turn of the century. In 1900, the peak year for Minnesota's lumber industry, more than a billion board feet were sent from these northern pineries to sawmills. After 1900, production dropped off dramatically as the state's virgin pine stands were harvested. A replica of a turn-of-the-century lumber camp includes a double horse barn; an office-store, known as a wanigan, where employees purchased personal belongings on credit; the bunkhouse; a blacksmith shop; a cook's shanty; and a filer's shack, where crosscut saws were sharpened. Each is appointed with period fixtures and furnishings, and guides in costume depict the life of a lumberjack. A museum has displays on the area's Indian heritage and the lumber industry. Trees along the Woodland Trail typify the forests of northern Minnesota, including the white pine, the chief commodity of the loggers.

LOCATION: Off Routes 169 and 2 in Grand Rapids. HOURS: Late May through mid-October: 10–5 Monday–Saturday, 12–5 Sunday; mid-October through late May: 12–4 Daily. FEE: Yes. TELEPHONE: 218–327–4482.

With the help of the Ojibwa guide Ozawindib, geologist and Indian agent Henry Rowe Schoolcraft located the long-disputed source of the Mississippi River in 1832. Schoolcraft named the source Lake Itasca, apparently by linking syllables from *veritas* and *caput*, the

Lake Itasca, where the Mississippi River begins its 2,552-mile course to the Gulf of Mexico.

Latin words for "truth" and "head." One of the oldest state parks in the country, the 32,000-acre **Itasca State Park** (Route 71, thirty-two miles southwest of Bemidji, 218–266–2100) was established in 1891 to protect the headwaters of the Mississippi River from the encroachment of the lumber industry. The park contains some of the largest and oldest white and red pines in the state.

CROOKSTON

The **Polk County Museum** (Route 2, 218–281–1038) traces the history and development of the surrounding area through artifacts ranging from a walking plow to a 1934 airplane. Also on the grounds are an 1880 schoolhouse, an 1872 log house, and a Burlington Northern caboose.

On October 2, 1863—after nearly two weeks of speechmaking, feasting, and being plied with rum—some Ojibwa chiefs ceded 9,750,000 acres of land in northwestern Minnesota and northeastern North Dakota to the federal government in exchange for reservation land and an annual fee to be paid over twenty years.

The treaty, which opened the fertile Red River Valley to white settlement, was signed at **Old Crossing Treaty Site,** where a pioneer oxcart trail crossed the Red Lake River. Located northeast of Crookston via routes 75 and 57, it is now a State Wayside Park.

MOORHEAD

Moorhead, set in the fertile Red River Valley, developed around a ford on the river, opposite Fargo, North Dakota. After 1872, when the Northern Pacific trains began to run through Moorhead, the frontier town became an important hub on this east–west line with many hotels and restaurants to serve the transient clientele. The **Solomon G. Comstock House** (506 South 8th Street, 218–233–0848) was completed in 1883, during the height of the boom years, by a financier who worked with Saint Paul tycoon James J. Hill to develop a rail system in the Red River Valley. Comstock's daughter Ada, a noted educator, was the first dean of women at the University of Minnesota and later served as president of Radcliffe College. The Queen Anne–style house has been restored to its 1883 appearance and contains most of the original furnishings.

The **Heritage Hjemkomst Interpretive Center** (202 North First Avenue, 218–233–5604) houses a seventy-seven-foot-long white oak replica of a Viking sailing ship called the *Hjemkomst,* built in 1971. In 1982 a crew sailed the vessel from Duluth to Bergen, Norway. The center also includes exhibits tracing the development of Moorhead and the other settlements in the Red River Valley.

CENTRAL MINNESOTA

MILLE LACS REGION

A large puddle left by the retreating glaciers, Mille Lacs is 200 square miles in area but only forty feet deep and is surrounded by a constellation of smaller lakes amid forested hummocks. In the mid-1700s, the Ojibwa and Dakota fought territorial battles in the area, the most decisive being the Ojibwa victory in the 1745 battle of Kathio. The battle site is now part of **Mille Lacs Kathio State Park** (off Route 169, 320–532–3523). After they succeeded in driving the Dakota south to the Minnesota Valley, the Ojibwa made the shores of Mille Lacs the cultural center of their forest homeland. The **Mille Lacs Indian Museum** (Route 169 at Vineland, ten miles north of Onamia, 320–532–3632) contains exhibits explaining the history and culture of the Dakota and Ojibwa, dioramas portraying the seasonal activities of the Ojibwa, and displays of Ojibwa crafts, including canoe making, beadwork, and weaving.

The French, British, and Americans were unusually eager to keep peace between Indian tribes in this region, since warring between the Ojibwa and Dakota was a hindrance to the fur trade and later to American settlement. Minnesota's second military post, **Fort Ripley,** was built some thirty miles west of the lake in 1848–1849 as part of the American surveillance effort. The fort is on the grounds of the Minnesota National Guard's **Camp Ripley Military Reservation,** also the location of the Minnesota Military Museum. Only a few stones remain of the original buildings; permission to see the site must be obtained from the camp commander at Camp Ripley (320–632–6631).

BRAINERD

Brainerd was established when the Northern Pacific Railroad built a bridge over the Mississippi at this site in 1871. Portions of the **Northern Pacific Headquarters** (vicinity of Laurel Street and Thirteenth Street South), built in 1871, have been restored for commercial use. The **Crow Wing County Historical Society Museum** (320 Laurel Street, 218–829–3268) has exhibits covering the Dakota and Ojibwa Indians, the fur trade, the logging industry, railroads, and pioneer settlement. **Lumbertown U.S.A.** (Route 77, twelve miles northwest of Brainerd, 218–829–8872), a group of twenty-four historic structures, depicts life in a Minnesota logging town in the 1870s.

LITTLE FALLS

Little Falls is situated on—and takes its name from—the eleven-foot drop in the Mississippi that attracted early settlers as a site for gristmills and sawmills. The first dam and sawmill were built in 1849, and the Pine Tree Lumber Company operated a large mill here from 1891 to 1919.

Charles A. Lindbergh House

Charles A. Lindbergh, the famed pilot who in 1927 made the first nonstop flight between Paris and New York, grew up on this 110-acre farmstead overlooking the Mississippi River. The family's first house burned down in 1905, and the 1906 Craftsman-style bungalow that replaced it was used mainly as a summer retreat during the ten years Charles A. Lindbergh, Sr., was a congressman in Washington, DC. The younger Charles managed the farm for two years

Charles Lindbergh grew up in this modest bungalow in Little Falls, where he spent hours "watching white cumulus clouds drift overhead" and dreamed of flying.

while he was completing high school. After he went to college in 1920, the house was seldom occupied, and following Lindbergh's trans-Atlantic flight, souvenir hunters made off with all movable objects. The restored house contains period furnishings, and exhibits explain Lindbergh family history.

LOCATION: Lindbergh Drive. HOURS: May through August: 10–5 Monday–Saturday, 12–5 Sunday; September through October: 10–4 Saturday, 12–4 Sunday. FEE: Yes. TELEPHONE: 320–632–3154.

SAUK CENTRE

Sinclair Lewis was born in Sauk Centre in 1885, grew up here, and later used the town, a trade center surrounded by farmlands, as the model for the fictional Gopher Prairie in his 1920 novel *Main Street*. The **Sinclair Lewis Boyhood Home** (810 Sinclair Lewis Avenue, 320–352–5201) a ca. 1880 frame house with Queen Anne elements, contains Lewis family items and other period furnishings, and the **Sinclair Lewis Museum** (Routes 94 and 71, 320–352–5201) displays memorabilia of the novelist.

SAINT CLOUD

The northernmost navigable stretch of the Mississippi River lies between Saint Anthony Falls and Sauk Rapids, sixty-five miles to the northwest. Saint Cloud, located in the largest dairy-producing region in Minnesota, grew up around this northern terminus of commercial traffic on the river. First settled in 1854, the river trading town served the outlying farms and was also noted for its granite quarries. The **Stearns County Heritage Center** (235 South Thirty-third Avenue, 320–253–8424) contains a variety of exhibits, including a natural history display, Ojibwa and Dakota dwellings, a two-story replica of a granite quarry, and a reconstructed log barn from the era of pioneer settlement. The **Fifth Avenue Commercial Buildings** (14–30 South Fifth Avenue, even numbers only) reflect the town's late-nineteenth-century prosperity.

Saint Johns University (Route 94, fourteen miles west of Saint Cloud, 320–363–2011) was founded by Benedictine monks who came in 1856 to minister to the German immigrants in the region. Most of the campus buildings are of locally made brick and date from 1866 to 1920, but eleven are modern structures designed by Bauhaus architect Marcel Breuer, including the **Saint Johns Abbey Church.** The bell tower, or "banner," is a 112-foot-high concrete slab supported by two concrete parabolas and containing the original monastery bells; its design is reminiscent of the flat facades of early Spanish missions. The walls and ceiling of the church are of corrugated reinforced concrete whose massive folds define the interior space.

OLIVER H. KELLEY FARM

Boston speculator and trader Oliver H. Kelley came to this site near the confluence of the Elk and Mississippi rivers in 1850 to help found the town of Itasca. When that venture failed, he turned to farming and in 1866 was appointed by the Department of Agriculture to report on the state of post–Civil War farming in the South. In 1867 he founded the National Grange of the Patrons of Husbandry, or the Grange, a national organization to protect farmers' interests. At its peak of influence in the mid-1870s, the Grange had nearly one million members.

The 189-acre farm is operated as a living history farm, with costumed guides doing domestic and farm chores as they would

Agricultural methods from the nineteenth century are still practiced at the Oliver H. Kelley Farm. OPPOSITE: *Trousers made from homespun fabric lie atop a crazy quilt in a bedroom at the farm.*

have been done in Kelley's time. The ca. 1875 homestead, a large frame house with Italianate elements, was built at a time when Kelley was largely occupied in Washington, DC, although his daughters lived here and farmed the land for another decade. The house contains period furnishings, and crops are grown in fields worked with oxen and horses using nineteenth-century implements. An interpretive center traces the life of Oliver Kelley and the history of the Grange.

LOCATION: Route 10, 2.5 miles southeast of the town of Elk River. HOURS: May through October: 10–5 Monday–Saturday; *Interpretive Center:* May through October: 10–5 Monday–Saturday; November through April: 10–4 Saturday, 12–5 Sunday. FEE: Yes. TELEPHONE: 612–441–6896.

SAINT CROIX RIVER VALLEY

Fur traders entered this region in the late 1700s, traveling from Lake Superior via the Brule–Saint Croix river system. The first permanent settlers were lumbermen from New England who arrived in the 1840s, lured by the extensive pine forests and the rushing Saint Croix, which provided a means of getting logs to market. Bringing with them Youlee styles of architecture and town planning, they built villages along the river in both Minnesota and Wisconsin that resemble towns in Vermont, Maine, and New York.

Halfway between the Twin Cities and Duluth, **Hinckley** was an important railroad stop in the nineteenth century. On September 1, 1894, the town was at the center of an immense firestorm, which killed more than 400 people and destroyed over 400 square miles of land. The **Hinckley Fire Museum** (106 Old Highway 61, 320–384–7338) is housed in the 1894 Saint Paul & Duluth Railway Station. Built to replace the one destroyed by the fire, the depot contains period fixtures and exhibits relating to the history of the disaster.

A family farm near Marine on Saint Croix, which was the second settlement in the state, after Mendota.

Near Pine City, a replica of the North West Company Fur Post has been constructed with the help of a journal kept by fur trader John Sayer during his residence here in the winter of 1804–1805.

North West Company Fur Post

Set on the banks of the Snake River, near the present-day town of Pine City, the North West Company Fur Post was occupied during the winter of 1804–1805 by fur trader John Sayer, his Indian wife, Obemau-Qnoqua, and a crew of *voyageurs*. Sayer was the dominant trader in the region from 1784 until 1805, and his journal of the winter he spent on the Snake River is a valuable record of the fur-trading era in Minnesota. A replica of the post, built by the Minnesota Historical Society, now stands on the original site. Surrounded by a stockade, the six-room log cabin contains furs and reproductions of goods and tools of the fur trade, and costumed guides demonstrate typical winter activities.

LOCATION: County Road 7, 1.5 miles west of the Pine City exit of Route 35. HOURS: May through Labor Day: 10–5 Monday–Saturday, 12–5 Sunday. FEE: None. TELEPHONE: 320–629–6356.

The sawmill town of **Taylors Falls** sits within view of the impressive rocky canyon called the Dalles of the Saint Croix. On a terrace overlooking the falls and the chasm is **Angels Hill Historic District**

A clapboard house in Taylor's Angels Hill Historic District, where in the 1850s and 1860s settlers from New England created a town reminiscent of a Vermont village. OPPOSITE: *Stillwater preserves a wealth of late-nineteenth-century residential and commercial architecture.*

(vicinity of Military and Government roads, and West and Plateau streets), a well-preserved mid-nineteenth-century village built around a central green. The structures, which are predominantly Greek Revival, include the **W. H. C. Folsom House** (Government Road, 612–465–3125). Folsom, a native of Maine, arrived in Taylors Falls in 1850 and made his fortune as a logger, merchant, and speculator. His large frame house, furnished with original Folsom family pieces, was built in the Greek Revival style with Federal elements and Southern-inspired verandahs.

One mile south of Taylors Falls is the headquarters of **Interstate Park** (Routes 8 and 95, 612–465–5711), the Minnesota counterpart to Wisconsin's Interstate Park on the east bank of the Saint Croix River. A **museum** at the headquarters explains the glacial geology of the valley. The tiny village of **Franconia** is nearby.

The **Gammelgarden Museum** (20880 Olinda Trail, 612–433–5053), in the Swedish community of **Scandia,** preserves several Swedish immigrant structures in an outdoor park. Among them is the first log sanctuary of the 1856 **Elim Lutheran Church,** the oldest extant church building in Minnesota.

Stillwater's Italianate Washington County Courthouse, which served the boisterous loggers of the Saint Croix Valley at the end of the nineteenth century.

Founded in 1843, **Stillwater** was the Saint Croix Valley's major logging and milling center and the site of the impromptu 1848 Territorial Convention held by the leading settlers—including Mendota fur trader Henry H. Sibley—which led to the formation of the Minnesota Territory in 1849. The site of the convention is marked by a **plaque** at Main and Myrtle streets. The town's commercial district retains numerous structures from the lumbering era, including the 1891 **John Karst Building** (125 South Main Street, private), the 1890s **Staples Block** (119 South Main Street, private), and the 1882 **Excelsior Block** (120 North Main Street, private). The 1867 **Washington County Courthouse** (101 West Pine Street, 612–430–6233), a monumental brick and stone structure with Greek Revival and Italianate elements, is one of the oldest public buildings in the state. The courtroom has been restored to the turn of the century with original furnishings, and photos detailing the history of the building are on display. The **Washington County Historical Museum** (602 North Main Street, 612–439–5956), housed in the 1853 state prison warden's house, contains Indian artifacts, lumberjack tools, nineteenth-century costumes and quilts, and early prison items.

THE   TWIN   CITIES

FORT SNELLING

Fort Snelling, built in 1819, was an impressive reminder to the British and Indians that America was bent on securing its claim to the Northwest after the War of 1812. The fort, largely rebuilt since 1950, stands on sheer bluffs at the confluence of the Mississippi and Minnesota rivers, a site Zebulon Pike purchased from the Dakota during his 1805 journey through the upper Mississippi region. The Fifth Regiment of Infantry was stationed at the fort and built mills at Saint Anthony Falls, planted crops, and inspected traders' goods in transit on the Mississippi. Missionaries gathered here to instruct Indians clustered in villages around the fort, while the Columbia and American fur companies built their headquarters nearby. Thus, the fort became a major focal point for trade, communication, and social life on the upper Mississippi and provided the nucleus around which Saint Paul and Minneapolis would grow. It declined in importance after 1851 when Indian treaties opened up lands to the west and other forts, such as Fort Ripley, assumed its responsibilities.

The garrison was originally called Fort Saint Anthony, but in 1825 the name was changed to honor Colonel Josiah Snelling, the commander responsible for its design and construction. Made of locally quarried limestone, the buildings within the diamond-shaped compound included barracks, commandant's and officers' quarters, a sutler's store, and a school (the first on the upper Mississippi). These structures were enclosed by a massive stone wall, punctuated at the four corners with sentry towers. Costumed interpreters rec act nineteenth-century life at the fort.

LOCATION: Fort Snelling exits off Routes 5 and 55. HOURS: May through October: 10–5 Monday–Saturday, 12–5 Sunday. *History Center:* May through October: 9:30–5:30 Monday–Saturday, 11:30–5 Sunday. Rest of year: 9–4:30 Monday–Friday. FEE: For History Center. TELE-PHONE: 612–725–2428.

OLD MENDOTA

The oldest permanent white settlement in the state, Mendota sits at the confluence of the Mississippi and Minnesota rivers and takes its name from the Dakota term for "meeting of the waters." Fur

traders worked at this strategic location in the late 1700s and had
established permanent camps by the early 1800s. The American
Fur Company set up a post at Mendota in 1824, and Henry H.
Sibley, second operator of the post and future first governor of
Minnesota, ran a store in one of the company warehouses that was
a spirited gathering point for Indians, French-Canadian *voyageurs*,
and traders. Troops from Fort Snelling, just across the Minnesota
River, also frequented Mendota.

The 1835 **Henry Sibley House** (1357 Route 13, 612–452–
1596) is the oldest stone residence in Minnesota, and when Sibley
lived here, from 1836 to 1862, it was the social and political hub of
the region. The vernacular house, constructed of locally quarried
limestone, contains period furnishings, some of them original, and
original items of clothing. Next door is the 1839 **Jean B. Faribault
House** (612–452–1596), a limestone structure that has a more
Greek Revival cast. Its central-hall interior allowed the residence to
be used as an inn. The French-Canadian Faribault began fur trading in Minnesota in the early 1800s, and his son Alexander, for
whom the town of Faribault is named, followed in his footsteps.
The house is now a museum of Indian artifacts, many of them
from the collection of Episcopal bishop Henry Whipple, a friend
and supporter of the Dakota Indians.

Nearby **Pilot Knob** (Route 13, west of Route 55), now the
Acacia Memorial Cemetery, is the highest point in the area. In
1851 it was the site of the signing of the Treaty of Mendota, which,
together with the Treaty of Traverse des Sioux, resulted in the
Dakota ceding to the United States 24 million acres of land in
southern Minnesota and adjacent parts of Iowa and South Dakota.
The Pilot Knob sessions, which involved the Mdewakanton and
Wahpekute tribes of the Dakota, began some days after the completion of treaty negotiations at Traverse des Sioux with the Sisseton and Wahpeton tribes. American negotiators deliberately separated the Dakota into two groups to reduce their strength and to
allow the federal agents to deal first with the Sisseton and Wahpeton, who were considered more malleable. Although there was
some resistance, the Mdewakanton and Wahpekute chiefs ultimately signed an agreement similar to the Treaty of Traverse des
Sioux. They were later assigned to reservation land around the
Lower Sioux Agency, while the Sisseton and Wahpeton were assigned to the Upper Sioux Agency.

SAINT PAUL

Saint Paul and Minneapolis may not be immediately distinguishable to the twentieth-century visitor, but the two cities had quite distinct origins and courses of development in the nineteenth century. Minneapolis grew up around Saint Anthony Falls as a lumbering and milling center, thus establishing itself as an industrial city. Saint Paul got its start at two river landings on the Mississippi below Mendota, and in the nineteenth century it was primarily a trading and transportation center and a point of entry for settlers and European immigrants.

Long before the arrival of either historic Indian tribes or white settlers, the bluffs along the Minnesota and Mississippi rivers were selected by prehistoric peoples as burial sites. Thousands of these mounds were destroyed by farming and urban development, but six have been preserved in **Indian Mounds Park** (Mounds Boulevard and Earl Street).

Saint Paul's 1888 Winter Carnival Ice Palace. OVERLEAF: *The city's origins as a Mississippi port are still visible in the late-nineteenth-century warehouses clustered at right.*

Saint Paul's first white settlers were French-Canadians and French-speaking Swiss refugees who had come to the area from Lord Selkirk's colony in Canada in 1838. Among them was an infamous French-Canadian trader named Pierre Parrant, whose main venture was selling whiskey. Parrant's disagreeable visage inspired the nickname Pig's Eye, which also served as the name for the early settlement. In 1841 the Catholic priest Lucien Galtier erected the Chapel of Saint Paul near the river landing and urged the more respectable saint's name on the village. The chapel site is marked with a **plaque** on Kellogg Boulevard near Minnesota Street.

Saint Paul, below the rapids and Saint Anthony Falls—at the head of navigation on the Mississippi—was a natural focus for steamboat traffic, and by the 1850s it was the busiest river port in the region. The city began on a narrow terrace along the Mississippi that linked the bustling river landing with Fort Snelling—this overland route can be traveled today by driving on West Seventh Street from downtown Saint Paul to the fort—and the strip of land also provided residential space convenient to the business district, such as **Lauer Flats** (226 Western Avenue, private), a group of townhouses built in 1887. In the downtown area the Richardsonian Romanesque **Landmark Center** (95 West 5th Street), constructed from 1894 to 1904 to serve as the federal courts building, is now an arts and cultural center, and the **Saint Paul Building** (6 West 5th Street), formerly the Germania Bank, has undergone an intelligent and respectful restoration. Most of the houses in the **Irvine Park Historic District** date from 1875 to 1900, and the most prominent is the 1872 **Alexander Ramsey House** (265 South Exchange Street, 612–296–8760). Home of the man who served as Minnesota's first territorial governor and second state governor, the Second Empire mansion is still furnished with original family pieces.

The 1896–1905 **Minnesota State Capitol** (Aurora Avenue between Cedar and Park streets, 612–296–2881) dominates the terraces north of the downtown area. The third of Minnesota's capitols (the first burned down in 1881; the second was razed in 1938), it is a monumental Beaux-Arts Classical structure typical of late-nineteenth-century statehouses but nonetheless a masterpiece of that genre. Designed by Cass Gilbert, who lived for many years in Saint Paul, it is a domed building with three projecting wings of granite and marble.

OPPOSITE: The Progress of the State, *a gilded four-horse chariot representing prosperity, adorns the base of the Minnesota State Capitol dome. It is the work of Daniel Chester French and Edward Potter.*

As Saint Paul outgrew its river terrace, it began to expand to the scenic bluffs overlooking the river. In the 1850s the first houses—more accurately country estates—were built on the promontory, but development was impeded by the panic of 1857, the Civil War, and the panic of 1873. With the boom years of the 1880s and improved city services permitting access to these bluffs, Saint Paul's wealthiest and most prominent citizens moved to **Summit Avenue** and commissioned the city's prominent architects, including Cass Gilbert and James Knox Taylor, to design mansions in the popular styles of the time. The eastern end of the avenue is a textbook of late-nineteenth-century residential architecture. While the largest houses were of the Richardsonian Romanesque style, most have gone; those that remain are Italianate, Second Empire, Queen Anne, and Jacobethan. The **Burbank-Livingston-Griggs House** (432 Summit Avenue, private), completed in 1865, is a fine example of the Italian Villa style. At the brow of the bluff stands the French Baroque **Cathedral of Saint Paul** (Summit and Selby avenues), completed in 1915. With its immense copper-clad dome, it is one of Saint Paul's most commanding structures.

Across from the cathedral stands Summit Avenue's other monumental structure, the **James J. Hill House** (240 Summit Avenue, 612–297–2555). The Canadian-born Hill moved to Saint Paul in 1856, when he was seventeen, to work as a stevedore and clerk on the Saint Paul levee and eventually amassed a fortune in the freight business. His paramount achievement was the completion in 1893 of the Great Northern Railroad between Saint Paul and Puget Sound; after he gained control, as well, of the Northern Pacific, Hill had a virtual monopoly on rail traffic between Chicago and the Pacific Northwest. He built his mansion between 1889 and 1891, at the height of his success. The 36,000-square-foot Richardsonian Romanesque structure is no masterpiece—Peabody and Stearns, its designers, were no Richardsons—but the interior contains elaborate woodwork and stained-glass windows.

F. Scott Fitzgerald grew up near, but not on, Summit Avenue, and his **birthplace** still stands at 481 Laurel Avenue (private). In 1919, while writing *This Side of Paradise*, he lived in an apartment in **Summit Terrace** (599 Summit Avenue, private), a Richardsonian Romanesque rowhouse he described as "a house below the average on a street above the average."

OPPOSITE: *Saint Paul's old Federal Courts Building, now the Landmark Center, was the scene of several trials of notorious gangsters in the 1930s.*

The **Gibbs Farm Museum** (Cleveland and Larpenteur avenues, Falcon Heights, 612–646–8629) is a seven-acre farmstead on land purchased by Heman and Jane Gibbs in 1849 and owned by the Gibbs family for nearly 100 years. On the premises are an 1854 vernacular farmhouse, an 1878 one-room school, and an 1890 barn, and the museum offers quilting, beekeeping, and blacksmithing demonstrations.

MINNEAPOLIS

Modern Minneapolis came into being in 1872 with the merger of two Mississippi River settlements: the city of Minneapolis, founded in 1849 on military reservation land on the west bank, and Saint Anthony, at Saint Anthony Falls on the east bank. The falls were first used for power by Josiah Snelling's troops, who built gristmills and sawmills at the cascades in the early 1820s. Franklin Steele, brother-in-law of Henry Sibley, realized the potential of the site and built a cabin at the falls in 1838 and a dam and sawmill in 1847. The 1849 **Ard Godfrey House** (Richard Chute Park between Bank Street and Central Avenue, 612–870–8001), the oldest extant residence on the east bank, was built by a millwright who worked for Steele and then started his own mill; the Greek Revival frame house contains mid-nineteenth-century furnishings.

The Pillsbury A Mill, Minneapolis.

The sawmills around the falls provided lumber for the rapidly developing farmlands to the west, lumber that was transported by an expanding network of railroads. These trains brought back the wheat that fed the flour mills, which had been financed largely by wealthy lumbermen. By 1870 a dozen mills were operating at the falls, and Minneapolis was the nation's leading producer of flour. Saint Anthony Falls was the industrial center of Minneapolis until World War I. The area is currently being revamped as a neighborhood of condominiums and shopping areas, but it still retains a strong sense of its industrial origins. A splendid remnant from that era is the **Pillsbury A Mill** (Main Street SE and Third Avenue SE), a looming limestone structure built in 1881 to use water from Saint Anthony Falls, which lie just below the mill. The falls, although obscured by a dam and hydroelectric facility, can be seen from the park that skirts the river on Main Street SE. Also visible from the park is the **Great Northern Railroad Bridge** (Main Street SE and Sixth Avenue SE), a series of massive stone arches spanning the Mississippi River constructed between 1881 and 1883. Against the southern sky, monumental grain storage elevators, including the ca. 1900 **Archer Daniels Midland Elevators** (29th Street SE, off 4th Street SE), form an impressive backdrop.

In the 1930s the Minneapolis skyline was dominated by the **Foshay Tower** (821 Marquette Avenue), a thirty-two-story obelisk with Art Deco elements constructed between 1927 and 1929. Upon its completion the tower was placed in receivership and its owner, Wilbur B. Foshay, was convicted of fraud. The **City Hall and Hennepin County Courthouse** (350 Fifth Street South), designed by Long and Kees, is a many-turreted Richardsonian Romanesque structure built between 1888 and 1905. The interior court has stained glass, iron stairs, and a monumental statue, *Mississippi, Father of the Waters,* by Larkin Goldsmith Mead. Turn-of-the-century commercial structures include the 1902 **Grain Exchange** (400 Fourth Street South) and the 1892 **Flour Exchange** (310 Fourth Avenue South).

The **Washburn-Fair Oaks Historic District,** south of downtown Minneapolis, contains many privately owned nineteenth-century houses, among them the 1888 **McKnight-Newell House** (1818 La Salle Avenue), one of the city's best extant Romanesque Revival structures; the 1912 Jacobethan **Charles Pillsbury House** (106 22nd Street East); and the 1903 **Alfred Pillsbury House** (116 22nd Street East), a mix of Gothic and Richardsonian Romanesque.

The museum and archives of the **American Swedish Institute** (2600 Park Avenue, 612–871–4907) are housed in a grandiose Romanesque mansion built between 1903 and 1907 by Swedish immigrant Swan Turnblad, who owned the Swedish-language newspaper *Svenska Amerikanska Posten.* The interior of the house contains elaborately carved woodwork, stained glass, painted plaster moldings, and Swedish furnishings, including porcelain-tile *kakelugnar* stoves. Exhibits throughout the mansion explain the history of Swedish immigrants in America.

A portrait of a sixteenth-century cardinal in his study, attributed to Lorenzo Costa, in the diverse collection of the Minneapolis Institute of Arts.

Pierre Bonnard's 1913 Dining Room in the Country *from the collection of the Minneapolis Institute of Arts (detail).*

Minneapolis Institute of Arts

One of the finest art museums in the Great Lakes region, the Minneapolis Institute of Arts opened in 1915 and now displays a large collection of ancient Greek and Roman statuary and pottery, Dutch and Italian paintings of the seventeenth and eighteenth centuries, French paintings of the nineteenth and twentieth centuries, and a variety of objects from Asia, South and Central America, and Africa. The institute's collections are strong in the areas of American and English silver and eighteenth-century French and Italian furniture. Among the American painters represented are Benjamin West, John Singleton Copley, Thomas Eakins, John Singer Sargent, Georgia O'Keefe, and Grant Wood. The institute also displays photographs by such noted masters as Alfred Stieglitz, Edward Weston, Lewis W. Hine, and Walker Evans.

LOCATION: 2400 Third Avenue South. HOURS: 10–5 Tuesday–Wednesday, Friday–Saturday; 10–9 Thursday; 12–5 Sunday. FEE: None. TELEPHONE: 612–870–3131.

The **Walker Art Center** (Vineland Place, 612–375–7622), one of the nation's most important museums of twentieth-century art, displays paintings, sculpture, and other works representing Social Realism, Cubism, Abstract Expressionism, Pop Art, Minimalism, and other movements. It is also an important venue for music, dance, poetry readings, film, and video.

The beauty of Minneapolis's design, on what was once the site of Dakota Indian villages along a string of lakes (Cedar Lake, Lake of the Isles, Lake Calhoun, Lake Harriet, Hiawatha Lake, and Lake Nokomis), is a testimony to the prescience of the nineteenth-century urban planners who argued successfully for the establishment of parks and parkways in this setting. The area has evolved as an impressive mix of residential neighborhoods, public parkland, and commercial developments. Many of the early-twentieth-century houses were designed by Prairie School architect William Gray Purcell in partnership with George G. Elmslie. Working with Elmslie, Purcell designed his own residence for a site overlooking Lake of the Isles. The 1913 **Purcell–Cutts House** (2328 Lake Place, 612–870–3131), a masterpiece of the Prairie School genre, is open the second weekend each month. Reservations must be made.

The beautiful fifty-three-foot **Minnehaha Falls,** located in **Minnehaha Park** (Minnehaha Avenue and Godfrey Road), on Minnehaha Creek just above its confluence with the Mississippi River, attracted explorers, traders, settlers, and such personages as Samuel Clemens in the early days of the Minnesota Territory. Accounts and a daguerreotype of the falls inspired portions of Longfellow's *Song of Hiawatha,* which in turn attracted more visitors. The oldest house on the west bank of the river, the 1849 **John H. Stevens House** (612–722–2220) originally stood in the settlement of Minneapolis, which Stevens founded in 1849. The house was moved to Minnehaha Park in 1896, pulled on ropes by 10,000 children and a team of horses in a remarkable display of civic pride.

Murphy's Landing (Route 101, one mile east of Shakopee, 612–445–6900), on the south bank of the Minnesota River, is an eighty-seven-acre outdoor museum containing a variety of structures assembled to depict frontier life between 1840 and 1890, including a fur trader's log cabin, a farmstead, and a one-room schoolhouse.

OPPOSITE: *One of eleven Swedish* kakelugnar *stoves—each of a different design—in the thirty-three-room Swan Turnblad mansion, now the American Swedish Institute.*

MINNESOTA RIVER VALLEY

MONTEVIDEO

Montevideo, settled in the late 1860s, sits on the bluffs overlooking the confluence of the Minnesota and Chippewa rivers. **Historic Chippewa City** (Routes 59 and 7, 320–269–7636) contains about twenty-five nineteenth-century structures gathered from the area, including an 1870 log house and an 1882 Norwegian Lutheran church; all are outfitted with period fixtures and furnishings.

The **Lac qui Parle Mission Site** (Route 13, eight miles northwest of Montevideo, 320–269–7636), near the junction of Lac qui Parle Lake and the Minnesota River, marks one of the earliest white settlements in the Minnesota Valley. This Protestant mission, established in 1835 to convert the Dakota Indians, stood near the American Fur Company post where Joseph Renville, the son of a French trader and Dakota woman, had been trading with the Indians since 1826. The mission declined after Renville died in 1846 and was abandoned in 1854. A replica of the chapel stands on the site, and markers indicate the location of various mission structures and Renville's trading post.

An 1882 Norwegian Lutheran Church, one of several nineteenth-century buildings that have been moved to Pioneer Village, near Montevideo.

THE UPPER AND LOWER SIOUX AGENCIES

The Upper and Lower Sioux agencies were established in the Minnesota Valley in 1853 to accustom the Dakota Indians to the settled life of farming after they ceded their homelands in the 1851 Treaty of Traverse des Sioux and Treaty of Mendota. Both agencies were thriving by 1860, and white traders and settlers lived in proximity to farming Indians, or "cut-hairs" as they were derisively called by Indians who chose to remain nomadic. The following year saw crop failure and a hard winter, however, and the Indians' U.S. government annuities arrived late, so they were nearly starving by the summer of 1862. The infamous statement of one storekeeper—"If they are hungry, let them eat grass"—exemplified the white settlers' lack of sympathy for the Indians' plight.

The Dakota Conflict was triggered some forty miles north of the Minnesota River on August 17, 1862, when several young Indians provoked and then killed five white settlers. Indians at the Upper Agency refused to participate in the conflict, and when fighting did break out they assisted the whites at the agency to safety. Most of the other Dakota chiefs were also reluctant to fight but were overruled by younger members of the tribe. On August 18, a band of Indians attacked the Lower Agency, killing some twenty people. The corpse of the outspoken storekeeper was found with grass stuffed in his mouth.

This confrontation led to a series of battles along the Minnesota River, culminating on September 23 with the Battle of Wood Lake, just south of the Upper Agency, when some 1,600 infantry and volunteers forced the Indians to retreat. Following the conflict, over 300 Indians were sentenced to death in hasty trials at the Lower Agency and were transported along the Minnesota Valley to Mankato for execution, threatened along the way by angry crowds. Between 500 and 800 settlers and soldiers were killed in the uprising; the exact number of Indian dead has never been determined. As historian Kenneth Carley wrote, "Measured in terms of the number of civilian lives lost, the outbreak was one of the worst in American history, and it launched a series of Indian wars on the northern plains that did not end until 1890 with the battle of Wounded Knee in South Dakota."

After the uprising the federal government canceled its treaties with the Dakota, allotted the Indians' annuities to white settlers claiming damage, and eventually removed most of the Indians to the Dakota Territory. Some were allowed to remain in the Minnesota Valley, and over time others returned. Small communities of Dakota descendants now live in the vicinity of the Upper and Lower agencies. The Upper Sioux Agency is located nine miles south of Granite Falls at the confluence of the Minnesota and Yellow Medicine rivers. An 1858 brick structure that once housed U.S. soldiers has been restored. Foundations of other buildings are visible, and interpretive markers describe the buildings and trace the history of the town. Films on local geology and ecology are shown. The site is part of **Upper Sioux Agency State Park** (Route 67, nine miles southeast of Granite Falls, 320–564–4777). One stone warehouse of the original compound remains at the Lower Sioux Agency, thirty miles downstream from the Upper Agency and seven miles east of Redwood Falls. The **Lower Sioux Agency History Center** (507–697–6321), on the grounds, recounts the history of the Dakota struggle in the region.

On September 2, 1862, a band of Dakota surprised a detachment of soldiers who had been sent from Fort Ridgely to bury dead settlers under the erroneous impression that the Indians had vacated the region. The ensuing battle lasted for thirty hours, and some twenty soldiers were killed. The rolling prairie where the conflict took place is now part of **Birch Coulee Park,** two miles north of Morton, at the junction of Routes 71 and 2. A **marker** on the grounds briefly describes the battle.

FORT RIDGELY

Fort Ridgely, on the north bank of the Minnesota River, is poorly situated from a military standpoint: It is on a promontory with ravines on three sides. In August 1862, during the Dakota uprising, settlers sought refuge at the fort. The Indians attacked on August 20 but were dispelled by artillery; they returned on August 22 with a larger force, but once again the howitzers kept them at bay. A stone powder magazine, restored stone commissary, and foundations of several original buildings are preserved at the fort's history center. The commissary contains exhibits on the Dakota Conflict and the history of settlement in the Minnesota Valley.

LOCATION: Off Route 4, 7 miles south of Fairfax. HOURS: May through Labor day: 8 A.M.–10 P.M. Daily. FEE: Yes. TELEPHONE: 507–426–7840.

OPPOSITE: *A monument to those who defended Fort Ridgely during the 1862 Dakota wars, erected near the fort in 1896.*

NEW ULM

Settled in 1854–1855 by two German colonization societies from Chicago and Cincinnati, New Ulm is situated on several broad terraces of the Minnesota River. The town played a key role in the 1862 Dakota Conflict, when more than 1,000 settlers from outlying areas poured in as a group of volunteers was setting up makeshift fortifications. The citizen soldiers were able to keep a band of about 100 Dakota at bay on August 19 and barely routed another force of 650 Indians on August 23. Thirty-four of the defenders were killed and sixty wounded, and the town was left in smoldering ruins. The settlers evacuated to Mankato, but their efforts at New Ulm, along with the standoff at Fort Ridgely, helped to ensure the eventual suppression of the Indian revolt.

The Greek Revival **Kiesling House** (220 North Minnesota Street, private), built in 1860, was used as a defensive outpost during the conflict. The **August Schell Brewing Company** (18th Street South, 507–354–5528), established in 1860 and still family run, includes a variety of nineteenth-century brick industrial structures and an 1880 Germanic-style brick residence with an octagonal gazebo set amid a large formal garden. It is said that the Schells' friendship with local Dakota spared the brewery from harm during the uprising.

Overlooking New Ulm from the highest river terrace is the **Hermann Monument** (Hermann Heights Park). The stone temple, built between 1887 and 1889, supports a thirty-two-foot statue of the ancient German chieftain who unified Germanic tribes and organized a successful rebellion against the Roman governor in the year A.D. 9. The **Brown County Historical Museum** (2 North Broadway, 507–354–2016) is housed in the 1910 Old Federal Post Office. Designed by James Knox Taylor, the building is notable for its alternating horizontal bands of brick and white terra cotta and its fanciful stepped gables, elements reminiscent of Dutch or Flemish design. The museum has exhibits explaining the Dakota Conflict and the crafts and trades of early Brown County settlers. A variety of nineteenth-century residences are found throughout the town, including the fortresslike **Niemann House** (827 North Minnesota Street, private).

OPPOSITE: *New Ulm's 1910 post office, now the Brown County Historical Museum.*

MANKATO

Mankato, founded in 1852 by land speculators from Saint Paul, is situated in a broad, deep valley where the Minnesota River takes a sharp dogleg north. Its name, which means "blue earth" in the Dakota language, refers to the color of the veins of soil along the banks of the Blue Earth River. French explorer Pierre Charles Le Sueur, who arrived in 1700, had hoped that the bluish soil indicated the presence of copper, but it turned out to be a type of clay. Flour milling and limestone quarrying were the town's chief industries in the nineteenth century.

The Dakota Conflict culminated in Mankato in December 1862, when the Dakota Indians convicted for their part in the uprising were brought here to await a review of the cases by President Lincoln. He commuted 265 of the sentences, and the remaining 38 Indians were hanged on December 26 under the gaze of a large gathering of settlers who, in turn, were watched by a peacekeeping force of some 2,000 Minnesota troops. A **marker** at Front and Main streets commemorates the hangings, the largest execution in the United States. The **Heritage Center** (415 Cherry Street, 507–345–5566) has Indian and pioneer artifacts and archives related to area history. The 1871 Second Empire **R. D. Hubbard House** (606 South Broad Street, 507–345–5566) is surrounded by Victorian gardens and filled with period furnishings. Next door, the 1890 **carriage house** houses horse-drawn vehicles and antique automobiles.

SAINT PETER

Saint Peter, on the banks of the Minnesota River, was settled in the 1850s. The river provided sites for flour milling, and the town soon became a market center for the outlying farms. A fine example of the Gothic Revival style, the 1871 **E. St. Julien Cox House** (500 North Washington Avenue, 507–931–4309) contains Victorian furnishings and Cox family items. The **Treaty Site History Center** (2 miles north on Route 169 at 1851 Minnesota Avenue, 507–931–2160, adjacent to the state park) focuses on the 1851 treaty between the United States and the Dakota; see next page. Old Main, an 1875 Second Empire structure, is the oldest building at **Gustavus Adolphus College,** founded in 1862.

Two miles north of Saint Peter, in **Traverse des Sioux State Park** (Route 169), is the **Traverse des Sioux Treaty Site,** located at a ford on the Minnesota River that was the site of a fur-trading post and Indian mission in the first half of the nineteenth century. For several weeks in the summer of 1851, the crossing was the site of a mass meeting between American negotiators and the Sisseton and Wahpeton bands of the Dakota. On July 23, thirty-five Dakota chiefs signed over 24 million acres of land in southern Minnesota and adjacent Iowa and South Dakota to the U.S. government. (A few days later, the Mdewakanton and Wahpekute bands signed a similar treaty at Pilot Knob.) In return, the Indians would receive $1,665,000 to establish schools and farms and provide individual annuities, but the chiefs were also coerced into signing a document that allowed fur traders' claims to be paid out of that money. This and other deceptions fostered the dissatisfaction that ultimately led to the 1862 Dakota Conflict.

LE SUEUR

Le Sueur, named for the French explorer Pierre Charles Le Sueur, was one of the many settlements that grew up along the banks of the Minnesota River in the 1850s. The **William W. Mayo House** (118 North Main Street, 507–665–3250) was the home of the country doctor and jack-of-all-trades whose later practice in Rochester led to the development of the Mayo Clinic. The 1859 frame house contains period furnishings and medical implements.

The Green Giant Canning Company, founded in 1903, is one of the town's major industries, and the history of vegetable canning is detailed in an exhibit in the **Le Sueur Museum** (705 North 2nd Street, 507–665–2050). The museum, located in a 1911 schoolhouse, also displays local farming and veterinarian's tools and artifacts from an early post office, school, and hotel.

Among the 1850s native limestone structures in **Ottawa Township,** five miles downriver from Le Sueur, is the **Ottawa Methodist Church** (Route 112), which contains period fixtures, an organ, books, and photographs. Near **Cleveland,** fifteen miles south of Le Sueur, is the 1860s **Geldner Saw Mill** (Route 15 at Route 1), the oldest extant sawmill in the region.

SOUTHERN MINNESOTA

PIPESTONE

Settled by homesteaders in 1873, Pipestone lies amid tall grass prairies that, despite the hardships of drought, blizzard, and grasshoppers, have proved to be excellent farmland. Serving the needs of people on the outlying farms, Pipestone boomed between 1880 and 1910, when it was served by four rail lines. A hub of activity during these years was the **Calumet Hotel** (104 West Main Street), built in 1888 of pinkish quartzite trimmed in red quartzite with Italianate features; it is still open as a hotel. The **Pipestone County Historical Museum** (113 South Hiawatha Avenue, 507–825–2563), in the 1896 city hall, contains a variety of Indian items, including ceremonial pipes, headdresses, beaded and quilled clothing from the Dakota and Ojibwa tribes, and early settlement artifacts, as well as exhibits on the artist George Catlin.

Pipestone National Monument

For centuries, Indians of the Great Lakes and the Mississippi and Missouri valleys traveled to this quarry to obtain red clay (or pipe-

Southwestern Minnesota contains several outcroppings of red quartzite that are associated with Indian history, including the Jeffers Petroglyphs, above, and those at Blue Mounds State Park, opposite.

stone) for carving calumets, the pipes used in important transactions and ceremonies. The vein of clay is twelve to eighteen inches thick and lies in shallow deposits along Pipestone Creek. In 1836 the artist George Catlin sketched the quarry and obtained a chemical analysis of the stone, which is now called catlinite in his honor. White explorers and historians have tended to romanticize the site, and legends that the quarry was sacred ground where all Indians came in peace are debatable. The area was controlled by the Yankton Dakota from the mid-nineteenth century until 1893, when the U.S. government seized the site for a federal Indian school.

The visitor center has exhibits of calumets and other pipestone objects. A scenic trail winds through a small section of virgin prairie past rocks inscribed by explorer Joseph Nicollet, who visited the site in 1838, and other adventurers and pioneers.

LOCATION: Route 75. HOURS: 8–5 Daily. FEE: Yes. TELEPHONE: 507–825–5464.

JEFFERS PETROGLYPHS

The Jeffers Petroglyphs comprise some 2,000 rock carvings, the largest collection of extant petroglyphs in Minnesota. The enigmatic pictures, etched in an outcrop of pinkish red quartzite, include stick figures—some in horned headdress and some engaged in warfare—various weapons, and such native animals as bison, rabbit, wolf, and turtle. Carved mainly by various Paleo-Indian groups, the petroglyphs appear to date from 3000 B.C., but some were created by Siouan Indians as recently as 1750. The rocks are surrounded by one of the few virgin prairies remaining in the state.

LOCATION: East of Route 71, 10 miles east of Jeffers, and north on Route 2. HOURS: Subject to change; call first. FEE: Yes. TELEPHONE: 507–697–6321.

FARMAMERICA

Farmamerica re-creates different periods in the history of the family farm in southern Minnesota: a farmstead of the period 1850 to 1860, with log buildings gathered from area farms; field crops and vegetables grown with nineteenth-century techniques and implements; a 1920s dairy and crop farm with a barn, granary, chicken coop, and milkhouse. The livestock and fieldwork techniques demonstrated here combine the use of horses and tractors. A contemporary farm employs modern methods and is used as a public forum for discussing current farm issues.

LOCATION: County Roads 2 and 17, 4 miles west of Waseca. HOURS: Mid-June through September: 10–4 Saturday–Sunday. FEE: Yes. TELEPHONE: 507–835–2052.

OWATONNA

Settled in 1854, Owatonna is the economic center for the surrounding farms. On the town square stands Louis Sullivan's 1908 **National Farmers Bank** (North Cedar Street and East Broadway), now Norwest Bank, a one-story brick and stone structure with large arched windows and terra cotta and mosaic ornamentation. The partially altered interior retains the original painted and gilded plasterwork, extensively stenciled walls, terra cotta ornaments, a large ornate clock, stained glass, chandeliers, and light fixtures. Two large murals of the rural landscape—one depicts a herd of Holstein cows—were painted by Oskar Gross, and much of the

The richly ornamented interior of Louis Sullivan's 1907–1908 National Farmers Bank was largely the work of George Grant Elmslie, the firm's chief designer.

ornamental design was the work of George Elmslie. The building is one of Sullivan's finest works and ranks among the genuine masterpieces of American architecture. More than any other single Midwestern building, it justifies a journey. Across the square is the 1891 **Steele County Courthouse** (111 East Main Street).

FARIBAULT

This small town on the banks of the Straight and Cannon rivers is named for its first resident, fur trader Alexander Faribault, who built the largest of his several trading posts here in 1826. The **Alexander Faribault House** (12 Northeast First Avenue, 507–334–7913), an 1853 frame structure with Greek Revival elements, contains period furnishings, some Faribault items, Indian artifacts, and pioneer articles. Other pioneer and Indian artifacts can be seen in the **Rice County Museum of History** (1814 Northwest Second Avenue, 507–332–2121).

Under the leadership of Bishop Henry Whipple, an indefatigable ecclesiastical leader and outspoken defender of the Dakota Indians, the town became the see of the Episcopal church and hub of its Indian missions in 1860. In 1865 Whipple founded **Shattuck School** (off Shumway Avenue) for boys; historic structures on the campus include New York architect Henry Congdon's **Chapel of the Good Shepherd.**

NORTHFIELD

On September 7, 1876, the James-Younger Gang attempted—unsuccessfully—to hold up a Northfield bank, killing an employee but fleeing with no money. Two of the outlaws were killed in a street fight, and the remaining six disappeared into the woods of southern Minnesota, with a posse of 1,000 men in hot pursuit. Frank and Jesse James managed to elude capture, but Cole, Bob, and Jim Younger and Charlie Pitts were apprehended near the town of Madelia on September 21. Pitts was killed during the ensuing melee, while the Younger brothers were taken alive and later sentenced to life in prison. The 1868 Scriver Building, where the robbery attempt took place, is now the **Northfield Historical Society and Museum** (408 Division Street, 507–645–9268).

Northfield was the home of Norwegian-American novelist O. E. Rölvaag, who wrote of the Norwegian immigrant experience in the United States; his house still stands at 311 Manitou Street (private). Several historic structures stand on the campuses of **Carleton College** and **Saint Olaf College** (Saint Olaf Avenue), including Carleton College's **Goodsell Observatory,** an 1887 Richardsonian Romanesque building still equipped with original nineteenth-century astronomical instruments.

The **William Gates LeDuc House** (1629 Vermillion Street), in the river town of **Hastings,** is a three-story limestone Gothic villa based on one of Andrew Jackson Downing's designs. The exterior is ornamented with fanciful carved verge boards, finials, and drip moldings in the classic Gothic style prescribed by Downing. The house, which was built between 1862 and 1866, is owned by the Minnesota Historical Society and has been restored.

RED WING

Red Wing, backed by majestic river bluffs, lies on a low plateau at the north end of Lake Pepin, a natural widening in the Mississippi River. This stretch of the Mississippi is a major flyway for migrating swan, and the town's name derives from a Dakota Indian chief whose name translated as "wild swan's wing dyed scarlet."

Many of the town's nineteenth-century buildings are clustered along the **Mall,** which runs along East and West avenues from the Mississippi River to 7th Street; these include the 1871 Gothic Revival **Christ Episcopal Church** (West 3rd Street) and the 1931 PWA Moderne **Goodhue County Courthouse** (West 5th Street). Notable private residences include the 1857 **Lawther Octagonal House** (927 West 3rd Street); the 1913 **Hoyt House** (300 Hill Street), a masterly Prairie Style residence designed by William Gray Purcell and George Elmslie; and the Italianate **Philander-Sprague House** (1008 West 3rd Street). A walking tour of the town can be obtained from the **visitor center** on Bush Street, adjacent to the 1874 **Saint James Hotel** (406 Main Street).

The **Goodhue County Historical Museum** (1166 Oak Street, 612–388–6024) has exhibits describing the geology and prehistory of the area, the Dakota Indians, nineteenth-century transportation, the development of local industries, and the immigrants who came to the area from Norway, Sweden, Germany, and the eastern United States between 1854 and 1874.

Ten miles southwest of Red Wing, in a secluded valley of the Cannon River, lies **Vasa,** a small Swedish Lutheran settlement that was established in 1855 and remains virtually intact. The 1869 redbrick Greek Revival **Vasa Swedish Lutheran Church** perches above a cluster of simple white frame buildings, including the 1861 **Vasa Museum** and the modestly Italianate 1875 **Town Hall.**

WINONA

Winona was established in the 1850s as a refueling spot for steamboats plying the river between Saint Paul and Galena, Illinois. In the nineteenth century it was a prosperous sawmill and gristmill town and an important shipping depot for wheat; the Italianate **Anger's Block** (116–120 Walnut Street, private) and **Kirch-Latch Building** (114–122 East 2nd Street, private), both built in the 1860s, recall this flourishing era, as does the 1857 **Huff-Lamberton House** (207 Huff Street, private), one of the best-preserved Italian Villa–style structures in Minnesota. The 1888 **Winona County Courthouse** (Washington Street and 3rd Street West) is an impressive Richardsonian Romanesque structure designed by Charles G. Maybury. The *Julius C. Wilkie* (Levee Park), a replica of a wood-hulled stern-wheeler, contains an exhibit of steamboat-era memorabilia.

Winona possesses two fine examples of early-twentieth-century banks designed by prominent Prairie School architects. The 1912 **Merchants National Bank** (102 East 3rd Street), designed by William Gray Purcell and George Elmslie, is a one-story brick structure with stained-glass curtain walls and extensive terra cotta ornamentation. The **Winona Savings Bank** (204 Main Street), now Winona National Savings Bank, is a blend of Egyptian Revival and Prairie School motifs designed in 1914 by Chicago architect George Maher. The interior includes inlaid stone and Tiffany windows.

The **Armory Museum** (160 Johnson Street, 507–454–2723) contains extensive archives and exhibits depicting a nineteenth-century parlor, kitchen, blacksmith shop, pharmacy, and dentist's office. The **Arches Museum of Pioneer Life** (Route 14, eleven miles west of Winona, 507–523–2111) consists of several historic structures, including a one-room schoolhouse, an 1850s log house, a ca. 1900 log barn, and a modern museum displaying antique farm and household articles. The Gothic Revival **William B. Bunnell House** (off Route 61, five miles south of Winona in Homer,

507–454–2723) was built in the 1850s by the first permanent white settler in Winona County; it is furnished with period items.

ROCHESTER

Rochester grew from the gristmills and sawmills built along the banks of the Zumbro River in the 1850s. The town was incorporated in 1858, its founder, George Head, naming it after his home city in New York state.

English-born physician William Worrall Mayo moved to Rochester in 1863 to examine inductees into the Union army and stayed to set up a private practice. His sons William and Charles, both surgeons proficient in the emerging techniques of antiseptic and aseptic surgery, joined him in the 1880s to form a family partnership that evolved into the Mayo Clinic. As other doctors were asked to join the practice, the Mayo brothers pioneered the concept of an integrated private group practice of medicine. Downtown Rochester is dominated by Mayo Clinic facilities, the most impressive being the 1928 **Plummer Building** (2nd Street SW and Second Avenue SW), a fifteen-story stone and brick structure in the Romanesque style.

The 1916 **William J. Mayo House** (701 4th Street), now occupied by the Mayo Foundation, is a mansion with a five-story entrance tower. While William chose to live within walking distance of the clinic, his brother Charles built his estate on 3,000 acres of land on the outskirts of town where he could pursue his agricultural hobbies. **Mayowood** (Route 125, 507–287–8691) sits on a wooded hillside overlooking the Zumbro River. Designed in large part by the doctor, the rambling stone and poured-concrete structure is eclectic in style and retains the original furnishings, many of them gathered by two generations of Mayos on world travels. Perched on a high bluff overlooking southwestern Rochester, the stone, brick, and stucco **Plummer House** (1091 Plummer Lane, 507–281–6183), built between 1917 and 1924, was the residence of the influential Mayo Clinic partner Dr. Henry Plummer, who was also a planner and inventor; it is furnished with original and period pieces.

The history of the region is detailed in the **Olmsted County History Center** (1195 County Road 22 Southwest, 507-282–9447) and the adjacent **Stoppel Farmstead,** which includes an 1860 vernacular farmhouse and various outbuildings.

468

Notes on Architecture

GEORGIAN

THE GEORGIAN, OH

Beginning in Boston as early as 1686, and only much later elsewhere, the design of houses became balanced about a central axis, with only careful, stripped detail. A few large houses incorporated double-story pilasters. Sash windows with rectilinear panes replaced casements. Hipped roofs accentuated the balanced and strict proportions inherited from Italy and Holland via England and Scotland.

GREEK REVIVAL

HENRY B. CLARKE HOUSE, IL

The Greek Revival manifested itself in severe, stripped, rectilinear proportions, occasionally a set of columns or pilasters, and even, in a few instances, Greek-temple form. It combined Greek and Roman forms—low pitched pediments, simple moldings, rounded arches, and shallow domes—and was used in official buildings and many private houses.

ITALIANATE

JOHN HAUCK HOUSE, OH

The Italianate style began to appear in the 1840s, both in a formal, balanced "palazzo" style and in a picturesque "villa" style. Both had round-headed windows and arcaded porches. Commercial structures were often made of cast iron, with a ground floor of large arcaded windows and smaller windows on each successive rising story.

QUEEN ANNE

PEORIA, IL

The Queen Anne style emphasized contrasts of form, texture, and color. Large encircling verandahs, tall chimneys, turrets, towers, and a multitude of textures are typical of the style. The ground floor might be of stone or brick, the upper floors of stucco, shingle, or clapboard. Specially shaped bricks and plaques were used for decoration. Panels of stained glass outlined or filled the windows. The steep roofs were gabled or hipped, and other elements, such as pediments, Venetian windows, and front and corner bay windows, were typical.

RICHARDSON ROMANESQUE

GLESSNER HOUSE, IL

Richardson Romanesque made use of the massive forms and ornamental details of the Romanesque: rounded arches, towers, stone and brick facing. The solidity and gravity of masses were accentuated by deep recesses for windows and entrances, by rough stone masonry, stubby columns, strong horizontals, rounded towers with conical caps, and botanical, repetitive ornament.

RENAISSANCE REVIVAL OR BEAUX ARTS

GEORGE ROGERS CLARK MEMORIAL, IN

In the 1880s and 1890s, American architects who had studied at the Ecole des Beaux Arts in Paris brought a new Renaissance Revival to the United States. Sometimes used in urban mansions, but generally reserved for public and academic buildings, it borrowed from three centuries of Renaissance detail— much of it French—and put together picturesque combinations from widely differing periods.

CHICAGO SCHOOL COMMERCIAL STYLE

CARSON PIRIE SCOTT BUILDING, IL

After the Great Fire of 1871 destroyed some 18,000 buildings in Chicago, the city's architects developed a type of commercial building, the skyscraper, using the new technology of steel-frame skeleton construction. A Chicago skyscraper frequently has three parts, with base, shaft, and cornice echoing the parts of a classical column. Rows of large rectangular windows are divided by narrow piers that reveal the skeletal structure.

PRAIRIE STYLE

HEURTHY HOUSE, IL

From about 1900 to 1920, Frank Lloyd Wright and several other Midwestern architects developed a style of residential building that attempted to reflect the rolling midwestern prairie. Wright claimed "The prairie

has a beauty of its own and we should recognise and accentuate this natural beauty, its quiet level. Hence, gently sloping roofs, low proportions, quiet sky lines, suppressed heavy-set chimneys and sheltering overhangs, low terraces and outreaching walls sequestering private gardens." Concentrated in Chicago suburbs such as Oak Park, Illinois, Prairie style houses were built until the end of World War I, when the fashion returned to buildings based on architectural styles of the past.

ECLECTIC PERIOD REVIVALS

EDSEL & ELEANOR FORD HOUSE, MI

During the first decades of the twentieth century, revivals of diverse architectural styles became popular in the United States, particularly for residential buildings. Architects designed Swiss chalets, half-timbered Tudor houses, and Norman chateaux with equal enthusiasm. Many of these houses were modeled on rural structures and constructed in suburban settings. Although widely divergent in appearance, they have similar plans, site orientations, and general scale, brought about by similarities in building sites and by clients' desires for spacious interiors.

I N D E X

PHOTO CREDITS

All photographs are by Balthazar Korab except for the following:

Cover
Main photo and inset 1: © Greg Ryan—Sally Beyer
Inset 2: Massillon Museum, Massillon, OH
Inset 3: Map by Guenter Vollath
Inset 4: Robert M. Lightfoot/ Nawrocki Stock Photo Inc.

Half-title page: Minnesota Historical Society
Page 13: Richard Hamilton Smith, St. Paul, MN
16: Cervin Robinson, New York, NY
21: David R. Barker/Ohio Historical Society
26-27, 32-33: James Westwater, Columbus, OH
38: James P. Rowan/Click Chicago
41: Chicago Historical Society (1914.1)
48-49: Public Library of Cincinnati and Hamilton County
58-59: Richard Alexander Cooke III, Eugene, OR
62 (left): Dirk Bakker/Detroit Institute of Arts
62 (right): Ohio Historical Society
65: Marietta College, Dawes Library/Hildreth Collection
74: James Westwater
82: Butler Institute of American Art
85: Ohio Division of Travel and Tourism, Columbus
88: Massillon Museum, Massillon, OH
100: Darryl Jones, Indianapolis, IN
103: Indiana University Auditorium, Bloomington
106: Jeff Gnass/West Stock
108, 112, 118, 119, 122, 123, 127: Darryl Jones
130: Bettmann Archive
133: Darryl Jones
136-137: Indiana Historical Society Library
138: Darryl Jones
141: Cathlyn Melloan/Click Chicago
143: Bettmann Archive
148-149: Peter Pearson/Click Chicago
150, 152: Darryl Jones
154: Culver Pictures
157, 161: Darryl Jones

162: Bob Daum, Chesterton, IN
165: Dirk Bakker/Detroit Institute of Art
168: University of Nebraska, Lincoln
171: Gary Irving/Click Chicago
174: Illinois Historic Preservation Agency, Galena
175: Bill Crofton, Wilmette, IL
177: Thomas Gilcrease Institute, Tulsa, OK
180: Don DuBroff/Sadin Photo Group
184: Terry Donnelly/Click Chicago
185, 186: Terry Farmer/Click Chicago
187, 189: Gary Irving/Click Chicago
200: Michael Bertan/Click Chicago
203: Bill Crofton
210: Illinois State Museum
215: Willard Clay/Click Chicago
216: Robert Frerck/Odyssey Productions
219: Chicago Historical Society
225: New York Public Library/ Prints Division, Stokes Collection
226, 233: Robert Frerck/Odyssey Productions
234-235: Art Institute of Chicago
244: Culver Pictures
251: C.D. Arnold/Chicago Historical Society (ICHi-02520)
253: Hedrich-Blessing
258-259: Jon Miller/Hedrich-Blessing/Courtesy of the Frank Lloyd Wright Home and Studio Foundation
263: Royal Ontario Museum, Toronto
270-271: Dale Fisher, Grass Lake, MI
273: Grand Rapids Public Museum, Pictorial Materials Collection
298: Marquette Mission Park and Museum of Ojibwa Culture
316: Bettmann Archive
318: New York Public Library/ Prints Division
324-325: Dirk Bakker/Detroit Institute of Arts
330-331: Robert M. Lightfoot III/Courtesy of *National Geographic Traveler*
338: Don DuBroff/University of Michigan, Ann Arbor, MI
335: Bob Kalmbach/University of Michigan News & Information Services
341: Newberry Library, Chicago
346-347: Richard Hamilton Smith
348: Wisconsin Dept. of Natural Resources, Madison

358: Ken Dequaine/Third Coast Stock Source
371: Darryl Baird/Third Coast Stock Source
372: Don DuBroff/Sadin Photo Group
374: Alan Magayne-Roshak/ Third Coast Stock Source
375: Ken Dequaine/Third Coast Stock Source
378: SC Johnson Wax
381: Ken Dequaine/Third Coast Stock Source
386: H.H. Bennett Studio Museum
387: Henry Hamilton Bennett
390: Zane Williams/Third Coast Stock Source
392: Chippewa Valley Museum
395: Bob Daum
398: Richard Hamilton Smith
403: Minnesota Historical Society, International Falls
410-411: Greg L. Ryan/Sally A. Beyer, St. Paul, MN
415: Richard Hamilton Smith
418: James P. Rowan/Click Chicago
421: Les Blacklock, Moose Lake, MN
425: Nathan Benn/Woodfin Camp
432, 435: Greg L. Ryan/Sally A. Beyer, St. Paul, MN
439: Henry Hamilton Bennett
440-441: Greg L. Ryan/Sally A. Beyer, St. Paul, MN
443: Steve Solum/Third Coast Stock Source
444: Greg L. Ryan/Sally A. Beyer, St. Paul, MN
446: Christian M. Korab, Minneapolis
448, 449: Minneapolis Institute of Arts
461: Greg L. Ryan/Sally A. Beyer, St. Paul, MN
463: Cervin Robinson
469 (top center): Hedrich-Blessing
Back cover: Darryl Jones

Composed in Basilia Haas and ITC New Baskerville by Graphic Arts Composition, Inc., Philadelphia, Pennsylvania. Printed and bound by Toppan Printing Company, Ltd., Tokyo, Japan.

The editors gratefully acknowledge the assistance of Ann J. Campbell, Rita Campon, Fonda Duvanel, Henry Engle, Ann ffolliott, Amy Hughes, Kevin Lewis, Carol McKeown, Catherine Shea Tangney, Linda Venator, and Patricia Woodruff.